WITHDRAWN

Drive to Hegemony

Drive to Hegemony

The United States in the Caribbean

1898–1917

David Healy

The University of Wisconsin Press

The University of Wisconsin Press
114 North Murray Street
Madison, Wisconsin 53715

The University of Wisconsin Press, Ltd.
1 Gower Street
London WC1E 6HA, England

5   4   3   2   1

Printed in the United States of America

Library of Congress Cataloging-in-Publication Data
Healy, David, 1926–
   Drive to hegemony.
   Bibliography: pp. 335–352.
   Includes index.
   1. Caribbean Area—Foreign relations—United States.
2. United States—Foreign relations—Caribbean Area.
3. United States—Foreign relations—1865–1921.
I. Title.
F2178.U6H43   1988   327.730729   88-40190
ISBN 0-299-11720-0

To Fred Harvey Harrington,
my teacher and friend of many years,
with respect and affection

Contents

Illustrations

Acknowledgments

I owe thanks to many people in the Golda Meir Library of the University of Wisconsin–Milwaukee, especially those in the Interlibrary Loan Office and the American Geographical Society Collection, who have helped me locate needed materials. I am also grateful to my colleagues in History and Political Science who have given me the benefit of their knowledge and critical judgment. Among them I should specifically mention professors David Buck, Howard Handelman, Ronald Ross, Donald Shea, and Walter Weare. Professor Bruce Fetter, who read each chapter as I wrote it, greatly increased my already large debt to him. Finally, my colleague and wife, Ann Erickson Healy, was once again invaluable as skillful editor, wise counselor, and perceptive historian.

Drive to Hegemony

Introduction

—————•◦⟨∞⟩◦•—————

After experiencing a heady victory in the Spanish-American War, the United States acquired a small but far-flung empire and embarked upon a more energetic course in foreign affairs. For the next generation its diplomatic efforts were focused principally on two regions, northern Latin America and the Far East. In both regions Washington sought to become a leading shaper of events and fount of influence, but with very different results. In spite of its pretentious Open Door policy, the United States repeatedly met with frustration and failure in its Far Eastern efforts; by 1917 it had little to show for them but an enduring rivalry with Japan and a Philippine colony already coming to be seen as a white elephant. In the Caribbean area, by contrast, it had established an effective regional hegemony.

The reasons for the nation's differing success rate in these areas are not hard to find, for they emerge clearly in even a superficial comparison of the two. First of all, in the Far East the United States was a latecomer to a long-standing rivalry involving a number of competitors: Great Britain, Russia, Germany, France, and the rising local power, Japan. Located halfway around the globe from the United States, the region was never regarded in Washington as vital, however intense the occasional burst of diplomatic involvement might become, and certainly no one at the time ever suggested that it had any bearing upon the security of the United States.

The Caribbean region, by contrast, was close to the United States and far from the other great powers. No other major power challenged United States hegemony there. Great Britain, with a large economic presence, the world's mightiest navy, and secure bases in Jamaica, Trinidad, the Lesser Antilles, British Guiana, and British Honduras, was best positioned to mount such a

3

challenge but consciously refrained. Although Americans* long feared that Germany would pick up the gauntlet, no significant opposition to Washington's growing power came from Berlin. The region was of secondary or marginal importance to the other nations of real weight, and of primary importance only to the United States. If necessary, the Americans were ready to fight for their aims in the Caribbean, and the other powers knew it. Locked into their own European tensions, they found nothing in the area worth a war with a rising naval and industrial power. As continental tensions rose steadily, then exploded into general war in 1914, Europe was increasingly debarred from any meaningful power commitments in the New World.

In addition to being the only major power with a free hand in the Caribbean, the United States possessed other regional advantages. Again, these emerge plainly from a regional comparison. American ambitions in the Far East initially included hopes of economic penetration, particularly into the markets of China. While these were at that time not large, Europeans and Americans alike shared a mistaken conviction that China was on the brink of rapid westernization and economic development which would make it a large consumer of western manufactures. In practice, China's trade with the developed world was not only rather static but overwhelmingly dominated by the British, while Japan emerged as a formidable regional business rival. As a result, the American economic stake in the Far East never became very large.

Once more the Caribbean was different. The British were also well entrenched in Caribbean trade, investment, and shipping in 1898, but not so strongly as in the Far East, while North American enterprise made steady inroads from the late nineteenth century on. By 1917 United States economic influence in the Caribbean had passed that of Great Britain, particularly in the countries in which Washington was most interested. The First World War clinched the American advantage by closing off the supply of European goods and money. Yankee businessmen quickly moved in to fill the void, making gains which substantially survived the end of the war.

A final contrast is even more striking: that between the vastness of China and the relative smallness of the Caribbean states. Both were vulnerable and disorganized at the turn of the century, but the teeming population of China had for centuries passively absorbed a succession of conquerors. To use force effectively in China might require considerable and expensive efforts extended over years, and the problem was compounded by the number of great-power rivals to be considered. The Russo-Japanese War of 1904–1905 was a grim warning of the price which the unwary could be obliged to pay; the winners as

---

*The use of *American* to mean *from the United States* is widely accepted in much of the world. In Latin America, *North American* is the term most used to denote United States origin. Since there is no generally satisfactory term available, I have used both interchangeably.

well as the losers suffered scores of thousands of casualties and paid dearly in gold as well as blood.

The scale of the effort required in the Caribbean was drastically smaller. Unchallenged by major rivals, Washington could overawe each small state one to one, in most cases not even needing to use its forces to make its point. When the United States did commit troops to action, seldom as many as two thousand were involved, and never more than three. There were normally enough marines stationed in the region or available nearby on the mainland to handle even small local wars without much extra expenditure, and never were they very bloody—for the North Americans, at any rate. Divided into many small, weak states, the Caribbean region posed little resistance to a determined great-power drive for hegemony.

Given these strategic and economic advantages, the United States quickly became dominant in the Caribbean. This book is an account of that rise to dominance, which began in 1898 and was substantially completed by 1917. The pages that follow do not, however, deal with the entire Gulf-Caribbean region. Mexico, important as it was, and however intimately entangled with the United States, constitutes another story. Like Colombia and Venezuela, it was not a part of the central system of Caribbean control erected in this period by the United States, but rather an indicator of the limits of that system. These larger countries also felt the weight of Washington's power and, in Mexico's case especially, played host to a myriad of North American enterprises, but never passed wholly within the circle of North American hegemony. Thus while Mexico's story has much in common with those of its neighbors, it is different in kind and will not be told here. Also omitted are the Caribbean colonies of Great Britain, France, and the Netherlands, with which Washington made no effort to interfere. This book is about United States relations, official and unofficial, with the independent states of Central America and the Greater Antilles, and the former Spanish colonies which passed under United States control in 1898. It is about the techniques developed to exercise hegemony over the small sovereign states of the Caribbean, the reasons why North Americans desired such hegemony, and some of the effects which resulted from its establishment. That is enough to attempt in one modest volume.

Part I

The Lodgment

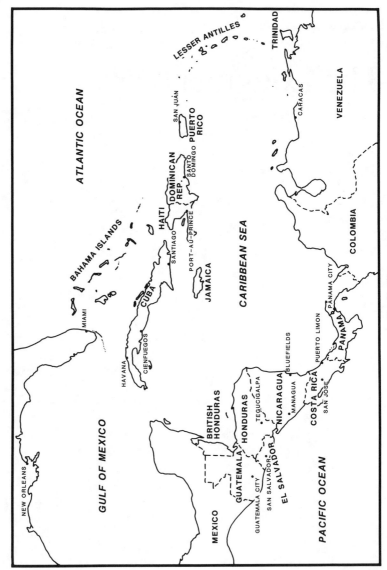

The Caribbean

Chapter 1

————··❦··————

The Caribbean in the 1890s

"The American Mediterranean," they came to call it, once the United States had actively established its hegemony there. But the Caribbean was no Mediterranean, no past or present world center or cradle of civilizations. Although once considered important by the great powers, it had long been peripheral, first to the interests and struggles of Europe, then to those of the United States. Seemingly colonial by nature, the region lacked power and unity, and in the 1890s was regarded as poor and backward as well. In an age when tropical peoples were branded as inferior by the newly industrialized societies of the north temperate zone, the very fact that the Caribbean Sea lay entirely in the tropics went far to explain its limitations to Europeans and North Americans. Yet it was undoubtedly a magnificent sheet of water, and the lands about it were widely acknowledged to be beautiful. In the 1890s, furthermore, they were once again thought potentially valuable to foreigners.

Although the Caribbean, like the Mediterranean, is largely surrounded by land, it too contains some very respectable distances. It is just under 2,000 miles from the Yucatán coast to the Windward Islands, and a little over 800 from Santiago de Cuba to Colón at the Caribbean end of the Panama Canal. From New Orleans, long a main gateway to the region from the United States, out through the Gulf of Mexico, Colón lies 1,600 miles to the south, Havana lies 700 to the east and south, and the principal ports of Guatemala and Honduras lie about 1,100 miles to the south. Cuba is by far the closest of these lands to the United States, its coast coming within 90 miles of Key West in Florida.

Around this vast watery expanse are strung a necklace of islands, the top of a continent, and the world's largest isthmus. In the 1890s the political status of all these lands was varied. Cuba and Puerto Rico were Spanish colonies, Jamaica was British. The smaller islands to the east and south belonged mainly to Great Britain and France, but also to the Netherlands and Denmark. Haiti and Santo Domingo were independent, as were the much larger South American nations of Venezuela and Colombia. In Central America, Panamá was a province of Colombia, British Honduras was a colony, and between them were the five independent republics of Guatemala, El Salvador, Honduras, Nicaragua, and Costa Rica. Their situations were by no means static, however. The Spanish colonies were restive under metropolitan rule, the Cubans beginning an independence revolution in 1895, the Puerto Ricans calling in softer tones for local self-rule. In Nicaragua a rising nationalism challenged the long-held British domination of that nation's east coast, while in Panamá a more local nationalism, which called for separation from Colombia, alternately flared and smouldered. Guatemala, Salvador, and Nicaragua routinely sought to dominate each other, singly or in combination, whenever possible using Honduras as a battlefield and client state. Mutually jealous, internally unstable, and resentful of foreign influence, Colombia and Venezuela strove to build effective nation-states on their large and rugged territories.

Culturally, the Caribbean region was the product of indigenous Indian societies, colonial transplants from Europe, and African slavery. Most of the region was Spanish speaking and racially mixed, but the mixtures and cultures differed widely from place to place. While Guatemala had a predominantly Indian racial stock diluted by Spanish settlement, the Cuban population was mostly white with a large infusion of Negro blood. Haiti and Jamaica were almost wholly black and mulatto, as were most of the Lesser Antilles and portions of the Caribbean coast of Central America. Spanish was the language most widely used, but Jamaica was English speaking, as were British Honduras, large stretches of the Central American coast, and many of the Lesser Antilles. Most Haitians spoke a French-African mixture called Creole, while the elite used pure French. While most of the remaining Lesser Antilles were culturally French, several Dutch- and Danish-speaking islands further varied the pattern. Thus cultural diversity combined with the physical separation of the islands and difficult communications on the mainland to keep the Caribbean region fragmented and complex, and to discourage any easy generalizations about it. Yet there were some commonalities. Most of the Caribbean peoples had been shaped in varying degrees by colonialism, slavery, sugar culture, and a two-class society dominated by a small hereditary elite.[1]

American travelers of the late nineteenth century found the region an area of both stagnation and change. The old sugar islands of the West Indies, once Europe's richest colonies, had lost their economic significance after the abolition of Negro slavery and the appearance of alternate areas and techniques of sugar growing. Yet in Cuba a new, modernized sugar culture was fast taking shape which promised partially to restore the former importance of the crop. In colonial days its plantation wealth made the Caribbean a principal arena for overseas European power struggles, but after the Napoleonic wars it had swiftly receded to a political backwater. However, a French attempt in the 1880s to build a canal across Panamá seemed to presage an equally sudden rebirth of strategic interest in the area. It was true that the Panama Canal Company was bankrupt by 1889, having failed at a magnitude unequaled in its time, but before doing so it had moved thousands of West Indian laborers across the Caribbean, temporarily galvanized the Central American economy, and inspired a rising United States interest in carrying through a similar project.

The lives of the region's people showed a similar ambivalence. Millions of West Indian and Central American peasants continued to survive on subsistence farming or traditional *latifundias,* living like their parents and grandparents in poverty and isolation. At the same time, thousands of their brothers were being harnessed to the production of export crops for the world market in new forms of plantation agriculture, as a swelling stream of European and North American investment transformed selected segments of the Caribbean economy. Economic change brought with it the penetration of outside ideas, methods, and influences. Thus what one saw in the Caribbean world depended very much upon where one looked, and the diverse impressions of outside observers before and after 1900 bring to mind the tale of the three blind men and the elephant.[2]

One American traveler at the turn of the century, for example, thought Nicaragua a neglected potential paradise: "Everything essential to the material wants of man is ready to his hand, and the earth needs but scant encouragement to bring forth its abundance." Yet, he declared, "amidst these fair surroundings four hundred thousand people are dreaming the years away." The country's natural resources were immense; it was the people who were wanting. "Only the innate laziness of the natives, intensified by frequently recurring civil wars and consequent conscription and oppression, prevents this country from blooming like a vast garden."[3] Another American who toured Central America in the 1880s found the Honduran peasantry the epitome of backwardness, a people living idly amid filth in the crudest of huts.

> A few stone jars of native work . . . , a couple of hammocks, and a few broken articles of furniture, constitute the equipment of a *peon's* house. The man of the house swings in a hammock while his spouse brings water from the stream in a large stone jar upon her head, and the pigs and chickens and children lie upon the floor indiscriminately mixed.[4]

In the capital city, Tegucigalpa, a town of perhaps twelve thousand people, he found no waterworks; every drop of water was carried upon a woman's head from a river at the bottom of a hundred-foot-deep gorge. Tegucigalpa had no carriages because it had no roads adequate for them. Travel between the capital and the seacoast was by oxcart or muleback. In sharp contrast, a recently installed telegraph system offered quick communication within the country and to outside points.

The same traveler judged Guatemala City the largest and "by far the finest" city of Central America, with paved streets and sidewalks, large and attractive houses, and an upper class dressed just as it would be in New York (the lower classes, of course, wore "native costume"). The police department had recently been reorganized and uniformed after the pattern of New York's Finest, while the railroad which served the city was so new that crowds still gathered to witness the arrival and departure of every train.[5] Everywhere, the overriding impression was of backwardness randomly penetrated by modernity. Regional modernization was particularly evident in the principal towns; Guatemala City and San José, Costa Rica, got the beginnings of electric street lighting in the 1880s, as did Havana and Santiago in Cuba. In the same decade some larger Caribbean towns received their first telephone lines and street railways. The affluent city dweller could by then introduce electric lights into his house, along with piped water from a private waterworks, and in places even piped sewer connections. If all of these were regarded as marvels, unknown outside of towns and available only to a privileged few, they were nonetheless harbingers of a great alien world that was already pushing its way into Caribbean life.[6]

The process was more advanced in Cuba than elsewhere. The eighties and nineties were notable there for the rapid expansion of sugar production, and the beginning of large-scale foreign investment. While much of the island was still characterized by small multicrop farming and grazing, growing sugar and tobacco for export was becoming the dominant economic pursuit. Sugar production in particular was becoming dependent upon capital-intensive techniques, for which Europe and the United States increasingly provided the needed capital. Long centuries of Spanish mercantilism were succumbing to the new economic currents, aided by a few years of tariff reciprocity with the United States in the early 1890s. Even Spanish colonial rule in Cuba had been shaken by the Ten Years' War of 1868–78, in reality less a war than a protracted series of raids and guerrilla actions carried on in the hope of political change. By 1890, autonomy was high on the agenda of popular discussion in Cuba and its sister colony of Puerto Rico, while more zealous Cubans cried openly for independence.[7]

On the neighboring island of Hispaniola, Haiti and Santo Domingo, already sovereign states, had not undergone the changes which were to remake Cuba. The Haitians, descended from black African slaves who had succeeded in driving out their French colonial masters a century earlier, had kept out white landowners and imperialists ever since. The great bulk of the people were poor peasants living by squatter agriculture, in a land already burdened by over-population and declining food production. An American observer of the early twentieth century, repelled by their teeming numbers and squalid condition, thought the Haitian peasantry "little above the animal," half-naked, ignorant, and devoid of modesty or sexual morality. To him the tiny French-speaking national elite was inadequate to redeem the country, elegant and well educated as it undoubtedly was. The judgment was harsh and unfair, but it reflected accurately enough the absence of any very significant change in the customary life of the Haitian masses.[8]

Though sharing an island with Haiti, Santo Domingo had a very different society. Haiti was black, Francophone (most Haitians spoke a French-African hybrid tongue), overpopulated, and backward. Santo Domingo was brown, Spanish speaking, and lightly populated. It too was poor, but the Dominican economy had been at least lightly touched by the new forces of the period. In some areas, modern sugar planting had been introduced by Cuban planters fleeing the vicissitudes of the Ten Years' War. A few North Americans had begun growing bananas for export, while tobacco, coffee, and cacao cultivation were also aimed at a world rather than a local market. Far behind Cuba in taking up these new enterprises, Santo Domingo nevertheless felt their impact politically as well as economically as new interests appeared among the still-crystallizing elite.[9]

The rise of coffee growing to prominence in the mid-nineteenth century also spurred agricultural production for export in Central America. First Costa Rica, then Guatemala and El Salvador, made coffee a principal export, and Central America became famous for the high quality and rich flavor of its coffee beans. This new source of income was generally accompanied by the rise of governments devoted to economic growth and material progress, which encouraged experimentation with additional crops: sugar, cotton, cacao, rubber, timber. Late in the century a new bonanza appeared in the form of bananas, raised on the region's Caribbean littoral. By this time railroads had begun to pierce the interior and stitch at least portions of the Central American republics into the patterns of world trade, while improved seaport facilities and other infrastructure were here and there in evidence.[10]

It must be emphasized that in the 1890s the Caribbean region was still overwhelmingly rural and largely outside the orbit of these changes. The entire region boasted only one large city, Havana. With about a quarter of a million people, the Cuban capital was several times larger than its nearest rival, and unquestionably the gayest and most cosmopolitan Caribbean city. With its visiting opera troupes, fine cafes, parks, handsome houses, and reputed two hundred brothels, Havana was the glittering center of the entire region. The other area capitals were mere towns, although Guatemala City had as many as sixty thousand inhabitants. In general, however, village life prevailed. Most agriculture was for subsistence or local exchange, and in some districts large areas lay almost unused; in 1898, only a fifth of the total land of Puerto Rico, for example, was under cultivation. In the 1890s, throughout the Caribbean, change was still far more promise and possibility than accomplished fact, a source alike of hope and greed, idealistic dreams and the most sordid schemes of enrichment.[11]

To many of the elite who shaped national attitudes and policies, it seemed clear that their countries could be brought to prosperity and progress only through the application of the new wealth-producing methods of Europe and North America. Science and reason were to be the tools of change, and foreigners their instruments. The Spanish colonial heritage was regarded, at least by the Liberals who had come to dominate the region's politics, as the dead hand of the past, and Indian culture as hopelessly decadent and backward. The United States was the epitome of modern progress, and the Mexico of Porfirio Díaz, with its low taxes and easy economic concessions, served as a model for the encouragement of foreign enterprise. Along with new mines and beef cattle, Mexico was getting railroads, the ultimate symbol of progress, the construction of which was in itself widely believed sufficient to release the anticipated riches of the future. The Mexican slogan of "order and progress" was taken up throughout Latin America, as was Mexican-style hospitality to foreign businessmen. While it all sounded very rational, the rhetoric of positivism and practicality disguised an almost mystic faith in economic development, and admiration for the material achievements of the United States was one of its major tenets. Thus regional governmental policies as well as economic opportunities helped to attract North American investment.[12]

There was, of course, far more British investment than American in the Caribbean of the 1890s. For decades the massive outflow of British capital to foreign lands had dwarfed all competition, while significant capital exports from the United States were just beginning. The British were much the largest takers of Caribbean government bonds and railroad securities; they dominated the region's banking and shipping, and were involved in every field of economic activity. French, German, and other European nationals were also active in the Caribbean on a lesser but still important scale. If American investment was still relatively small before 1898, however, it was by no means insignificant. Mexico had for a generation past been the largest foreign recipient of United States direct investment, which one careful estimate put at two hundred million dollars by 1897. In the same year, in the Caribbean proper, Cuba led with something over thirty million dollars, while total American investment for the West Indies and Central America came to some sixty or seventy million dollars. Most of this was in agricultural enterprises, particularly sugar planting in Cuba and banana growing in Central America. United States participation in Caribbean railroad building was also fairly widespread, although British enterprise still dominated that field. While mining ventures were launched in Cuba and Central America, except in Honduras they had never constituted a main thrust of American activity. There was some effort to sell North American consumer products in the region, such as hardware, shoes, sewing machines, and canned goods, but European imports generally did better up to the turn of the century. In Cuba, where American investments became especially large, American products exchanged more briskly with local ones. In 1894 the United States took 87 percent of Cuba's exports and provided 38 percent of its total imports, slightly more than Spain itself. The value of United States–Cuban trade in that year reached the impressive total of one hundred million dollars.[13]

Quite directly, it was the sale of Yankee goods in Cuba that led to large-scale American investment there. Many Cuban sugar planters had been accustomed to buying their supplies on credit in New England or Spain and paying for them when their crop was marketed. The foreign middlemen involved became, in a small way, merchant bankers as well as commission merchants. One such entrepreneur was Edwin F. Atkins of Boston, whose career illustrates the process by which North American capital first entered Cuba. Atkins was the son of Elisha Atkins, founder and head of the grocery firm of E. Atkins and Company. This company developed a large Cuban trade in the generation before the Civil War, broadening its operations into a wide range of consumer goods. Besides selling supplies, the firm advanced money at interest on future sugar crops, which in turn were contracted to the company to sell in the United States for a commission. The elder Atkins prospered greatly and diversified his interests, becoming a director of the Union Pacific Railroad and other large enterprises. Edwin, or Ned as he was called in the family, was a sharp-nosed, sharp-eyed Yankee lad who entered his father's business late in 1868. After a year's apprenticeship in its Boston countinghouse, Ned's father sent him to Cienfuegos, a sugar town and port on the south coast of Cuba, to learn the Spanish language and local business methods. The Atkins' company's Cuban correspondents were the Torriente brothers of Cienfuegos, and to them the elder Atkins entrusted his son. For the next fifteen winters, Ned Atkins lived and worked with the Torriente family, thereby gaining an intimate knowledge of Cuban business and society. In 1875 he took entire charge of the Cuban end of the Atkins business, and by the end of the Ten Years' War in 1878 he was prepared to find opportunities in the continuing economic crisis that gripped the island.[14]

Desultory and partial as it was, the Ten Years' War was the most formidable Cuban challenge to Spanish rule that the island had yet seen. Although not a major military conflict, it traumatized the Cuban economy in several ways. The rebel forces concentrated on property destruction, burning cane fields to destroy the sugar crop, and sometimes estate buildings as well, wrecking railroads and bridges, and sending interest and insurance rates soaring. Cumulatively, this wartime destruction and disruption hit many planters hard. Moreover, as the upper classes lost interest in the prolonged struggle, its leaders switched their appeal to the large Negro population, calling on the slaves to join the rebellion as they made the abolition of slavery one of its chief objects. This was in fact the only one of the movement's goals actually realized in the negotiated peace which ended the fighting. As a result, the planters felt added pressures from the need to restructure their work force after the slaves gained their freedom. In the long run the new system of seasonal wage labor may have been cheaper than the slave system, but the immediate effect was to place more strain upon the planters' resources. On top of this, Cuban growers faced strong competition from government-subsidized European beet sugar, which forced down prices on the world market.[15]

All over Cuba, sugar estates were in trouble, and firms like E. Atkins and Company had great difficulty in collecting their cash advances, which had often accumulated over several years. Both the Atkins and Torriente concerns faced large potential losses, while the Torrientes owned large sums to the Atkins' company as well. In 1880 the two families acted together to foreclose on one of the largest sugar estates in the Cienfuegos district, and after two years of court battles the junior Atkins took charge of its management. In 1884, when the Torrientes were forced to give up most of their share in the property in order to cover their own debts to Atkins and Company, Atkins was left in sole charge of a major sugar complex.[16]

Edwin Atkins saw that to raise sugar at a profit, lower costs, greater efficiency, and increased centralization were required, and he had both the resources and the foresight to make his newly acquired Soledad estate the most modern in Cuba. Extensive physical improvements were only the beginning; not the least of Atkins' achievements was the creation of a skilled management staff. In addition to his estate manager, an American engineer with long experience in Cuba, Atkins hired a German sugar master, a mill engineer, and a full-time industrial chemist, who soon devised an improved sugar-making process. Shrewdly, Atkins built a large sugar mill of advanced design on the estate, and gave it a capacity well beyond his own needs. As grinding mills became more complex and expensive, most planters ceased to grind their own cane and became mere suppliers of these central mills, or *centrales,* each of which threw out a radial network of narrow-gage railways to bring in the crop. Such suppliers, who owned or leased nearby land, were known as *colonos* when they contracted to deliver their entire crop to the mill at a price previously agreed on. Atkins, at the forefront of this movement, benefited from the shift of economic power from planter to millowner; it was the latter who set the terms between them.[17]

By the time the elder Atkins died in 1888 and Edwin succeeded him as head of the firm, the old commission business in sugar was virtually dead in the

Edwin F. Atkins. Courtesy of the American Geographical Society Collection, University of Wisconsin–Milwaukee

United States. The American sugar-refining industry had coalesced into large units which sent their agents to Cuba to buy sugar directly, eliminating the numerous traditional jobbers and wholesalers to whom commission merchants like Atkins had sold. After Henry O. Havemeyer consolidated a number of refining firms into the American Sugar Refining Company, popularly called the "sugar trust," he also moved to control his sources of supply by acquiring sugar lands in Cuba. By 1890 the Havemeyer company controlled from 70 to 90 percent of the United States' refined sugar market, and Atkins found it expedient to come to terms with it. He sold Havemeyer his refining interests in Massachusetts, but the sugar king really desired the benefit of Atkins' knowledge of Cuba and his expertise in cane production and management. The latter's Soledad estate was regarded as a model of productivity. In 1893 it covered, with its dependencies, over twelve thousand acres; there were twenty-two miles of private railroad on the estate, and twelve hundred workers lived on it during the harvesting and grinding season. It was this operation which Havemeyer wished to emulate, and in 1892 Havemeyer, Atkins, and Havemeyer's cousin, Charles H. Senff, organized the Trinidad Sugar Company, with Atkins as president. The new firm rapidly leased and bought thousands of acres of sugar lands in the vicinity of Trinidad, another south coast town not far from Cienfuegos, and worked them with up-to-date planting methods. The day of the traditional planter had passed; big foreign-owned companies like Trinidad represented the shape of the future.[18]

Most of the Cuban sugar crop was sold in the United States, but Cuban-American trade was hampered by the protective tariff policies of both Spain and the United States, as well as by Cuba's Spanish export taxes. In 1890, however, the United States adopted the McKinley Tariff, which put sugar on the free list and included reciprocity provisions with Spain. This was a boon to the sugar business which greatly advanced the interests of the Atkins and Trinidad companies during the four years when it was in effect. The Cuban sugar crop leaped from 632,000 tons in 1890 to a million in 1894, while other Americans, including Claus Spreckels, the California- and Hawaii-based sugar baron, moved into Cuban sugar growing. The incursion of these Americans had considerable impact, for they were among the largest and most efficient producers, and like Atkins were usually associated with millownership. Atkins wrote Senator Nelson Aldrich of Rhode Island in 1894 that American-owned estates produced about ten percent of all Cuban sugar. Nevertheless, North Americans did not own or control the Cuban sugar industry in the 1890s; they controlled only the market for sugar, but that control was to prove fundamental.[19]

While some Americans moved into the Cuban sugar business, others helped pioneer in marketing a newer tropical product, bananas. In 1866, when Carl B. Frank began importing small quantities of bananas from Panamá to New York, the fruit was a little-known oddity in Europe and the United States. At the Philadelphia Centennial Exposition of 1876, bananas wrapped in tinfoil sold at ten cents apiece. After 1870, Captain Lorenzo Dow Baker of Massachusetts tested the market by bringing bananas from Jamaica to Jersey City. Finding sales good, he enlarged his operations and moved his distribution point to Boston, where he sold his fruit through an agent, Andrew Preston. In 1885 Baker, Preston, and seven others founded the Boston Fruit Company, which continued to find its main supply in Jamaica, but looked also to Cuba and Santo Domingo.[20]

By the 1880s, Central America also shipped a modest quantity of bananas from several ports on the Gulf of Honduras and from Bluefields, Nicaragua. Italian immigrants had pioneered in the trade, buying their fruit from small local producers and arranging its shipment to the United States. Once more, however, it was an American who turned these prosaic transactions into big business. Minor C. Keith first arrived in Costa Rica in 1871 at the call of his older brother, Henry Meiggs Keith. The two were nephews of Henry Meiggs, the legendary Andean railroad builder after whom the elder brother was named, and it was his influence which had secured for H. M. Keith a government contract to build a railway from Costa Rica's central plateau to Puerto Limón on the Caribbean coast. Costa Ricans had long dreamed of connecting their central highlands, where most of the population lived, with an Atlantic seaport, in the faith that export costs would plummet and agricultural profits would soar once interior products could readily reach the outside world. When pressed, the Costa Rican president who negotiated the railroad loan admitted receiving a kickback of £100,000 from the London bankers, but at its inception the project was so popular that nothing could discredit it, while the prestige of the Meiggs name smoothed the way for his nephews.[21]

Minor Keith was still in his early twenties when he joined the railroad enterprise, but he was no stranger to management, having begun a successful lumber business at the age of sixteen. Born in Brooklyn, New York, he was raising cattle on the Texas coast when his brother's call reached him, and on arriving in Costa Rica he took charge of the project's commissariat. The work went badly, however. While one portion of the projected route lay among mountains and steep canyons, the coastal section ran through almost impassible swamps. Costs and problems multiplied, while the government funds ran out. Railroad construction ceased in 1873 amid mutual recriminations between the elder Keith and the Costa Rican government, which had already been badly cheated by its English bankers. H. M. Keith left the country in disgust, leaving his claims in the hands of his younger brother.[22]

By then Minor Keith had already diversified his business activities in Costa Rica, and unlike his brother was not solely dependent upon his railroad post. Keith had arrived with forty thousand dollars of his own money, realized from the sale of his Texas properties, and from the first had promoted several enterprises on the side. As buying and distributing agent for the railroad, he found it easy to move into private trading in local products, and he soon opened a line of retail stores as far along the coast as British Honduras. Settling in Puerto Limón, the hot, mosquito-infested village where the railroad was supposed to reach the sea, Keith also edged cautiously into the fruit trade, sending bananas north to New Orleans along with shipments of coconuts and other products.[23]

More surprisingly, Keith soon reentered the railroad field. In the later 1870s he personally contracted to build another short segment of the line, and his completion of this contract helped to dissipate the sense of failure and scan-

Minor C. Keith. Courtesy of the American Geographical Society Collection, University of
Wisconsin–Milwaukee

dal created by the previous stoppage of the work. Thereafter, each time the
impecunious government raised a little money, Keith took further contracts to
push the railroad forward a few more miles. Rumor had it that four thousand
men died in building the first twenty miles through the fever-ridden coastal
swamps, but there was never a shortage of West Indian Negroes to do the

work, and in time the roadbed climbed out of the coastal littoral and into the highlands.

Keith had a way with men, inspiring an almost fanatical loyalty in his workers. At one point when money ran short, some fifteen hundred of Keith's laborers worked without pay for nine months, relying simply on his promise to make good in time. The Costa Ricans admired his physical courage, which he liked to demonstrate with dangerous-looking acts like being let down the face of a cliff on a rope, or riding on the front of the first locomotive to cross a newly completed high bridge. Unlike most United States enterprisers in the Caribbean, Keith lived there full-time, became a member of Costa Rica's innermost social and political circles, and was at least half an adopted Costa Rican—all of which added to his influence and aided his business ventures. In 1883 he married Cristina Castro Fernández, whose father, José Maria Castro, had been twice president of the country, chief justice of the supreme court, minister of foreign relations, and holder of other lofty positions.[24]

His growing social and political influence never distracted Keith from his main purpose. In 1882 the railroad, built from both ends toward the middle, lacked only twenty-five miles of being complete. In that year Keith contracted with the government to lease it for five years, and to have first priority for building the completing segment. He was already shipping quantities of timber, coconuts, and most importantly, bananas to Puerto Limón for export, and he believed that control of railroad transportation would ensure his ultimate success. To complete the road, Keith became an international financier, periodically spending months in London to negotiate the necessary loans for the Costa Rican government. When the complex arrangements were finally completed in 1886, Keith headed a company which held a ninety-nine-year lease on the completed railroad and title to 800,000 acres of public land near the coast. It was 1890 before the line was finished, but the transportation monopoly to the east coast which it gave Keith was crucial.

Up to this point Keith had actually lost money on his railroad ventures, and he tried for years to get reimbursement from the government. The Costa Rican congress adamantly refused, but a sympathetic president once irregularly advanced him £80,000 of government funds at a moment of need, arguing when the act was exposed that Keith's bankruptcy would be a national disaster! Yet the railroad projects brought all else in their wake, including the huge land concessions; as the largest single landowner in Costa Rica, Keith's fortunes soon came to rest solidly on the humble banana.[25]

Between 1883 and 1900, the annual banana exports of Costa Rica increased from 110,000 stems to over a million, and the increase in production was almost entirely Keith's. Instead of buying local bananas from small producers, as had been customary, Keith made banana growing a plantation industry. Until then, the coastal lands were considered worthless, and few Costa Ricans would live there; with Keith's political connections it was both cheap and easy to acquire almost any number of these empty acres. The same black Jamaicans who had built his railroad, and their newly arrived cousins, provided a cheap and ample supply of labor for the new banana farms. Instead of the wild native banana, his trees grew the superior Gros Michele strain. Since bananas were cheap to grow but quick to spoil, fast transport was the key to their marketing. His domination of the railroad ensured that Keith's bananas would always have cars to move them, no matter what else waited on the sidings—and his competitors accused him of deliberately arranging at times that their shipments did just that. Even when he transferred the road to an English syndicate, Keith retained preferential treatment, including lower rates, special trains, and favorable schedules. By the 1890s Keith's operations were rivaled only by those of the Boston Fruit Company, though competition between the two leaders in the trade was reduced by the fact that Keith's base of operations was primarily in New Orleans and only secondarily in the northeast.[26]

Minor Keith's burgeoning success was gravely threatened when his New Orleans distributors failed in 1898. He held their bills for one and a half million dollars, and lost his largest United States outlet as well. Hard pressed, he sought a new marketing agreement with the Boston Fruit Company, and this association soon led to the merger of the Keith and Boston concerns, which combined in 1899 to form the United Fruit Company. In 1900 the new corporation had assets of almost seventeen million dollars, and operated 66,000 acres of banana plantations in five Caribbean countries and Jamaica. At birth it controlled about 60 percent of the growing United States banana market. Spurred by such giant enterprise, bananas soon became to coastal Central America what sugar was to Cuba.

In spite of United Fruit's instant success, Minor Keith finished his career as he had begun it, building railroads. After the first few years he left the fruit company's management to others, while he concentrated on efforts to build a Panamá-to-Mexico rail system. He had completed only portions of the ambitious scheme when he died at eighty-one in 1929. His preoccupation with railroads, however, had brought forth a new field of tropical export agriculture comparable to the sugar-and-railroad complex in Cuba. Like sugar and coffee, bananas would tie portions of Caribbean society into an international market economy.[27]

While Atkins and Keith represented the main currents of Caribbean development in the 1890s, North American investment patterns in the region could vary widely. In 1892, for example, a New York syndicate headed by John Wanamaker, President Benjamin Harrison's postmaster general, bought out the defaulted foreign debt of the Dominican Republic and organized the San Domingo Improvement Company. Along with the debt, the new company acquired the right to float new Dominican loans, secured by the government's customs revenues. Next the Improvement Company bought control of the National Bank of Santo Domingo from a French group. Within a few years the company had twice refunded the national debt, the second time with loans totaling over four million pounds in face value; it had gotten involved in a government railroad-building project; and it was not only deep into national politics but itself a major political issue in the Dominican Republic.[28]

Besides such involvement in banking and finance, North American enterprise in Caribbean countries built electric plants, ice-making plants, and waterworks; paved streets and improved docks and harbors; mined gold and iron and copper. In company with European capitalists, United States entrepreneurs were everywhere beginning to penetrate the economies of the region, and those who made government policy in Washington were already aware of it. Yet except for diplomatic support in time of crisis, and periodic attempts at tariff reciprocity treaties, few of these early economic enterprises owed much to the United States government or its policies. Washington's policy makers, on the other hand, had Caribbean interests distinct from those of the private sector, and these interests also engaged their attention. These too were expanding by the 1890s, and it is necessary next to see what drew the government of the United States into its own increased activity in the Caribbean region.

Chapter 2

The Background of
United States Policy

While private American businessmen were moving into the late-nineteenth-century Caribbean world on a broad front in sugar, bananas, merchandising, railroads, and other enterprises, the region figured regularly in United States foreign policy as well. The reasons for this went beyond narrowly economic considerations. From the Reconstruction era to the 1890s, there was rarely a time when the nation's policy makers were not concerned about one Caribbean issue or another. The battle smoke of the Civil War had barely cleared away before successive administrations were attempting to acquire Caribbean territory, worrying about rival European penetrations in the area, and pursuing the possibilities of an isthmian canal. Until the 1890s, these efforts were part of an admittedly fitful and ineffective foreign policy carried out by a government which let its armed forces decline to insignificance. The nation's attention was inward centered, external affairs often being regarded as almost irrelevant. Yet events in the Caribbean continued to spur at least sporadic interest in Washington, and coherent national policies were evolving in regard to that region well before 1898.

Over the years, the Caribbean question which most persistently titillated Americans was the feasibility and status of an isthmian canal. Anyone looking at a map could see the possibilities of such a canal, which could eliminate the long and dangerous voyage around South America, or the need to unload cargo for land transit across the isthmus and to subsequently reload it upon ships on the opposite side. An American-built railroad carried such transshipments across the narrow neck of Panamá from 1855 on, but interest in the canal remained lively; eastern merchants emphasized that any isthmian canal would cut at least six thousand miles from their shipping distance to the orient.

The opening of the Suez Canal in 1869 seemed to indicate that the advance of technology had also made possible a sea route through Central America. Moved by this faith, President Ulysses S. Grant initiated a program of naval expeditions to survey and evaluate the best isthmian canal routes, and seven such expeditions went out between 1870 and 1875.

In practice, only two prospective canal routes received consistent backing. One ran across Panamá, roughly on the line of the Panama Railroad. The other followed the San Juan River along the southern border of Nicaragua until it reached Lake Nicaragua, ran across that inland sea, then penetrated the coastal hills to emerge on the Pacific. The Panamá route was the shorter, but required cutting through or going over a considerable range of highlands. The Nicaragua route was judged more practical for a sea level, as opposed to a lock, canal; it took advantage of existing natural waterways, and offered a location somewhat nearer the United States. On the other hand, it was substantially longer than the Panamá route, and the San Juan River would require drastic enlargement and dredging before it could carry oceangoing ships. The Grant administration signed a treaty with Colombia in 1870 giving the United States the exclusive right to build a Panamanian canal, but the Colombian senate attached amendments which were unacceptable in Washington, and the treaty was allowed to die. In 1876 the president's interoceanic canal committee recommended the Nicaraguan route, and thereafter until 1900 Nicaragua triumphed in each new American survey or reevaluation.[1]

The activities of a French concern, the Universal Interoceanic Panama Canal Company, brought urgency to the isthmian canal issue. Headed by Ferdinand de Lesseps, prestigious hero of Suez, the Panama Canal Company bought out the Panama Railroad and began actual construction in 1881, after about two years of publicity and preparation. By the autumn of 1883 the work force totaled ten thousand men, and a year later approached twenty thousand, over three-fourths of them black laborers from the West Indies. This great work force, the abundance of modern machinery, and the huge sums of money spent made it necessary to take de Lesseps' venture very seriously, and to President Rutherford B. Hayes it represented an actual crisis. An isthmian canal, Hayes said in a special message to Congress, constituted virtually a part of the United States coastline, being of peculiar importance to American trade and shipping as well as American security. "The policy of this country is a canal under American control," Hayes declared. "The United States can not consent to the surrender of this control to any European power or to any combination of European powers." [2]

Hayes undoubtedly remembered the French incursion of the 1860s into Mexico, when Napoleon III established a client state in that nation under the short-lived regime of the Emperor Maximilian. Although Napoleon withdrew his troops in 1867, abandoning Maximilian to his fate, the incident had done much to keep alive American fears of European intervention in the New World. Attempting to allay such fears, the French government quickly dissociated itself from the Panamá canal project, explaining that de Lesseps represented only a group of private citizens from several nations. The leadership and most of the capital for the venture were nevertheless French, and many Americans believed that the company must inevitably look to official French protection in time of need, thus constituting a standing menace to the Monroe Doctrine.[3]

While the issue was never resolved diplomatically, it was removed for practical purposes by the massive failure of the French canal attempt. Although French accomplishments were impressive, the job proved vaster than anyone had imagined, and the canal company went into receivership in December 1888. It had been vanquished by tropical diseases, shaky financing, and most of all, by the enormous costs of the project, which soared to $287 million before the company finally collapsed. Its fall created a national scandal and brought down a French government, as well as impoverishing thousands of investors, while as many as twenty thousand human beings may have died of disease in the canal zone during its operations. The French liquidators persuaded the Colombian government to extend the canal concession to 1904, but only on condition that a new company should be organized to carry on the work. Accordingly, the New Panama Canal Company was chartered in 1894, inheriting the property and charter of its predecessor. This concern carried on token operations through the remainder of the nineties, but it appeared that building an isthmian canal was beyond the capacity of private enterprises; only a major government could command the vast sums required for its completion.[4]

In 1887, shortly before the Panamá canal project lapsed, a United States syndicate organized the Maritime Canal Company of Nicaragua and received a charter of incorporation from Congress. The company was formally launched in 1889 with a paper capital of $250 million. Only $6 million of this imposing sum were actually paid in, but a subsidiary firm began preliminary construction work with that. However, the American enterprise was no more successful than the French one had been. By 1893 the original funds had run out, while the business panic of that year made it impossible to raise more. The promoters had from the first counted on federal funding, and they received warm support from the Harrison administration in their quest. In both 1891 and 1892, however, Congress failed to act on bills which provided for the United States government to guarantee up to $100 million of the company's bonds in return for a share in the ownership and control of the canal. The tide began to turn in 1895 when Congress appropriated $50,000 to investigate the practicality of the company's scheme, and in 1897 it authorized further investigation by a new commission which enjoyed a large budget and ample time to carry out its work. By then there was at least serious consideration in the United States for building an isthmian canal as a national project, while as yet few seemed to question that it would be located along the Nicaragua route.[5]

Even without a canal, the United States had a long-standing isthmian commitment of a special kind. The 1840s had seen a growing rivalry between the United States and Great Britain for control of prospective canal routes. When the British in 1844 claimed a protectorate over Nicaragua's Mosquito Coast, both United States and Caribbean policy makers took alarm. In an effort to forestall British expansion, the government of Colombia in 1846 offered Benjamin Bidlack, the American minister in Bogotá, a treaty which guaranteed to the government and citizens of the United States the right of free passage across the Isthmus of Panamá, and over any subsequent railroad or canal which crossed it. In return the United States was to guarantee the neutrality of the Panamá isthmus and ensure Colombian sovereignty there. Uncertain of his government's desires, Bidlack signed the treaty and sent it home for ratification or rejection. Not surprisingly, the United States Senate long hesitated to take on the unprecedented commitments entailed in this so-called Bidlack Treaty, but finally ratified it in 1848 in the flush of enthusiasm which accompanied the successful conclusion of the Mexican War. By that time the British had forcibly seized the outlet of the San Juan River, through which the contemplated Nicaraguan canal route reached the Atlantic, and tensions were rising rapidly.[6]

The Anglo-American contest for strategic positions was quieted in 1850 by the Clayton-Bulwer Treaty, the major provision of which pledged that neither party would fortify or exercise exclusive control over any isthmian canal. This seeming guarantee of a neutralized international canal went far to end the mutual scramble for spheres of influence, but did not do away with the prior commitments of either party; the treaty's provisions as to these were deliberately vague. Thus the United States continued to adhere to the Bidlack Treaty and to act from time to time on its obligations under it.[7]

In practice, the principal obstacle to a neutral Isthmus of Panamá, and to free and unobstructed transit across it, was the frequent political unrest which stemmed from Panamanian separatism. Isolated from Colombia by interests, sentiment, and geography, Panamá was a hotbed of revolutionary hopes. By one count there were fifty rebellions in Panamá between 1830 and 1903, almost all of them aiming at autonomy or independence. A major uprising in 1855–56 succeeded in securing home rule until 1863, but while the province's constitutional status varied over the years, the Panamanians never achieved any long-term satisfaction of their aspirations.[8]

At times, the revolts in Panamá threatened foreign life and property. Since the American-built Panama Railroad was the crucial communications link across the isthmus, rebels often seized it to deny its use to Colombian government troops. It took time for Bogotá to gather forces and transport them to the isthmus to reestablish control; meanwhile it was usual for American naval commanders to take a hand in events. In order to protect foreigners and guarantee free transit, these naval officers customarily insisted that the railroad must be unhampered in its operations, and that Panamá's cities were out of bounds as battlefields; actual fighting must take place well away from them. Since these demands necessarily hampered the Panamanian rebels, they were not always obeyed. In such cases the United States Navy was apt to land bluejackets and marines to enforce its rules, citing the Bidlack Treaty as its authority. Whatever its qualms about such outside interventions, the Colombian government found them important safeguards to its own authority in Panamá, and therefore did not contest the Americans' version of their treaty rights.[9]

This was the case even in the largest of such North American interventions. In 1885 Panamanian dissidents took advantage of an uprising elsewhere in Colombia to make a new try for independence. With the French canal project at its peak of activity, the world's eyes were on Panamá, while Panamanian self-government had even greater attractions for the locals. The United States became interested when the rebels temporarily interrupted service on the Panama Railroad, as well as reportedly seized American-owned vessels and property. The Colombian authorities, caught short of available troops, found the rebellion unusually difficult to crush. When they removed their limited garrison from Colón on the Caribbean coast to oust resistance in Panamá City, new rebel forces seized Colón; when the government troops returned to Colón the rebels burned that city and withdrew, while the original insurgents retook Panamá City. These uprisings on two fronts put the isthmus in an uproar, and in Washington the newly installed administration of President Grover Cleveland decided on a large-scale intervention to impose order. Within a few weeks a landing force of over twelve hundred men occupied the key points of Panamá. Overawed by the American admiral in command, the principal rebel leader surrendered to government authorities, and the disorders on the isthmus ended. Thus even under the first Cleveland administration, which showed a minimum of interest in overseas activism, the United States occupied a unique place in the affairs of Panamá and took drastic action to preserve its special position there.[10]

By the late 1880s, America's Caribbean interests and isthmian canal projects were also associated with a new development, the birth of a modern United States Navy. Congress had appropriated funds for a handful of new steel warships in 1883, after having allowed the navy virtually to disappear as an effective fighting force. In 1885 the secretary of the navy announced that the nation still possessed no single warship which could keep the sea against any modern opponent, and even when Benjamin Harrison came to the presidency in 1889 the United States ranked a lowly twelfth among the world's naval powers, surpassed among others by Sweden, Turkey, China, and the Netherlands. By this time, some forty new vessels had been either built or authorized, but most of them were relatively small and lightly armed. It was under Harrison and his energetic secretary of the navy, Benjamin Franklin Tracy, that the official goal of the building program changed from a merely modern navy to a major one.[11]

At first glance, Benjamin Tracy was an unlikely figure to become one of the fathers of American navalism. A lifelong friend and political ally of Thomas Collier Platt, the "easy boss" of New York's state Republican machine, Tracy was put into the cabinet to assuage a quarrel between Platt and the incoming president. His knowledge of warfare was gained on land, not water; he had served in the Civil War, seen combat at Spotsylvania, and eventually received a Congressional Medal of Honor for his actions there. Mustered out of the service as a brevet brigadier general, he pursued a successful career at law, serving for a time as chief justice of the New York Court of Appeals and building a lucrative private practice. He was known to the general public for none of these things, however, but as a prominent breeder and racer of trotting horses.[12]

Although initially ignorant of naval affairs, the new secretary began a vigorous self-education campaign upon his arrival in Washington. Determined to be more than a figurehead in office, he sought guidance from the best professional minds available. This soon brought him into contact with Admiral Stephen B. Luce and Captain Alfred Thayer Mahan, two of the foremost naval thinkers of their day. These men and others converted Tracy at the outset to the doctrine of all-out naval expansion, while Mahan's theories of sea power guided Tracy's thinking even before they were known to the world at large. In his first annual report, Tracy called for the construction not only of more lightly armed commerce raiders, but of a battleship force capable of contesting the approach of an enemy fleet to American shores. At that time without any fighting ships of the heaviest class, the navy needed at least twenty, Tracy declared in his revolutionary report. While Congress never was willing to go nearly as far or as fast as the impatient secretary desired, it did accept his call to begin building capital ships. Once set on this course, the nation never turned back; only twenty years after Tracy took office, the United States Navy would rank third in the world.[13]

A great nation, Captain Mahan wrote, needed extensive foreign trade to ensure economic strength, a large merchant marine to carry it, and a powerful navy to protect it. Furthermore, to be effective in key strategic areas or in distant parts of the world, a navy needed coaling stations and secure bases overseas. Mahan's insistence on the importance of overseas bases was fully accepted by his superiors. As President Harrison wrote Secretary of State James G. Blaine in 1891, "I do feel that in some directions, as to naval stations and points of influence, we must look forward to a departure from the too conservative opinions which have been held heretofore." Blaine in turn advised that only three overseas points were of sufficient importance for the United States to acquire them, namely, Hawaii, Cuba, and Puerto Rico. Hawaii alone required speedy action, Blaine thought, while the other two could wait. To Tracy, however, this seemed much too complacent; in his opinion both more bases and more speed were necessary.[14]

Their divergence of views on such matters was to lead to a thinly veiled rivalry between Blaine and Tracy over the shaping of foreign policy. As secretary of state, and a formidable party chieftain of long standing, Blaine enjoyed obvious advantages, but these were offset by a stroke of fate. Early in 1890 Tracy's Washington residence was struck by fire, and in one dreadful night the naval secretary lost his wife and a daughter, while a second daughter and a grandchild were badly injured when they jumped to safety. Tracy himself was severely hurt and carried from the house unconscious. Shocked by the tragedy, President Harrison had Tracy brought to the White House to recover; normally a chilly, rather distant man, the president opened his heart to his stricken subordinate and the two became fast friends. When Tracy recovered from his long ordeal, he plunged back into his work with obsessive energy, and overseas bases were high among his priorities. Aided by his new intimacy with Harrison, his views often overrode those of the secretary of state, and the government soon embarked upon a search for West Indian naval stations.[15]

Such a quest was by no means new; President Andrew Johnson's secretary of state, William H. Seward, had pursued similar goals immediately after the Civil War. The problems of blockading the Confederacy had convinced Seward that the navy needed one or more Caribbean bases, and in 1867 he negotiated a treaty for the purchase of the Danish West Indies. The Senate withheld its ratification, however; having just approved the purchase of Alaska, it was unwilling to spend another seven and a half million on the tiny Danish islands. Nothing daunted, Seward shifted his base campaign to Samaná Bay in eastern Santo Domingo. A few years earlier a weakened Dominican government, wracked by bitter domestic dissidence and afraid of reconquest by Haiti, from which it had broken free only in 1844, had sought stability by reannexing the country to Spain. But the period of Spanish rule from 1861 to 1865 saw the growth of armed popular resistance to this retreat to colonial status, so that in the end the Spanish withdrew rather than face a prolonged struggle to maintain their authority. Again independent but with an empty treasury, the new government offered to sell Samaná Bay to the United States, and Seward was as anxious as they to close the deal. By what seemed a happy coincidence, the Haitian government also approached Seward with a proposal to sell the Môle Saint Nicolas, a protected anchorage on Haiti's northwest tip which commanded the Windward Passage between the islands of Hispaniola and

Cuba. By this time, however, the Dominican leaders were talking of annexing their entire country to the United States, in a renewed search for security and stability under the protection of a stronger power. Once again Congress demurred; in January 1869 the House of Representatives roundly defeated a resolution which would have authorized United States protectorates over both Haiti and Santo Domingo.[16]

President Grant inherited these projects upon taking office, and was soon won over to another attempt to annex the Dominican Republic. The new president was surrounded by ambitious men who hoped to profit personally from Dominican annexation, his own secretary, General Orville Babcock, being one of them. It was Babcock who went to Santo Domingo in 1869 as Grant's executive agent and negotiated terms under which the United States would pay two million dollars for Samaná Bay, and an additional million and a half to retire the Dominican national debt after annexation. A rigged national referendum in Santo Domingo purported to show that the people of that country favored annexation to the United States, and a formal treaty went forward to the Senate. That body, however, showed as little enthusiasm for Grant's territorial schemes as for Seward's. Though Grant fought with his usual dogged stubbornness, the Senate rejected his treaty in June 1870. He sought for another year to gain Senate approval, but in vain. Nevertheless, only a few votes in the Senate had prevented the annexation of a Caribbean country to the United States.[17]

Unlike Grant, neither Harrison nor Tracy attempted to annex entire Caribbean countries; their ambition ran no further than acquiring one or two naval bases. Even in this they encountered at first the reluctance or opposition of Blaine, who preferred to concentrate on his Hawaiian schemes. When late in 1890 the Danish government made new overtures to sell Saint Thomas and Saint John in the Danish West Indies, Tracy was eager to look into the matter, but Blaine successfully argued that those small islands should wait until "by fate we own the larger West Indies." Tracy continued to insist upon the importance of West Indian bases, however, both to support a stronger Atlantic fleet and to protect a future isthmian canal. The canal in turn would strengthen America's naval posture by making it easier to defend both coasts with one fleet. Since Harrison and Tracy both believed that an isthmian canal was vitally important and certain to be built, the president bypassed Blaine to support the Caribbean initiatives of his navy secretary.[18]

Tracy accepted Captain Mahan's judgment that Cuba was the best location for an American naval base, but no one believed it possible to secure a base concession from the Spanish authorities. There remained the old alternatives of Seward's and Grant's day, Haiti's Môle Saint Nicolas and Santo Domingo's Samaná Bay. Oddly enough, Blaine helped to focus attention on the former, claiming that his predecessor had made a secret agreement by which the United

States would ensure the delivery of arms to Haitian revolutionist Florvil Hippolite in return for the lease of a naval base at the Môle when Hippolite had made himself president. The revolt succeeded, and Blaine asserted that the Haitians were now obligated to negotiate the base concession. President Hippolite denied the existence of such an arrangement, and in fact no record of it has ever been found. Nevertheless, Tracy eagerly took up the claim, and early in 1890 he sent Admiral Bancroft Gherardi to Port-au-Prince to speak directly for the navy. At first Gherardi attempted to camouflage his intent by talking only of a coaling concession for the Clyde Line, a New York shipping firm to which Hippolite owed money, but the Haitian president was wary of any foreign concession at the Môle. On a second visit in January 1891 Gherardi tried a blunter approach, presenting the Haitians with what amounted to an ultimatum. When Hippolite stalled, Tracy sent the navy's new White Squadron to his capitol as an implied threat. This attempt at open intimidation set off a strong patriotic reaction in Haiti which made further negotiations appear hopeless. Virtually ignoring the State Department, the navy had tried its own version of diplomacy, but Tracy's heavy-handedness had outraged the Haitians while also alienating opinion in the United States.[19]

The Americans then turned to Samaná Bay, finding the Dominican dictator Ulises Heureaux hard pressed for funds and ready to make a deal. In 1892 the two governments agreed upon a draft treaty giving the United States a ninety-nine-year lease on the bay, but the *New York Herald* broke the story before the treaty was signed, setting off a patriotic reaction in Santo Domingo similar to that in Haiti the previous year. Fearing a threat to his power, Heureaux broke off negotiations, and the Harrison administration was forced to give up any immediate plans for a Caribbean naval base. In this respect, Tracy's efforts had come to nothing, while his attempts at naval diplomacy had been distinctly inept. Like the battleship campaign, however, the search for Caribbean bases would long outlive Tracy, and achieve fuller success later under other men.[20]

In the mid-nineties American concern about Caribbean naval bases was joined by a fear of supposed British expansionism in the area, which culminated in the Venezuelan crisis of 1895–96. In the late nineteenth century the great powers of Europe were well along in partitioning the eastern hemisphere among themselves, and concerned Americans began to fear that European imperialism might next turn toward the New World. Many Latin American states were weak and vulnerable, most notably those of the Caribbean. Europeans already had large financial interests there, and the British had great diplomatic influence as well. A series of events in 1894–95 persuaded many Americans that Great Britain was threatening to violate the Monroe Doctrine, and the result was a diplomatic showdown between the two nations.

Great Britain had long claimed a special position on the east coast of Nicaragua, first under the so-called Mosquito Protectorate, later through her self-appointed role of defender of the native Indians in its successor, the Mosquito Reserve. United States leaders had never ceased to resent this; in 1888, then Secretary of State Thomas F. Bayard publicly accused the British of maintaining their hold on the reserve only because it commanded the eastern end of the Nicaraguan canal route. Although the area was formally under Nicaraguan sovereignty, the Nicaraguans had never been able to exercise control over it; the real authority in the reserve was British. When Nicaragua finally rejected this status in 1894 and moved troops into the region, a diplomatic crisis arose, in which President Cleveland's State Department vigorously backed Nicaragua. Not wanting a confrontation with the United States, Great Britain reluctantly withdrew from its former protectorate.

The turmoil which accompanied the extension of direct Nicaraguan rule to the Mosquito Coast brought riots and disorders there, after which the Nicaraguan authorities arrested and deported a number of British subjects. Already dangerously disgruntled, the British government demanded an indemnity for the property losses to these people resulting from their enforced sudden departure, but the Nicaraguan government refused to pay. To reassert its prestige in the region, in 1895 Great Britain seized Nicaragua's Pacific seaport of Corinto and occupied it with a naval force. Thus coerced, the Nicaraguans paid the indemnity, and the British promptly departed.[21]

This sudden exercise of force in Central America alarmed American observers, however; the press and public overlooked Britain's significant retreat from the Mosquito Coast and saw only its muscle flexing at Corinto. Republicans in particular attacked President Cleveland for failing to take some action during the Corinto affair. Senators Cushman Davis of Minnesota and Henry Cabot Lodge of Massachusetts, both Republicans, and Democratic Senator John T. Morgan of Alabama, all warned the Senate in full-dress speeches that Great Britain was embarked upon a plan to extend its domination in the Americas. In particular, all three senators saw further menace in the long-standing British dispute with Venezuela over the boundary between the latter state and the colony of British Guiana.[22]

The Venezuela-Guiana boundary dispute involved a large but lightly populated piece of jungle in which precise borders were understandably lacking. After years of wrangling, the British had simply announced that much of the disputed area was no longer subject to negotiation. The alarmed Venezuelans hired a skilled lobbyist and former diplomat named William L. Scruggs and began to publicize their case in the United States. Their most effective argument was that the British were pushing forward the borders of their empire under the guise of a boundary dispute, using tactics already successful in India, Burma, and Africa, and that these actions constituted a veiled threat to the Monroe Doctrine. The charge was shrewdly selected, for it matched emerging American fears about British intentions. Senator Lodge, among others, promptly raised the alarm at European imperialism in the Americas. In Lodge's words, "These powers have already seized the islands of the Pacific and parcelled out Africa. Great Britain cannot extend her possessions in the East. She has pretty near reached the limit of what can be secured in Africa. She is now turning her attention to South America." If the United States ignored the challenge, Lodge warned, it would soon find the European powers camped on its very doorstep, and the Monroe Doctrine a dead letter.[23]

Convinced that there was substance in these fears, President Cleveland in July 1895 approved the dispatch by Secretary of State Richard Olney of a startling message to London. The president called it "Olney's twenty-inch gun," and in fact it was intended to set off something of an explosion. Olney too viewed the British course with Venezuela as thinly veiled expansionism, and he declared that "the safety and welfare of the United States are . . . concerned with the maintenance of the independence of every American state as against any European power." Any European threat to the integrity of American states, Olney said, would "justify and require the interposition of the United States." Furthermore, the secretary of state claimed, "Today the United States is practically sovereign on this continent, and its fiat is law upon the subjects to which it confines its interposition." This was because "its infinite resources combined with its isolated position render it master of the situation and practically invulnerable as against any and all powers." All this would change, however, if European imperialism were allowed a free hand in the Americas. If even one European state were allowed to seize American territory, the others would follow. It was therefore up to the British to explain themselves, Olney concluded. If the Venezuelan issue were really only a boundary dispute, then the British could prove it by submitting their claims to arbitration. A refusal to do so, on the other hand, would strongly suggest that American suspicions were justified.[24]

Nonplussed by this amazing communication, the British cabinet delayed its reply for months, and then flatly rejected Olney's argument. In December, Cleveland himself took charge, sending a special message to Congress which caused a further sensation. If Great Britain would not submit to arbitration, he stated, then he would ask Congress to approve sending a United States commission to the disputed area which would itself determine what territory rightfully belonged to each party in the dispute. When this had been done, the president promised, his government would then "resist by any means in its power" any British attempt to take more territory than the commission allowed them. This virtual threat of war set off an intense debate in the United States in which the embattled president found as many supporters as critics. In London, the astonished British finally realized that the United States government was seriously aroused, and eventually decided to concede the arbitration which Olney and Cleveland had demanded. This was less the result of fear of the United States, whose armed forces were as yet no match for those of the British, than the result of a far-sighted decision to seek friendship with the rising power of the New World rather than implant a source of long-term hostility. The disputed territory, London decided, was simply not worth the enmity of the United States, especially after the Americans made important concessions on the limits of the arbitration.[25]

Whether wise or foolish, Cleveland's ringing assertion of hemispheric supremacy was, in the end, substantially accepted by the only power well placed to challenge it. Even more important, it reflected a new determination in the United States to play a larger role in hemispheric matters, and to tolerate no interference from across the Atlantic. It was ironic that this bold expansion of American pretensions should come from the antiexpansionist Cleveland, who believed that he was simply meeting the threat of foreign aggression. Yet, having faced down Great Britain itself, American policy makers were more prone to believe that their word should be obeyed when hemispheric issues drew their attention. In a very real sense, the incident seemed to validate United States intervention in Caribbean affairs.

At the same time, a new mood of expansionism was visible in the country, in part reflecting the national self-image. A nation becoming conscious of its growing power, and confident in its righteousness, wanted to be received more fully into the inner circle of great powers. Colonial empires were currently the premier status symbols in that circle, and as they looked on at the territorial scramble which then engaged the European powers over much of the world, Americans too began to yearn for status. They were as virile and progressive as any other people; they too could carry enlightenment to the earth's darker corners. American democracy and Protestant Christianity, American technology and know-how, could do their part to speed up the world's progress. Scattered voices began to call for a greater American role in international affairs, even as the disastrous industrial depression of the 1890s added economic concerns to those of national pride. The Panic of 1893 and subsequent collapse of domestic markets brought urgency to the search for buyers abroad. Foreign markets for industrial products appeared most promising in areas lacking their own industry, for it was feared that the highly industrialized nations of Europe would bar American goods if pushed too hard at home; they could, after all, manufacture what they needed for themselves. The best export markets, therefore, were assumed to be in the large economically undeveloped countries. Many of these had been annexed to European empires, however, and could no longer be considered open to equal competition from outsiders. By elimination, American theorists isolated two regions as holding the most promising markets for an expanded United States export trade: the Far East and Latin America, the latter already a lively field for American enterprise.[26]

Accordingly, American leaders were soon sketching the outlines of a more active Caribbean policy. Senator Lodge called in 1895 for a much enlarged navy, the acquisition of a major naval base in the West Indies, some form of United States control over Cuba, and the construction of an isthmian canal under United States control. The Republican platform of 1896 included an isthmian canal plank, which was echoed in a resolution of the recently organized National Association of Manufacturers. The debate over Hawaiian annexation after 1893, as well as increasing talk of a "China market," added urgency to the canal issue by suggesting a larger future role for the nation in the Pacific. The Caribbean was seen as gaining in importance to the United States, and further interventions there appeared increasingly likely.[27]

By 1896, the place where United States intervention seemed most needed was Cuba. An insurrection against Spanish rule began on that island in the previous year, and spread rapidly among a people hard hit by economic depression. Spain quickly assembled a large army to crush the rebellion, but the guerrilla tactics of the *insurrectos* proved effective against conventional armed forces. The guerrillas raided outposts and destroyed property, and in response Spanish forces rounded up the civil population of entire districts into concentration areas, while both sides freely used terrorism to intimidate the uncommitted. This unpleasant struggle, of a kind since painfully familiar to the world, soon fell into what appeared to be a permanent deadlock, the Spanish securely controlling the cities and the rebels roaming the countryside with relative freedom.[28]

A year and a half of such stalemate had reduced Cuba to serious distress, cut deeply into its sugar production, and threatened foreign life and property on the island. The outgoing Cleveland administration regarded the situation as a threat to American interests, and strongly desired the restoration of peace and order. In his last annual message to Congress, President Cleveland spoke at length of American interests in Cuba. United States concern with Cuba's troubles, the president stated with his usual directness, was "by no means of a wholly sentimental or philanthropic character," since "our actual pecuniary interest in it is second only to that of the people and government of Spain." United States citizens had invested from thirty to fifty million dollars in Spain, Cleveland estimated, while before 1895 United States–Cuban trade had been running at around one hundred million dollars per year. With such substantial interests now in jeopardy, the United States wanted an end to the struggle. The most satisfactory solution, the president suggested, might come through a Spanish offer of autonomy, or local self-government, to the Cubans. An end to the fighting was all that the United States wanted, Cleveland said; he offered America's good offices, and denied any ambition for Cuban conquest.

Thus far the president had been reiterating a well-known policy, but the end of his message held a warning: it should not be assumed, he said, that the "hitherto expectant attitude of the United States will be indefinitely maintained." If it became clear that Spain was unable to restore order in Cuba, the obligation of the United States to respect Spain's sovereignty would be superseded by "higher obligations." A time might come when "a correct policy and care for our interests," as well as general humanitarian motives, would demand United States intervention in the Cuban war in order to stop the fighting. If Spain could not restore order in Cuba within a reasonable time, Cleveland's message indicated, the United States would have to do so.[29]

As a lame-duck president, Cleveland could hardly speak for future administrations. Neither did he wish an armed intervention in Cuba on the part of the United States; he had done all that he could to avoid such an action. Yet events had already run so far that he clearly foresaw the possibility, and within eighteen months it would become a reality under his successor. Grover Cleveland, like William McKinley after him, found himself caught up in an accelerating current of diplomatic activism and expansionism. Like Benjamin Harrison, Cleveland would denounce imperialism and colonial rule when they came; yet like Harrison, he had unwittingly played his part in leading the country toward them. Under their administrations the United States had rapidly expanded its navy and its overseas interests. It aimed at a larger role in the Americas, an isthmian canal, Caribbean naval bases, Hawaiian annexation, and if necessary, even direct intervention in Cuba. It only took the Spanish-Cuban-American War to carry the country beyond even these ambitious goals. While wartime developments were sudden and far-reaching, they were also the culmination of a decade of steady change in American foreign policy, of growing economic interests in overseas areas, and of the rising tide of navalism and expansionism which had already appeared during the nineties.

Chapter 3

———··⟨∞⟩··———

War in Cuba and Its Fruits

William McKinley had as little desire to see the United States drawn into the Cuban struggle as his predecessor in the presidency, and he made serious attempts to prevent it. Late in 1897, he advised Congress that his administration had for the present rejected formal recognition of Cuban belligerency, much less independence, as well as any United States intervention in the Cuban crisis. As to forcible annexation of Cuba by the United States, McKinley sternly opposed it; that, he said, "would be criminal aggression." Instead, the new Liberal ministry which had recently come to power in Spain should be allowed time to attempt a compromise solution, presumably that experiment in Cuban autonomy which Washington's diplomacy had consistently come to favor. However, the chief executive inserted a muted warning note reminiscent of his predecessor's a year earlier: "If it should hereafter appear to be a duty . . . to intervene with force," it would only be because the need for such action had become "so clear as to command the support and approval of the civilized world." [1]

Four months later the United States and Spain were at war over Cuba. The speed with which events moved has bemused both contemporary observers and later historians, many of whom have accused McKinley of a weak-kneed reversal of his policies in the face of an aroused public opinion. Public opinion was indeed aroused; the United States has never entered a war with as much enthusiasm as it did the war with Spain. The Cuban revolutionary junta, whose headquarters were in New York, had proven itself a master of propaganda, successfully depicting the struggle in Cuba as one between brave Cuban freedom fighters and brutal, cowardly Spaniards who practiced murder and atrocity with sickening abandon. The junta's releases were avidly reprinted by the American press, and gave specific shape to the mounting national concern over the undoubted tragedy in Cuba.[2]

The members of Congress both shared and fueled this rising emotionalism. Some forty-eight resolutions, introduced in the House of Representatives and the Senate during the Fifty-fourth and Fifty-fifth Congress, called for the recognition of Cuba's belligerency or independence, or for some form of United States intervention in Cuba. While such resolutions had bipartisan support, they tended more often to originate with members of the Democratic or Populist parties than with Republicans. This was especially true after the bitterly fought election of 1896 and the return of the presidency to Republican hands; the congressional opposition then increasingly implied that a callous administration, interested only in the profits of big business, ignored a moral obligation to end Cuban suffering. From first to last, two-thirds of the Cuban resolutions, or thirty-two of them, were introduced by Democrats and Populists, while one-third, or sixteen, were introduced by Republicans. There was nevertheless a strong group among congressional Republicans which favored active aid to the Cubans, challenging President McKinley's contrary position.[3]

Furthermore, the existence of an armed conflict so near home created unavoidable diplomatic issues. Cuban *insurrectos* found their principal source of weapons and ammunition in the United States, where a bold group of gunrunners made lucrative profits by violating the neutrality laws. This understandably irritated the Spanish, who demanded more effective federal enforcement of the ban on this arms traffic. But the enormous length of American coastlines coupled with the federal authorities' slender resources in ships and men ensured that much of the contraband would reach Cuba. Additional frictions arose from the need to protect bona fide American citizens injured or endangered by the fighting, a task complicated by the efforts of Cuban revolutionaries to gain protection by claiming to be naturalized citizens of the United States. When one added the substantial property damages resulting from the war, frequently caused by Cuban actions but laid at the door of Spain, and the crippling effects of the contest on Cuban-American trade, Washington's diplomatic burden became substantial. Even a tactful tone could not smooth away all of these rising tensions, and the nation's representatives in Spain and Cuba were by no means always tactful.[4]

Events, moreover, suddenly moved far beyond these major but familiar diplomatic concerns. On February 15, 1898, the U.S.S. *Maine* was destroyed in Havana harbor by a tremendous explosion which killed some two hundred and sixty of its crew. It was never possible, then or later, to establish the cause of the explosion, though informed opinion has swung increasingly to the view that it was one of those internal eruptions in the powder magazine which were endemic in the navies of the period. At the time, however, the United States Navy rejected this view as a reflection on its own competence, and American opinion generally accepted that the source of the explosion was external. Many, including numerous newspaper editorialists and politicians, leaped to the conclusion that the vessel had been treacherously destroyed by the Spaniards in retaliation for growing American support for the Cuban revolution. To cooler heads the disaster signified simply that the Cuban crisis was spinning out of control, and must quickly be resolved in one way or another. The *Maine*'s dramatic death mobilized an already formidable feeling that "something ought to be done about Cuba," and fed a dangerously strong anger against Spain. It further coincided with a growing conviction that the United States must be more active in the Caribbean and increase its influence there. Rather than an isolated event, the *Maine* disaster was the spark which lit a tinder already prepared.[5]

McKinley did his best to calm his public, and to delay action until emotions had abated. Meanwhile Stewart L. Woodford, his ambassador in Madrid, began a diplomatic offensive aimed at persuading the Spanish government to sell Cuba to the United States. Neither was successful; no Spanish regime dared sell Cuba and risk the wrath of its own people, while in the United States there was an inexorable drift toward war. A desperate Madrid offered at the last minute to suspend Cuban hostilities in order to seek a peaceful solution, but the Cuban rebels saw no point in halting their struggle when victory was in sight. While the Cuban leaders would accept nothing less than independence, that was the one thing which Spain would not concede, and the president's hopes for a diplomatic resolution of the crisis began to fade toward the end of March 1898.[6]

William McKinley now faced a dilemma: much as he disliked going to war with Spain, his public and Congress demanded an early resolution of the Cuban question which did not seem attainable through diplomacy. The New York lawyer Elihu Root, to whom McKinley had originally offered the post of ambassador to Spain, summarized the situation at the beginning of April in a letter meant for the president's guidance. As Root saw it, McKinley had won general respect for his courageous efforts to restrain events, but those efforts had clearly failed:

> Fruitless attempts to hold back or retard the enormous momentum of the people bent upon war would result in the destruction of the President's power and influence, in depriving the country of its natural leader, in the destruction of the president's party, in the elevation of the Silver Democracy to power.[7]

The advice struck a responsive ear. Having finally lost faith in diplomacy, McKinley was assessing not only the domestic political risks of his antiwar policy, but the harm which might come to American interests abroad through the conjunction of a continuing Cuban war and a seemingly impotent United States. Like Grover Cleveland before him, McKinley had made it known that his patience about Cuba must necessarily have limits. These limits were now reached, and on April 11, 1898, the president sent a war message to Congress.

Historians have long disagreed as to just what forces drove the government to war in 1898. Ernest R. May echoed Elihu Root in singling out an eruption of public emotion so formidable that political leaders had no choice but to defer to it. Richard Hofstadter suggested that this unique surge of feeling resulted from a national frustration, or "psychic crisis," brought on by the economic depression of 1893–97, the social strains of headlong industrialization, and the numerous other tensions of an uncomfortable transition period in American history. Frustration found release in aggression, Hofstadter asserted in an attempt at applied psychology. From a differing perspective, William Appleman Williams and Walter LaFeber have emphasized the desire of businessmen for markets abroad, made urgent by the recent depression and by growing industrial productivity. According to this approach, war with Spain could serve the nation's material interests by enabling it to seize valuable entrepôts in the Caribbean and Far East, and thus expand America's exports along with its influence. Yet another analysis, that of H. Wayne Morgan, depicts the president as serving a more complex and sophisticated kind of national interest. Morgan stressed the essential consistency of McKinley's course, which he saw as combining a steady and increasing pressure on Spain with a rational, cool-headed diplomacy until it became certain that United States goals regarding Cuba could not be achieved without the use of force. According to Morgan, these goals were economic, strategic, political, even ideological, and were not easily summarized.[8]

What is certain is that the movement for war gained very strong and widespread support during the early months of 1898, independently of the business world's positions; that national leaders saw the Cuban crisis as affecting important national interests; and that few responsible observers still believed that when the nation opted for war the conflict in Cuba could be ended through peaceful agreement with Spain. The role of economic interests is less clear. A classic work by Julius Pratt depicted big business leadership as strongly opposed to the drift toward war until overtaken by events in 1898, and then swept along like other citizens by the tidal wave of feeling set off by the *Maine* disaster. Another classic work by Walter LaFeber held that the conversion of the nation's top management circles to belief in the merits of forcible imperialism, however late it came, was a decisive factor in moving McKinley to intervention. Perhaps both erred in making "business" appear to speak with a single voice, instead of its more usual diversity.[9] Furthermore, no real evidence is available to show that the president's actions regarding Cuba represented a response to dominant economic interest groups. On the other hand, McKinley certainly shared the widespread concern for the future health of the economy propagated by the depression of the 1890s, and had long-standing and close ties with the country's business community. This alone would have placed economic concerns among the complex of forces which shaped his policies, but it does not prove that these concerns were more than one factor among several at play in the events leading to war.

While the president was forced to accept the necessity of war with Spain, the nature and purposes of that war were by no means a matter of general agreement. Not only did a contest about Cuba quickly become an expansionist war, but even as to Cuba there were widely differing intentions. In his war message to Congress, McKinley rejected the claims of the Cuban republic, the revolution's political arm, to be the legitimate government of Cuba. It was insufficiently stable and representative, he argued, while its authorities ruled no fixed territory. Refusing to recognize the revolutionary regime or to accept any obligation toward it, the president asked Congress for authority to impose peace and stability on Cuba through "hostile constraint" on both parties there, Cuban and Spanish alike. He justified such action on four grounds: the need to end suffering and death in a closely neighboring country; the need to protect United States lives and property; the national interest in reviving the formerly important trade with Cuba; and the general trouble and expense laid upon the United States government by the enforcement of its neutrality laws, the protection of its citizens, and the relief of the suffering. He used the destruction of the *Maine* as a graphic illustration of the unacceptable level which the Cuban problem had reached, while carefully not charging Spain with direct responsibility for it. The president closed by appealing to "humanity," "civilization," and "endangered American interests" for the right to restore peace through the use of force.[10]

This carefully crafted message was unwelcome to many members of Congress. By emphasizing "endangered American interests" and general humanitarian considerations, while refusing to endorse Cuban self-government under the only existing Cuban regime, McKinley made it clear that he wished an intervention for United States purposes and under United States control, not merely a crusade to win freedom for the Cubans. The future of Cuba would presumably be decided in Washington, and the Cuban revolutionaries would seem to have little to say about it. Some senators and congressmen had long been committed to support of the Cuban republic, while others shared the popular sympathy for Cuban aspirations to self-government; the president's position both jarred and angered these groups. It was also possible that some members of Congress were influenced by the lobbying of those who had invested in the Cuban republic's bonds. Issued in enormous quantities, this paper had been the object of considerable speculation in the United States, creating an interest group whose chances of profit were directly dependent upon the success of the Cuban revolutionaries in achieving political control.[11] Thus instead of following the president's lead, each house of Congress adopted its own goals for the war. The Democrats in the House of Representatives brought in a minority resolution to recognize the Cuban republic, but the administration's supporters defeated it by a vote of 190 to 150. On the other hand, the final House resolutions included a stated intention to establish "by the free action of the people thereof a stable and independent government of their own in the Island." [12]

The Senate, like the House, began by authorizing the president to use the nation's armed forces to expel Spanish authority from Cuba, but went on to defy the White House by recognizing the Cuban republic as the "true and lawful government of that island." This action was carried through largely by Democrat and Populist votes, but was based on wording previously provided by the Republican Senator Joseph B. Foraker of Ohio, a pro-Cuban and political rival of the president. To this, Colorado's Senator Henry M. Teller added his famous amendment which stated

> that the United States hereby disclaims any disposition or intention to exercise sovereignty, jurisdiction, or control over said island except for the pacification thereof, and asserts its determination when that is accomplished to leave the government and control of the island to its people. [13]

Hurriedly passed without debate, the Teller Resolution was presumably the work of those in the Senate who feared that the administration harbored designs for the eventual annexation of Cuba, and wished to spike such schemes in advance. At any rate, since the Senate had already recognized the Cuban republic as the legitimate government, Teller's additional stricture would have seemed to make no material difference. As a result, five days after McKinley's call for the imposition of a unilateral United States solution to Cuba's problems, the House of Representatives was committed to the freedom and self-determination of the Cubans, while the Senate insisted that the control of future events there rested solely with the current revolutionists! Furthermore, the Teller Resolution aimed to preclude any United States role whatever in postwar Cuba, leaving the single national war aim that of driving out Spain and delivering power to the Cuban republic.

In the face of this rebellion the embattled president marshaled his forces, and after an intense application of his quiet but effective persuasions, the lines began to shift. The war resolutions went to conference committee, where after a hard fight the Senate dropped its recognition of the Cuban republic. The House members, on the other hand, accepted the Teller Amendment, leaving the president's policy of complete United States control in Cuba on visibly unfirm ground. Despairing of anything better, McKinley signed the resolutions on April 20, 1898, and the nation was formally at war. [14]

The United States had gone to war specifically about events in Cuba. The conflict would quickly spread its effects across the Pacific Ocean as well as the Caribbean Sea, but few had foreseen such a widening at the outset. To an important degree it was William McKinley who would determine where, and how far, these new currents would run. Having unsuccessfully resisted the coming of war, he was determined at least to make it serve the interests of the United States. In particular, the president intended to enhance his country's influence in the Caribbean, the Pacific, and the Far East, and while still uncertain as to methods, he soon showed an unmistakable purpose in his wartime dispositions. The dispatch of troops to Cuba, Puerto Rico, and the Philippine Islands laid the foundation for a surge of colonial expansion, although the special circumstances of the Cuban case made the exact outcome unpredictable there.

There had been little preparation for the war now beginning. True, more than a decade of steady naval expansion had given the United States a fleet superior to Spain's, and the navy had even given thought to how it could use its forces in case of a Spanish war. The army, however, was very small—some twenty-eight thousand officers and men at the beginning of 1898—and gravely unprepared for war. Forced with little warning to ingest over two hundred thousand volunteers in only four months, the War Department fell into near-chaos, from which it was only beginning to emerge when hostilities ended. Since Spain had two hundred thousand regulars in Cuba alone, it began to seem less easy to impose a forcible solution there than recent oratory had suggested. The public and press nevertheless called for and expected an immediate descent in force upon the Pearl of the Antilles, while the army's commanders wished several months at a minimum in which to drill and equip their raw recruits and to await the end of the unhealthy rainy season in Cuba. In view of the army's unreadiness, the navy proposed simply to blockade the Spanish in Cuba, cutting off their supplies and reinforcements, while conveying much-needed weapons and supplies to the Cubans. The naval planners hoped that this in itself might tip the balance against Spain and end the Cuban stalemate, but their simple approach was soon overrun by events.[15]

There was at first no plan for a large-scale summer campaign, but rather than waste the summer entirely, and in view of the popular clamor for action, the president and his service advisers sought a more modest task for the ground forces. A plan soon evolved to land about five thousand regulars in southeastern Cuba, where the revolutionary forces were strongest, for a brief reconnaissance in force. The regulars could deliver supplies to the Cubans and gain reliable knowledge of military conditions in the area, returning to Florida after a few days. Orders for this project were actually drawn up at the end of April, but it was delayed by news that a Spanish naval squadron was heading for Caribbean waters and had eluded interception by the United States Navy. In May, however, the navy located the enemy's warships in harbor at Santiago

Street scene, Santiago de Cuba, 1890s. Courtesy of the American Geographical Society Collection, University of Wisconsin–Milwaukee

de Cuba and blockaded them there with its heavy armored units. Reversing its earlier assessment of the army's readiness, the navy now urged that a substantial ground force be sent to Santiago to threaten the port and force the Spanish cruisers out of their refuge. After a brief discussion, the White House planners adopted the scheme.[16]

General William R. Shafter, who commanded a concentration of troops at Tampa which contained most of the regular army and a smaller number of volunteers, was therefore directed to embark some seventeen thousand men as soon as possible and sail for Cuba. This force, designated the Fifth Corps, reached the vicinity of Santiago on June 20 and prepared to effect a landing. Shafter's first move toward this end was to establish contact with the Cubans. In theory the United States was in the process of imposing a "hostile constraint" on Cubans and Spaniards alike, at least according to the president's view of the matter, but in practice the army needed Cuban cooperation and was glad to accept it. The offered aid came from General Calixto García, who commanded the revolutionary forces in eastern Cuba. Shafter followed García's advice on where to land, and the Americans found fifteen hundred Cuban troops holding the landing beach when they reached it. Thus the campaign began with the Cubans in the role of de facto allies, whatever their theoretical status.[17]

Late in June the Fifth Corps moved inland, and on July 1 they attacked and captured the outer defenses of Santiago in an engagement known as the Battle of San Juan Hill. Thus threatened, the Spanish squadron attempted a dash to freedom on July 3, only to be totally destroyed in the naval battle of Santiago. Seeing their situation as hopeless, the Spanish land forces in and about Santiago surrendered to Shafter on July 17. While this brief campaign broke the Spanish will to continue the war, it also saw the collapse of the original Cuban-American friendship. At San Juan Hill, the only major land action in which the Americans fought in Cuba, the Cubans were in evidence only as guides and scouts, playing little part in the fighting. The American soldiers, already disillusioned at finding ragged and barefoot irregulars instead of the dashing heroes described in the popular press, were further alienated when the Cubans constantly begged for food and appropriated unguarded supplies. Furthermore, the United States was an overtly racist society in 1898, and the Cuban army contained a high proportion of Negroes and men of mixed blood. In an almost instantaneous reversal, the heroic Cuban freedom fighters became, in Yankee eyes, useless "dagoes" who would neither work nor fight. This view was quickly picked up and propagated in the United States by the numerous press corps members who had followed the army to Cuba. Soon editorials across the nation were declaring the Cubans unfit for self-government, calling them "good-for-nothing allies," and charging that they had "displayed their worthlessness." Some went further, to suggest that the Teller Amendment had been based upon an unrealistically high estimate of Cuban capabilities and should therefore be ignored.[18]

All of this, of course, reflected a deep ignorance of the nature of irregular warfare and of the military achievements of the Cubans during the previous three years. With the slenderest of resources, the Cuban Liberation Army had stalemated masses of Spanish regulars. Its soldiers had endured suffering, hunger, wounds, and death without losing heart. And they had performed valuable services for the Fifth Corps, from screening its initial landing and providing it with detailed local knowledge to carrying supplies and digging trenches. In addition, much of García's force had been occupied in preventing some eight thousand Spanish troops at Holguin, about seventy miles to the northwest, from joining the Santiago garrison. Another Cuban force aided the United States Marines in immobilizing several thousand Spaniards at Guantánamo, forty miles to the east. Only a few of the Americans in Cuba were aware of these facts, or understood very clearly the difference between hit-and-run partisan warfare and conventional campaigning. The Cubans were clearly not regulars, but they had proven themselves effective fighters in their own fashion.[19]

Thus Cubans, then and later, resented the American assumption that it was solely United States efforts which evicted Spain from the island. The Cuban historian Emilio Roig de Leuchsenring most fully developed the counterargument, which pictured the Spanish-Cuban-American War as the brief final phase of a thirty-year struggle for Cuban freedom which began in 1868 with the onset of the Ten Years' War. The seventeen years from the end of that struggle to the start of the final uprising in 1895 was an era of revolutionary conspiracy and preparation, the maturing of a national leadership, and the perfection of new organizations for renewing the fight. After 1895, the Cubans had fought Spain for three years, the United States for three months. By 1898, Roig insisted, the Spanish government was bankrupt and despairing, and a new ministry had come to power in Madrid which was already considering making major concessions in order to buy peace. In short, the Cubans had almost won their long struggle when the United States intervened, not to ensure Cuban freedom but to prevent it. For, thwarting the generous impulse which initially moved the American public, President McKinley successfully opposed the unconditional independence of Cuba under its revolutionary leadership. So runs the argument, which is most controversial in its assumption that Spanish concessions to an unaided Cuba would soon have gone as far as granting it independence. The recent work of Louis A. Perez, Jr., however, makes a persuasive case that the Spanish government was near the end of its rope in 1898, and could not greatly have prolonged the Cuban war even without United States intervention.[20]

While United States troops campaigned in Cuba, the war with Spain rapidly spread its effects to other areas as well. The conflict had hardly begun before it took on an expansionist character. Admiral George Dewey's May 1 victory over a Spanish squadron in Manila Bay was followed by the dispatch of an American army to the Philippines, leading ultimately to their annexation and to a United States bid for great-power status in the Far East. By increasing the strategic importance of the Pacific Ocean, this development weakened congressional opposition to the annexation of Hawaii, and a joint resolution of annexation passed both houses early in July. These events visibly increased the urgency of building an isthmian canal to connect the Atlantic and Pacific, and as a consequence brought the Caribbean directly into an emerging strategic overview. As Massachusetts Senator Henry Cabot Lodge wrote in mid-June, "The whole policy of annexation is growing rapidly under the irresistable pressure of events."[21]

By that time, Spain's colony of Puerto Rico had become another of the objects of expansion. Swiftly, almost spontaneously, leaders and press alike came to see that island as a natural prize of victory. General Nelson Miles, the Commanding General of the Army, had from the first given priority to the conquest of Puerto Rico, preferring an opening campaign there rather than in Cuba. In this he was overruled, but the attractions of Puerto Rico were widely seductive. Theodore Roosevelt, by then a lieutenant colonel of volunteers, wrote his friend Senator Lodge in May, "Do not make peace until we get Porto Rico [sic]." In June, Lodge gleefully reported to Roosevelt that the secretary of state had told him that "there is of course no question about Puerto Rico, everyone is agreed on that." Lodge himself favored annexing Hawaii, part or all of the Philippines, and Cuba, in addition to Puerto Rico. And late in June, *New York Tribune* editor Whitelaw Reid, soon to be appointed to the United States delegation to make peace with Spain, privately declared that "the judgment of the American people is so fixed" for retaining Puerto Rico "that the Administration could not make peace on any other terms if it wanted to." All that remained was to take the island, which was easily done, for Spain had been able to spare it few troops from the fighting in Cuba. General Miles sailed late in July with the vanguard of an invasion force which soon exceeded thirteen thousand men, and had four columns advancing across the breadth of the island when an armistice ended hostilities on August 12.[22]

The peace conference to end the war with Spain began in Paris on October 1, 1898. The Spanish representatives understood well enough that Spain was to lose Cuba and Puerto Rico, for that had been stated in the armistice protocol, but they found to their dismay that they must give up the Philippines as well. As a final bitter draught, they faced an adamant American refusal to accept any of Cuba's financial liabilities. For many years, the Spanish government had segregated those financial obligations which pertained specifically to Cuba and carried them as charges on the Cuban treasury, secured by Cuban revenues and embodied in special bond issues which had reached the enormous total of $400 million. The Spanish position was that this debt belonged to Cuba, and should pass intact to whatever government exercised power there. The debt, in short, went with the island, and since the United States was to take charge of the latter, it should assume the former as well.

The United States commissioners, however, refused to acknowledge any such thing. They held that most of the Cuban debt represented the cost to Spain of combating rebellions there, which hardly benefited Cuba. Furthermore, they denied that the United States was to possess sovereignty over Cuba. Their Spanish opposite numbers nevertheless urged that the United States assume responsibility for the debt as long as it governed the island, after which the debt could be passed along to the Cubans as part of the cost of self-government. When this effort failed, the Spaniards offered to adjust the amount, but always the American response was a resolute negative. The issue came at last to threaten the very existence of the conference, and was finally resolved by a stipulation in the treaty that the United States would pay to Spain the sum of $20 million. Nothing in the wording connected this sum with the debt; it was, nevertheless, the price of agreement. As to Cuba, Spain agreed to relinquish her sovereignty and title, along with government property there, while "any obligations assumed in this treaty by the United States with respect to Cuba are limited to the time of its occupancy thereof." [23]

The United States was formally to take over control of Cuba from Spain on January 1, 1899. As the date approached, it was by no means clear whether the forthcoming American occupation would be long or short, whether it would end in complete Cuban independence or something less. The president's annual message to Congress in December spoke of the need for "a just, benevolent, and humane government, created by the people of Cuba," but also declared that the military occupation would continue until there was "complete tranquility in the island," which a cynical British press took to mean that the Americans were to stay indefinitely. The expansionist Senator Lodge had long since concluded that Cuba should be annexed as a territory because the Cubans were not capable of establishing a stable government, and a protectorate would be "too complicated and too unnatural for our form of government." General Shafter spoke for the veterans of the Santiago campaign when he declared the Cubans unfit for self-government, while McKinley's minister to Spain had taken that view from the beginning. The latter wrote McKinley even before the war began, "If we have war we must finally occupy and ultimately own the island." Robert P. Porter, a personal agent of the president sent to Cuba in the autumn of 1898 to gather information, likewise came quickly to favor Cuba's annexation, not as a colony but for eventual statehood within the American union. Many Americans, on the other hand, still regarded the Teller Amendment as a solemn pledge and favored Cuban independence under the revolutionary organs which McKinley had refused to recognize.[24]

The Cuban leadership was only less divided. Many of the wealthier upper-class Cubans who had advocated autonomy under the Spanish flag were now ready to accept annexation to the United States, or internal self-government under American tutelage. Most of them actively preferred such ultimate control from Washington to the unchecked authority of the turbulent Cuban Liberation Army. More notably, even some of the revolution's top leaders reflected a cautious mixture of hope and apprehension. Tomás Estrada Palma, who had headed the Cuban junta in New York and was to be the first president of an independent Cuba, desired and expected the United States to ensure internal order on the island while the Cubans learned to rule themselves. In the longer run he favored eventual annexation, but only through the free choice of the Cuban people. General Calixto García, who had aided the Fifth Corps in its campaigning, was so disgusted with the political leadership of the Cuban republic in the spring of 1898 that he privately endorsed McKinley's refusal to recognize it. The commander in chief of the Cuban army, General Máximo Gómez, also distrusted the bulk of Cuba's civilian leadership. He envisioned a future government to be headed by Estrada Palma, with the firm support of the army, after order and discipline had been restored to the country. Meanwhile, he believed that the Americans could best carry out that restoration, and Gómez hoped to work with them during a transitional period of up to two years, though in the end he meant to secure full Cuban independence. A large and articulate body of military and civilian leaders were equally devoted to full independence, but wished it immediately and viewed the American presence with suspicion. While reassured by the Teller Resolution, these more thoroughgoing *independentistas* were prepared only to tolerate, not welcome, a temporary foreign administration in their country.[25]

The United States occupation of Cuba was to last for over three years, from the beginning of 1899 to May 20, 1902. It was embodied in a military government, run by officers of the United States Army and directed by the president of the United States through his secretary of war. While Cubans made up the mass of bureaucrats and functionaries who carried on its work, they acted wholly under United States authority. Major General John R. Brooke served as military governor throughout 1899; thereafter, Major General Leonard Wood held that position. The pivotal post, however, was that of secretary of war. It was in that office that policy formation centered after August 1, 1899, when the able and vigorous Elihu Root replaced an ineffective predecessor to become the principal arbiter of Cuban affairs, and to give shape and direction to the army's efforts there.[26]

According to Root's well-known account, he received a telephone call from the White House in the summer of 1899, and was told by an intermediary that President McKinley wanted him to become secretary of war. Root's answer was that he knew nothing of war or the army, but his informant, after a pause for consultation, reassured him: "President McKinley directs me to say that he is not looking for anyone who knows anything about the army; he has got to have a lawyer to direct the government of these Spanish islands, and you are the lawyer he wants." [27]

The new secretary of war found no existing consensus on Cuban policy when he took up his duties, but rather a kaleidoscope of opinions. Senator Henry M. Teller of Colorado, for example, the very man who had sponsored the Teller Resolution guaranteeing Cuban independence, had come by the end of 1898 to advocate a long-term United States protectorate over Cuba. On the other hand, Senator John C. Spooner of Wisconsin, one of the most influential Republicans in the Senate, countered early in 1899 with a demand for the exact fulfillment of the Teller Resolution as soon as possible. While both positions commanded support, there were other congressmen who favored outright annexation, notably Senator Lodge of Massachusetts and Senator Albert J. Beveridge of Indiana.[28]

Among programs proposed by the army commanders in Cuba, the most comprehensive and detailed came from General James Harrison Wilson, a well-connected veteran of the Civil War who had left the army between wars to pursue a business career and become a Republican National Committeeman from Delaware. Wilson regretted the Teller Resolution, for he favored the annexation of Cuba. Once adopted, however, the resolution must be honored, and when the Cubans had written a constitution the United States must withdraw from the island as promised—at least formally. But according to Wilson's scheme, the new Cuban government should then be made to sign a treaty which would establish a de facto United States protectorate. The Cubans would retain the substance of internal self-government, but maintain a common postal service with the United States, allow Washington to supervise customs and sanitation services, and cede it a naval station. Of central importance was a customs union which would give Cuban sugar guaranteed free entry into the United States and set a common tariff against outsiders. These provisions, Wilson believed, would adequately protect United States interests in Cuba while tightly binding the Cuban economy to that of its larger neighbor. Drawn by economic self-interest and impressed by the continued demonstration of Yankee efficiency, enjoying an unprecedented prosperity and stability, the Cubans would ultimately seek voluntary annexation, Wilson predicted.[29]

The rising general Leonard Wood advocated a more direct route to Cuban annexation. Let the military occupation continue indefinitely, he urged, with no more promises about independence, nor indeed any comment of any sort about future developments. Happy to enjoy peace and clean, efficient government, the bulk of the Cuban people would soon stop dreaming of independence, and settle for the status quo. In time the issue would simply fade away, and eventually Washington could formalize matters through outright annexation. Already, Wood declared, the Cubans were "rapidly realizing that annexation is the best thing for them." [30]

Presumably, the president was the ultimate policy maker, but it was by no means clear where he stood on the Cuban question. He had listened noncommittally to everyone's schemes for Cuba without betraying a plan of his own, although in the summer of 1899 Theodore Roosevelt believed that he favored Wood's idea of an indefinite occupation leading to annexation.[31] By that time, however, non-Cuban complications limited the president's options. The greatest of these was the outbreak of a large-scale uprising in the Philippines against American rule, in February 1899, which set off what was to be a three-year armed struggle.

Beginning as a conventional military contest, the so-called Philippine insurrection evolved into brutal guerrilla warfare after the Filipino army had been broken in formal battle. At its peak it required a United States force of over seventy thousand men, while news of the atrocities committed on both sides shocked the American public and made this distant and unexpected war ever more unpalatable.[32] Clearly, the administration in Washington could not risk a second colonial war in Cuba; such a catastrophe would utterly discredit the McKinley foreign policies. With a presidential election looming in 1900, the lesson was clear that nothing could be done in Cuba which seriously risked an armed challenge from a reconstituted Liberation Army. Cuba, like the Philippines, was the seat of an armed independence movement, one amply endowed with experienced military leaders and veteran troops who had only recently proved their effectiveness against Spain.

Elihu Root therefore lived in apprehension of a Cuban revolt against American rule, at the same time that much of the American press called insistently for annexation. In November 1899, rumors swept Cuba that the avowedly temporary military occupation was to be replaced by a permanent civil colonial regime. The result was a wave of unrest and mass meetings and a blizzard of Cuban telegrams, resolutions, and editorials denouncing such a change and demanding to know United States intentions. Determined to avoid a crisis, Root published the text of his annual report on December 1, setting forth in it assurances for the Cubans. The United States occupation was indeed temporary, Root said, and would continue no longer than was necessary. The military government would give way in due time to a democratic and independent Cuban regime, freely chosen by its people. In the meantime, however, a necessary sequence of steps must be taken. The military government's recent census of Cuba must be tabulated in order to provide correct data on suffrage and representation for the coming elections. Further, no elections could properly be held until after April 11, 1900, when the year of grace expired during which residents of Cuba could elect either Cuban or Spanish citizenship, according to the terms of the peace treaty. Once the census was completed, however, and it was known who the citizens of Cuba were, municipal elections could be held, followed by the choosing of a constituent assembly to write a constitution for the new government. When this new government was ready for installation, the United States would end its occupation and withdraw.[33]

This clear, step-by-step program went far to quiet Cuban doubts, as did Root's promise that relations between the Cuban republic and the United States would "be a matter for free and uncontrolled agreement between the two parties." However, the Cuban portion of the president's annual message to Congress, delivered only a few days later, was distinctly less definite as to the future. The creation of the new Cuba must not be a "hasty experiment," the president said, while the nature of relations between it and the United States was left uncertain. McKinley was sure that "the destinies of Cuba are in some rightful form and manner irrevocably linked with our own, but how and how far is for the future to determine in the ripeness of events." At the moment, he could not even say "whether those ties shall be organic or conventional," leaving official policy far from settled on the most important point of all.[34]

Root nevertheless proceeded with his announced program of census completion, municipal elections, and constitutional convention. The latter began its sessions in November 1900, and progressed steadily in its task of framing the future instrument of government. Before it had finished, however, some further aspects of United States policy became visible. In January 1901 the secretary of war began private consultations with the secretary of state, the president, and congressional leaders about the nature of postoccupation Cuban-American relations. Root was determined to end the occupation and get out of Cuba, but it now became clear that he meant to replace the military government with an American protectorate. Borrowing elements from General Wilson's scheme and adding new ones of his own, Root sketched the outlines of such a protectorate. Senator Orville Platt of Connecticut, chairman of the Senate's Committee on Relations with Cuba, was impressed; he suggested that Root help the committee to formulate "a resolution authorizing the President to discontinue the military occupation of Cuba whenever certain things should have been agreed to and incorporated into the constitution of Cuba, making it certain that results which are essential are assured." Root was by now ready to write a draft statement, and blending in some ideas of their own, the senators quickly produced the so-called Platt Amendment, which they introduced in the Senate in February.[35]

The Platt Amendment contained seven articles, which collectively gave to the United States formidable controls over the new Cuban republic. Cuba was forbidden to make treaties with other foreign governments which in the judgment of the United States might tend to impair its independence or permit foreign lodgment or colonization. It could not borrow beyond its ability to repay from the ordinary revenues of its government, a provision intended to eliminate the principal reason for European intervention in the Caribbean. The new government was required to validate all the acts of the United States military occupation, and to carry out the occupation's plans for the sanitation of the island. The United States must be given a naval base or bases to enable it "to maintain the independence of Cuba, and to protect the people thereof," as well as for more purely national purposes which the senators did not choose to mention in the document. Most important of all, Cuba must grant to the United States "the right to intervene for the preservation of Cuban independence, the maintenance of a government adequate for the protection of life, property, and individual liberty, and for discharging the obligations with respect to Cuba imposed by the Treaty of Paris on the United States." This last condition was apparently to be interpreted and applied at the sole discretion of the United States. It aimed in particular to ensure political stability in Cuba by virtually outlawing revolution, in Yankee eyes the bane of Caribbean politics.[36]

These demands were clearly inconsistent with the Teller Resolution, as well as with Root's earlier assurance that postoccupation relations would "be a matter for free and uncontrolled agreement between the two parties." They shocked the delegates to the Cuban constitutional convention, in which members of the former revolutionary apparatus were strongly represented. Leonard Wood, now military governor, had the task of securing the convention's acceptance of the Platt Amendment and seeing its provisions incorporated into the new constitution. This was not to be easy, for even the more amenable delegates were impressed by the uproar of popular dissent in Cuba. However, the effect of this was undercut somewhat by the highly equivocal positions of Máximo Gómez and Tomás Estrada Palma, two of the most prominent national leaders. Both held aloof from the fight, a circumstance which no Cuban could fail to notice. Furthermore, the occupation authorities began a skillful campaign to minimize the significance of the required terms. To help matters along, Root provided Wood with a written statement that the proposed right of intervention was "not synonymous with intermeddling or interference with the affairs of the Cuban government," but would be exercised only in extraordinary cases.[37]

In any case, the Cubans were in a vise and they knew it. If they refused to accept Washington's terms, the American occupation might continue indefinitely. Of course, they could always remobilize the Liberation Army, which had been disbanded shortly after the occupation began, and attempt a military challenge to United States power; it was this potential threat which gave the Cubans what bargaining power they had, and may well have saved them from outright annexation. In practice, however, few Cubans were eager for a new war so soon after the three-year struggle with Spain which had so devastated their island. Further, they perceived in the United States a more formidable opponent than Spain, while a war with the northern giant would obviously be fought without the American aid and supplies which had been so important in the earlier struggle. There was therefore little else to do but bargain for concessions, and perhaps bluff a little.

Root and Wood had little patience with bargaining, however, and brusquely rejected Cuban counterproposals which would have watered down the American demands. The Cubans were the most disturbed by the proposed United States right of intervention, even after Root's attempt to soothe them on that score. Independence at Washington's discretion was hardly independence at all, they maintained with some justice. Ultimately, the convention arranged to send a special commission to Washington to seek further understanding of the more unpalatable terms. The commission reached the American capital late in April 1901, to confer mainly with the author of their troubles, Secretary of War Root. At two afternoon conferences, Root again played down the importance of the right of intervention and justified it in any case as implicit in the Monroe Doctrine. Stalemated on political issues, the Cubans turned to the question of economic concessions. When the commission inquired anxiously into the possibility of tariff reciprocity between the United States and Cuba, which would ensure a preferential American market for Cuban sugar, Root insisted that the subject must await negotiation with a competent Cuban government. In short, there could be no tariff concessions until the Platt Amendment had been ratified. Nonplussed, the commission returned to Havana, where after several more weeks of futile maneuvering a majority of the delegates adopted the Platt Amendment without modification.[38]

Meanwhile, the United States Congress had approved the amendment as well, removing the Cubans' last hope for better terms. In a surprisingly short debate, a bloc of Democratic senators failed signally to modify the conditions set down for Cuba. The opponents were joined by the Republican Senator Foraker, who pointed out prophetically that in the long run the right of intervention might well prove self-defeating as a measure to ensure Cuba's internal stability. More likely, Foraker said, it would lead the losing parties in Cuban elections to foment disorders in order to force American intervention and thereby prevent their rivals from exercising power. Shrewd as was Foraker's estimate, it seemed to influence no one. During the debate Senator Teller gave qualified support to the Platt Amendment, while even Senator George F. Hoar of Massachusetts, a leading Republican antiimperialist, found it a proper measure. In the end, Foraker and Teller reversed positions, Teller voting against the amendment and Foraker for it, as party discipline reasserted itself, and the amendment passed by a two-thirds majority. The House of Representatives followed suit a few days later, though by a reduced margin, and the measure became law.[39]

The failure even of committed antiimperialists to make a strong fight over the Platt Amendment stemmed from a general perception that it represented the middle course in the Cuban case. While their independence was seriously compromised, the Cubans would at least get the substance of internal self-government and the symbolism of a president, congress, elections, and flag of their own. United States interests in Cuba, both economic and strategic, would be securely safeguarded. Both sides would be spared the trouble, expense, and tensions of a long-term American administration in Cuba, yet internal stability would presumably be ensured. Each country got at least its minimum demands, while neither was prepared to grant much more. That being true, the congressman may well have asked, what other sort of settlement could have been reached?[40]

Central as it was, the Platt Amendment was not to provide the entire structure of Cuban-American relations. Leaders on both sides had shown concern for future commercial relations between the two countries, while Leonard Wood's occupation government did what it could to ease the way for American investment in Cuba. Underlying other economic issues was the question of tariff reductions for Cuban sugar imported into the United States. Cuban spokesmen insisted that such preferential treatment of its sugar was essential for the island's prosperity, while Root considered tariff preference an essential part of the implicit bargain which he had struck while pushing through the Platt Amendment. Thus Cuban planters and politicians, American investors like Edwin Atkins, and the War Department and military government presented a united front in urging Cuban reciprocity on Congress. Wood worked in Cuba to orchestrate a flood of resolutions, petitions, and letters from political officials and planters' and merchants' organizations, while Root saw to it that the president was firmly enlisted in the cause.[41]

The assassination of William McKinley in September 1901 temporarily interrupted this reciprocity campaign, but the new president, Theodore Roosevelt, was soon equally committed to the fight. The American beet sugar industry, however, was politically potent and determined to prevent such favors to its principal foreign competitor. Sugar beets grew in large areas of the upper midwest, the Rocky Mountain region, and the Pacific coast, and the growers pointed out that this cultivation had been vigorously encouraged by the United States Department of Agriculture. With the powerful support of farm bloc representatives in Congress, the beet sugar lobby could raise a formidable opposition to Cuban reciprocity.

Hearings on a reciprocity bill began early in 1902, and the battle lines developed rapidly. Strongly backed by President Roosevelt, supporters of reciprocity held that the United States had a moral obligation to foster Cuban prosperity, that such prosperity was necessary for order and stability in the island, and that reciprocity would open a lucrative market for American exports to Cuba. Their opponents claimed that American farmers would lose the chance to expand their domestic beet sugar market if the bill passed. More tellingly, they charged that the American "refining trust" had bought up Cuban sugar crops in advance, and that reciprocity would therefore mean cheap raw materials, and consequent higher profits, for refiners without greatly improving the lot of the Cuban planter, who had already contracted to sell his product. The result was a deadlock. The House of Representatives passed a bill in April which offered a 20 percent reduction on Cuban imports in return for an offsetting Cuban concession on United States goods. The Senate, however, never got its bill out of committee, in spite of a strongly worded appeal from Roosevelt urging action. When the Congress adjourned on July 1, nothing had been done.[42]

Having failed at legislation, the administration turned to treaty making. The United States occupation of Cuba ended on May 20, 1902, when the Cubans took over their own governance. During the following summer, the State Department negotiated a reciprocity treaty with Cuba whose terms paralleled those of the failed bill. The treaty was signed in December and at once submitted to the Senate for approval. When the Senate adjourned in March 1903 without having acted on the treaty, President Roosevelt called it into special session, to consider the Cuban treaty and the new isthmian canal treaty which had just been concluded with Colombia.

Meanwhile, Cuban bargaining power had suddenly increased. In March 1902 a conference of European states had agreed to stop supporting beet sugar production through government export bounties. This decision meant an easing in the current world oversupply of sugar, a resulting improvement in sugar prices, and a prospective new market for Cuban sugar in Europe to supplement that in the United States. If Cuba sold more to Europe, it might buy more there, cutting its American imports in the process. All of these considerations weakened congressional opposition to Cuban reciprocity. It was weakened even more by a sudden shift in the position of the beet sugar lobby, which dropped its former objections. The American Sugar Refining Company, or "sugar trust," had been busily investing in sugar beet concerns for months, and had succeeded in virtually buying out the opposition. Although a strongly protectionist Congress still contained enemies of the Cuban treaty, it was ratified at the end of 1903.[43]

Cuban reciprocity never opened up as large a market for Yankee goods in Cuba as its proponents had promised, but it tied Cuba's principal crop to the United States market under conditions ultimately controlled from Washington. It thereby offered an additional lever on Cuban actions to complement the controls conferred by the Platt Amendment, as well as benefited both Cuban and foreign sugar growers and stimulated further American investment in the island. A child of both intervention and sugar, the Cuban republic would develop in an environment heavily influenced by the arrangements with the United States arrived at in 1901–1903, and offer a model and a precedent for further United States expansion in the Caribbean.

Chapter 4

―――――・・・◈・・――――――

Assumptions, Biases, and Preconceptions

As the twentieth century got under way, the United States stood poised to extend its interests far beyond the initial Caribbean stepping-stones of Cuba and Puerto Rico. Even as this process began, many of the nation's people and policy makers already harbored a set of shared assumptions which would condition their future actions in the area. These assumptions touched upon the relations between the powerful industrialized states and the weaker and less developed ones, the economic potential of the Caribbean region and the capabilities of its peoples, and the probability of a European threat to the region's security.

Such preconceptions did not necessarily originate in the United States; some were borrowed from European views and experience, while many were jointly held on both sides of the Atlantic. By 1900, the European powers had a long history of interaction with other societies in every part of the world, and had established an extensive set of behavioral norms, many of which were accepted in the United States as a matter of course. The Old World was still a world of empires, and the thirty years before 1900 had witnessed a massive advance of European colonialism across Africa and Southeast Asia. Europeans of the Victorian age tended to divide the peoples of the world into the civilized and the barbarous, and their nations into the progressive and the stagnant. They saw non-European peoples lacking modern industrial societies as not merely different, but inferior, and worse yet, obstructive. These peoples, they felt, had no right to stand in the way of the world's development; "civilization" needed their raw materials, their agricultural production, and the economic opportunities which they represented. British Colonial Secretary Joseph Chamberlain regarded the tropical expanses of the empire as "undeveloped estates," and urged their development in the interests of world commerce. It was assumed to be both necessary and mutually beneficial for modern business enterprise to push its way into the preindustrial world, and it must necessarily do so on terms compatible with the western world's legal and corporate practices.[1]

This assumed need raised problems in dealing with preindustrial nations. This was especially true of those with exotic legal and commercial codes, those prone to political violence, and those whose magnates or governments failed to honor contracts with the outside world. Once European men and money had committed themselves to enterprises in such places, their home governments must be ready to protect their lives and property against local misbehavior. The Palmerston Circular, issued by the government of Great Britain in 1849, formally claimed the right to intervene for its citizens abroad either in their individual capacity or as members of corporate organizations. Other governments claimed the same right, and the diplomatic protection of citizens' economic activities abroad became an increasingly important function of foreign offices and their legations and consulates.[2]

It was not always clear when a citizen or corporation had been wronged, of course; frequently the disputes were murky, with much to blame on both sides. Furthermore, the issue may have been formally decided after due process by the legal system of the host country, but the imperial powers refused to accept this as decisive. A leading authority on international law explained that even though an alien received all of the rights granted by local law, and full equality of treatment with native dwellers, the results were not binding if local usages fell "below the requirements of the international standard of civilized justice." The writer noted that this principle had been applied most energetically "to some of the weaker countries of the world," and that "powerful states have at times exacted from weak states a greater degree of responsibility than from states of their own strength." The exaction could result from conventional negotiation, gunboat diplomacy, or outright invasion; the "civilized" state claimed the right to use any means that proved necessary. The abuse of this principle, our legal expert declared frankly, had resulted "in securing for aliens in some of the weaker states of the world a privileged position as against nationals, a condition against which some of the Latin-American countries . . . have, at times . . . protested." The European powers, however, argued that special protection for their citizens was essential, for without it the risks involved in foreign investment and enterprise would be prohibitively high, and the economic development of the world would thereby lag.[3]

Since the great powers insisted that their actions were based on international law, the Latin Americans in particular attempted to create their own version of such law. In the later nineteenth century the theories of the Argentine diplomat Carlos Calvo grew rapidly into the so-called Calvo Doctrine, which was quickly espoused by Latin American governments. At the heart of this doctrine lay two simple propositions. The first was that sovereign states had a right to freedom from outside interference of any sort. The second held that aliens were not entitled to rights and privileges not available to nationals, and must therefore seek justice only from local authorities. Together the two propositions would virtually eliminate the diplomatic protection of aliens abroad, and the developed states therefore resisted the Calvo Doctrine, the United States among them. Since few industrial countries would sign treaties which embodied it, the Latin American states adopted the expedient of making the doctrine a provision of their contracts with foreign concerns. To secure government contracts or concessions, the foreign enterprise was obliged to sign away its right to appeal to its own government in contract-related disputes. Even this action, however, by no means ended the matter. In a typical great-power response, the United States government took the position in 1888 that its citizens could not renounce the obligation of their government to protect them, and refused to regard such contract clauses as binding. In reality, therefore, the Calvo Doctrine had little effect on the actual practices of the great powers.[4]

The powers particularly insisted that the governments of economically undeveloped countries repay the debts which they contracted in Europe. Everyone knew, of course, that not all such debts could withstand close scrutiny, for irregularities abounded on both sides. European bankers, for example, often drastically discounted the government bond issues which they floated. An early Mexican government loan was marketed at 58 percent of its face value, and while this was rather low, some discount below par was the norm for Caribbean public bond issues. The bankers involved routinely subtracted advance interest and commission charges as well from the funds realized by bond sales, and these also could become onerous. In 1859 the Swiss-French firm of J. B. Jecker and Company sold 75 million francs in Mexican government bonds, which after subtracting a heavy discount and other highly inflated charges brought the Mexicans only 3.75 million francs! Yet governments which borrowed were expected to repay the entire face value of their bond issues plus the stipulated interest, however little cash they actually realized on a loan.

The borrowers soon learned the tactics of evasion. Some Latin American governments regularly defaulted on their loans, and most did so at least once. Almost all of them contracted new loans to repay the old, usually enlarging the total in order to have fresh funds in hand for current needs. Governments regularly pledged specific sources of revenue—most often customs collections or export taxes—to the service of existing debts, then used them for other purposes in violation of their promises. It was not long before the whole process of contracting such debts became a vicious game without rules, in which each side tried to take advantage of the other. By the turn of the century some semblance of order began to emerge, as the complex and sordid controversies of the past were increasingly settled by compromise. In such settlements the debtor government paid only an agreed fraction of the sometimes fantastic totals charged against them by the bondholders. Even in 1900, however, the whole field of Caribbean government loans was still dangerous to the uninitiated, and too often tarred with scandal.[5]

Whatever the abstract merits of their case, lenders were naturally determined to recover what they could from recalcitrant debtors, and at times they turned to their governments for support. On a number of occasions in the second half of the nineteenth century, European lenders got their governments to help them collect defaulted public debts abroad. One method, which quickly became widespread, was to place the defaulted state's finances under the partial or entire control of a consortium representing the foreign bondholders and backed by their governments. Such foreign financial groups were central to the fiscal operations of Egypt after 1876, Turkey after 1881, Peru after 1883, Serbia after 1895, Greece after 1898, and Persia after 1907. Debtor states which resisted might be coerced; the French occupation of Mexico between 1862 and 1867 grew out of a joint attempt at forcible debt collection by Great Britain, France, and Spain in 1861. Again, however, the approach was not applied equally, but only to weaker states. When Spain, Italy, Austria-Hungary, and a number of state governments in the United States suspended or reduced their debt obligations over the same period, no foreign government considered taking action on behalf of its citizen-lenders.[6]

This complex of expectations, exactions, and precedents was codified over the course of time as "international law," and was soon regarded by the industrial powers as setting a general standard of economic decency and morality. It was true that the standard was not equally applied, but its upholders argued that it was the unstable countries of the undeveloped world which most needed foreign enterprise and a stabilizing hand. As historian Robert F. Smith has pointed out, the main thrust of this portion of the new international law can be summed up in five main principles: (1) The resources of undeveloped countries must be made available to industrial nations. (2) The markets of undeveloped countries must be open to exports from industrial nations. (3) Investments in undeveloped countries must be protected, since they were vital elements in trade expansion and the growth of general prosperity. (4) Excessive domestic upheavals, or hostility to foreign enterprise, harmed trade and investment and must be curbed. (5) The industrial-creditor nations therefore had the right and duty to police underdeveloped areas in order to secure all of the above aims. All this was common doctrine and practice before the United States itself became active in undeveloped areas abroad, and the Yankees adopted it whole.[7]

If belief in special enterprisers' rights under international law commanded a consensus in the United States, so did confidence that the Caribbean countries contained a rich field for enterprise. American travelers of the period almost invariably saw vast economic promise in the region. The genuinely fertile island of Cuba set the standard, while the lush foliage of the tropics suggested a similar productivity for most of the other areas. Thus Nicaragua, for example, was widely regarded as having equal possibilities. Speaking of that country, a traveler of the 1880s concluded: "Nature has blessed it with wonderful resources, and a few years of peace and industry would make the country prosperous without comparison. . . ." Some years later the navy's Admiral James G. Walker echoed the sentiment: "The country's natural resources are immense. Millions of acres of rich land . . . need but little development to yield enormous harvests." In 1906 the United States minister drew a dismal picture of the present state of the country, then went on to contrast this with its latent potential: "This lamentable picture is one of the most fertile, beautiful countries in tropical America, which would rapidly advance in wealth and population were there security of life or property." A half dozen years later, another transient Yankee saw the future prosperity of the land in the cultivation of sugar and rubber by foreign investors, once political stability should be restored. "For these people and for this country as much can be done as we did for Cuba," he wrote, "and without firing a shot." [8]

In 1899 the noted journalist Murat Halstead depicted the prospects for Puerto Rican development in equally glowing terms. The island had a "delightful" climate, he asserted, and its soil was "exceedingly rich," while "in natural resources it is of surpassing opulence." His optimism reached its peak when he cited another writer's claim that "precious metals abound, although systematic effort has never been directed to the locating of paying veins." More prosaically, he judged that coffee growing would yield annual returns of 10–15 percent on the capital invested, while assuring his readers that coffee plantations could readily be bought "at fair valuation." [9]

In like vein, other wayfarers found comparable promise in Santo Domingo. A 1903 report of the United States minister spoke of large bodies of copper ore, the possibility of mining gold, valuable hardwood forests, and rich agricultural lands which could produce coffee, tobacco, and cacao when opened up by a proposed railroad project.

> All that is needed is a stable Government and peace, so that the capitalists who may desire to invest may have no fears as to the future results. In a few years thereafter the republic by the aid of these new enterprises, will be able to pay the enormous debt that threatens to engulf it.

Secretary of State Elihu Root corroborated this forecast for Santo Domingo in a 1907 speech: "With her phenomenal richness of soil her people ought to be among the richest and happiest on earth; but the island has been the scene of almost continual revolution and bloodshed." [10]

American pronouncements on this subject ran parallel to current English thinking. A correspondent of the *Times* of London, in a long dispatch from Santo Domingo, commented in 1905 on "the extreme richness of the landscape," and reiterated the theme with variations. "The country is exceptionally rich in timber." "The mineral resources of the republic are exceptionally rich." "Many estates produce high-grade crops and make good profits." A contemporary British diplomat had in the meantime included the whole of Central America in the golden circle. "All five Central American Republics," he reported in 1902,

> possess very great resources both in agricultural possibilities and in minerals, but this is especially the case with the two largest, Guatemala and Nicaragua. With only three to four years' honest administration and encouragement of industry, both these Republics could not only free themselves from their present embarrassments, but they could become wealthy and flourishing.[11]

These views were reinforced by the recent record of economic growth in Mexico, where a vast influx of foreign enterprise had begun in the 1880s. Even the chaos of the Mexican Revolution failed to dampen American faith in the country's future. John Lind, one of Woodrow Wilson's early presidential agents in Mexico, reported in 1913 that the nation was "phenomenally rich," though brought to a deplorable state by revolutionary disorder. Three years later, Wilson himself asserted:

> Mexico is one of the treasure houses of the world. It is exceedingly to be desired by those who wish to amass fortunes. Its resources are indeed serviceable to the whole world and are needed by the industries of the whole world. No enterprising capitalist can look upon her without coveting her.[12]

Such generalized optimism seemed to survive almost any kind of negative experience and to fasten upon the most unlikely places. Thus, as late as 1920, a veteran American travel writer took the same expansive tone toward Haiti, then as now the poorest country in the western hemisphere. With a sufficiency of Yankee enterprise, he assured his readers, Haiti would soon be as rich as Cuba, which was then still awash with sugar profits from an unprecedented wartime boom. But everything, he warned, must be done from scratch, for the Haitians had neglected or destroyed everything while creating nothing.[13]

The comment was characteristic. Almost invariably, each glowing forecast of future prosperity was accompanied by harsh criticisms of the current society of the country under discussion. Thus Nicaragua had heretofore failed to flourish because "so much attention has been paid to politics that little is left for anything else," and frequently recurring civil wars disrupted labor and production. Bad government was reputed to be almost universal. The same British diplomat who saw such material promise in all of the Central American states found in their rulers a major obstacle to development. "Their dishonest methods, total lack of justice, and their shiftiness make it almost useless to endeavor to deal with these Governments as with civilized nations," he declared. "Presidents, Ministers, Judges, police and all other Government or local officials appear to have but one object, namely, to extort and steal as much as possible during their term of office." Elihu Root dismissed the public life of Santo Domingo in a sentence: "Her politics are purely personal, and have been a continual struggle of this and that and the other man to secure ascendancy and power." [14]

To these outside observers, the failure of government was closely associated with the defects of the population. Witness after witness testified that the Caribbean peoples were ignorant, lazy, backward, perhaps vicious. The London *Times* correspondent who gave such a favorable report of Santo Domingo's land and resources described the people as "easy-going and improvident," devoid of initiative or enterprise. When he asked a rural cultivator why he did not dig a ditch and irrigate his field, the man replied that if such a thing were necessary, God would have made it. Admiral Walker saw the Nicaraguans as "dreaming the years away" without past traditions or future ambitions to inspirit them. The American author of a 1910 travel book on Central America did not attempt to conceal his contempt for the people of that region: "Barbarism, enervated by certain civilized forms, without barbarism's vigor, tells all in a word. Scenes of disgust I might repeat to the point of nausea; utter lack of sanitation, of care of body as well as mind, expose a scrofulous people to all the tropical diseases. . . ." To this writer, Central America was not properly a part of the larger Latin American whole, for the South Americans were civilized and progressive, the Central Americans not so. They would be better called "Indo-Americans," he thought, to indicate their inferiority.[15]

Perhaps the most sweeping indictment of Latin Americans as people was contained in George W. Crichfield's *American Supremacy: The Rise and Progress of the Latin American Republics and Their Relations to the United States under the Monroe Doctrine*. This remarkable work was published in two volumes by Brentano's of New York in 1908. A massive compendium of facts, legend, biased history, personal experience, and diatribe, its contents were inadequately foreshadowed by its title. One chapter was entitled "Entire Lack of Good Faith among Latin-American Dictatorships," another "Valuelessness of Spanish-American Statistics." The author saw "infamy, perfidy, intrigue, and scoundrelism covering Spanish-America as with a pall." Mestizos, who made up a large portion of the Caribbean population, were bad enough, but "an infusion of Negro blood into this peon mixture generally brings about a product which is wholly and irretrievably bad." The common folk in the towns were "usually lazy, insolent, and good-for-nothing," while people in the mountains were violent as well. "A Latin American may profess undying affection for a person, but he may be at the same time planning literally to cut his throat at the first opportunity. . . . Bad faith is universal." While a reviewer in *The Nation* condemned Crichfield's "embittered and violent tone" and "wild" conclusions, a prominent scholar of Latin America took no such exception in *The Annals of the American Academy*. Chester Lloyd Jones found Crichfield's information useful, objecting merely to the work's excessive length and poor organization.[16]

The truth was that the American public of the early twentieth century expected to find inferior qualities in nonwhite peoples from tropical societies. Racism in the United States was older than the nation itself; Indians and blacks had suffered from the stigma of inequality since early colonial times. The legacies of the frontier and slavery had long since hardened into fixed attitudes, only superficially changed by the passing of Indian resistance or the episodes of the Civil War and Reconstruction. By the late nineteenth century the South was resubmerging its black population under grandfather clauses, Jim Crow legislation, and lynch law, while Indians were consigned to segregated "reservations" and forgotten. Even the newer European immigrants, flocking in from Southern and Eastern Europe and bringing different cultural backgrounds into the mainstream, were received with deep suspicion and scarcely concealed intimations of inferiority. The inequality of peoples was a pervasive idea in turn-of-the-century America; the Indians, mestizos, and blacks of the Caribbean could hope for little from United States public opinion.

The period entertained not only racial, but geographical biases. A widely read book entitled *The Control of the Tropics* appeared in 1898 with a large impact in both England and America. Written by an Englishman named Benjamin Kidd, its thesis centered on the allegation that the tropical peoples were always and everywhere incapable of self-government and economic development, and their societies were typically characterized by anarchy and bankruptcy. The roots of this alleged condition were not merely racial; white men of "high efficiency," living too long amid slack standards in an enervating climate, were themselves in danger of degeneration. Such men must return regularly to their homelands to renew their mental, moral, and physical vigor, or succumb in time to the universal tropical decay. If tropical areas were to be developed, therefore, they must be governed and managed by career executives and civil servants sent out from the vigorous societies of the north, and regularly replaced by new blood. Since the last great field for the world's economic growth lay in the tropics, Kidd declared, the matter was of more than theoretical importance, and scores of reviewers and readers in the United States agreed with him.[17]

Carl Schurz, the German-American editor, politician, and reformer, had actually anticipated Kidd's argument when he opposed Grant's scheme to annex Santo Domingo in 1870–71. "Show me a single instance of the successful establishment and peaceable maintenance . . . of republican institutions, based upon popular government, under a tropical sun," he told the United States Senate. "But, more than that, show me a single instance in any tropical country where labor . . . did not exhibit a strong tendency to run into shiftlessness. . . ." Schurz noted, as Kidd would later, that Anglo-Saxons themselves tended to go downhill when they settled in the tropics; the climate led inevitably to slavery, violence, and degeneration, he concluded. The fact was that Kidd's views were widely familiar before he stated them, which is why they were so compelling to his readers. As Carl Schurz preceded Kidd in condemning tropical peoples, American public men continued to do so after 1898. Woodrow Wilson reechoed the theme, declaring of the Filipinos in 1901 that "they are children and we are men in these deep matters of government and justice." And in 1914 Theodore Roosevelt listed Mexico, Venezuela, Honduras, Nicaragua, Haiti, and Santo Domingo as "not fit to be trusted in international matters, even so far as themselves are concerned." [18]

To examine the newspaper editorial cartoons of the first quarter of the twentieth century is to see the biases of the age made visual. In them, the peoples of the Caribbean are most often depicted as children, Negroes, or both, while Uncle Sam is consistently portrayed in a fatherly, benevolent role, always dominant and often disciplinary. A 1907 cartoon showed a smiling Sam about to give a doll labeled "freedom" to a very black "pickaninny" girl representing Cuba, with a warship significantly visible in the background. Another, from the same year, showed Uncle Sam administering "mediation soothing syrup" to two squalling brats in nursery beds identified as "Mexico" and "Guatemala." A 1910 cartoon had Sam cutting a willow switch outside the "Monroe Doctrine woodshed" to whip a sullen and unrepentant "bad boy" labeled "Nicaragua." In a 1912 sample, a small black "Cuba" child apprehensively viewed a broken milk pitcher on which was lettered "self-government," while a vision of the United States flag reminded him of coming punishment. Countless cartoons showed the various Caribbean peoples as grotesque Negro stereotypes, replete with thick lips, ragged clothing, lazy and irresponsible habits, and watermelons. Like so many of the travelers' reports, the cartoonists conveyed graphically that the human stock of the Caribbean region could not by itself be expected to achieve much.[19]

Potentially rich, but peopled by inferior stocks and retarded by inimical tropical conditions, the future of the region lay primarily with outsiders: that was the message, implicit or explicit, received by public opinion in the United States. Yet a plethora of witnesses asserted their confidence in the area's future. Given even a modest degree of order and stability, they chorused, foreign business enterprise would soon be able to tap the varied riches awaiting its fulfilling hand. With economic development under way, a generalized prosperity would soon transform the lives, the institutions, perhaps even the nature

"Cuba's Freedom Is Not Far Off," Thomas May, *Detroit Journal*, 1907

"More Trouble in the Nursery," Osborn, *Milwaukee Sentinel*, 1907

"Cutting a Switch for a Bad Boy," McKee Barclay, *Baltimore Sun*, 1910

"Golly, I've Gone an' Did It Again!" J. H. Donahey, *Cleveland Plain Dealer*, 1912

of the local populations. For the benefits of economic growth would assuredly be mutual; the native peoples of the Caribbean would gain at least as much as the entrepreneurs who came from abroad to invest their money and talents. A rising level of wealth would bring peace, education, and progress to currently benighted areas, provided of course that the developers enjoyed a relatively free hand. Furthermore, the glowing prospects so often described were typically placed, not in the remote future, but in the next decade or sooner. The driving engine of this economic miracle was to lie primarily in tropical agriculture: the sugar, coffee, bananas, or tobacco in which foreign investors were already so interested. In addition some infrastructure would be needed, particularly in the form of railroads and public utilities, while mining and lumbering represented further fields for action.[20]

Writing near the turn of the century, Joseph Conrad made a character in his novel *Nostromo* argue that foreign enterprise brought social benefits in its wake in spite of its admitted lack of philanthropic purpose. Published in 1904, *Nostromo* depicted the impact of foreign development on the fictional Latin American state of Costaguana. The largest outside enterprise in that country was an Anglo-American mining company, whose English chief executive defended its presence in these words:

> What is wanted here is law, good faith, order, security. Anyone can declaim about these things, but I pin my faith to material interests. Only let the material interests once get a firm footing, and they are bound to impose the conditions on which alone they can continue to exist. . . . your money-making is justified here in the face of lawlessness and disorder . . . because the security which it demands must be shared with an oppressed people. A better justice will come afterwards.[21]

In the unsparing light of hindsight, it is easy to indict these prophets of progress and prosperity for their hypocrisy. After a century of partial and selective foreign development, the Caribbean region is not rich, but poor. While the enterprisers often made money, and local elites received a more modest share, their activities produced nothing like a generalized prosperity. On the contrary, a vast inequality of incomes left many in penury and most barely above the subsistence level. And in the long run, even the investors' profits were limited; most of the twentieth century has seen agricultural products exchange at a disadvantage with industrial goods, the terms of trade being largely controlled by the industrial and financial centers.[22] World market surpluses of sugar, coffee, and other tropical staples have further driven prices down, so that only during major wars does a true agricultural prosperity bloom in the tropical world.

In the light of these facts, it is tempting to conclude that the claims and promises by which foreign enterprisers justified themselves in the early twentieth century were insincere and self-serving. Self-serving they certainly were, but not necessarily insincere. It is, after all, easiest to believe what is welcome; belief and self-interest typically run hand in hand. More seriously, the enterpriser of 1900 or 1915 had persuasive reasons to believe in the viability of an agriculturally based economic development. At that very time, Argentina was rapidly emerging as the most prosperous and "modern" of Latin American states, making a major success of selling wheat and beef to a hungry Europe. Since the bulk of Argentina's population sprang from recent European immigrants, the lesson seemed to be that the more efficient "races" could indeed wring wealth out of the soil, and that the process was inhibited elsewhere mainly by the deficiencies of the natives. Furthermore, Argentine economic development had been managed and financed to a notable extent from England, demonstrating the efficacy of foreign enterprise. With a fast-growing productive base, a solid infrastructure, and a relatively stable political system, Argentina was widely seen as a role model for all of Latin America.

Closer to home, the enterprising Yankee had an even more compelling example of the possibilities of market agriculture. The United States itself had long flourished through the export of huge agricultural surpluses, which had played an essential role in financing nineteenth-century industrialization. Nor was this a phenomenon of the past; American food and fibers still dominated the world market, and their profitability had continued to spur the development of large sections of the nation. The Great Plains constituted the last great agricultural frontier, and in 1900 that region was just approaching full development. Within the memory of millions of living Americans, vast areas west of the Mississippi had been settled and broken to the plow. With startling speed, railroads were built, cities founded, churches, opera houses, universities created—an entire new society, comprising numerous states of the union, had appeared as if by magic in a few decades, quickly achieving American standards of wealth, productivity, and material consumption.

The undeniable fact was that United States economic development had historically been tightly linked to a varied and prosperous agriculture. Its modern industrial economy was built on a foundation of soil-based wealth; its citizens took it as a given that the one was a natural precondition for the other. What they had done at home, right up to the early twentieth century, they assumed they could do anywhere else where a reasonable resource base existed. They had little reason to doubt that a healthy economic development could spring from the export of agricultural surpluses to a world market, and every reason to have faith in the process.

In retrospect, of course, there are obvious flaws in this assumption. The relatively favorable terms of trade enjoyed by agricultural products at the beginning of the century were to disappear almost permanently after the First World War. A crop like sugar, considered as an enterprise, differed significantly from grain or meat, given sugar's special demand for cheap seasonal labor and its wildly fluctuating world price. Large-scale corporate farming by foreign businesses was hardly the same as the family farming which prevailed for so long in the United States. And nowhere in the Caribbean, except perhaps in Cuba, were there large tracts of land possessing anything like the incomparable richness of soil and climate which characterized the more prosperous farming areas of the United States. At the time, however, it appeared otherwise. The Great Plains, with their harsh climate, insect plagues, lack of trees, and inadequate rivers seemed the ultimate in nature's resistance to exploitation. Surely the nation which had brought such a region to productivity could repeat its success in the lush, warm valleys of the Caribbean, where the limitations of tropical soils were still imperfectly understood. Flush with surplus capital, confident of their new technology, and glorying in past success, it never occurred to Yankee enterprisers to doubt their ability to pluck riches from the neighboring lands to the south. Neither did they doubt that their success in this would bring the region progress and prosperity. What had happened so often at home was now to be duplicated abroad, they believed, and so did their contemporaries.[23]

   What American businessmen and policy makers feared in the Caribbean was not economic failure, but the challenge of their transatlantic rivals to United States control of the region. If they saw the principal barrier to Caribbean development in the supposed deficiencies of the native peoples, they were only slightly less concerned with the threat of European intervention in the area. France's invasion of Mexico in the 1860s, the French Panamá canal project of the 1880s, and the events leading to the Venezuelan crisis with England in the mid-1890s all mobilized long-standing fears in the United States that Europe's imperial rivalries might spill over into the Americas. As Richard Olney's "twenty-inch gun" note of 1895 had so dramatically stated, most Americans would regard such outside intervention in the hemisphere as disastrous, threatening United States security, prestige, and future economic growth. The Monroe Doctrine's dictum against the possibility had long expressed a central tenet of United States foreign policy, and commanded the most widespread popular support.

   There were, as always, a few dissenters. The ever-idiosyncratic George Crichfield urged a strong United States hegemony over most of Latin America, but if Americans were not willing to take the hemisphere in hand, then he thought it better that the Europeans do so rather than leave the region in its current intolerable state. "It would be better for the United States, from every viewpoint, that England should have Central America and the whole continent of South America than that they should remain in their present condition," Crichfield declared, "And this I would assert for Germany also." Some years later, Colonel Edward M. House, the confidant and adviser of President Woodrow Wilson, formulated a variation of Crichfield's view. In a 1915 conversation with Secretary of State Robert Lansing, House stated that there were no objections whatever to the Germans going to South America in great numbers and getting peaceful control of the governments, and in continuing them under republican forms of government . . . it would probably be of benefit to the Americans rather than a detriment, for the German population would be in every way preferable to the population now in the majority of South American countries.[24]

In general, however, contemporary Americans were united in their opposition to European expansion in the New World, and after 1900 they came quickly to focus their strongest fears and suspicions, no longer on France or Great Britain, but on the rising power of imperial Germany. From the beginning of the twentieth century, this perceived "German threat" constituted one of the ongoing assumptions behind United States policies in the Caribbean.

Belief in a German threat to the Americas was growing rapidly even before Theodore Roosevelt became president in 1901, and it became pervasive in the policy-making circles of the Roosevelt administration. As early as 1898, Roosevelt himself believed that "of all the nations of Europe it seems to me that Germany is by far the most hostile to us." By 1901, he was certain that only a major naval building program could deter the kaiser's ambitions. "I find that the Germans regard our failure to go forward in building up the navy this year as a sign that our spasm of preparation, as they think it, has come to an end," he wrote,

that we shall sink back, so that in a few years they will be in a position to take some step in the West Indies or South America which will make us either put up or shut up on the Monroe Doctrine; they counting upon their ability to trounce us if we try the former horn of the dilemma.

To an English correspondent, Roosevelt confided that "as things are now the Monroe Doctrine does not touch England . . . the only power that needs to be reminded of its existence is Germany." In particular, he feared the Germans would find ways to acquire the Dutch and Danish possessions in the Americas to use as bases for the insertion of their power. By 1905, however, the president felt that his firm stance, accompanied by a continuing program of naval expansion, had become an effective deterrent: "I think I succeeded in impressing on the Kaiser, quietly and unofficially . . . that the violation of the Monroe Doctrine by territorial aggrandizement on his part around the Caribbean meant war, not ultimately, but immediately, and without any delay." It was, however, a deterrent which required continual alertness and preparation, he thought.[25]

Roosevelt's thinking was mirrored in that of his most influential advisers. His lifelong friend, Senator Henry Cabot Lodge, had only a few years earlier sounded the alarm against British expansionism in the Americas, but he soon shifted his fears to Germany. He doubted, he wrote Roosevelt in 1901, that Germany would attack the United States, as "it would be a pretty dangerous undertaking under any circumstances, but at the same time it is well within the range of possibilities, and the German Emperor has moments when he is wild enough to do anything. . . . Our only safety is in being thoroughly prepared," Lodge concluded. "The Navy is the vital point. . . . If we have a strong and well-equipped Navy, I do not believe Germany will attack us." [26]

Secretary of War Elihu Root entertained similar suspicions. He announced in 1900 that "the American people will within a few years have to either abandon the Monroe Doctrine or fight for it, and we are not going to abandon it." In time his concern diminished somewhat, but the source of his fear was never in doubt. As he wrote nine years later, after ending his term as Roosevelt's secretary of state, "Germany, under her present government, is the greatest disturber of peace in the world." Another shaper of Roosevelt's thinking, the naval theorist Alfred Thayer Mahan, believed from the 1890s on that "Germany . . . represents the probable element of future trouble for us." Like Roosevelt and Lodge, he was convinced that security lay only in maintaining a stronger navy than that of the Germans, and he became deeply concerned in 1909 when Congress began to slow down the naval building program. Projecting current programs in both countries, he concluded that the German navy would have a clear lead by 1912, after which there would be serious danger to hemispheric security. Germany had come late to the race for colonies, he pointed out, and could not hope to secure much of an empire without venturing a war somewhere. The Germans particularly wanted a foothold in the Americas, and the Monroe Doctrine was therefore only as good as the United States power to enforce it. [27]

These fears of hostile German intentions were not confined to administration insiders, but were matters of common knowledge and objects of frequent discussion in the press. They outlived the end of the Roosevelt administration, to be reinvigorated by the events of the First World War. Why were Americans so sure that Germany's power was dangerous to them, and how accurate was their assumption?

Germany, like the United States, was a fast-rising industrial power and a relative newcomer to the imperial scramble for colonies. Also like the United States, it had recently entered the international competition to become a leading naval power. Its flamboyant kaiser, fond of military show and symbolism, talked altogether too freely at times of his grandiose ambitions. The Prussian military tradition dominated the new German Empire, and if its navy aimed to become one of the strongest in due time, the position of its army was already fixed at or near the top. This was, in short, a formidable, energetic state, which appeared both ambitious and menacing to powers with established claims.

An initial source of anti-German feeling grew out of the United States conquest of the Philippines. Prior to the Spanish-American War, the German government had hoped to secure bases in those islands if Spain could no longer hold them under its control, which seemed a distinct possibility by the 1890s. This hope was no secret, and in fact a spokesman for the German foreign office unofficially stated it to the United States ambassador in 1898. If the United States chose not to take the archipelago, he suggested, or did not want all of it, Germany would be anxious for a chance at any appropriate base area. Once the Americans were militarily involved, however, there is no evidence of any intent in Berlin to challenge whatever decision Washington made about the disposition of the islands.[28]

A contrary impression nevertheless arose in the United States from the actions of a German naval squadron which arrived at Manila Bay shortly after Admiral Dewey's victory there. The German admiral was tactless and abrasive, angering Dewey and his subordinates. Some of the latter read the most sinister implications into what were in reality minor incidents, and their comments soon found their way into the home press. Dewey himself, who became the long-time chairman of the navy's influential General Board, was intensely anti-German for the rest of his life. These naval biases and rumors were reinforced by diplomatic gossip at the State Department, where reports from various European capitals speculated that the Germans might strongly contest the transfer of the Philippines to any one of their European rivals. Such reports encouraged the conclusion that the United States must keep the entire territory of the Philippines, for a failure to do so would presumably mean either sharing them with Germany or risking a general struggle for control over whatever portion the United States left unclaimed.[29]

There were also reasons to tie a prospective German threat to the Caribbean. Admiral Alfred von Tirpitz, the powerful German naval chief, wished to acquire bases in the western hemisphere to match those already held by Great Britain and France. He thought of finding such bases on the coast of Brazil, where three hundred thousand German immigrants had settled in the recent past, or in the Galapagos Islands on the Pacific side of South America. He also talked, however, of gaining possession for Germany of the Dutch or Danish colonies in the Caribbean area and thereby gaining a base at Curaçao, Surinam, or the Virgin Islands, a possibility that worried American naval strategists.[30]

Between 1897 and 1905, German naval staff officers elaborated a series of war plans involving an attack upon the east coast of the United States. Their original concept of a direct descent upon New York, Norfolk, Boston, or elsewhere was eventually modified to include the prior seizure of an advanced base in Puerto Rico or Cuba. Such a staging point would make an invasion less risky, and had the added advantage that its seizure would force the American fleet to come out and fight at a time and place chosen by the Germans. By 1901 the Army General Staff had joined the Admiralty Staff in joint planning, General Alfred von Schlieffen originally estimating that fifty thousand men

would be required to take and hold Cuba. A later version of the plan substituted Puerto Rico for Cuba, and reduced the troop strength for its seizure
to something over twelve thousand men. Finally, in 1906, the war operations
plan was reduced to a mere theoretical exercise, as rising tensions in Europe
made it too dangerous to consider committing Germany's entire naval strength
to operations in another part of the world. The continued increase in United
States naval strength also acted to discourage German planners, and in 1909
the German navy's Caribbean–South Atlantic squadron was discontinued.[31]

   While Germany's war plans were kept secret, some idea of their nature
leaked through to the United States, where American naval leaders added a
real fear of invasion to their earlier anti-German bias. Repeated rumors of the
German General Staff's hostile activity confirmed Theodore Roosevelt in his
belief in a Teutonic threat and his determination to keep the navy strong. Inter-
estingly, his conviction in 1905 that he had succeeded in deterring the kaiser's
ambitions through a policy of firmness and strength came reasonably close to
the moment when Berlin itself ceased to consider an American adventure. By
1909 President William Howard Taft would call talk of German aggression
in the hemisphere "absurd," and even the navy became less convinced that a
clash was imminent.[32]

   By that time, however, Americans perceived another kind of threat, as
Germany's economic penetration of Latin America and success in selling its
exports there identified her as a leading trade rival. The large German immigration to South America and the prominent role of resident German businessmen in many Latin American cities reinforced the picture of a drive for
economic domination. Such domination was achieved in fact only in tiny,
poverty-stricken Haiti, where German merchants did control the great bulk of
international trade. Elsewhere, however, the growth of United States trade out-
paced that of its rivals, including Germany; rapid Latin American economic
growth in the early twentieth century had in fact increased the exports of all
the leading suppliers to the area, but none more than the United States.[33]

   Whether there really was a "German threat" to the United States or its
Caribbean interests is still a matter of debate. H. H. Herwig and David Trask
have argued that the intensive German war planning at the beginning of the
century indicated a serious interest in naval and military circles in an aggressive war against the United States. Admiral von Tirpitz made no secret of his
ambitions in the western hemisphere, and he had considerable influence over
the impressionable kaiser. True, such a war now appears adventurist and dangerous, risking German power far from home for distinctly marginal purposes,
and the Germans themselves eventually thought better of it. However, they
long discounted American naval, and more especially military, strength on the
assumption that the United States armed forces were weakened by indiscipline
and inefficiency. Thus, according to this view, it was only the growing crisis

in Europe itself that finally acted to cancel out Berlin's aspirations in the New World.[34]

Melvin Small agrees that Americans long feared a German attack, but concludes that the decision makers in Berlin never seriously considered Latin American conquest or North American aggression. Whatever intellectual gymnastics the service leaders undertook, they did not reflect actual government policy, his argument implies. Certainly after 1903, he says, the kaiser's government hoped for good relations with the United States, not confrontation. All in all, Small believes, the "German threat" had been more apparent than real.[35] Yet Small omits a close scrutiny of the period from 1898 to 1903, where lay the strongest indications of a hostile German purpose. On the other hand, no one has made much of a case for a German threat after 1906, even if one existed earlier. One is forced to conclude that the *continuation* of the fear of German designs in the hemisphere was ill founded, even as one concedes the sincerity of most of its prophets.[36]

Justified or not, fear of Germany played a significant part in American thinking about the area as a vital security zone. Concern for the national security blended in turn with economic objectives, status ambition, and even reforming zeal to motivate a quest for United States hegemony. As they looked southward, Americans saw a potentially rich area awaiting development. They believed its resident peoples backward and inferior, incapable by themselves of achieving progress or material development. They feared that European rivals might challenge American power and policies in the region, and in particular that Germany would do so, or perhaps go even further and unleash armed aggression against the United States. And they accepted a European-made concept of international law which upheld the rights and interests of foreign enterprisers in undeveloped countries. All of these assumptions, singly and together, encouraged Americans to feel that they should play a leading role in the Caribbean, in order to benefit themselves, develop the region, and forestall foreign threats. Most Americans soon came to see United States hegemony as practical, right, legally justified, and even necessary.

Chapter 5

The Isthmian Canal

The initial United States movement toward Caribbean hegemony came in two principal steps. The first was embodied in the Spanish-Cuban-American War and the consolidation of long-term positions in Cuba and Puerto Rico. The second grew out of the quest for an isthmian canal, and the resulting creation of further commitments which amplified and extended United States power in the region. The development of the canal factor, following hard on the heels of the victory over Spain, made the years 1898–1903 crucial ones in the growth of Caribbean policy.

Until 1898, the widespread interest in an isthmian canal had centered about its commercial importance. The traumatic economic depression which hit the United States in 1893 popularized the view that the domestic market was saturated, that America's industries had come to produce more than its people could consume. To find an outlet for its surplus production, went the argument, the nation must cultivate foreign markets. Salvation lay in exports, and promising fields for export must lie outside of Europe and its colonial empires, for the imperial powers could be expected to discriminate against any serious foreign competition. So ran the assumptions of the day, and given such assumptions, Americans came to view Latin America and the Far East as the logical fields for cultivating expanded markets. China seemed especially promising, for it had a huge population, and the western powers had collectively imposed a kind of joint protectorate upon it which opened its ports to their trade on favorable terms. Western economic and cultural penetration of Japan had already brought far-reaching changes in that country, encouraging the expectation that China would likewise modernize and develop western-style needs and consumer patterns. By the turn of the century, faith in an imminent trade boom in the Far East was deeply implanted in current thought.[1]

Confidence in a booming transpacific trade underscored the need to cut down the distance and cost of shipping goods from the eastern United States across that vast ocean. The Suez Canal gave an advantage to Europe, until a New World counterpart should restore the balance. Eastern manufacturers, Southern textile interests, and seaport elites hoped for direct advantage from a successful isthmian canal project. An additional expectation was that a cheaper coast-to-coast shipping route through an isthmian canal would force down transcontinental railroad rates to the benefit of shippers, farmers, and consumers all over the nation, but particularly in the West.[2]

All of these hopes were especially intense in the South. In the post–Civil War era, Southern leaders stressed the need for a new, more industrialized Southern economy, which could take advantage of the region's cheap labor and plentiful farm production. By the late nineteenth century, the South's textile industry was challenging that of New England, while seeking additional markets for its product. To Alabama's Senator John T. Morgan, an isthmian canal was a necessity for an economically developing South. In 1888 he announced in the Senate that he would "advocate any and every scheme that [might furnish] to the Gulf States and the South Atlantic States this coveted outlet to the Pacific Ocean," and he was as good as his word. From that time on, Morgan was the leading proponent in Congress of an isthmian canal. In 1891 he became the Senate leader in the drive to secure government financial support for the Nicaragua canal project, emerging as well as the ranking Democrat on the Senate Foreign Relations Committee. Morgan served on the latter body from 1878 until his death in 1907, acting as chairman from 1892 to 1894, when his party held a majority. One of the most influential Democrats of his day on foreign policy, Morgan also espoused Mahan's prescription of a large navy, overseas bases, and a subsidized merchant marine to expand American export markets, but the canal was to Morgan the central point of the entire conception.[3]

Other isthmian canal backers included the Gulf seaports, and especially New Orleans, which competed with New York at an increasing disadvantage for the trade of Latin America. New Orleans would be far closer to an isthmian canal than any major Atlantic coast port, and civic leaders there hoped to reestablish the old north-south trade routes up the Mississippi valley to Chicago and southward through the Caribbean. At times they attempted to enlist the aid of other Mississippi valley river and rail centers like Memphis, Saint Louis, and Chicago, which could also benefit from an alternative to the existing east-west trade axis now running through the great northeastern ports. The Gulf-to-Chicago rail lines constituted further potential allies, the Illinois Central in particular. While the major part of this campaign came after 1900, by 1890 business leaders throughout the Mississippi valley were aware of these isthmian canal factors. In December 1891, for example, the head of the Nicaraguan Canal Company visited Chicago to assure that city's business and railroad executives that a completed isthmian canal would give them direct access to the trade of Central and South America.[4]

A typical statement of canal support came from United States Senator Donelson Caffery of Louisiana in 1899:

> This canal ought to be built. . . . It will double the commercial power of the United States. It will cut by half the distance from our trade centers to the distant lands that we hope to supply with our manufactures and our products. It will reduce the land transportation costs of the entire United States by a considerable per cent.

But after this standard litany of hopes, Caffery went on to include another kind of benefit from the canal: "It will double the power of the American navy. It will greatly assist in the coast defense on both oceans. For every consideration," he concluded, "I think this canal ought to be built."[5]

After 1898, the strategic significance of an isthmian canal began to override its commercial importance in public discussion, as the recent war experience reshaped opinion. While strategic arguments gained in urgency and acceptance, however, they were hardly new. Ever since the 1880s, the case for naval expansion had been closely tied to the need to protect a future canal. The newborn Naval War College quickly developed a strategic doctrine for the canal, and by 1887 its lecturers expounded the need to control approach routes and outer entryways as well as the canal itself. Other navalists pointed out that in case of a war involving maritime powers, the one with the stronger navy would attempt to deny the canal to its enemy. If the United States were one of the belligerents with its then weak fleet, its fighting ships would be confined to one side of the nation or the other. Thus Secretary of the Navy Benjamin Tracy had argued in 1890 that the United States must build either an isthmian canal or two separate fighting fleets, one to defend each coast.[6]

These strategic premises became familiar to those Americans with any interest in such matters, and had the unwavering support of the prestigious Captain Mahan himself. By 1890, Mahan regarded an isthmian canal as vitally necessary to the United States. Yet the current weakness of the navy made the canal potentially dangerous:

> Militarily speaking . . . the piercing of the Isthmus is nothing but a disaster for the United States, in the present state of her military and naval preparation. . . . The United States is woefully unready . . . to assert in the Caribbean and Central America a weight of influence proportioned to the extent of her interests.

When the canal became a reality, it would give the Caribbean area such strategic importance as to draw in the naval strength of the great powers, while the United States would be left helpless by its weakness. Thus to Mahan, an isthmian canal and a strong naval fleet were the two indispensable needs for the national security, and each leaned heavily upon the other.[7]

The new expansionism of the 1890s added urgency to these factors. As Senator Morgan wrote in 1897, "The annexation of Hawaii would make the canal a necessity as the construction of the canal will make annexation a necessity." Navalists insisted that if the United States were to become a Pacific power, a canal would be essential to allow the navy to concentrate quickly in the Pacific in time of need. The recent war with Spain had begun with a dramatic illustration of the problem. The battleship *Oregon* was stationed on the west coast when war threatened, and in March 1898, she began a "dash" to join the other heavy armored ships at Key West. Her epic voyage of 17,500 miles in eighty-one days, closely followed in the daily press, educated the nation in the need for a shorter sea route between the coasts.[8]

The weaknesses made evident by the war itself, and the accompanying acquisition of Hawaii and the Philippines, brought a national consensus in favor of a government-built isthmian canal. In January 1899, the United States Senate passed Senator Morgan's bill providing for federal construction of a Nicaraguan canal. Its defeat in the House of Representatives resulted from no lack of canal enthusiasm in that body, but rather the complications arising from a rival House bill, the issue of the Nicaraguan versus the Panamanian route, and the obstacle embodied in a long-standing agreement with Great Britain which limited America's freedom of action. Congressional support for some kind of isthmian canal project was virtually unanimous, while the McKinley administration pressed ahead to resolve these initial problems.[9]

The first problem was essentially diplomatic. With the exception of Grover Cleveland, every American president from Hayes to McKinley had declared that the United States must have exclusive control of any isthmian canal. Yet the Clayton-Bulwer Treaty of 1850 contained a mutual pledge by the governments of the United States and Great Britain that neither would build such a canal alone, or claim sole control of it. For half a century the nation had been bound by this promise, and several diplomatic efforts had failed to persuade the British to modify its terms. By 1898, both public and official opinion in America held that the treaty had become obsolete, and must be altered or abrogated. Fully aware of the strength of this feeling, the British cabinet pondered the proper response. The prime minister, Lord Salisbury, reported its discussions early in 1899 to Sir Julian Pauncefote, the British ambassador in Washington. The cabinet, he said, were reluctant to obstruct the creation of a major artery of commerce, but were equally reluctant to yield such an important concession to the United States without some reciprocal gain. He therefore wished Pauncefote to investigate the possibility of resolving the canal issue and the current Canadian-Alaskan boundary dispute in a single treaty, obviously in the hope that British concessions on the one question would elicit American concessions on the other. Another avenue might be to seek increased British trade opportunities in Puerto Rico, Cuba, and the Philippines. In short, the British were ready to deal, but wanted a quid pro quo.[10]

The British attempt to link the canal issue with other Anglo-American concerns met with consistent rejection in Washington, however, and in the end London gave ground. The Hay-Pauncefote Treaty, signed in February 1900, allowed the United States to build an isthmian canal unilaterally. But it would be permanently neutralized, as was the Suez Canal, and open to the ships of all nations in peace and war. Neither could it be fortified, for its militarization would violate its neutrality. The terms of the treaty aroused a storm of opposition in the United States. As Theodore Roosevelt, then governor of New York, wrote Secretary of State John Hay,

> If that canal is open to the warships of an enemy it is a menace to us in time of war; it is an added burden, an additional strategic point to be guarded by our fleet. If fortified by us, it becomes one of the most potent sources of our possible sea strength. Unless it is fortified, it strengthens against us every nation whose fleet is larger than ours.[11]

Like Roosevelt, the Senate put the strategic factor foremost, and refused to accept the treaty without changes which would allow for the defense of the canal. Hay was dismayed, the British taken aback. In London's eyes the use of bases in Puerto Rico and Cuba already went far to guarantee American control of the sea approaches to the canal, while the Admiralty advised the Foreign Office that control of the isthmus depended much more on local naval supremacy than on any possible canal fortifications. While the Admiralty still opposed an American canal, the Foreign Office concluded that the fortification issue was not vital, and decided at last to give in on it. Whitehall had despaired in any case of preventing a canal on American terms. The consequence was momentous: a British acceptance of United States strategic control in the Caribbean. Acting on this basis, the two governments made a new treaty which simply abrogated the old agreement of 1850 and said nothing whatever about fortifications; the United States now had a free hand on the isthmus. The second Hay-Pauncefote Treaty was signed in November 1901 and promptly approved by the Senate.[12]

Having successfully dealt with the only great power in a position to obstruct the canal scheme, United States policy makers expected little difficulty from the small Caribbean states involved. They saw their problem as simply deciding where to place the canal, in Nicaragua or in Panamá. The former route had dominated American thinking since the 1880s, and in Washington Senator Morgan headed a strong congressional lobby which was wholly committed to Nicaragua. Many Americans regarded Panamá as the "French" route, tainted by disease and failure. Nevertheless, the Panamá site always had proponents. In February 1899 the *Scientific American* compared the routes in detail and found strongly in favor of Panamá, as did an occasional spokesman for the engineering profession. Before the Spanish-American War, common reference was to a "Nicaragua canal"; that after 1898 the term "isthmian canal" was more current indicated more openmindedness on the question. And in March 1899 Congress instructed a reconstituted Walker Commission to recommend a choice between the two main routes, as well as two lesser locations which were quickly eliminated.[13]

Admiral Walker and his colleagues set off a new debate when they reported in favor of a Nicaraguan route. Not only the decision, but its equivocal basis, encouraged dissension, for the commission found Panamá in most respects superior. A Panamá canal would be 134 miles shorter than its Nicaraguan counterpart, and there were engineering advantages in that route which had long been evident to specialists. However, the New Panama Canal Company, successor to de Lesseps' failed enterprise, still held the Colombian government's charter for the Panamá location, as well as a great deal of machinery and other property, all of which they valued at $109 million. If forced to buy out the French firm at that price, the commission estimated, the United States government would spend over $60 million more to build in Panamá than in Nicaragua. They therefore favored the cheaper project, noting that they valued the French concession and property at no more than $40 million. Taking the hint, the French company soon offered to sell out for the $40 million, while President Theodore Roosevelt found that the best engineering advice favored Panamá. His direct influence, added to the sudden $69 million reduction in cost for the Panamá project, induced the Walker Commission to change its recommendation early in 1902.[14]

All of this enraged Senator Morgan and the Nicaragua lobby. Morgan favored Nicaragua in part because he had long been close to the American entrepreneurs who had promoted a canal there, in part because the Panamá project bore the onus of scandal. He favored it even more for the simple reason that a Nicaraguan canal would be seven to eight hundred miles closer to the Gulf ports of Mobile, New Orleans, and Galveston than to Boston or New York. It would favor the South, he thought, and that was enough for him. The Senator and his allies fought hard for their project, but were ultimately defeated by a congressional compromise which favored Panamá. This compromise, known as the Spooner Act, authorized the president to negotiate the necessary canal arrangements with the government of Colombia. If unable to do this within a "reasonable" time, however, he must then shift his efforts to Nicaragua. This victory for Panamá benefited from the efforts of three shrewd men: William Nelson Cromwell, a persuasive New York lawyer hired as a lobbyist by the French canal company; Philippe Bunau-Varilla, a

French engineer representing that company, who had had a significant role in de Lesseps' earlier canal project and was determined to vindicate it; and Senator Marcus Alonzo Hanna of Ohio, a Republican party bigwig who became an enthusiastic convert of the other two. All three had lobbied effectively in Washington, while it was Bunau-Varilla who persuaded his colleagues in the French canal company to sharply reduce the asking price for their remaining Panamá assets.[15]

In mid-1902, with the Spooner Act behind it, the Roosevelt administration began serious negotiations for a canal treaty with Colombia. The act specified that the president should acquire from Colombia "perpetual control of the canal strip," and authorized him to buy the rights and property of the French canal company for $40 million. The negotiations with Colombia, however, quickly ran into difficulties. In the autumn of 1902, while the proposed treaty was under discussion, Roosevelt sent marines into Panamá to put down a disturbance without bothering to get the prior consent of the Bogotá government, which the United States had always done before. Worse yet, the United States admiral who took charge at the isthmus at first refused passage to Colombian troops on the Panama Railroad, though the State Department ultimately intervened to reverse the decision. These and other high-handed measures immediately aroused Colombian fears about Washington's behavior once it had title to a canal strip, which the clause about "perpetual control" did little to alleviate. Furthermore, the Colombians told Hay that Bogotá must get a portion of the $40 million paid by the United States to the New Panama Canal Company. The talks dragged, and when Hay at last threatened to break off negotiations with Colombia and look to Nicaragua, the Colombian minister in Washington resigned rather than approve the current draft treaty, which was finally signed by Chargé d'Affaires Tomás Herrán.[16]

The Hay-Herrán Treaty, signed in January 1903, granted to the United States a canal strip ten kilometers wide along the alignment of de Lesseps' canal. Although Bogotá refused to grant the strip in perpetuity, the treaty provided for a 100-year lease which was renewable at the option of the United States. This seemed long enough for all practical purposes, and the American Congress made no objection to it. In return for this leased zone, the United States was to pay Colombia a down payment of $10 million, and an annuity of $250,000 per year beginning after nine years. The United States was to have the right to intervene militarily without the previous consent of Colombia in case of imminent danger to the canal. While Colombia would retain its legal sovereignty over the canal zone, police and judicial functions within it would be exercised jointly by the two governments. The treaty appeared to meet all the legitimate needs of the United States, and was approved by the Senate in March 1903. The Colombian senate, however, hotly debated the treaty, then rejected it decisively in August.[17]

While Roosevelt and Hay were shocked at this reverse, they themselves were largely to blame for it. Warned of strong Colombian opposition to the treaty, they made little effort to understand the political situation in Bogotá, where the end of a bitter three-year civil war in November of 1902 left a tense atmosphere in which the new government was forced to move cautiously. At any rate, the treaty posed some serious issues for that government. All previous canal treaties had specified a privately owned canal wholly under Colombian sovereignty; now effective sovereignty in the zone would be shared with the United States. Deep Colombian suspicions of American imperialism accompanied widespread disapproval of alienating the national territory; yet Panamanians were eager for renewal of the canal enterprise and desperately afraid that Colombian intransigence would force its removal to Nicaragua. There were also financial considerations. The United States minister in Bogotá believed that the money question was central; if the French company paid Colombia $10 million of its $40 million in American purchase money, he reported, the treaty could probably be ratified. Otherwise the Colombian government might simply wait until the French canal charter expired, then make the sale itself and keep *all* of the money. The canal charter was originally scheduled to expire in 1904, but had been extended for six years in 1900 by an emergency decree of the then president. By the summer of 1903 some Colombian senators were talking of invalidating the recent charter extension and repatriating the canal rights a year hence. To prevent this, the State Department had warned that under the terms of the Spooner Act, such a delay would probably force the abandonment of the Panamá route for that in Nicaragua. While many, perhaps even most, Colombians really wished to see a Panamá canal built, they regarded the financial terms of the Hay-Herrán Treaty as niggardly, and expected to benefit in one way or another from the bonanza involved in the United States purchase of the canal concession and properties.[18]

In short, Washington may well have had its treaty simply by allowing Bogotá to appropriate a portion of its payment to the French company. The expense to the United States would have been the same either way, and no American interest would have suffered. But the French canal interests were determined to keep all of the money, and their able representative, William Nelson Cromwell, prevailed on Hay to intervene on their behalf. Colombia had formally notified the New Panama Canal Company that it must obtain permission from Bogotá to sell its rights to the United States, and that it must pay part of the sale money to the government from which it had received the canal concession. Cromwell argued that it was improper to make a United States treaty contingent upon prior Colombian arrangements with private interests, and persuaded Hay that the Hay-Herrán Treaty settled the matter. Under that treaty, he claimed, Washington already had the right to buy out the French, and Colombia was no longer free to attempt separate deals with third parties.

Old and ailing, Hay leaned on Cromwell's expertise and found his reasoning persuasive. The secretary of state insisted that Colombia must get no more than what was specified in the treaty, and thereby doomed his agreement over an irrelevancy.[19]

If Hay was nonplussed at the treaty's defeat, Roosevelt was furious, referring to the Colombians as "foolish and homicidal corruptionists," "jack-rabbits," and worse. The angry president was at a loss for a course of action. He could turn to Nicaragua, as Hay had so often threatened and the Spooner Act might soon require, but "the great bulk of the best engineers" had agreed on the superiority of Panamá. Furthermore, the Nicaraguan government, though eager for a canal, had steadfastly refused to share its legal jurisdiction in the proposed canal zone with the United States. Alternatively, Roosevelt could do nothing at present, and hope for eventual progress at Bogotá. This was not an unrealistic course, but as a follower of Mahan, the president saw no real security for the United States until an isthmian canal should be completed, and his impatient nature chafed at delay.[20]

It might be possible, Roosevelt cryptically wrote Hay in September, to secure the Panamá route without dealing with the Bogotá government at all, for "I am not inclined to have any further dealings whatever with those Bogotá people." This comment could only have referred to the possibility of a successful Panamanian independence revolution. Given the long history of Panamanian revolts, everyone half expected a new uprising over this latest isthmian disappointment, and indeed some Panamanians had openly warned Bogotá of the risks of rejecting the canal treaty. Yet, in his private correspondence, Roosevelt rejected the option of helping to foment a Panamanian revolution. "Whatever other governments can do," he wrote, the United States could not employ

> such underhanded means. . . . Privately, I feel free to say to you that I should be delighted if Panamá were an independent State, or if it made itself so at this moment; but for me to say so publicly would amount to an instigation of a revolt, and therefore I cannot say it.[21]

In spite of these expressed scruples, the possibility of a Panamanian revolt was much in the minds of Washington policy makers. In September, Hay wrote the president about such an occurrence in terms that seemed to leave all of the options open: "It is altogether likely that there will be an insurrection in the Isthmus against that regime of folly and graft that now rules at Bogotá," he reflected. "It is for you to decide whether you will (1) await the results of that movement, or (2) take a hand in rescuing the Isthmus from anarchy, or (3) treat with Nicaragua." In case of an isthmian uprising, Hay noted, the United States would be obliged to act in any case "to keep the transit clear. Our intervention should not be at haphazard nor, this time should it be to the profit, as heretofore, of Bogotá." The secretary of state closed his advice by suggesting that Roosevelt "let [his] mind play a little about the subject for two or three weeks." [22]

While the president and his secretary of state speculated, others were already doing the work which they would welcome. Philippe Bunau-Varilla, the French lobbyist and former canal engineer, played a central role in bringing about an isthmian revolt. Bunau-Varilla had spent several years shuttling between Paris, New York, and Washington, and in the summer of 1903 he had sounded out the State Department on the Panamá issue. Though he got no promises, he shrewdly concluded that the United States would move under its 1846 Bidlack Treaty, which empowered it to keep the transit route open, to prevent Colombia from crushing any serious independence movement on the isthmus. He therefore notified the ardent but fearful Panamanian nationalists that he had secret assurances from the highest North American circles that they would be protected from Colombian wrath when they proclaimed their new state. This dramatic news, though probably untrue, served its purpose well. Fortified by a new sense of security, the original revolutionary plotters, who were mostly connected in some way with the American-run Panama Railroad, were able to convert the isthmian oligarchy to the cause. Assured of imminent action, Bunau-Varilla even managed to acquire the authority to act as the diplomatic representative of the Panamanian revolution.[23]

On November 3, 1903, the secessionists in Panamá proclaimed their revolution. On the previous day, United States naval commanders in the area had received orders to keep the transit route open and to prevent the landing of any armed forces, either government or insurgent. The order came too late to prevent the arrival of several hundred Colombian soldiers who had been dispatched in anticipation of trouble, and for a moment the revolution was in jeopardy, but the officials of the Panama Railroad saved the day. They temporarily lacked the cars needed to take the soldiers across the isthmus, they explained, but could provide a private car at once for the troop commander and his staff, while the main command would follow as soon as the rolling stock arrived. Arriving at Panamá City without his troops, the government commander was promptly arrested by the revolutionists, while his soldiers were left leaderless and immobilized on the Caribbean shore. With a cash bribe and the support of the United States Navy, the new Panamanian junta persuaded these stranded troops to return to Cartagena, and thereafter American naval vessels sealed off the area effectively. The State Department gave de facto recognition to the new isthmian state on November 5, at the same time warning the government of Colombia that no further attempts to land troops would be permitted. These measures ensured the success of the revolution, while observers could not help but notice the speed with which Washington had acted.[24]

In Washington, meanwhile, Philippe Bunau-Varilla presented his creden-

Steam shovels at work on the Panama Canal. Courtesy of the American Geographical Society Collection, University of Wisconsin–Milwaukee

tials as minister from the newborn state, and conferred with Secretary Hay about a canal treaty. After laboring for two weeks, the two produced an agreement which was strikingly favorable to the United States. In his memoirs Bunau-Varilla claimed authorship of this document, with the avowed motive of offering the United States Senate a bargain too attractive to refuse. He allotted only a passive role to Hay, while Hay in turn was presumably glad to have it seem that the treaty's one-sided terms resulted from concessions freely offered by the other side. Historians long accepted this version of the story, but the recent scholarship of John Major has established a very different sequence of events. It was not true, as Bunau-Varilla asserted, that Hay presented a treaty draft for his consideration which was little changed from the Hay-Herrán Treaty rejected by Colombia. In fact Hay had made sweeping changes in the former document, feeling that Washington's bargaining power with the new regime in Panamá was far stronger than it had been in the earlier case. Now the United States demanded a grant *in perpetuity* rather than a renewable 100-year term; the Canal Zone was widened from ten kilometers to ten miles; all mention of Panamanian sovereignty in the Canal Zone was omitted, and Panamá lost all legal jurisdiction there; there was to be no $10 million lump sum payment, merely the annual rental of $250,000; and the terminal ports of Panamá City and Colón were to be included in the Canal Zone.[25]

Bunau-Varilla in turn secured a number of changes in Hay's new draft. On behalf of Panamá he successfully argued for the restoration of the $10 million and the exclusion of the terminal cities from the zone. As further giveaways the Frenchman added clauses which allowed for United States acquisition of any lands and waters *outside* the Canal Zone needed for canal purposes; gave the United States a perpetual monopoly on any future isthmian canals or railroads; and allowed Washington to enforce sanitation measures in the terminal cities, even though they were no longer to be included in the zone. Significantly, it was Bunau-Varilla who wrote the famous clause which described United States powers in the Canal Zone as those it would have had "if it were the sovereign." Later he added still more concessions, most notably a United States right of intervention to preserve order in the terminal cities in case Panamanian authorities failed to do so.[26]

The treaty signed on November 18, 1903, was therefore the work of both negotiators, the State Department, far from being a passive recipient of Panamanian largess, having aggressively sought favorable terms. It is true that the compliancy of the Frenchman ensured Hay's success; Bunau-Varilla was eager to see the canal treaty written and ratified as soon as possible, and careful to meet possible Senate objections in advance. He was a man in a hurry, for he knew that a two-man diplomatic commission was on its way from Panamá to join him in the treaty negotiations. These men would undoubtedly bargain for Panamá's advantage; there might be difficulties in reaching agreement. The Frenchman cared little for Panamá's interests, however, being wholly interested in seeing the canal completed and the French canal company $40 million richer. Having fostered the necessary revolution in Panamá, he now meant to ensure an early diplomatic agreement that would allow the other arrangements to go forward. He confided much of this to Hay, with the result that the two were just able to complete a treaty and sign it before the unsuspecting Panamanians arrived. When the latter protested, they were told that the matter was closed. Furthermore, as Bunau-Varilla cabled the junta in Panamá, the Colombians were rushing a delegation to Washington to attempt to reopen canal negotiations; if the Panamanian government delayed matters, Roosevelt might abandon it to strike a better bargain with Bogotá. Caving in quickly, the new regime agreed to accept Bunau-Varilla's treaty before its leaders had even seen it! As good as its word, the junta formally ratified the treaty the day after a copy of it reached Panamá.[27]

The president sent the Hay-Bunau-Varilla Treaty to the Senate early in December 1903, and it was approved by a wide margin on February 23, 1904. This success did not come by consensus, however. Senator Arthur Pue Gorman, the Senate minority leader, had formulated a scheme to withhold the thirty-three Democratic votes in the Senate until the Republican leadership agreed to a congressional investigation of Roosevelt's actions regarding the Panamá revolution. Having presumably scored political points against the administration, the Democrats would then approve the treaty, making clear their support of the canal. Gorman's plan failed when almost half of the Senate Democrats deserted him to vote for the treaty at once. Since all the Republican senators did the same, the necessary two-thirds majority was easily achieved. As the astute Bunau-Varilla had intended, Democrats could see as clearly as Republicans that the treaty was uniquely favorable to the United States, while the financial terms to which Colombia had objected were accepted unchanged by Panamá. As Hay wrote to a member of the Senate, the treaty was "vastly advantageous to the United States, and . . . not so advantageous to Panamá. . . . You and I know too well how many points there are in this treaty to which a Panamanian patriot could object." [28]

The one-sided nature of the canal treaty, the role of the United States Navy in securing the success of the Panamá revolution, and the remarkable speed with which Washington acted throughout convinced many critics that the Roosevelt administration had played an active part beforehand in planning and organizing the Panamanian independence movement. Despite his supposed statement that "I took the Canal Zone," however, Roosevelt always denied any complicity in the revolutionary movement. It was untrue that he or his subordinates had given any prior assurances to the Panamanians, he wrote a correspondent early in 1904; Bunau-Varilla had simply made some very shrewd estimates and then acted upon them.

> He is a very able fellow, and it was his business to find out what he thought our government would do. I have no doubt that he was able to make a very accurate guess, and to advise his people accordingly. In fact, he would have been a very dull man had he been unable to make such a guess. . . .[29]

If the Panamanians had revolted, Roosevelt had been prepared to support them against Colombia, he admitted, but he had done nothing to bring about the revolt. In an attempt to prove this, he released to the press the text of an intended message to Congress in November 1903. The substance of the presumed message was that continued and unreasonable delay by Colombia in ratifying the canal treaty would mean that the United States "must forthwith take the matter into [its] own hands." If the Panamanians had not revolted, Roosevelt wrote a private correspondent a decade later, "I should have recommended Congress to take possession of the Isthmus by force of arms; and . . . I had actually written the first draft of my Message to this effect." These confessions hardly upheld the president's virtue, but they did strengthen the presumption that he was unaware of the status of the secession plans in Panamá.[30]

If the Rough Rider was innocent of starting a revolution, he nonetheless acted in a very arbitrary manner toward Colombia. The official argument justified the navy's intervention against the movement of Colombia's troops within its own territory by invoking the United States' duty under the Bidlack Treaty to keep the isthmian transit route open. That same treaty gave the United States the further duty of protecting Colombian sovereignty in Panamá, but the State Department asserted that this provision applied only to foreign aggressors, not to internal divisions within the nation. Whatever the merits of this legal sleight of hand, it could not hide the fact that United States action toward Colombia had been swift and brutal, and that Washington had at no time tried seriously to respond to legitimate concerns in Bogotá. The American course had rested at bottom on bullying, and virtually all of Latin America saw it that way.[31]

Theodore Roosevelt faced some harsh criticism over Panamá, which was reflected in the dissenting portion of the press. The antiimperialist *New York Evening Post* called the Panamá affair "a vulgar and mercenary venture," and held up the president's moralistic posing to ridicule: "And this blow below the belt is dealt by the vociferous champion of fair play! This overriding of the rights of the weaker is the work of the advocate of a 'square deal.' " The *New York Times* asserted that the nation was treading "the path of scandal, disgrace, and dishonor." The *Springfield Republican* condemned "one of the most discreditable performances in our history," and added a charge of hypocrisy to that of false dealing. These and many other newspapers editorially accused the administration of cynically using the nation's power to defraud a smaller neighbor. Yet whatever the critics said, most Americans approved of their government's course on the isthmus. Not only did most Republican newspapers support the president's actions, but so did many Democratic organs; in the nation's press as a whole, approval of the Panamá affair outweighed disapproval by a wide margin. Some editors had speculated freely about a possible Panamanian revolution before the event, and most assumed that the administration would utilize such an event to achieve the nation's purposes. According to the *St. Louis Republic*, the administration had "done no more than its duty," a sentiment echoed by scores of journals all over the country. Whatever Roosevelt's sins, he reflected the thrust of contemporary opinion in committing them.[32]

As might have been anticipated, the very faithfulness with which the Hay-Bunau-Varilla Treaty mirrored the desires of the United States was certain to create long-term problems in Panamá. As the junta and other national leaders studied the terms which had been imposed upon them, they could only feel betrayed. The treaty guaranteed Panamá's titular sovereignty over the Canal Zone, but what could this mean when the United States exercised all of the authority there which it would have "if it were the sovereign," and exercised it not for some limited term but "in perpetuity"? What could be left of Panamá's sovereignty? In effect, the Canal Zone belonged to the United States in full and, presumably, forever. From the start, the new Panamanian state would be bisected by an American colony which wholly contained that small nation's principal national asset.

Building the Miraflores Locks. Courtesy of the American Geographical Society Collection, University of Wisconsin–Milwaukee

Worse yet, the Panamanians soon came to believe that they had given up the Canal Zone for a pittance. The annual rental of $250,000 was no more than what the Colombian government had long received for the Panama Railroad alone; it failed to reflect the immensely greater value of a canal.[33] Even the $10 million initial payment looked trifling when one reflected that the French canal company received four times as much. And for these bargain prices, the United States claimed not only the Canal Zone, but the right to take extensive additional territories which it unilaterally determined to be "necessary and convenient" to the project in almost any way. The vigorous application of this clause would poison Panamanian–United States relations for generations to come.

Whatever their frustrations, however, the Panamanians had little choice but to accept the treaty, and the United States protection which came with it. Colombia's leaders showed themselves desperately anxious to retrieve their loss; the Conservative party leader, General Rafael Reyes, soon to be president, announced that he would see the Hay-Herrán Treaty ratified if he had to declare martial law and ratify it himself.[34] If Panamá was tardy in sealing her agreement with the United States, Washington had only to turn back to Colombia, a possibility of which Bunau-Varilla constantly reminded them. Thus there was no disposition in Panamá to reopen the question of ratification, however disappointed they might feel.

The canal treaty ensured that Washington would play a large role in the affairs of Panamá, through its control of crucial territories in that small state, the magnitude of the canal project, and the strategic importance attributed to the canal. Moreover, Panamá's constitutional assembly seemed openly to invite a Yankee protectorate when in January 1904 it adopted Article 136 of its new constitution. This provided that "the Government of the United States of America may intervene in any part of the Republic of Panamá to re-establish public peace and constitutional order in the event of their being disturbed. . . ." In return, the article said, the United States must guarantee the independence and sovereignty of Panamá. United States Minister William I. Buchanan was known to favor this provision, and many believed that he had forced it on the convention at the command of the State Department. Article 136 was not popular in Panamá, and it provided the occasion for the first open attacks on the United States by press and politicians.[35]

In reality, the State Department had believed the provision unwise and unnecessary, for the United States had ample power to defend its canal under the Hay-Bunau-Varilla Treaty. Hay was wary of an arrangement which obligated his government to put down revolts in Panamá, and so notified Buchanan. The intervention clause was in fact the product of Panamá's ruling Conservatives, who feared a Liberal uprising against their political control. Borrowing the idea from Cuba's Platt Amendment, they hoped it would awe their opponents with the fear of North American power. Buchanan favored it as a way to strengthen Washington's hand, but he did not reflect the views of his government. The constitutional assembly adopted the measure on a largely partisan vote of seventeen to fourteen, most Liberals voting nay, and the infant republic lost another portion of its sovereignty.[36]

Meanwhile Washington pushed on toward the ultimate purpose of all these diplomatic complications. In 1904 the United States government began the decade-long effort to complete the canal, and while it lasted, the project captured the national imagination as had no comparable activity: not the National Road, the Erie Canal, or the transcontinental railroad. The *Readers' Guide to Periodical Literature* listed 546 articles on some phase of the canal published in American magazines between 1900 and 1914, while 32 more came under the earlier heading, "isthmian canal." Newspaper stories and editorials were even more numerous. In the latter stages of construction, thousands of sightseers actually journeyed to Panamá to look at the huge project; besides all other motives, the sheer size of the effort attracted a people who admired bigness for its own sake. By the end of 1906, about twenty-four thousand people were working on the canal, and at the peak in 1911–14, nearly fifty thousand, brought there from a hundred different countries. The Caribbean itself furnished the lion's share, for many of its islands suffered from a chronic labor surplus, and canal wages were considered good for the time and place. The extensive use of black laborers from the West Indies created an exodus from Barbados, Martinique, Guadeloupe, Jamaica; about 40 percent of the adult males of Barbados worked on the canal at some point. The dollar costs reached

Panama Canal workers at mealtime. Courtesy of the American Geographical Society Collection, University of Wisconsin–Milwaukee

the majestic total of two-thirds of a billion dollars, an astronomical sum for the time, while despite improved health measures, nearly five thousand canal workers died of disease during the ten years of construction.[37]

These costs merely made the ultimate triumph more impressive. Americans saw themselves as having succeeded where the most advanced technology of Europe had failed; the promise of "American know-how" was redeemed. Most also considered the great work in Panamá a contribution to that universal progress in which they so firmly believed, and to which each nation must give its best effort. The greater the contribution, the greater the contributing society; the canal was a visible proof of American greatness. In 1915 the *Ladies' Home Journal* ran an article on the canal entitled "America's Gift to the World."[38] The title reflected popular thinking at the time. As is so often the case, the popular mind was inconsistent, for the Panama Canal, though the *Journal*'s "gift to the world," was simultaneously seen by the public as enhancing United States power and influence, profiting her merchants and producers, and justifying further American penetration in the Caribbean; in short, in advancing purely national purposes.

Beyond that, the Panama Canal was a compelling demonstration of Yankee willingness to use the national power in peacetime. Washington's thinly veiled threat to defy the Clayton-Bulwer Treaty if it could not be altered left Great Britain with the choice of giving in to American wishes or taking on the burden of an unwanted confrontation with the United States. In the end, London chose a graceful acquiescence, once it became clear that the United States government was not even prepared to grant reciprocal concessions for the favor. The prompt use of naval force to insulate Panamá's revolutionaries from Colombian reprisals was a further portent for Caribbean peoples. With the British in retreat and American power rapidly advancing, an era of United States hegemony in the area was at hand.

Part II

The Search for Stability

Chapter 6

———⸘∞⸘——

Toward Caribbean Security

In his book on the Panama Canal, Walter LaFeber has cautioned that it is too easy to explain United States activism in the Caribbean simply in terms of canal security, as is sometimes done. The nation's Cuban involvement clearly predates the canal project, while contemporary developments in Venezuela and Santo Domingo had little to do with Panamá, he argues. Policies toward these countries represented instead a larger and prior pattern into which Panamá also fit, even though the canal obviously increased United States interest in the region. Thus, LaFeber concludes, the Panama Canal was more a symptom than a cause of Washington's Caribbean policy.[1]

This is a useful warning against one kind of oversimplification, if one discounts LaFeber's parallel conclusion that real concern about canal security was never very great. In fact, security factors in the broad sense played a role in Caribbean policy wherever it applied, and the Panama Canal project sharpened and enhanced American concern about security. Since the defense of the canal was defined to include regional naval superiority and control of access routes, as well as the denial of effective Caribbean bases to a potential enemy, the issue of canal security affected policy makers' thinking about the entire Caribbean region. Very soon, a concept of "lifeline diplomacy" developed that was directly comparable to British security doctrine for the Mediterranean.

The new strategic view of the Caribbean began to emerge clearly in a report submitted to the secretary of the navy by the navy's General Board in 1898, shortly after the Spanish-American War. The General Board was an advisory committee created during the war to do strategic analysis and planning, with Captain A. T. Mahan as its most prominent member. Though abandoned after the war, it was recreated on a permanent basis early in 1900 under the chairmanship of Admiral George Dewey, the victor of Manila Bay, and long remained the navy's chief center for strategic thought. The original board's final report in 1898 laid out some of the navy's basic thinking. The Caribbean, the board declared, was the most strategic single region for the United States, for it was there that hostile naval powers could most seriously threaten U. S. interests. From the first, naval strategists believed that no European power could defeat the United States in its own hemisphere without securing a Caribbean base of operations. Furthermore, the report assumed that an isthmian canal was now a national necessity, and therefore certain to be built. Once such a canal existed, the Caribbean, already vital to the United States, would assume "surpassing influence" in the affairs of the rest of the world as well. Thus a completed isthmian canal would almost automatically draw in European rivalry and threats, the board members thought, while Germany soon emerged in American eyes as the leading European rival. The navy's top priorities were therefore to protect the future isthmian canal, and to prevent the appearance in the Caribbean of either European or local threats to the position of the United States.[2]

The Caribbean is a landlocked sea, entered through a few main channels between the islands of the West Indies. By far the most important of these was the Windward Passage between Cuba and Hispaniola; others included the Yucatán Passage at the western end of Cuba, the Mona Passage between Hispaniola and Puerto Rico, and the Anegada Passage between the Virgin Islands and the Leeward Islands. In 1898 the General Board recommended the development of a chain of bases to guard these channels, plus the establishment of additional strong points along the isthmus and on the Pacific coast of Central America. The board's report suggested several acquisitions for this purpose: Saint Thomas in the Virgin Islands, then known as the Danish West Indies, or alternatively Samaná Bay in Santo Domingo; a base at Guantánamo Bay or Santiago in Cuba; Almirante Bay in Panamá; and a Pacific coast base yet to be selected. During the next decade, other possible base areas were added to the original list, including Port Elena in Costa Rica, the Pearl Islands in the Gulf of Panamá, Havana and Cienfuegos in Cuba, Chimbote in Peru, and Ecuador's Galápagos Islands, which lay some eight hundred miles out in the Pacific from Panamá.[3]

Secretary of State John Hay gave serious attention to the navy's wishes, and for some years the exploration of possible base acquisitions was a routine chore at the State Department. Ultimately, the navy's chiefs had second thoughts about spreading their bases broadcast. Each would have to be defended, and the resulting dispersal of forces would contradict the fundamental principle of concentration. By 1903 the General Board, under the vigorous leadership of Admiral Dewey, was moving rapidly toward the concept of only a few bases in key positions. This essentially strategic decision was reinforced by the reluctance of Congress to appropriate funds for base development, and the board eventually narrowed its emphasis to Cuba. That island alone dominated two of the major outlets of the Caribbean, while the terms of the Platt Amendment already guaranteed the navy one or more bases there. Guantánamo Bay on the Windward Passage was by far the best base site in Cuba, but the General Board decided that the navy should have others at Havana, Cienfuegos, and Nipe Bay as well. Both John Hay and Theodore Roosevelt gave full support to these demands, but the Cubans were adamantly opposed to an American naval presence at Havana, while showing impressive skill at evading most of the other claims. In a 1903 treaty, Cuba finally ceded base rights at Guantánamo, and at Bahía Honda on the north coast west of Havana. Considering the latter site of little value, however, the Americans traded it off in the end for an enlarged naval reservation at Guantánamo Bay. Thus the result of several years of naval planning and diplomatic negotiation was one major Caribbean base at Guantánamo, and very little else. The quest for American bases had been largely converted to a determination to prevent the development of potentially hostile bases, especially on the part of Germany.[4]

This did not mean that concern for canal security had abated; rather, thinking as to how to achieve that goal continued to evolve. The navy believed from the beginning that overall fleet strength was more important for canal defense than either regional naval bases or canal fortifications. American fleet strength had grown dramatically in the years after the war with Spain; sixteen new battleships were commissioned from 1899 to the end of 1906. These, with the four prewar battleships, gave the United States a total of twenty, to be supplemented by a continuing program of new construction. If these twenty American battleships looked modest in 1906 compared with Great Britain's forty-nine, they matched the strength of any other navy; Japan had eleven, France twelve, and Germany, like the United States, twenty. In the years after 1906, Germany and the United States vied for second place in fleet strength. Although the Germans would pull ahead by the First World War, the Americans still held the advantage in their own home waters.[5]

With their faith placed in fighting ships, American service chiefs were less upset about the first Hay-Pauncefote Treaty's ban on canal fortifications than were civilian political leaders. The General Board's thinking concentrated increasingly on the idea of a showdown battle between the entire United States battle fleet and an enemy main force rather than a prolonged war of position; such a showdown battle would probably be decided far from the Panama Canal and possibly outside of the Caribbean. Between 1904 and 1906, naval planners also embraced the concept of seizing advanced bases as needed, rather than holding them in peacetime. Boldly innovative, this plan entailed keeping a fully equipped expeditionary force on call at Philadelphia's League Island station, ready to be transferred on demand to any place in the Caribbean.

While enthusiasm for this approach had waned by 1912, it was a temporary solution to the paucity of fixed bases.

Though the fleet itself was to be the first line of defense, everyone agreed on the need for some sort of fortifications in the Canal Zone. Aside from the threat of attacks by great powers, both Roosevelt and William Howard Taft thought a fixed defense system necessary to prevent some reckless Caribbean regime from attempting a sudden strike at the canal during a confrontation with the United States. The civilian authorities, however, were slow to make up their minds how much local defense would be needed. The issue came to a head during the Taft administration, the president disapproving War Department fortification plans which he thought too ambitious. When Taft left office, something like a consensus emerged. Henry L. Stimson, Taft's secretary of war, wrote in 1913 that the Canal Zone required fixed coast artillery installations at either end to hold an enemy fleet at a distance, and a mobile army garrison of six or seven thousand men to guard against small-scale raids, and if possible to delay a major invasion until reinforcements could arrive. This forecast the general shape of Canal Zone defenses in the ensuing years.[6]

Military and naval thinking varied somewhat regarding the details of Caribbean defense, and both services changed their planning in some respects over time. The central themes were constant, however, and civilian policy makers were as loyal to them as service leaders. As Secretary of War Elihu Root wrote in 1902, "The great thing is to recognize the inevitable trend and consequences of American public policy in the large sense, which must certainly bring the West Indies . . . under the political and naval control of the United States."[7] Root's view was to be the general one, as Americans assumed that the United States had become, and must remain, supreme in the Caribbean.

Washington was not long, however, in perceiving a new challenge to its Caribbean supremacy. During the very months in which the Roosevelt administration was negotiating the abortive Hay-Herrán Treaty with Colombia in its attempt to acquire the Panama Canal Zone, it became involved in the second Venezuelan crisis. As the first Venezuelan crisis, that of 1895–96, had reflected American fears of an expansionist Britain, this 1902 crisis was closely tied to burgeoning suspicions of Germany, as well as generalized American security fears in the Caribbean. The episode forced Theodore Roosevelt into some rapid policy formulation, and ultimately resulted in a formal claim of United States hegemony in the region. Like so many Caribbean crises, it stemmed from the failure of a local government to pay its European debts, and the consequent resort to gunboat diplomacy by the Europeans involved.

Venezuela's foreign obligations took several forms. Its government had floated large loans in London in 1881 and in Berlin in 1896, together totaling over five and one quarter million pounds sterling, which went into complete default in 1901. There were also snowballing damage claims by foreign citizens who had suffered harm in person or property from the civil strife which regularly erupted in that country. Also, from 1901 on, Venezuelan gunboats seized a number of small British-flag coasters from Trinidad which plied local waters, charging them with smuggling and revolutionary activity. And finally, railroad promoters and other European businessmen were increasingly involved in disputes with the Venezuelan government. Mounting British and German protests about these issues were rebuffed by Venezuela's feisty and xenophobic President Cipriano Castro, who ruled his country with a strong hand and showed open contempt for the rest of the world. The German government was considering forcible measures by 1901, and made a point of getting an early clearance from Theodore Roosevelt. Sounded out by his old friend Hermann Speck von Sternberg of the kaiser's diplomatic service, Roosevelt warned against any attempt at territorial aggrandizement, but had no objection to the proper punishment of Castro's misdeeds. "If any South American State misbehaves toward any European country," he wrote Sternberg, "let the European country spank it; but I do not wish the United States or any other country to get additional territory in South America." [8]

The British government, which was also considering forcible action against Castro's regime, repeatedly inquired in Berlin about German intentions. In the summer of 1902 the Germans proposed a joint naval intervention by the two powers, and since Castro had now refused even to acknowledge any of the numerous British notes of protest, London agreed. The new allies decided not to seize Venezuelan customhouses for fear of antagonizing the United States. Instead they would seize or immobilize the gunboats which constituted Venezuela's navy, and if necessary impose a naval blockade of that country's coast. The powers duly notified the United States government of their intention, giving assurance that they would seize no territory. Secretary of State Hay replied in November 1902 that his government could not object to the redress of injury, though it regretted the need to use force, and repeated the usual strictures against taking possession of territory.[9]

By December 7 the two capitals had agreed upon parallel ultimata and delivered them to Caracas. Anglo-German naval forces were already at hand, and when the twenty-four-hour deadline for the satisfaction of demands expired without an answer, the Europeans launched their campaign against the Venezuelan navy. On December 20 the powers implemented a full coastal blockade, while the government of Italy presented its own demands to Castro and withdrew its diplomats from the capital. Rather than giving in to the formidable coalition ranged against him, President Castro astutely asked the United States to arbitrate the dispute. Though Castro was as unpopular in the United States as in Europe, and faced protests from Washington too, he rightly guessed that the Americans would be uneasy at the allies' use of force, and would prefer to substitute their own initiatives for those from across the Atlantic. A German cruiser had already sunk two Venezuelan gunboats, while a pair of warships, one belonging to each ally, had shelled and destroyed a coastal fort with the aid of landing parties. The American press had fully reported these events, while public opinion in the Great Republic grew restive.[10]

President Roosevelt too reacted strongly, though he had given the punitive enterprise his prior approval. While no one seemed seriously alarmed about British motives, the navy had been suspicious from the first of German designs in Venezuela. Beginning early in 1901, naval commanders in the Caribbean had forwarded persistent reports of a German scheme to acquire the island of Margarita, which lay near the Venezuelan coast about one hundred and fifty miles west of Trinidad. The State Department made official inquiries about these rumors, but the navy remained unconvinced by Berlin's denial that they were true. So, presumably, did the president, who ordered the navy to prepare a base of operations at Culebra, a small island belonging to Puerto Rico, "in case of sudden war." [11]

When word reached America of plans for an Anglo-German intervention in Venezuela, naval commanders reacted with alarm. In a memorandum to the president written in late November 1902, Admiral Henry C. Taylor drew some grim conclusions about the action's probable results. The forcible debt-collecting action, Taylor believed, was likely to lead to war between Germany and Venezuela. While the Germans did not seek such a war, it might well be thrust upon them by the fiery Castro, and to preserve their prestige they must win a clear-cut victory. Having done so, they would probably demand indemnity, and given Venezuela's empty treasury this must necessarily take the form either of territory or a lien on Venezuelan revenues, both equally unacceptable to the United States. The result would be a dangerous confrontation between the United States and Germany.

In light of these risks, the memo argued, Washington must not tolerate Germany's occupation of any Venezuelan port or fortification which could be useful to her in a war with the United States. Furthermore, the navy should maintain a force in readiness at Culebra large enough to match the German forces in the Caribbean. If Germany sent troops to the region, American troops in corresponding strength should be sent to Puerto Rico. "Our aim must be at all times to be in a better state of preparation for war than Germany is, and her every move must be met by corresponding preparatory action on our part." [12]

A combination of these naval warnings and his own deep-seated suspicions led Roosevelt to regret his approval of the Venezuelan intervention almost as soon as it got under way, and to push for the arbitration which Castro had requested. Late in December he wrote a friend that "the chances of complication from a long and irritating little war between the European powers and Venezuela were sufficiently great to make me feel most earnestly that the situation should be brought to a peaceful end if possible." By a useful coincidence, large-scale fleet exercises had already been scheduled in the Caribbean for December of 1902, and a rapid naval buildup soon found the North Atlantic Squadron, with most of the navy's battleships, gathered at Culebra. The Caribbean Squadron joined the heavy ships there, while the South Atlantic and European squadrons rendezvoused at Trinidad. Thus the bulk of the United States fighting fleet rapidly concentrated in the eastern Caribbean, while Admiral Dewey, the navy's top-ranking commander, sailed on December 1 to take personal command. Clearly, the presence of so much naval force in the immediate area gave Roosevelt a unique advantage in the Venezuelan situation.[13]

Events peaked on December 16, after Washington learned that a full blockade of the Venezuelan coast was imminent. On that day, Hay formally called upon the governments of Great Britain and Germany to accept arbitration of their dispute with Venezuela. On the same day, Roosevelt ordered four battleships to move down to Trinidad and two cruisers to Curaçao, both islands just off the Venezuelan coast and within the blockade area. Two days later, London announced that the British would yield to Hay's request, the Germans making a similar announcement on the following day. The blockade would still go into effect until the Venezuelans had agreed to the rather stringent conditions of the arbitration, including liability in principle for any claims for injury or wrongful seizure of property. There would even be further armed clashes in January between Venezuela and the allies. For the Americans, nevertheless, the crisis was almost over, and in fact the blockade would end early in February. Admiral Dewey left the fleet for home on January 5, though all of the fleet's battleships stayed on in the Caribbean until April.[14]

Pressure from Washington had undoubtedly been effective in cutting short the allies' naval operations. British public opinion, and its reflected expression in Parliament, also played a major role in London's changing policy. Germany was suspect in England as well as America, and the British public recoiled at the apparent sight of their government courting Berlin while antagonizing Washington, a course just the reverse of what many Britons desired. Whitehall soon found its position politically embarrassing, and was openly eager to find a way out of the Venezuelan venture. The Germans were less ready to arbitrate, but were almost forced to do so by the potential unreliability of their British ally. Upon Roosevelt's initiative, the arbitration was shifted from Washington to the Hague Court. President Castro agreed to immediate payment of the most pressing claims, and all those of the first priority were paid in full by 1907.[15]

Only later did it become known that there might be more to the story. On August 21, 1916, Theodore Roosevelt wrote author William Roscoe Thayer a letter in which he told of his hitherto secret actions in the Venezuelan affair. According to this account, Roosevelt had seen Germany as the leader in the punitive action, while "England was merely following Germany's lead in rather half-hearted fashion." Confident that Britain would never back Germany in a showdown with the United States, Roosevelt had applied private pressure solely to the Germans. After gathering the fleet in the danger zone, he claimed, he had called in German Ambassador Theodor von Holleben and given him an ultimatum: the kaiser's government must accept arbitration of its dispute within ten days, or Roosevelt would order Dewey and the fleet to Venezuela "and see that the German forces did not take possession of any territory."

Holleben was upset, Roosevelt's narrative continued, suggesting that such an action could lead to war. Nevertheless, when the two next met a week later, Holleben still had no word from his government. Roosevelt then told the German that further delay was useless, and moved his deadline forward by twenty-four hours. Under this renewed pressure Holleben soon brought a favorable reply from the kaiser, after which the president publicly expressed great gratification at Germany's action. Thus the story ended, though two supplementary letters from Roosevelt to Thayer shortly afterward modified a few details and contained an admission that the former president's memory was vague about the exact dates and time periods involved.[16]

Roosevelt's story of his secret threat to the kaiser became public through Thayer. At first accepted by historians, it later became the object of prolonged controversy. How reliable was the word of the volatile ex-president regarding events which had occurred over fourteen years earlier? Why was there no documentation of any of this anywhere in official files? Was it not true that the navy's concentration in the Caribbean conformed to a plan for general fleet maneuvers drawn up months earlier, before the crisis emerged, and that the navy continued to hold annual large-scale winter maneuvers in the same area for years to come? Why had the Rough Rider told no one else of his actions in all this time?[17]

In the first place, Roosevelt had in fact foreshadowed the story at earlier points in his private correspondence. A briefer and more modest account than that in the Thayer letters appeared in a 1906 letter from the president to the diplomat Henry White. In this version, Roosevelt told the German ambassador that "the popular feeling was such that I should be obliged to interfere, by force if necessary, if the Germans took any action which looked like the acquisition of territory there [in Venezuela] or elsewhere along the Caribbean. . . ." In contrast to his later story, Roosevelt did not claim definite credit for the German change of course: "I do not know whether it was a case of *post hoc* or *propter hoc*, but immediately afterward the Kaiser made to me the proposition that I should arbitrate myself, which I finally got him to modify so that it was sent to the Hague." Roosevelt had written Ambassador to England Whitelaw Reid a similar version about two months earlier, while in 1915 he sent another correspondent a short preview of the account which Thayer received the following year.[18]

The historian Frederick Marks makes the most interesting argument in favor

Theodore Roosevelt. Courtesy of the National Archives

of the accuracy of Roosevelt's story of a naval threat to the kaiser. Looking more closely at the absence of documentary evidence, Marks found that absence so complete as to constitute evidence in itself. Systematically checking the relevant archives, he discovered that a void existed in the German diplomatic records corresponding to the period of the Venezuelan crisis, as well as in the published diaries and letters of the top German policy makers involved. In addition, the British Foreign Office records were missing nine telegrams from the British ambassador in December 1902; the John Hay Papers showed a similar gap; even United States Embassy records in Berlin were missing notes whose existence was indicated in State Department files. There appeared to have been a "laundering" of the documents of all three powers involved, which strongly suggested to Marks that there must have been something important to hide.[19] The argument is persuasive, and indicates that Theodore Roosevelt put a very high priority indeed on the containment of European security threats in the Caribbean. It is possible that he later exaggerated the severity or specificity of his expressions to the German ambassador, but there is ample evidence that he became deeply concerned during the second Venezuelan crisis, and that this concern had a visible effect upon the policy of two great powers.

Nor did the president's concern end when the danger of confrontation receded, for the policy makers of both Great Britain and Germany helped to keep the issues alive in Roosevelt's mind. In a public speech in February 1903, on the day the allies' naval blockade of Venezuela ended, British Prime Minister Arthur J. Balfour called for the United States to assume greater responsibility in the Caribbean. He declared that "it would be a great gain to civilization if the United States of America were more actively to interest themselves in making arrangements by which these constantly recurring difficulties between European powers and certain States in South America could be avoided. . . ." The Americans could be most helpful "by doing their best to see that international law is observed, and by upholding . . . the admitted principles of international comity." Behind the prime minister's courteous phraseology lay a serious point: if Washington was averse to the actions of European powers to redress their legitimate grievances in the Americas, then Washington had better be prepared to redress such grievances itself.[20]

The message from Germany was not quite the same. In March, a month after Balfour's speech, Roosevelt was again visited by his friend Hermann Speck von Sternberg. Sternberg proposed a scheme to create an international syndicate to take over Venezuela's government finances. This step, he said, would tend to stop the outbreak of revolutions there and make the country peaceful and prosperous, presumably because potential rebels could no longer hope to seize public funds. It would also end the need for European punitive expeditions to collect debts. The German proposed that the Americans take the lead in such a movement. Roosevelt replied, as he promptly wrote Hay, that "my judgment was very strongly that our people would view with the utmost displeasure any such proposal," for "it would pave the way for reducing Venezuela to a condition like that of Egypt, and . . . the American people interpreted the Monroe Doctrine as meaning of course that no European power should gain control of any American republic." In a forthcoming speech which he planned on the Monroe Doctrine, the president noted, he had better state plainly that his country would "never consent to allowing one of the American Republics to come under the control of a European power by any such subterfuge as . . . a pretense to the guaranteeing or collecting a debt." [21]

Balfour had proposed that the United States make itself directly responsible for enforcing "international law" in the western hemisphere, with an obvious reference to debt collection; Sternberg had suggested that Washington join with the European powers to do so, as merely a partner in a multilateral enterprise. There could be no question as to which course Roosevelt preferred, though it would be another year before he was ready to express himself fully on the matter. He did so finally on May 20, 1904, through the medium of a letter to be read aloud at a banquet in New York celebrating the second anniversary of Cuban independence. Former Secretary of War Elihu Root, who had presided over the birth of the Cuban republic, read the letter to the assembled guests, who may not have realized that they were hearing the first announcement of the Roosevelt Corollary to the Monroe Doctrine.

The president began by denying that the United States entertained any ambition for further territory or dominion. "All that we desire is to see all neighboring countries stable, orderly and prosperous," he wrote.

> Any country whose people conduct themselves well can count upon our hearty friendliness. If a nation shows that it knows how to act with decency in industrial and political matters, if it keeps order and pays its obligations, then it need fear no interference from the United States.

If these conditions were not met, however, no such promise could be made. "Brutal wrongdoing, or an impotence which results in a general loosening of the ties of civilized society, may finally require intervention by some civilized nation, and in the Western Hemisphere the United States cannot ignore this duty. . . ." [22]

This claim on behalf of the United States to a generalized right of intervention in its own hemisphere did not escape notice in the antiimperialist press. Three weeks after the Cuban dinner, Roosevelt wrote Root that he was "rather amused at the yell about my letter." It had stated, he insisted,

> the simplest common sense. . . . If we are willing to let Germany or England act as the policeman of the Caribbean, then we can afford not to interfere when gross wrongdoing occurs. But if we intend to say "hands off" to the powers of Europe, then sooner or later we must keep order ourselves. [23]

The august *Times* of London editorially agreed. Some people spoke as though intervention in the affairs of another country violated international law, the *Times* writer noted, but in fact there was no authoritative international law. There was only international practice, and in practice the kind of "wrongdoing" or "impotence" of which Roosevelt spoke did eventually require that some nation intervene. Examples were plentiful; the editorial cited Turkey,

Egypt, China, and Cuba, among others. In the absence of any accepted world authority, individual nations must act or no one would. If the United States meant to maintain the Monroe Doctrine, it must take responsibility for having justice done in the western hemisphere. Apart from questions of justice, some future case might see a mischievous European power improperly attempt to use a South American state for its own purposes, which the president's statement would rightly block. Like Roosevelt, the *Times* clearly regarded the new doctrine as no more than common sense.[24]

One scholar has concluded that the president's famous statement was formulated with reference to the presidential campaign of 1904, in which Roosevelt ran for reelection. Having acted strongly in Venezuela and Panamá, he wished to present to the voters a general justification based on American principles and sound moral grounds. The original declaration of the Roosevelt Corollary had nothing to do with future events in the Dominican Republic, for in May 1904 Roosevelt had no intention of taking major action there, at least until after the election. Rather, the president wished to claim credit for the foreign policy achievements of his first administration, in both the Caribbean and the Far East, and to tie his Caribbean policies firmly to the hallowed Monroe Doctrine. The latter tactic might also help to make the administration's methods in Venezuela and Panamá seem less unorthodox than they were.[25]

This analysis seems perceptive, but the Roosevelt Corollary was to be no mere electioneering exercise. In December, after his reelection, the president expanded his statement somewhat and included it in his annual message to Congress. This revised version stated that "in the western hemisphere the adherence of the United States to the Monroe Doctrine" might force it "however reluctantly . . . to the exercise of an international police power."[26] A year later, in his annual message for 1905, Roosevelt stated: "We must make it evident that we do not intend to permit the Monroe Doctrine to be used by any nation on this Continent as a shield to protect it from the consequences of its own misdeeds against foreign nations." By then the Rough Rider was deeply involved in a debt crisis in the Dominican Republic to which his letter of May 20, 1904, had an obvious relevance.

The question of unpaid debts, Roosevelt confessed in this latter message to Congress, was a thorny one. The United States itself had never been willing to use force in order to ensure the fulfillment of a foreign government's contracts to American citizens, and it was to be wished that other governments would show a similar forbearance. Unfortunately, they did not, which posed a dilemma.

> On the one hand, this country would certainly decline to go to war to prevent a foreign government from collecting a just debt; on the other hand, it is very inadvisable to permit any foreign power to take possession, even temporarily,

of the custom houses of an American Republic in order to enforce the payment of its obligations, for such temporary occupation might turn into a permanent occupation.

There was only one solution: the United States must be ready at need to make the necessary arrangements for repayments and secure the agreement of the interested parties. This, the president wrote, was "the only possible way of insuring us against a clash with some foreign power." [27]

As Roosevelt wrote a friend earlier in 1905, "I believe with all my heart in the Monroe Doctrine and have, for instance, formally notified Germany to that effect." But the doctrine, he said, must not "be used as a warrant for letting any of these republics remain as small bandit nests of a wicked and inefficient type. This means that we must in good faith try to help them . . . , and be ready if the worst comes to the worst to chastize them. . . ." [28] By inventing an "international police power" to serve his purposes, Roosevelt drastically reshaped the Monroe Doctrine. What had been a declaration that Europe's powers must keep their hands off the independent states of the Americas became the justification for unilateral United States intervention in the hemisphere at its own discretion. In the name of security, the nation now claimed a regional hegemony.

Chapter 7

———⸻❧⸻———

The Deepening Quest for
Security: The Dominican
Republic

The Venezuelan crisis of 1902–1903 had done more than mobilize the Roosevelt administration against the threat of European intervention in the Caribbean; it had dramatically illustrated the connection between local instability and the danger of such intervention. Venezuela's government finances had fallen into chaos and European bondholders had at last secured action from their governments. Venezuela's internal political struggles had brought foreigners under risk to life and property, again leading them to appeal to their governments for support. Thus fiscal and political disorders in Venezuela had triggered the Anglo-German initiatives to which Theodore Roosevelt had objected, and which led him to formulate his famous corollary. At first glance, the Roosevelt Corollary seemed to resolve the issue; in the future, when Caribbean disorders threatened foreign interests, the United States would intervene on behalf of all.

In practice, however, the issue was not that simple. Washington was not eager to involve itself in an endless series of interventions in the Caribbean and Central America, nor was it certain that every European power would always be content to accept the United States as a surrogate in its disputes. A better solution would be found in an essentially peaceable Caribbean where governments succeeded one another in orderly fashion, avoided civil strife, and regularly paid their foreign debts. Regional security, in short, could best be secured through regional stability. Fiscal and governmental stability in the Caribbean would also create a favorable climate for foreign investors, while stimulating international trade and economic growth. At the same time, such stability would satisfy North American notions of decent national behavior and help to disarm a growing animus in the Colossus of the North against Latin American society and culture.

Unfortunately, the Caribbean region was not characterized by such stability, but by its opposite. Newly committed to policing the area, the Roosevelt administration found political turbulence, civil war, and unpaid debts all too common throughout it. President Roosevelt wrote a friend early in 1904 that "the attitude of men like myself toward the weak and chaotic governments and people south of us is . . . that it is our duty . . . to police these countries in the interest of order and civilization." [1] The question was how to achieve an acceptable level of order over the region as a whole. The coming years would see a systematic attempt by the United States to develop mechanisms, principles, and techniques for stabilizing the Caribbean. Stability, in fact, soon became the chief goal of American policy there, for it was considered to contain in itself almost all that was needed to further United States interests in the region.

This quest for stability and for insurance against European intervention explained Washington's reaction to the Dominican Republic's financial crisis of 1904. Coming soon after the Venezuelan debt crisis and the Panamá revolution, the Dominican affair forced United States policy makers to further refine their techniques and methodology. To meet the crisis, the Roosevelt administration adopted tools of fiscal control designed to be used not only in the Dominican case, but in any similar situations which might arise in the Caribbean region. The new case was a challenging one: a small nation torn by revolution, hopelessly in debt, and beset by threatening foreign powers. By the beginning of 1904, a deeply troubled Dominican Republic faced problems which appeared beyond its power to resolve.

The roots of these troubles dated back to the lengthy dictatorship of Ulises Heureaux, who had ruled the country as a tyrant from 1882 to 1899. Hoping to build a railroad system and needing funds to keep himself in power, Heureaux had arranged a succession of European loans, periodically refinanced at increasingly drastic discounts. An 1897 debt consolidation and loan had seen new bond issues selling for as little as 24 to 32 percent of face value; in all, the Dominican government borrowed about one and a quarter million pounds sterling in new debt, in addition to refinancing old loans, but raised less than half a million pounds in actual new funds. The dictator faced bankruptcy by the late 1890s, and tried once more to sell Samaná Bay to the United States during the Spanish-American War.[2]

Heureaux's assassination in 1899 left the treasury in default on its foreign debts, which by then were held in both Europe and the United States. A New York syndicate called the San Domingo Improvement Company had bought out the government's European debts in 1892, and later established a

Dominican National Bank and a Central Railroad Company as subsidiaries. The Improvement Company had been forced to refinance the foreign debt in 1897 to stave off national bankruptcy, and the new bond issues floated at that time added large blocs of French and Belgian investors, while British, German, and Spanish bondholders had also participated in one or another of the loans. As a series of short-lived governments slipped increasingly into arrears on their payments, European creditors appealed to their own governments for support. The French bondholders were most successful in this, but aggressive demands from Paris were regularly checked by Washington, which also gave strong backing to the American-owned Improvement Company. In 1900 a new contract gave the Improvement Company virtual control of customs, supposedly on behalf of all of the foreign creditors, but this arrangement was short-lived. It was not only extremely unpopular with the Dominican public, which had come to see the Improvement Company as the source and symbol of the nation's financial troubles, but was decisively rejected by the European bondholders as uniquely favorable to the Americans. European governments once more expressed support for their citizens, and a general scramble to take over the custom houses seemed possible.[3]

Desperate to find a solution to the crisis, in January 1901 the Dominican government terminated the functions of the Improvement Company and attempted to negotiate a settlement of its debts. The French and Belgian bondholders refused an offer of 50 percent of face value for their bonds, but the Americans agreed to sell out all of the Improvement Company's interests for four and one-half million dollars in gold. The money was to be paid in monthly installments, and the customs revenues of Puerto Plata and three other northern ports were pledged as security. In case of default, the United States government would appoint an agent who would take over customs collection on the north coast in the interests of the Improvement Company shareholders.[4]

By early 1904 the Improvement Company settlement had been formally accepted on both sides, but the question of European debts was very much unresolved. Resenting the privileged position of the Americans under the Improvement Company settlement, the European representatives seemed to favor the creation of an international commission representing the governments whose citizens held the largest portions of the Dominican debt. This agency would take over financial control of the country as receivers in bankruptcy. Something similar had been done in Greece, Egypt, and elsewhere, and some Dominican leaders were prepared to accept such an arrangement. In October 1903, the Belgian chargé d'affaires in Santo Domingo proposed to William F. Powell, the United States chargé, that a Dominican debt commission should be formed of three members named by the United States, France, and Belgium, because their citizens made up the largest groups of creditors.[5]

Preoccupied with events in Panamá, where the new Panamanian state was proclaimed in November, the State Department had no immediate response to Powell's report. Meanwhile the Carlos Morales government which came to power in Santo Domingo in that same month preferred another plan. In December and January, Morales and his cabinet elaborated a scheme by which the United States would lease Samaná Bay, and Manzanillo Bay in the northwest corner of the country, for fifty years, with the right to fortify them and build naval bases. The United States would also assume a long-term protectorate over the Dominican Republic, taking control of its governmental finances, guaranteeing the foreign debt, and helping to maintain internal order. The rental from the two bays would be applied to foreign debts along with the customs receipts, which would be divided between the debtors and the government. Finally, the Dominicans offered a reciprocity treaty modeled on that between Cuba and the United States. Morales thus rejected an international debt commission for a straightforward American protectorate which, by implication, would protect the Morales government against its enemies, both domestic and foreign. Powell himself had informally suggested the provisions for leasing the two bays and for the reciprocity treaty; the former president, Heureaux, had repeatedly offered the bays for naval bases, and had suggested a protectorate arrangement to Washington shortly before his death. The Morales proposals therefore contained little that was not familiar in outline to both parties.[6]

Fresh from his Panamá adventure and facing a reelection campaign, Theodore Roosevelt was cautious in his public posture concerning the Dominican troubles. In an oft quoted statement, he assured a correspondent that "as for annexing the island, I have about the same desire to annex it as a gorged boa constrictor might have to swallow a porcupine wrong-end-to. . . . If I possibly can I want to do nothing to them. If it is absolutely necessary to do something, then I want to do as little as possible." As for establishing a protectorate, or taking charge of Dominican finances, the president said, "we could not possibly go into the subject now at all." To his son he was equally cautious, if somewhat franker. "Santo Domingo is drifting into chaos," he wrote in February 1904, "for after a hundred years of freedom it shows itself utterly incompetent for governmental work." He had been obliged to investigate the situation there, Roosevelt said, but hoped it would "be a good while before I have to go further." Yet sooner or later, Roosevelt predicted, "it seems to me inevitable that the United States should assume an attitude of protection and regulation in regard to all these little states in the neighborhood of the Caribbean." In yet another private statement, the president confessed that he did not immediately intervene in Santo Domingo "chiefly because if I did many honest people would misunderstand my purposes and motives; and so I feel obliged to put off the action until the necessity becomes so clear that even the blindest can see it."[7]

While Washington remained inactive, the situation in the Dominican Republic grew ever more complex. The death of the dictator Heureaux had added political chaos to financial disaster. Heureaux's assassination and the political revolution which followed it in 1899 had been carried out by Horacio Vásquez and Ramón Cáceres, the latter personally killing Heureaux. Having seized power as provisional president, Vásquez called for elections and threw his support to Juan Isidro Jiménez, a formerly rich merchant who had dissipated his fortune in repeated efforts to overthrow Heureaux. In November 1899, Jiménez became president and Vásquez vice-president of the country. These two men were to dominate Dominican politics for many years, while Cáceres would also be a leading figure until his death in 1911.[8]

Beset by financial chaos, foreign pressures, and rampant factionalism, the new leaders soon fell out among themselves. Vásquez and Cáceres strongly disapproved of Jiménez' unpopular decision to grant control of the customs to the San Domingo Improvement Company, and even though this was later reversed, tensions mounted steadily until they took to arms to oust Jiménez by force in the spring of 1902. Vásquez again became provisional president, with Cáceres once more his principal adviser and lieutenant. During these struggles almost all Dominicans divided into two political camps, known as "Horacistas," the followers of Don Horacio Vásquez, and "Jimenistas," who supported Juan Isidro Jiménez. The division would long endure, but constant defections from one camp to the other, and breakaway factions under leaders ambitious for their own advancement, always kept the dividing lines unstable. Thus it was typical that Vásquez's new policy of rigid economy in government alienated the local political bosses whose customary subsidies he ended, setting off a spate of local rebellions in the second half of 1902. Despairing of uniting the endless factions, Vásquez called for new elections and announced his retirement from politics.[9]

The proposed elections never occurred, for Heureaux's old generals seized the moment to launch a powerful assault on the capital, which succeeded only after weeks of bloody combat in the spring of 1903. The resulting new regime, headed by General Alejandro Woss y Gil, lacked popular support, however, and fell in turn to another revolt in the autumn of 1903. This uprising was the work of Carlos Morales, a Jimenista whose announced intent was to restore Jiménez to the presidency. He soon decided to keep power for himself instead, wooing the support of Cáceres and other Horacistas to offset the outrage of his abandoned party. With Cáceres as his running mate, Morales won an election early in 1904, leaving political groupings confused and the government surrounded by potential enemies. Meanwhile, revolutionary conflict had grown so fierce in 1903 that the United States, Germany, Italy, and the Netherlands had all sent warships to the capital to protect their citizens, while French, American, and other foreign naval vessels had appeared repeatedly between 1899 and 1904.[10]

Not one but several revolts had broken out since Morales seized power, and the resulting disorders spread across the entire country. Powell granted formal recognition to the Morales government in January 1904, but by that time the largest of the opposing forces was already besieging the capital. Early in February, insurgents fired on a launch from a United States warship in Santo Domingo's bay, killing a seaman. A similar incident a week later led the local American naval commander to shell the insurgent camp and land three hundred men to drive off the troops there. Shortly after this incident, Morales himself was able to raise the siege and clear the enemy from his capital. This, along with other military successes in the interior, gave increased credibility to his government.[11]

In the course of reporting these events, Powell also raised a new spectre. Late in February he obtained a copy of a letter purportedly written to the local German consul by the rebel general whose men had fired on the navy's boats at Santo Domingo. The letter accused Morales of selling out his country to the United States, and offered the Germans a secret treaty making them, rather than the Americans, protectors and financial supervisors of the country. In Powell's view, this letter was added proof of the generally pro-German bias of the major opposition faction, and another reason to deal with the pro-American Morales. Powell also reported rumors that the German representative at the capital had proposed the cession of one or more Dominican ports to his government for a naval station. Reports in high places even had it that the German government was considering buying up Spanish, Italian, and Belgian claims against the Dominican Republic and occupying the ports whose customs receipts were pledged to those claims, in order to get control of the country. Neither the navy nor the State Department took such reports lightly. Once again, a debt crisis seemed to be opening the way for a German threat in the Caribbean.[12]

Emboldened by his military successes, President Morales felt strong enough by late February to make public his plan for American customs control. Predictably, this brought a flood of denunciations from the government's enemies, as well as arousing a good deal of genuine concern for the country's independence. The Panamá revolution was only three months past, the Spanish-American War with its subsequent annexations barely five years gone, and many in the Caribbean feared a continuing American campaign of annexations and protectorates. Dominican fears were reinforced from Haiti, whose government saw a Yankee take-over of its neighbor as a prelude to its own absorption in a growing United States empire. A Haitian delegation appeared in Santo Domingo in March, threatening to support Morales' foes if the president persisted in negotiating away the country's independence.[13]

In the midst of these alarms, Powell sent the State Department some advice. With Washington dragging its feet, he was uncertain of the shape of future policy toward the Dominican Republic, but he ventured to suggest what it should be. First and foremost, forcible annexation must be ruled out, for it would unite all the quarreling factions in an anti-American front. "We would have a sullen foe that would constantly give us trouble on every occasion," he declared, at least until the country was "completely subjugated," and to do that would require "the sacrifice of many lives and the expenditure of large sums of money." It would also drive the Haitians into common cause with the Dominicans for mutual defense. A far better course would be to lead the Dominicans along by gradual steps until the country had been regenerated; by that time, recognition of the vast benefits the Americans had brought would bring the people to desire annexation. The first step was to secure the consent of the Dominican government to American control of customs collection and disbursement, a step which the Morales regime already advocated. The customs revenue, which represented most of the government's income, should be divided between the government and its creditors. With the United States present to guarantee the arrangement, foreign lenders and their governments would be satisfied. Such a course would also practically end insurrections, for both the object and the funding of local revolutionaries lay in the seizure of customs houses. Denied this ready source of cash, future revolutionary leaders would never be able to mobilize support or procure arms.[14]

Furthermore, once an honest system of collection was instituted, customs receipts would mushroom, for at present enormous sums were lost to officially tolerated smuggling and graft. Powell estimated that total customs revenues would leap from their current level of about two million dollars per year to from four and a half to five and a half million. Thus everyone involved, the Dominican government included, would get more money. In addition, by controlling customs the United States could also watch port traffic to prevent the landing of arms, a further safeguard against revolts. With insurrection a thing of the past, the army could be disbanded, to be replaced by an urban police force and a rural guard like that recently created in Cuba. These would be cheaper than an army, and the new system could also eliminate the numerous district *jefes* whose political importance had required every past government to buy them off in order to keep the peace.

Given peace and order and a reduced cost of government, the Dominicans could devote themselves to developing their ample agricultural and mineral resources. A reciprocal trade treaty would ensure that they bought and sold in the United States. They would soon grow so prosperous, Powell declared, that they would request to be annexed. Within ten years the people would be educated in the new order of things. Roads and railroads would be built, opening up whole new districts to production. The national debt could be halved, and the country could become the United States' richest possession. The Morales government approved of such a course, though its opponents did not. In addition, many leading citizens throughout the country were willing to see it adopted, as were almost all of the business men, Powell concluded.[15] While Powell's talk of annexation went beyond Washington's intentions, his discussion of a customs receivership marshaled almost all of the arguments that would ultimately be used to justify it.

By April, Morales appeared to have won the military struggle against his enemies, and began arranging to transform his provisional government into a fully constitutional regime. These developments led Powell to urge quick action on a treaty giving the United States control of the customs, which Morales continued to urge upon him. Once the congress was reconstituted, it would contain many opponents of such a treaty; better to treat with the pro-American president now while he still had a free hand. But the State Department was unconvinced, as it soon demonstrated. Hearing rumors (which later proved false) that Italian warships were to seize customhouses to secure debt repayment, Morales and his foreign minister called on Powell to ask that the United States frustrate any such move by taking over all the customhouses in the country. Powell agreed to a purely temporary takeover only if the Italians acted, and simply to protect American interests pending a general settlement. When he reported this to the State Department, however, his action was disapproved; Washington would not yet sanction a general take-over under any conditions.[16]

At about this time, Morales asked the State Department to name an American financial expert who could direct a general revision of the government's fiscal laws and administration. The chief executive said that he wished to see Dominican law and practice regarding government finance conform as closely as possible to that of the United States. The State Department accepted this modest step, ultimately selecting Professor Jacob H. Hollander, an academic economist and financial expert.[17]

In the spring of 1904, Theodore Roosevelt sent a commission headed by Admiral Dewey to investigate the situation in the Dominican Republic. Assistant Secretary of State Francis B. Loomis, who was one of Dewey's group, reacted strongly to what he saw. In a private memo to the president, Loomis wrote: "The frequent and sometimes bloody civil wars in the Dominican Republic . . . are shameless sordid struggles for the privileges of controlling customhouses and disposing their revenues. The country is largely in the grasp of desperately selfish irresponsible political brigands." Like earlier American observers, Loomis favored ultimate United States control of customhouses to establish financial order and end revolutionary activity. Meanwhile the Navy should maintain at least three warships in Dominican waters, and Santo Domingo should be raised from its present subordinate status to an independent diplomatic post under a new minister.[18]

The United States had long sent a single diplomat to represent it in both Haiti and the Dominican Republic, as minister to the former and chargé d'affaires in the latter. This diplomat, who was customarily a black man, resided at the legation in Port-au-Prince and usually worked in Santo Domingo through the resident United States consul general. All this had been true of William Powell, a black appointee whose sustained sojourn in Santo Domingo had indicated the serious nature of the crisis there. Loomis was therefore urging that Powell return to his duties in Haiti and a full-time minister be appointed for the Dominican Republic alone. Roosevelt agreed, and early in July the new United States minister, Thomas C. Dawson, reached his post. Dawson was a white Iowa lawyer who had already spent seven years as secretary of legation in Brazil. He spoke Spanish fluently, and the Dominican post was to be his first of several Caribbean area appointments as head of mission before his premature death in 1912.[19]

While Roosevelt was willing to make the diplomatic change suggested by Loomis, he preferred to put off more active involvement in Dominican affairs. The presidential election campaign of 1904 was in full swing, and the president feared that forceful new moves in the Dominican Republic, coming so soon after his display of the big stick in Panamá, would give ammunition to his democratic opponent, Alton B. Parker. He also hoped that the gradual improvement in the Dominican political situation would continue as the Morales government gained strength and legitimacy. The Dominicans continued to seek State Department approval for a United States customs take-over, but Roosevelt was determined to avoid direct involvement for the present. Significantly, however, he suggested to Secretary of State John Hay that Morales might be given a hint to renew his requests in eight months—that is, after the election.[20]

The new minister, Thomas Dawson, spent his first months in Santo Domingo largely in seeking compliance with the agreement on the Improvement Company, but the financial situation was hardly promising. By the autumn of 1904, the foreign debt of the Dominican Republic totaled about $32 million, of which all but $5 million had been "liquidated"; that is, the Dominican government had agreed with the claimants on the amount owed and promised to pay it. It was another matter, however, actually to produce the money. The government owed almost $900,000 immediately, and about $1.7 million more within the next year. Yet revenues for the coming year were estimated at only $1.8 million while government expenses were expected to take $1.3 million, leaving only $0.5 million dollars for debt service. "The condition is one of hopeless bankruptcy," Dawson reported, "unless there is a radical change in the system of collecting revenues, and a great reduction in current expenditure."[21]

According to Dawson, the loss in customs revenues resulted not only from widespread official graft and smuggling, but from the government's need for constant short-term borrowing. Foreign merchants regularly loaned the government money at exorbitant rates of interest in return for credit against future

customs payments for the goods they would import. By 1904, Dawson estimated that half of all customs revenues were lost in honoring these loans. Thus
short-term lenders prospered at the expense of long-term bondholders, whose
loans were in theory secured by these same customs receipts. Furthermore,
none of this borrowed money, from whatever source, did much to help the
country. It was not spent for roads, schools, sewers, or similar purposes, but
went almost entirely to pay the salaries of a bloated bureaucracy and to prevent or put down revolutions. If left under Dominican management, Dawson
concluded, public revenues would never produce enough surplus to retire the
foreign debt.[22]

In September, Morales' government announced that it could not meet the
scheduled payments for the Improvement Company award, and invited the arbitration agent to make his demand for possession of the Puerto Plata customhouse, which he promptly did. The minister of foreign affairs told Dawson
that United States control of one or more customhouses would help to prevent
new revolutions. However, the regime would continue to need some of the
money from the northern ports, and thus hoped that it would not be required
to meet the payments in full. In fact, Morales wanted to keep 60 percent of
north coast receipts to pay his soldiers there, putting only 40 percent toward
the Improvement Company award. This began a prolonged quarrel with the
Improvement Company's management, which insisted upon full payment.[23]

It began other quarrels as well. The Dominican public was deeply upset over
the prospective take-over of customs control by the United States, and again
fears of annexation were freely expressed. During November, Morales' most
substantial supporters began to desert him, many accusing him of betraying
his country. The government had planned to transfer three more north coast
customhouses to the Americans, in addition to that at Puerto Plata, but it now
reversed itself and began to waver on the whole matter. Meanwhile the French
chargé had called upon Dawson to ask whether the United States meant to
take over the customhouses on the south coast too, or whether it preferred that
the French and Belgian governments do so under terms analogous to those of
the United States in the north. The Frenchman's drift seemed unmistakable:
if the United States did not soon take entire charge of the debt crisis, the other
creditor nations would be forced to act on their own.[24]

By the end of 1904, the Morales government faced a renewed threat of revolution with its former political backing in shreds, while foreign governments
once more prepared to take debt collection into their own hands. Morales saw
his only hope in timely United States action to satisfy the Europeans and overawe the regime's domestic enemies. At long last, Washington responded; with
the election over and the Dominican crisis at a crucial point, it was finally
time to act. On December 28, 1904, the State Department instructed Dawson
to "ascertain whether the Government of Santo Domingo would be disposed

to request United States to take charge of the collection of duties and effect an equitable distribution of the assigned quotas among the Dominican Government and the several claimants." (Since Morales had been seeking such an arrangement for most of the year, this was hardly a stab in the dark.) "Already one European Government strongly intimates that it may resort to occupation of some Dominican customs ports to secure its own payment," the message informed Dawson, but the State Department had reason to believe that a general United States take-over would be acceptable to the other powers. Such an arrangement would serve "as a practical guarantee of the peace of Santo Domingo from external influence or internal disturbance." [25]

Before acting to resolve the Dominican debt crisis, the United States had, of course, shared with European governments the responsibility for intensifying it. The State Department had originally obtained the Improvement Company settlement through heavy diplomatic pressure in Washington and Santo Domingo. When Morales' predecessor, President Woss y Gil, sought to reject the previous government's pledge to arbitrate the debt, the State Department sent an ultimatum demanding immediate compliance with the earlier arrangement. The Dominican foreign minister had complained bitterly at this, but William Powell replied that his government was now through negotiating, and must have satisfaction. When General Morales overthrew Woss y Gil and sought diplomatic recognition, Powell warned him that a principal condition of American recognition was that all previous agreements with the United States must be "sacredly" observed; the attempts of each new regime to evade prior commitments for debt settlement must end.[26] By thus holding the Dominicans to arrangements which favored United States creditors over their European fellows, the State Department helped to create the dissatisfactions to which so many European governments finally found it necessary to respond.

Given a green light at last from Washington, President Morales was eager to complete arrangements for an American-run customs receivership, in spite of mounting dissension within his cabinet. There were, however, numerous sensitive details to be negotiated, while the real challenge was to complete a treaty along the desired lines without precipitating the overthrow of his regime. As Dawson wrote a friend: "There is always the dread that the men I have been at so much pains to negotiate with may suddenly be standing up against a wall instead of sitting in the Minister's arm chair." Though Dawson never explicitly used the threat of force to promote the treaty, two United States naval vessels remained anchored at the capital throughout the negotiations, exerting what the minister described as "a powerful moral effect on the rash and ignorant elements." [27] In addition, at President Roosevelt's order, the navy's Commander Alfred C. Dillingham joined Dawson as a partner in the negotiations. Dillingham had been patrolling the Dominican coast for over a year, and had often brought about meetings between Dominican politicos designed to keep or restore the peace. Tough but respected, he was well known to political leaders of all factions.[28]

One of the sticking points in reaching agreement was the question of how to divide customs receipts between the Dominican government and its creditors. The Dominicans wanted to keep 60 percent while using 40 percent for debt servicing, but the State Department desired the proportions to be just the opposite; in the final treaty, the Dominican government received 45 percent of the revenues. The State Department also demanded a fixed limit on government spending, and an assurance that the Dominicans could change their customs laws only with United States approval. As the negotiations dragged on, public alarm in Santo Domingo reached dangerous levels, many believing that the end result would be American annexation of all or a part of the country. To calm its people, the Dominican cabinet leaked the main treaty provisions in advance of final agreement, an irregular but essential course which proved effective at reducing the excitement. Also, at the request of the Dominicans, an opening clause was added to the treaty draft in which the United States guaranteed the territorial integrity of the Dominican Republic.[29]

The treaty, signed on February 7, 1905, faced strong opposition in the United States Senate. In an attempt to minimize this, the State Department had announced in January that the Dominican customs agreement constituted neither a United States protectorate nor an American guarantee of the Dominican debt. It also stressed that the treaty was made at the formal request of the Dominican government. On February 15, the president transmitted the treaty to the Senate with a carefully worded message. "It has for some time been obvious," he wrote, "that those who profit by the Monroe Doctrine must accept certain responsibilities along with the rights which it confers." The current intent, however, was to hold those responsibilities to a minimum. "We do not propose to take any part of Santo Domingo or exercise any other control over the Island save what is necessary to its financial rehabilitation." Nevertheless, the necessary minimum must be done, for it was unfair for the United States to forbid other countries to collect their just debts if it was not prepared itself to act in the matter. In addition to providing equity for foreign lenders, the prosperity of the Dominican Republic itself was an issue, Roosevelt said. In an artful bid for the support of Southern Democrats, he coupled Dominican prosperity with "the interests of the South Atlantic and Gulf States, the normal expansion of whose commerce lies in that direction." [30]

In spite of its careful preparations, the administration faced a coalition of Democrats and anti-Roosevelt Republicans which was just able to block the ratification of the treaty. Roosevelt raged in the privacy of his correspondence:

> After infinite thought and worry and labor with Root, Taft and Hay as my chief advisers, I negotiated a treaty which would secure a really satisfactory settlement

... of the Santo Domingan matter ... the result is that by a narrow margin we find ourselves without the necessary two-thirds vote in the Senate for confirming the treaties. . . . I am then left to shoulder all the responsibility due to their failure.[31]

The prospect that the Senate would fail to approve the treaty filled Carlos Morales with despair. It would result in the fall of his government, the Dominican president predicted, just as the government of President Buenaventura Báez had fallen in 1873 when the United States Senate finally rejected the proposed treaty of annexation. Dawson concurred, reporting that

the opponents of the Protocol and of the Morales Government have been becoming more encouraged and active every day that has passed . . . without news of ratification. The impression has been gaining ground that the Senate will refuse to ratify and even that a revolution against Morales could count on a considerable moral support in the United States.[32]

When the Senate adjourned without ratifying the Dominican treaty, the desperate Dominicans offered to name a temporary United States receiver of customs for the south coast ports while the northern ports would be administered under the Improvement Company award. This would achieve some United States customs control pending treaty ratification, and thus might stave off foreign creditors and domestic enemies. Dawson's quick canvassing showed most foreign representatives favorable to such a move, while he himself thought "some modus vivendi absolutely necessary." The State Department quickly endorsed the idea of a modus vivendi, but wanted a single unified system for the entire country. Working fast, Washington and Santo Domingo soon agreed upon a plan for a temporary collection system based on the provisions of the treaty. If the treaty should be ratified, the system would become permanent; in case it was not, all surplus funds would be held in escrow in a New York bank, to be returned to the Dominican government upon final Senate rejection. The Dominican government was pleased at Washington's promptness in resolving the matter, putting the modus vivendi into effect by decree on April 1.[33]

The customs receivership was soon organized, running under the modus vivendi for almost two years before the United States Senate finally approved it. One of the objections voiced by the treaty's opponents was that it would make the United States government, as disburser of debt payments, responsible for determining the amounts of the various claims. While these had already been fixed by many negotiations prior to 1905, the results were hardly definitive. As Roosevelt admitted in his message transmitting the treaty to the Senate, "Some of these debts . . . are without question improper or exorbitant." It was generally assumed that further adjustment was needed, and the critics held that the treaty, if ratified, would put Washington squarely in the middle of a disreputable scramble of international creditors, American bondholders included. To remove this objection, Roosevelt announced that the Dominicans alone were responsible for debt adjustment. Ultimately, Jacob Hollander, the American-nominated financial expert, played a key role in helping the Dominicans to scale down their debts, but the State Department took no official part in the process.[34]

During 1906 the Dominicans achieved major successes in new debt negotiations, reducing a nominal debt of over thirty million dollars to about seventeen million. Hollander then negotiated a refunding loan of twenty million dollars on reasonable terms from Kuhn, Loeb and Company of New York. As a result, by 1907 the Dominican financial picture was far brighter and clearer than it had been in 1905, and alarmist predictions about the risks of ratifying the treaty had lost much credibility. Also, the treaty was reworded to make it more pleasing to the Senate, and the new version, signed on February 8, 1907, was promptly ratified.[35]

In spite of the State Department's denials, the extension of United States control over the governmental finances of the Dominican Republic created a de facto protectorate, as both sides well understood. In regard to a treaty clause limiting Dominican government expenditures to an indispensable minimum, Thomas Dawson explained to his superiors that the provision "opens the door to a real superintendence of all administrative matters, which in wise hands can be used to great advantage." Theodore Roosevelt wrote Secretary of War William Howard Taft when the modus vivendi went into effect that "American citizens in the custom houses are there to stay until we ourselves take them out, and no revolutionaries will be permitted to interfere with them." Roosevelt told Hay that "beyond a doubt we shall have flurries in connection with revolutionary uprisings and filibustering enterprises," but he did not "think that Santo Domingo . . . will give us much trouble." [36]

The Dominican customs receivership was conceived from the start to be more than merely financial; it was expected to bring stability to the country under United States tutelage. Many of the Americans involved in Dominican affairs believed with William Powell and Francis Loomis that a customs receivership would almost automatically end the constant revolutionary outbreaks in the country. Not only did revolutionaries depend upon the seizure of a customhouse and its collections to finance their operations, the argument ran, but the customs revenues themselves were a principal object of revolution. Denied access to customs money, prospective revolutionaries would lose both means and motive for insurrection. Thomas Dawson quickly came to believe this, as did the navy's Commander Dillingham. The latter reported early in 1904 that control of the customs would not only block their seizure by rebels, but end the foreign merchants' habit of financing rebellions at exorbitant interest rates. These loans were either repaid from customs revenues, or more often by forgiving the lenders' future customs duties on the goods which they imported to sell. If the customs system were removed from local control, there would be no prospect of repayment and therefore no merchants' loans; and without loans or customs receipts there would be no rebellion. Washington's men on the spot thought it as simple as that.[37]

The customs receivership and its consequences formed a part of the new pattern of United States activity in the Caribbean, but it grew equally from an older pattern in Dominican affairs which began with the temporary reannexation to Spain in 1861. A tendency to seek protection from some stronger power had subsequently brought the United States into the picture when the Baéz regime sought annexation in 1870. President Heureaux had repeatedly sought a closer American connection, and secretly proposed a protectorate to Washington in 1898. Theodore Roosevelt wrote of the Dominicans early in 1904 that "their government has been bedevilling us to establish some kind of a protectorate." [38] The extreme vulnerability of successive Dominican governments and their need of protection from both foreign and domestic threats led them to subordinate nationalism to the quest for a reliable foreign patron. Spain had been tried and failed; some Dominicans may have favored Germany, but power realities in the region left the United States as the most logical nation to play that role.

Doubts soon arose whether the new customs agreement would end the endemic turbulence in the Dominican Republic. In spite of the United States presence, the Morales government fell to a host of enemies late in 1905. For a time, this event gave pause to United States policy makers and led even Thomas Dawson to question whether customs control alone could bring Dominican stability. Determined not to be drawn into the country's factional struggles, however, the State Department made no move to protect Morales, whose political support had in any case virtually disappeared. Elihu Root, who had become Secretary of State upon the death of John Hay, even indicated privately that the new Dominican government would be allowed to abandon the modus vivendi if it chose. To everyone's relief, the political situation rapidly stabilized under the leadership of the new president, Ramón Cáceres, and for the next five years the Dominican Republic enjoyed a rare period of peace and relative prosperity. The customs receivership seemed to fulfill the most optimistic predictions, for under American management, receipts doubled. The Dominican government received more money than it had ever known even though 55 percent of collections went to debt servicing. Assured of a dependable income, Cáceres was able to crush the inevitable uprisings with little difficulty, while embarking upon a modest but popular program of public works.[39]

It became an article of faith in Washington that the customs receivership had solved the Dominican problem, and policy makers awaited similar cases to which the new technique could be applied. Echoing the general mood, Theodore Roosevelt predicted that the Dominican customs treaty would "prove literally invaluable in pointing out the way for introducing peace and order in the Caribbean and around its borders." [40]

Chapter 8

————⟨∞⟩————

Interventions and Alternatives

When United States policy makers committed themselves to the goal of stability in the Caribbean, they accepted the prospect of a vigorous gunboat diplomacy to impose it, including military interventions when necessary. It was obviously desirable, however, to limit the use of force to the lowest level consistent with United States policy goals. Too much actual fighting would be expensive, destructive, and politically counterproductive both at home and abroad, while even "peaceful" occupations carried the risk of igniting local resistance. The Dominican customs receivership represented a major attempt to find a nonmilitary means for bringing order to turbulent countries, and its apparent success suggested that the use of force could be reserved for the rare special case.

A 1904 incident in Panamá, however, indicated that the threat of force, as opposed to its actual use, might be needed more frequently. On that occasion the commander of Panamá's tiny standing army attempted to take control of the government from the country's frightened and elderly president. He was thwarted by the United States minister, who called in three warships and a small marine contingent to confront the ambitious general. Recognizing defeat, the general peaceably resigned, after which the Panamanian government paid off and disbanded his army. Since the marines had stayed in the Canal Zone and no one had fired a shot, the method employed could be optimistically regarded as moral suasion rather than force.[1]

Nevertheless, force remained in the Panamanian picture. The presidential election of 1908 was accompanied by partisan bitterness and potential conflict. When the government of President Manuel Amador Guerrero attempted to prevent the registration of known opposition voters, his political opponents threatened revolution. Instead, Theodore Roosevelt sent a sharp warning that the United States would not tolerate election fraud, and would if necessary invoke its right under Panamá's constitution to intervene to preserve peace and constitutional order. To give weight to his words, Roosevelt ordered the secretary of the navy to "have on the Isthmus . . . twelve hundred marines in connection with the approaching elections." Under strong pressure from Washington, President Amador reluctantly requested United States supervision of the election. Certain of defeat, his faction boycotted the voting, and its opponents won unopposed.[2]

Although the Roosevelt administration used or implied the threat of force in Venezuela and Panamá, and more subtly in the Dominican Republic, the only large military intervention which it undertook was in Cuba in 1906. This unwanted and unforeseen episode represented a breakdown in the United States plan for that island, and boded ill for Washington's schemes of political reformism in the Caribbean. Whatever else it was, the Cuban occupation of 1898–1902 had been a serious attempt at state building. As Washington saw it, the new Cuba had begun life as a healthy, functioning democracy, and those who had overseen its birth had high hopes for its future. Theodore Roosevelt expressed these hopes in his annual message to Congress for 1904: "If every country washed by the Caribbean Sea would show the progress in stable and just civilization which . . . Cuba has shown since our troops left the island, . . . all question of interference by this Nation with their affairs would be at an end."[3]

Unfortunately, this rosy picture soon took on more somber hues. Cuban President Tomás Estrada Palma, though honest and well-meaning, lacked both popular support and political skills. Seventy years old in 1905, he had played a prominent part in the Ten Years' War of 1868–78, been captured by the Spanish, jailed, and released into exile. He returned to prominence by heading the Cuban junta in New York during the war of 1895–98. When he returned to Cuba in 1902, he had been out of the country for twenty-five years, mostly in the United States. As president, he emphasized fiscal honesty and debt reduction, quickly coming into conflict with a congress whose members sought personal gain from the return of postwar prosperity. One of the first acts of congressional leaders was to introduce a bill providing for bonus payments to Cuban army veterans. While this bill unaccountably languished, the congressmen bought up the veterans' claims at half price; having acquired enough to satisfy their greed, they then passed the bill. The ensuing scandal put one prominent leader, Alfredo Zayas, briefly in prison.[4]

Estrada Palma's term ended in 1905. After a period of rapid evolution, two parties dominated that year's presidential election campaign. The Liberal party, containing many whom the president regarded as hopelessly corrupt, ran a ticket headed by José Miguel Gómez with Alfredo Zayas as his running mate.

Both men were deeply involved in the veterans' pay scandal. Their opponents, the so-called Moderates, decided to support the reelection of Estrada Palma. As president, the latter had attempted to avoid identification with any one party, with the result that he had had little influence with congress. But, regarding the Liberals as unfit to rule, Estrada Palma merged his fortunes with the Moderates and reorganized his cabinet along partisan lines to prepare for the coming election. Unfortunately for the president, the charismatic Gómez was extremely popular with the voters, a problem which the Moderate faction set itself to solve. A key part of the election process was a preliminary election to select the registration boards for all of the country's individual wards. Held in September 1905, this election was marred by widespread fraud, as everywhere the government's entrenched officials prevented Liberals from voting. Once in control of ward registration, the Moderates padded the rolls with fictitious supporters. Correctly claiming that they had no chance for a fair election, the Liberals boycotted the voting for president in December, giving Estrada Palma victory by default. His victory was generally discredited, however, a leading newspaper of his own party complaining that 300,000 eligible voters had somehow managed to cast 432,000 votes.[5]

By this time political passions in Cuba ran dangerously high. Confident of their popular support, the Liberal leaders fully intended to mount an armed challenge to Estrada Palma's regime, but the *zafra* was currently under way, the period of the sugar harvest, when much of the population were busily earning their income for the coming year. The time to make revolutions was in the *tiempo muerto,* the "dead time" when the countryside was full of seasonally unemployed *quajiros* and everyone had time to listen to stirring appeals. The coming revolution was the talk of Havana by the summer of 1906, the Liberals' plans seeming to be the worst-kept secret in Cuba. When the rising began in August, the authorities moved rapidly in Havana to arrest almost all of the principal revolutionary leaders. It mattered little; local military chieftains took charge in every district, filling their ranks with the idle rural work force. The government, lacking popular support and effective armed forces, appeared indecisive and vulnerable. Left to itself, Estrada Palma's administration had little chance of survival.[6]

Given the strength of their position, the Liberals' program was not extreme. They planned to depose Estrada Palma, set up a provisional government, and hold new elections. If the government could be coerced into major concessions, perhaps even this would not be necessary. On the other hand, if the government stood fast and events dragged on, the United States might well intervene under the authority of the Platt Amendment. This, too, could be made to serve the purposes of the revolution. An American occupation would mean the ouster of Estrada Palma and, presumably, an honest, American-supervised election which the Liberals were virtually certain to win. If things went badly and Washington failed to act, the Liberals could simply threaten to destroy foreign property, ensuring American intervention. Once in charge, the American occupiers would find it difficult to resist the cry for an honest election.[7]

While the revolutionaries fitted the prospect of American intervention smoothly into their plans, Estrada Palma and his cabinet were at first confident that such an intervention would maintain them in power. Unwilling to void the 1905 election and hold a new one, the president dug in and looked to Washington for help. Since the United States opposed revolution in Cuba, he assumed that it would defeat his enemies for him. Early in September he sent the State Department confidential notice that he planned to request United States intervention to restore order. Paradoxically, each of the two opposed factions in Cuba expected the United States to guarantee its success.[8]

Washington's initial move was to dispatch warships to Havana and Cienfuegos, as requested by Consul General Frank Steinhart. This encouraged both sides in Cuba to think in terms of an American intervention, and hardened Estrada Palma's stance toward the Liberals. President Roosevelt quickly forbade the landing of any troops, however, and ordered the recall of a small marine force hastily put ashore at Havana. Roosevelt showed a deep reluctance to pursue military involvement. He told the Cuban government in confidence that he did not welcome its proposed request for United States troops. The United States had "kept everything straight and decent in the island" during the occupation, Roosevelt wrote a friend, but now all was in jeopardy: "On the one hand, we cannot permanently see Cuba a prey to misrule and anarchy; on the other I loathe the thought of assuming any control over the island such as we have over Porto Rico or the Philippines."[9]

To publicize his position, Roosevelt sent an open letter to the Cuban minister in Washington which was reprinted with considerable editorial approval in the Cuban press. For seven years, the president declared, Cuba had enjoyed peace and a growing prosperity, four of those years under its own independent government. Now, however, the threat of chaos loomed. "Whoever is responsible in any way for the condition of affairs that now obtains, is an enemy of Cuba," Roosevelt charged, for "there is just one way in which Cuban independence can be jeopardized, and that is for the Cuban people to show their inability to continue in their path of peaceful and orderly progress." The United States had no wish to intervene, and would do so only if the Cubans showed that they had "fallen into the insurrectionary habit" and lapsed into anarchy. In that case the president would be obliged to do his duty under the Platt Amendment, and intervene to restore order. Also noting that there had been some injury to American property in Cuba, he called for an immediate end to the fighting there.[10]

This blunt warning was designed to make Cuba's warring leaders more amenable to compromise, while strengthening the administration's position in case it had ultimately to send in troops. Meanwhile, Roosevelt sought counsel from his principal advisers. By an unfortunate coincidence, two of those to whom he would have turned first were unavailable. Secretary of State Elihu Root had gone to South America to attend a Pan-American conference at Rio de Janeiro and make other goodwill visits, while Edwin V. Morgan, the able and respected United States minister in Havana, was in Europe on vacation. The president did consult his army chief of staff, General J. Franklin Bell, who was distinctly pessimistic about the problems of suppressing the guerrilla warfare which was likely should the Cubans resist an American take-over.[11]

With Morgan absent from his post in Cuba, Roosevelt's most prominent source of advice there was the United States consul general, Frank Steinhart. Born in Germany, Steinhart came to the United States in his youth, joining the army in the 1880s. While an enlisted clerk, he became a stenographer for General Philip Sheridan, studied law at night school, and came to Havana in 1899 as chief clerk in the office of the American military governor. With the aid of Leonard Wood he secured his appointment as consul general when the occupation ended. By 1906 he was a close friend of Estrada Palma, a power in Havana, and an advocate of strong United States action to uphold the Cuban president. It was Steinhart who had called in the warships which so encouraged the Cuban regime, warning Washington of a general collapse without the early use of force. Vigorously urging further action, he soon found himself out of harmony with his superiors. Assistant Secretary of State Robert Bacon cabled him: "The President directs me to state that perhaps you do not yourself appreciate the reluctance with which this country would intervene." The government would not act until the Cubans had exhausted every alternative, Bacon said.[12]

Roosevelt had so far assumed that Cubans of all parties were eager to escape United States intervention under the Platt Amendment, and that they would compromise in the end rather than undergo it. Knowing that Tomás Estrada Palma had been reelected through the use of official fraud, and that the Liberals commanded the bulk of popular support, he was unwilling to use force to uphold the incumbent government. Furthermore, he feared that forcible support of Estrada Palma would push the Liberals into guerrilla warfare against the United States Army, a catastrophe to be avoided at all costs. Roosevelt therefore wanted and expected a resolution of the Cuban crisis by means of a deal between the contending parties which gave the Liberals at least a part of their demands. As all this dawned on Estrada Palma, that tottering leader decided to resign and force Washington to fill the resulting vacuum in Havana. Only thus could he exclude the Liberals from power and safeguard the treasury surplus in which he took such pride.[13]

In this emergency, Roosevelt sent a special mission to Cuba headed by

Robert Bacon, then standing in for Root at the State Department, and Secretary of War William Howard Taft. The two arrived in Havana on September 19, 1906, and were met by a naval squadron and a transport full of marines. Demanding an immediate truce in the hostilities, they proposed that the congressional elections of 1905 be voided and reheld, which would undoubtedly give the Liberal party control of the legislature. Meanwhile Estrada Palma would stay on to finish his second term as president, but with many of his own Moderate officials replaced by Liberals. The Liberals might well have accepted this compromise, but Estrada Palma flatly refused it, and was deaf to the repeated appeals of the Americans. Even when Roosevelt begged him "not to conduct yourself so that the responsibility . . . for the death of the Republic can be put at your door," the Cuban president refused to continue in office.[14]

Puzzled as to what to do, Theodore Roosevelt thought of simply holding new elections, which the Liberals would presumably win, and allowing them to take power. Taft disagreed; he felt that the United States must restore order more securely before new elections would be appropriate. The Liberals had, after all, made a revolution, and put arms into the hands of the country's poor and uneducated classes. Bacon would have preferred initially to back the incumbent government against all comers, even at the risk of war; he still saw the Liberals as revolutionaries, and therefore illegitimate. Thus divided, the Americans offered no new options, while the Cubans rejected the original one. Estrada Palma refused to resume office, nor would the Cuban congress meet to choose an interim president. The resulting deadlock left Cuba without a government until the Americans gave up hope. On September 29, Taft proclaimed himself provisional governor of Cuba and ordered the marines ashore. Roosevelt announced that the new occupation would be purely temporary, while the Cuban public took this final blow quietly, having foreseen it for weeks. In October a "permanent" provisional governor, Charles E. Magoon, took charge in Havana.[15]

Roosevelt had moved cautiously and reluctantly, carefully preparing public opinion in both countries and emphasizing throughout that the Cubans were forcing him to act against his will. In general he was successful at forestalling criticism, but as usual some senators were hostile. Senator Joseph B. Foraker of Ohio, a Republican opponent of the president, protested that the new intervention needed congressional sanction. Roosevelt professed to agree, but argued that the collapse of government in Cuba made it impossible to wait until Congress was back in session before he acted. When Congress reconvened, he declared, it could decide on a long-run policy. Another Republican, the expansionist Senator Albert J. Beveridge of Indiana, mounted a campaign for immediate annexation on the ground that the Cubans had demonstrated their incapacity for self-government. He wrote Roosevelt that it was "nonsense to keep on setting up one Cuban government after another." Patiently, the president pointed out that only one Cuban government had fallen so far; it would require more cases than that to justify forcible annexation. Furthermore, such a step would require that Cuba be occupied for at least a year by a minimum of twenty-five thousand troops, and should therefore not be undertaken in haste.[16]

Despite the moderate tone of his reply to Beveridge, Roosevelt was thoroughly disillusioned with the Cubans, and by no means certain of their long-term future. Taft and Bacon had come home from Havana "tired out," he wrote his son; "They said they never could tell when those ridiculous dagos would flare up over some totally unexpected trouble and start to cutting one another's throats." Six months later he opined that "the best, most intelligent, and most thrifty and industrious Cubans wish us to stay," but concluded that "the Cubans are entitled to at least one more trial for their independent republic." To Taft he confided his fear that the Liberals' success in procuring the ouster of the Estrada Palma government left little hope that the next really discontented faction would refrain from insurrection, but concluded that "there is a slight chance and in my opinion we should give them this chance." After that one last chance, however, the president left the future open to developments; while still reluctant to impair Cuban independence, his faith in the Cubans' ability to manage their own affairs was badly damaged.[17]

The second Cuban occupation began in September 1906 and ended in January 1909. It was unwelcome in the United States and soon unpopular in Cuba. Yet Roosevelt and his advisers felt that they had had no choice but to intervene, especially given the terms and intent of the Platt Amendment. They were shocked to find Cuban party leaders so lacking in patriotic feeling that they would turn their country over to foreign rule for partisan advantage; to them the Cubans were entirely to blame. Their views have been substantially reflected by United States scholars, like David A. Lockmiller in the 1930s and Lester D. Langley in the 1980s, who have stressed the culpability of the Cubans and Roosevelt's reluctance to intervene. Some Cuban scholars have agreed. Writing soon after the event, Enrique Collazo held President Estrada Palma solely responsible for the second occupation, while exonerating the leaders of his own Liberal party. Even Emilio Roig de Leuchsenring, a Cuban historian generally critical of United States policies, for years blamed his own countrymen rather than the Yankees. Another Cuban scholar, however, Herminio Portell-Vilá, suggested in the 1930s that the American legation at Havana deliberately worsened the election crisis of 1905 by encouraging Estrada Palma in his measures against the Liberals. A fourth Cuban, Manuel Márquez Sterling, faulted Roosevelt for intervening at all; if he had held aloof, the Cuban factions would have been forced to work out a settlement for themselves, Márquez Sterling argued in 1941.[18]

In conjunction with the other factors involved, it is now easy to see the

Platt Amendment itself as a principal cause of the second occupation. Since Cuban political leaders knew that real power resided ultimately in Washington, it was natural that they should attempt to enlist the United States government in their graver clashes; that both sides did so in 1906 sufficiently demonstrates the point. As sole and self-appointed arbiter of Cuba's internal disputes, the United States was automatically involved in them. Politics is the art of manipulating power; the Cubans had therefore to consider the uses of United States power as it touched their affairs. Elihu Root unwittingly expressed this as early as 1902. "The trouble about Cuba," he noted then, "is that, although it is technically a foreign country, practically and morally it occupies an intermediate position, since we have required it to become part of our political and military system, and to form a part of our line of exterior defense." [19]

It is ironic that while Roosevelt had been forced by events to intervene in Cuba against his will, he never felt able to mount an intervention much closer to his heart. Venezuela's President Cipriano Castro had gone into Washington's black books during the Venezuelan crisis of 1902–1903, and had done little afterward to redeem himself. In June 1904 the Venezuelan government seized the property of an American asphalt-mining company on the ground that its management had aided a rebellion. The United States minister in Caracas recommended the use of force to restore the company's property, and Roosevelt was receptive. He suggested to Secretary of State John Hay that the mining company's confiscation should serve as justification for seizing a Venezuelan customhouse. This could be turned over to representatives of the Hague Court, who would disburse the revenues to all foreign claimants. This arrangement would remove any pretext for European intervention, and would also "show those Dagos that they will have to behave decently." But this was late in the summer of 1904, well into the presidential campaign season, as the president noted: "Of course I should want action deferred until after the election." [20]

By March 1905, the State Department had decided to support the claims of several more United States citizens or firms who had lost property to Castro's regime, including another dispossessed asphalt company. The Venezuelans stood fast on the Calvo Clause, which they inserted into all foreign contracts and concessions, forbidding the parties involved to appeal for redress to any foreign government in case of dispute. Washington refused to be bound by this clause, and as negotiations bogged down, the American minister again called for the use of force. In March, Hay sent down an unusually strong note to Caracas, but Castro stood fast. Roosevelt privately described Castro as "an unspeakably villainous little monkey," and confessed that he "should like to send an expedition against him." However, with the Dominican customs take-over imminent, and the Senate proving difficult, any new Caribbean adventure was obviously ill timed. Even so, the frustrated president was sorely tempted. He had already had the navy plan a Venezuelan operation to seize customhouses, and in the spring of 1905 it was ready to implement; the Cruiser Division could sail at once with six hundred marines. Only the domestic political risks stayed Roosevelt's hand, particularly the certainty of opposition in Congress.[21]

During 1905, Castro also became embroiled in a dispute with a French cable company which eventually moved Paris to action. The French government sent two cruisers to the area, and by December, only United States influence deterred France from launching a naval attack. Even so, France broke relations with Venezuela early in 1906. Meanwhile, Castro had added new disputes with the United States to the old ones. However, Elihu Root, who had succeeded Hay as secretary of state, was intent on keeping to purely diplomatic methods. Root was convinced that Castro would eventually be ousted by domestic foes, and preferred to keep the path clear for successful negotiations with the next Venezuelan government. In this he showed wisdom and foresight, but it was only with difficulty that he restrained his chief. Roosevelt asked the Army General Staff early in 1906 for operational plans for a Venezuelan intervention, and was still actively considering armed intervention as late as 1908. In March of that year he proposed to Root that marines land to seize the customhouses, and sent the evidence of Castro's sins to the Senate Foreign Relations Committee. To the president's disappointment, the senators were unmoved by the documents, and chilly to an intervention in Venezuela. Lacking the political support he needed to go ahead, Roosevelt contented himself with breaking diplomatic relations.[22]

As Root had foreseen, the problem eventually solved itself. By late 1908 Venezuela had lost diplomatic relations with the Netherlands as well as France and the United States, and was embroiled in a boundary dispute with Colombia. The Dutch sent naval vessels to Curaçao and sought Washington's permission to chastize Castro. This they received, with the usual admonitions about taking territory, and late in the year they prepared to take action. In November Castro suddenly sailed for Europe to get needed medical treatment, leaving the government in the hands of Juan Vicente Gómez, his vice-president. When the Dutch squadron showed up off the coast, Gómez assumed emergency war powers; once in control, he declared himself president, and ousted Castro in a bloodless coup. Unlike his predecessors, Gómez desired good relations with the major powers, and especially the United States. Almost at once he took steps to resolve the issues between the two countries, largely on Washington's terms. An effective strong man, Gómez kept power for many years, during which there were no further crises between the United States and Venezuela.[23]

While Root's waiting game paid off in Venezuela, Roosevelt left office still unreconciled to the restraints imposed on his actions by public opinion. Toward the end of his presidency, he penned a general complaint:

In Cuba, Santo Domingo and Panama we have interfered . . . . I would have interfered in some similar fashion in Venezuela, in at least one Central American State, and in Haiti already . . . if I could have waked up our people so that they would back a reasonable and intelligent foreign policy which should put a stop to crying disorders at our very doors. . . . But in each case where I have actually interfered . . . I have had to exercise the greatest care in order to keep public opinion here with me . . . , and I have been able to lead it along . . . only by minimizing my interference and showing the clearest necessity for it.

In short, the public and Congress would accept Caribbean interventions, but only within limits, and only if they were convinced of their need.[24]

While Roosevelt fretted at the limits on his use of intervention, the closing years of his presidency saw an attempt elsewhere in his administration to develop alternatives to it. Elihu Root became secretary of state after the death of John Hay in 1905, and at once he began consciously to change the tone of the administration's Latin American policy. He also took the burden of making that policy from the president's shoulders. As Hay's health had failed, the load on Roosevelt had become very heavy, increasing steadily until the former's death. "I deeply mourn Hay," Roosevelt wrote Taft, "but for two years he has done little or nothing in the State Department. What I didn't do myself wasn't done at all." Root had already worked closely with Roosevelt as secretary of war, when he had been in charge of Philippine, Cuban, and Puerto Rican affairs. An able administrator and skilled lobbyist with Congress, Root was also a strong leader and a man whose judgment had won respect in Washington. Henry Cabot Lodge predicted regarding his new appointment that "he will be a tower of strength indeed."[25]

In many ways Root and Roosevelt saw eye to eye. As the father of the Platt Amendment, Root had prepared the way for further United States intervention in Cuba, though it had been his hope that the mere existence of the amendment would make intervention unnecessary. It was Root who had first announced the Roosevelt Corollary to the world at the Cuban-American dinner in May 1904; Root approved of the corollary, and had probably discussed it with Roosevelt before its release. A few months before he became secretary of state, Root had written of the Caribbean: "The inevitable effect of our building the canal must be to require us to police the surrounding premises. In the nature of things, trade and control, and the obligation to keep order which goes with them, must come our way. . . ." Like Roosevelt, Root feared a German threat and believed in an effective navy. His views and goals were fundamentally those of the president, and the latter was therefore willing to give Root an unusually free hand. As his administration came to a close, Roosevelt asserted that its most important diplomatic activity of 1905–1908 had been that involving Latin America, and that "this work has been entirely Root's. My part in it has been little beyond cordially backing him up."[26]

The new secretary of state, however, also brought perceptions which his president did not share. Throughout his tenure in the State Department, for example, Root labored to improve the tone of United States relations with Latin America, as distinct from their substance. Like Theodore Roosevelt, citizens of the Colossus of the North tended to regard their Latin American neighbors with scarcely concealed contempt. Typical was John Hay's comment that nobody much had attended a recent diplomatic reception, for "they were mostly dagoes and chargés."[27] Latin American representatives could hardly fail to note this attitude, which increased their dislike and suspicion of the United States. Root faced this problem squarely. "The South Americans now hate us," he stated late in 1905,

> largely because they think we despise them and try to bully them. . . . I think their friendship is really important to the United States, and that the best way to secure it is by treating them like gentlemen. If you want to make a man your friend, it does not pay to treat him like a yellow dog.[28]

The solution, Root thought, was to adopt a consistently courteous tone toward the southern neighbors, find occasions for friendly initiatives toward them, and cultivate social ties with their diplomats. Shortly before Estrada Palma's fall in Cuba, Root had asked the president of Harvard College to arrange an honorary degree for him. "I think the effect on the Cuban people would be good," he noted. "They are . . . an affectionate, sensitive people, easily impressed by marks of consideration and courtesy, and they are too frequently treated with rudeness by Americans." On another occasion he wrote of the Central Americans that "it is delightful to see how readily and gratefully they respond to a little genuine interest combined with respectful consideration. . . . If we can maintain for a time the right sort of relations with them, we can exercise an enormous influence over their conduct. . . ." Root accordingly set himself to cultivate the Latin American diplomatic community, while somewhat softening the tone of the State Department's expressions. The objects of this attention noticed the difference and appreciated it, though it is difficult to demonstrate how much the change may have lessened their resistance to Yankee influence.[29]

It is also hard to say whether Root's goodwill campaign reflected genuine sentiment or was merely another example of his proverbial shrewdness and lobbying skills. Referring to the Latin Americans, he asserted that "I really like them and intend to show it." In private, however, he sometimes complained of the burdens of socializing. On the eve of a major goodwill visit to South America, Root confided to a friend that the social side of the trip would be "dreadful." "I hate banquets and receptions and ceremonial calls and drinking warm, sweet champagne in the middle of the day," he lamented. "All these are the fate of an honored guest in South America." More directly, Root charged in a retrospective statement toward the end of his life that "all of the Latin Americans have a genius for misrepresentation." But whatever his real feelings (and they were probably mixed), he single-mindedly worked to eliminate the gratuitous and unnecessary strains placed upon Latin American relations by North American discourtesy.[30]

At first sight, Root's course regarding the Second Hague Conference in 1907 might appear to be just another case of flattering Latin sensibilities, but to Root it was far more than that, and in fact illustrates another facet of his policies toward Latin America. The First Hague Conference had met in the Netherlands in 1899, with the object of furthering international peace. The government of Russia called for a second peace conference to meet at the Hague in the summer of 1906, the time already selected for the Third Inter-American Conference to meet in Rio de Janeiro. Root had decided to attend the latter conference, and therefore faced a conflict in regard to the Hague meeting. Through talks with the Russian ambassador in Washington, he succeeded in getting the Hague Conference delayed for a year. Once this was accomplished, he campaigned to have all of the American republics invited to participate in it. This was not easy; the Latin American states had rarely participated in European conferences, and never as a bloc, but at Root's insistence the Russians gave in. Twenty Latin American nations received invitations, and eighteen actually sent delegates to the Hague. This unprecedented recognition aroused pleasure and excitement throughout the hemisphere, as well as gratitude to the secretary of state who had brought it about.[31]

Root's intentions were more than cosmetic, however. His major aim at the conference was to create a permanent court of international justice to hear and resolve international disputes. Root believed deeply that world peace could best be achieved through the strengthening and development of international law. He saw an international court as potentially a crucial mechanism for conflict resolution. Its judges were to be selected from among the world's prominent jurists and authorities on international law. The Latin American nations had produced a number of such distinguished authorities; with their representatives present at the court's creation, it could be assumed that they would be directly represented on the court's judicial panel. In the long view, Root hoped that an effective system of international justice would help to eliminate the need for European intervention in the western hemisphere, while the Latin Americans' participation in its machinery would ensure them fair treatment.[32]

Root's international court plan ultimately failed of adoption, though Great Britain and Germany supported it, but he had meanwhile sponsored another initiative designed to shield the Americas more directly from Europe's armed intervention. This involved the Drago Doctrine, a by-product of the second Venezuelan crisis of 1902. At that time the Argentine foreign minister, Luis María Drago, proposed to Washington a joint hemispheric policy prohibiting

Elihu Root. Courtesy of the State Historical Society of Wisconsin

the use of armed force by any European power against any American state for the collection of a public debt. While the State Department had taken no action on the suggestion at the time, Root became intrigued with the idea, and advanced it in an altered form at the Hague Conference. In Root's version the doctrine was global, rather than confined to the western hemisphere. While broader in application, however, it was watered down to allow the forcible collection of debts if the debtor nation refused to arbitrate the dispute, or to carry out an award resulting from arbitration. This modification fostered Root's purpose of strengthening arbitration procedures, but was unacceptable to the Latin American delegates, who wanted no loopholes in the ban on armed intervention. The conference nevertheless adopted this modified Drago Doctrine as Root desired, the Latin Americans voting en bloc against it.[33]

In the light of hindsight it is easy to belittle Root's achievements at the Hague conference, for the subsequent development of international law failed to justify his hopes. However, Elihu Root regarded them as genuinely important. He had managed to get the Latin American states included for the first time in the councils of the world's powers, and he had attempted to create legal mechanisms to protect them from arbitrary force. His goals were multiple: to win the Latins' friendship by espousing their cause, to give them a larger international voice in safeguarding their own interests, and to erect new barriers against European interventions in the western hemisphere. While it was meant to serve United States purposes, Root's course represented enlightened self-interest, for it was intended to serve the needs of others as well.

Root believed that the United States had a right to intervene in the Caribbean, and that it would probably need to do so at times. He was nonetheless determined to hold such occasions to a minimum, and to allow the Caribbean states as much freedom of action as he thought possible. His restraint of Roosevelt's plans to intervene in Venezuela is merely one example of this determination. Another case had occurred when the Morales government in the Dominican Republic weakened in the autumn of 1905. Roosevelt had ordered the navy to stop any revolution against it. Root, however, who was just taking hold at the State Department, pursued a policy of neutrality in such factional struggles, allowing Morales' enemies to assume power. He was even prepared to let the new Dominican regime abandon the customs receivership if it chose to do so, though Roosevelt had been ready to use force to keep it in effect. By 1906 Root's State Department subordinates were acutely aware of his reluctance to resort to interventions. Robert Bacon reflected this when his mission to Havana ended in the second Cuban occupation. "I shall be ashamed to look Mr. Root in the face," Bacon then confessed. "This intervention is contrary to his policy and what he has been preaching in Latin America." [34]

Since Root fully believed in the need to establish order and stability in the Caribbean, but rejected the routine use of force to achieve it, he worked hard to develop alternate methods to fulfill United States goals. His principal efforts to do so centered on Central America, where international tensions reached the crisis point during Root's tenure in the State Department. The five Central American republics which developed after independence from the short-lived Central American Federation included Guatemala, El Salvador, Honduras, Nicaragua, and Costa Rica. Together they had long constituted a miniature state system characterized by quarreling and turbulence. In the time of Root and Roosevelt, two strong and ambitious dictators dominated the Central American arena, Guatemala's Manuel Estrada Cabrera and Nicaragua's

José Santos Zelaya. The two were mutually jealous and hostile; both meddled in the affairs of their neighbors, especially if they saw an opportunity to install governments friendly to themselves. The most frequent victim of this practice was Honduras, which lay between the rivals and was relatively weak and vulnerable, but none of the five was immune from the others' machinations. Internal revolts and external wars reached a peak shortly after the turn of the century, when Washington's concern about canal security made disorders on the isthmus particularly unwelcome.[35]

In May 1906, when Root was about to leave on his South American tour, anti-Cabrera exiles were gathering on the borders of Guatemala in preparation for an assault on the dictator. They were supported by the government of El Salvador, which had reason to fear its ruthless neighbor, and war seemed imminent. Root tried to head it off through an offer of mediation, and to make this approach more persuasive he arranged through the Mexican ambassador to have Mexico cosponsor the offer. As the nearest large nation, Mexico had long had influence in Central America; under President Porfirio Díaz Mexico had enjoyed several decades of political stability and in Root's eyes constituted a good example; finally, the participation of a leading Latin American state might help take the curse off an initiative from Washington. This attempt to work in tandem with Mexico was one of Root's early contributions to Central American policy, and suggested a possible modification of American unilateralism.[36]

In spite of these efforts, a Central American war began in July 1906, after Root had left on his long trip. It came when General Tomás Regulado, former president, current minister of war, and still strong man of Salvador, led a force across the Guatemalan border in a drunken rage. Regulado was killed by the Guatemalans in the initial assault, but Honduras joined with Salvador in what quickly became a bloody struggle. The comic-opera image of "banana wars" often concealed a harsher reality; some nine hundred men were killed and about twenty-five hundred wounded in the Salvadoran army alone in ten days of fighting. In Root's absence, Roosevelt sent messages to the belligerent governments urging a prompt end to hostilities. When these failed, he invited Mexico's President Díaz to join him in a joint venture at mediation. After much discussion the mediating powers were able to arrange a peace conference aboard the United States cruiser *Marblehead*, offered as a neutral meeting place.[37]

The so-called Marblehead Conference convened aboard the cruiser on July 20, 1906. Participants included not only delegates from the three warring countries, but the two United States ministers accredited to Central America, the Mexican minister to the area, and representatives from Costa Rica and Nicaragua. The latter two participated in the discussions without voting, while the Mexican and the two Americans acted as neutral mediators. In a single day the conferees agreed to stop the fighting and disarm, while pledging to attend a more general conference in the near future. Oral tradition at the State Department long held that this speedy agreement owed much to the rough seas in which *Marblehead* rolled at her anchor that day; the diplomats, it seemed, were not good sailors, and were eager to go ashore.[38]

As agreed, the Central American states held another conference in San José, Costa Rica, in September 1906 to strengthen their peace-keeping arrangements. The meeting was marred by the refusal of Nicaragua's President Zelaya to participate, but the other four states concluded a general treaty of peace, friendship, and commerce, and reestablished a Central American Tribunal of Arbitration which had first been agreed upon in 1902 but had not yet heard a case. This effort seemed wasted, however, when a new crisis developed early in 1907. In January an insurrection broke out in Honduras, whose president blamed Zelaya for aiding and instigating it. The Hondurans chased the rebel force back into Nicaragua, killing some Nicaraguans in the process. Zelaya went to the Central American tribunal to demand indemnity, but that body demanded that both sides disarm before it would render a decision. Zelaya refused, successfully invaded Honduras, and replaced the president with one friendly to himself. Guatemala and El Salvador objected, seeing a pro-Zelaya government in Honduras as a threat to their own security. When the three neighboring states failed to agree on a Honduran regime, Zelaya prepared to invade Salvador and a general Central American war seemed unavoidable. Vigorous United States diplomatic efforts, however, managed to secure a fragile peace agreement in April.[39]

Elihu Root, who suffered from exhaustion in the summer of 1907 and spent part of it in a health sanitarium, found these developments discouraging. In July he summarized his thoughts on Central America: "The trouble is that there is no real controversy to be settled there," Root declared.

> Zelaya is bent on conquest and if driven from one pretext immediately finds another or goes on without any. Cabrera seems to be a cruel tyrant under whom the political activity of Guatemala is confined to assassination. . . . We can join with Mexico in urging peace but it is merely a form. . . . Nothing would be of any real use except a long period of armed intervention. That we cannot undertake.[40]

Soon, however, Root conceived a more constructive approach to the isthmian problem. In August 1907, Roosevelt and Díaz once more summoned the Central American states to a conference, with the purpose of ending their constant disputes. The State Department preferred that the meeting be held in Mexico City, but Guatemala's long-standing fear of Mexico, her own Colossus of the North, dictated Washington as the site. The conference met there from November 14 to December 20, 1907, Root opening the proceedings as temporary chairman. An early proposal by the Honduran delegates for a new Central American federation almost broke up the proceedings but was soon dropped. After that, the conferees worked steadily and with impressive success, under Root's watchful eye, to erect a new framework for regional stability. Once the region possessed its own peace-keeping institutions, to be operated by the Central Americans themselves with United States encouragement, Root hoped for a major improvement in Central American relations.[41]

In all, the five attending states adopted eight treaties and conventions. The most important of them provided once more for a Central American Court of Justice to resolve all disputes between member states, made arbitration of disputes compulsory, neutralized Honduras, and guaranteed it against invasion. Other provisions barred political refugees from border regions near their own countries, and forbade the diplomatic recognition of any government which came to power by overthrowing a constitutional regime. The states also signed a ten-year treaty of peace and amity. All of the treaties were quickly ratified by the five governments concerned, in itself a remarkable achievement for an area where treaties were regularly signed but rarely ratified.[42]

When the conference closed, Root sent a circular letter to the editors of eight leading United States newspapers and magazines soliciting editorial support for the new arrangements. Heretofore, he told the editors, Central American peace efforts had been confined to general agreements and empty promises. By contrast, the new treaties "contain(ed) a number of specific, practical provisions" well calculated "to begin a progressive growth of common sense conduct leading towards a real union." This was to the benefit of both Central America and the United States, for "the building of the Panama Canal puts these Central American countries in the front yard of the United States" so that "their conduct is important to us."[43]

The new regional system was quickly tested. In June 1908, a rebellion in Honduras led that government to accuse Guatemala and El Salvador of complicity with the rebels. The case went to the Central American court, amid a general perception that the failure of the new peace-keeping machinery might open an era of United States intervention. The court held that Honduras had failed to prove its case, and firmly closed the incident. For the next several years the court and the other regional arrangements succeeded in averting wars among the five republics, and the concept of regional self-regulation under United States auspices appeared to be successful.[44]

In 1909, Root explained to a former colleague that he had left office with one further objective in Central America unachieved. Since attempts to control Honduras had so often ignited regional conflicts, Root desired a joint guarantee of Honduran neutrality by the United States and Mexico. The guarantee should be in such form that "the President could use our naval force to prevent violations of that neutrality without himself over-stepping the constitutional limitations upon his power." Root believed that the very existence of such power would make its use unnecessary, as he considered to be the case in the Dominican Republic, and had once thought to be true in Cuba as well. Washington should not impose this Honduran guarantee on the Central Americans, however, but await their invitation to exercise it. "I have felt sure that the psychological moment would come when such a thing could be brought about upon Central American initiative," probably as a result of revulsion at the continuing misbehavior of Zelaya and Estrada Cabrera. Once in place, "such a guarantee would be the pivot upon which the whole political life of Central America would turn." [45]

As secretary of state, Root worked consistently to limit forcible intervention in the Caribbean and to find substitutes for it in the task of keeping the region politically stable. He approved of the Dominican customs receivership, which had already begun operating before he came to the State Department. To this he added several new devices. The inclusion of the Latin American states in the world's councils, as achieved at the Hague Conference, and the adoption of a watered-down Drago Doctrine were aimed at improving hemispheric relations with Europe and diminishing the possibility of European interventions. Efforts to work in partnership with Mexico in Central American affairs could put a better face on United States initiatives there, and also ensure that Washington would consider the Latin American viewpoint in its planning. The Central American Conference of 1907 was an ambitious attempt at regional stabilization through international agreements and shrewd diplomacy, so that United States influence would play the role of upholding the peace-keeping efforts of the local states. Bringing a resourceful legal mind to his problems, Root meant to provide, not ad hoc responses, but long-term solutions, at the same time that he avoided reliance on armed force.

Theodore Roosevelt remarked in 1911 that Cuba and the Dominican Republic "can remain independent always if only they will not be too foolish, will not contract debts they cannot pay, and will not indulge in revolutions." It might be said that Roosevelt meant to use intervention to avert annexation, while Root hoped to achieve stabilization without intervention. It is easy to exaggerate the differences between Roosevelt and Root, however. Root always regarded armed intervention as an essential final recourse, while Roosevelt was generous in his praise for Root's innovations. As he was about to leave office, the president wrote Andrew Carnegie, financial underwriter of peace movements: "No European statesman of whom I have heard has done as much for peace in any quarter of the world as Elihu Root has done in the Western Hemisphere in the last three years." [46]

Furthermore, Roosevelt eventually developed some of Root's willingness to work as an equal with the more advanced Latin American countries. Several years after leaving the presidency, he publicly suggested that the United States' unilateral "custodianship" of the Monroe Doctrine could in time be shared with the southern sisters as they achieved stability and prosperity. While this was not yet foreseeable for "the lands and waters through which the Panama Canal and its approaches run, where our interests are vital," it was already possible in large parts of South America.

> Brazil, the Argentine, Chile, have achieved positions of such assured . . . progress, of such political stability and power and economic prosperity, . . . it is safe to say that there is no further need for the United States to concern itself about asserting the Monroe Doctrine so far as these powers are concerned.

This definition dovetailed neatly with Captain Mahan's dictum that United States security concerns ended at the Amazon River, making it unnecessary to apply the Monroe Doctrine south of it.[47]

In its later years, the Roosevelt administration evolved two contrasting methods for seeking stability in the Caribbean: armed intervention under the Platt Amendment and the Roosevelt Corollary, and a variety of nonmilitary alternatives ranging from the Dominican customs receivership to the Central American peace system. There is no question that Elihu Root hoped that the latter would be the more central approach, and to a considerable extent Roosevelt shared that hope. They both thought the second Cuban occupation an aberration brought on by the irresponsibility of Cuba's leaders. Neither yet suspected how readily limited interference led to major intervention, or how measures originally designed to avert the use of force would at times draw the nation into ever escalating entanglements.

Chapter 9

---·····⌒⌒✑⌒·····---

Dollar Diplomacy:
Theory and Practice

On March 4, 1909, William Howard Taft succeeded Theodore Roosevelt as president of the United States. Taft, like Root, had been a central figure in Roosevelt's cabinet; the three referred to themselves as the "three muske-teers" and grew personally close. The Rough Rider had handpicked Taft as his successor and, using his domination of the Republican party, had virtu-ally imposed his choice on the 1908 convention. The new president, however, had ideas of his own, particularly regarding foreign policy. While the Taft administration would continue the Caribbean policies of its predecessors, it would do so with its own methods and in a framework of somewhat differing assumptions.

For his secretary of state, Taft chose Philander C. Knox, a successful corpo-ration lawyer from Pennsylvania who had served both McKinley and Roosevelt as attorney general. Knox went to the United States Senate in 1904, and con-tended against Taft for the presidential nomination in 1908. He nevertheless became Taft's closest adviser, and Taft delegated to him virtually complete control of American diplomacy, with more independence than either McKinley or Roosevelt had been willing to give any subordinate. As Taft was the heaviest American president, Knox at five feet five may have been the shortest Ameri-can secretary of state; Roosevelt had called him "Little Phil." Cold, formal, impassive, and impeccably dressed, the new secretary liked to work at home, spending little time at the State Department. To fill the gap at headquarters, Knox leaned heavily on a younger man, Francis M. Huntington-Wilson, who had spent nine years as a diplomatic secretary in Tokyo before coming to Washington as an assistant secretary of state in 1906. Huntington-Wilson was energetic and hardworking, but had a genius for antagonizing people. Root disliked him, but Knox admired his ability and made him his chief assistant.[1]

These three men, Taft, Knox, and Huntington-Wilson, shared a common world view and held similar visions of the United States' world role. While Roosevelt's foreign policy formulations never strayed far from the realities of power and the possibility of armed struggle, the new team believed that war among the great powers was no longer a serious threat. Though watchful for German machinations, Taft dismissed fears of actual German aggression in the Caribbean as groundless. He and his subordinates stressed economic rather than military factors in their policies. The press soon referred to the Taft-Knox approach as "dollar diplomacy," a term which the two then defiantly adopted as their own. Their purposes were multiple: to aid the business community; to safeguard domestic prosperity by finding foreign markets for the nation's excess industrial production; to bring economic growth and political stability to strategic third-world areas; and to harness United States economic strength to the task of achieving the nation's various goals abroad, while depending less upon military force.[2]

Huntington-Wilson explained the administration's interpretation of dollar diplomacy in a 1911 speech:

It means the substitution of dollars for bullets . . . the creation of a prosperity which will be preferred to predatory strife . . . [and] taking advantage of the interest in peace of those who benefit by the investment of capital. It recognizes that financial soundness is a potent factor in political stability; that prosperity means contentment and contentment means repose. This thought is at the basis of the policy of the United States in Central America and the zone of the Caribbean.

Many years later, Huntington-Wilson complained that the critics of dollar diplomacy had

missed the whole point. . . . They refused to distinguish between old-fashioned selfish exploitation and the new and sincere and practical effort to help. They refused to accept the plain fact that our Government was using Wall Street to serve our national interest and to benefit other countries. They even pretended that Wall Street was using the Government. . . .[3]

To their efforts in the Caribbean, Knox and Huntington-Wilson brought a renewed contempt for the region's population and impatience with much of Elihu Root's legacy there. Stiff and reticent, Knox was personally agreeable only among a small circle of intimates. He was at his worst with Latin American diplomats, for he had a low opinion of their countries and made no effort to conceal it. Huntington-Wilson was even worse; humorless, arrogant, and suspicious, he was excessively demanding and insulting during negotiations. He wrote in his memoirs that there was no natural affinity between Latin Americans and the people of the United States; Pan-Americanism must be viewed as a marriage of convenience, not of sentiment. Huntington-Wilson had little use for what he called "the sweetness and light aspect of Root's policy, the beautiful speeches and the toasts in champagne." During the Taft years, the administration had merely insisted "that the respected must act respectably," he declared.[4]

Others were more severe in their judgments. In old age, Elihu Root recalled Knox as "a peppery sort of fellow" who was "absolutely antipathetic to all Spanish-American modes of thought and feeling and action." More basically, Root thought that Knox had relied much too heavily on Huntington-Wilson, whom Root regarded as a baleful influence on Caribbean policy. More acid comment came from the British ambassador to the United States, Lord Bryce. Bryce had respected Root and Roosevelt, but he disliked Knox and Huntington-Wilson. "The trouble with the Secretary of State," he reported to London,

> is that he is hopelessly ignorant of international politics and principles of policy, and is either too old or too lazy to apply his mind to the subject and try to learn. Nobody in his miserably-organized department is competent to instruct or guide him. No country but the U.S. could get on under such conditions.

If this was too severe, it contained a kernel of truth; the two State Department leaders were impatient of protocol and cared little for the views of other governments.[5]

The two also insisted on the primacy of United States economic interests. Under Knox, the State Department brought pressure to bear on the government of Panamá to discourage a proposed commercial treaty between that government and Great Britain which might have cut into United States trade on the isthmus. Similarly, it dissuaded the Cuban government from removing the tariff on sugar mill machinery and railroad materials, a move which would have lost United States manufacturers the advantage of the Cuban reciprocity treaty and thereby opened the market to German producers. The State Department believed that the government must help the business community to find export markets and to best foreign competitors. It could help in other ways as well. As an incidental side effect of sending some marines to Guantánamo during a Cuban rebellion in 1912, the government saved a nearby New York–owned sugar estate the difference between charges of 5.5 percent and 1.5 percent of assessed value on war risk insurance, which amounted to a considerable sum. Thus even the deployment of the armed forces could have a cash value.[6]

The use of overt economic diplomacy, of course, was not an invention of the Taft administration, but represented a growing trend. John Hay had maintained in 1904 that the United States government "does not interfere with the management by foreign governments of their own fiscal systems," and had refused to become involved in a proposed refunding of the Honduran foreign debt. Six months later, however, both Root and Roosevelt urged Hay to support

Philander Knox. Courtesy of the State Historical Society of Wisconsin

a proposed loan by New York bankers to the government of Costa Rica. Root stressed the importance of having "the next door neighbor of Panamá under the financial control of Americans, with a power of ultimate control by the United States." Roosevelt pointed out that "it is to our advantage to gain by the free offer of these republics just that power over their finances the lack of which is causing us such trouble at this very moment in San Domingo [sic] and Venezuela." Nothing came of this loan scheme, but Hay must have become aware that the climate of opinion on such matters had changed.[7]

Like previous administrations, the Taft-Knox regime made stability the cornerstone of its Caribbean policy, and Knox had clear ideas about how to seek it. "True stability is best established not by military, but by economic and social forces," he declared in 1910. "The problem of good government is inextricably interwoven with that of economic prosperity and sound finance; financial stability contributes perhaps more than any other factor to political stability." The proper financial tools to ensure Caribbean stability were ready at hand, particularly customs receiverships similar to the one already established in the Dominican Republic. Knox and Huntington-Wilson saw the Dominican customs receivership as a brilliant success. It had satisfied European creditors and met repayment schedules, yet the Dominican government had a larger revenue than before. Even after cutting tariffs in half, the Dominicans had seen the duties collected rise from $1.8 million in 1904 to over $3 million in 1911. In the same period Dominican foreign trade had grown from about six million to over seventeen million dollars per year. Most important of all, the years 1906–11 had been characterized by domestic peace and political stability in the Dominican Republic.[8]

Now it was time to apply the remedy elsewhere. Internal strife prevented Caribbean states from developing their economies and forced them to contract ruinous loans abroad. Progress could come only by breaking the cycle of revolution, and by achieving financial stability. This accomplished, the doors would be open to foreign investment, and economic and social development would follow. The answer lay in customs control, Knox explained, because "the customhouses have ever been the objective point of the revolutionists and successive contests for their control have marked the national existence." Knox told the British ambassador that, far from progressing, Central America had actually retrogressed in the past century. In his view, progress could come to the troubled Central American states only "by regulating their monetary system, and by placing the customs under the management of a competent official from outside."[9]

Knox targeted Honduras as the first new beneficiary of this rehabilitation program. Having undergone seven revolutions in the previous fifteen years and defaulted on a large foreign debt, that nation exemplified the kind of political and financial disorder which Washington sought to end. The State Department was initially inspired to act, however, largely because it appeared that the British would act first, leaving control of Honduran public finance in London rather than Washington. Since one of the goals of the Taft-Knox policies was to replace European loans to Caribbean governments with loans from United States bankers, this was particularly unacceptable to them.

For some years, Honduran administrations had seen the need to improve their international credit and rationalize their customs collection. Hoping to achieve both of these aims, the government of President Miguel Dávila had opened negotiations in 1908 with the British bondholders who held most of the foreign debt. The British minister proposed a plan by which Honduras would pay off the bondholders in forty annual installments, using revenues from import duties and income from rail and dock facilities at Puerto Cortés, at that time the country's chief port. This proposal offended United States entrepreneur Washington Valentine, president of the largest mining company in Honduras, who concurrently held the Puerto Cortés rail and wharf concessions and would lose control of them under the British plan. Valentine therefore sought support from New York banks, and ultimately put forward an alternate proposal to refund the Honduran debt through an American loan.[10]

When the Taft administration took office in March 1909, Second Assistant Secretary of State Alvey Adee, a long-time fixture in the State Department, called Knox's attention to the Honduran situation and suggested that it might offer an opening for a Dominican-style customs agreement. Knox was quick to take up Adee's suggestion. The United States minister to Honduras protested the British debt repayment scheme while Knox successfully brought pressure on London to disown it. With an empty treasury, mounting domestic opposition, and the British demanding repayment, Dávila saw no alternative to Valentine's American-loan scheme. His own negotiators actually suggested a "Santo Domingo-type guarantee" which would ensure United States financial control, apparently hoping that this would also bring State Department support of the president against revolutionary threats. Knox and Huntington-Wilson were delighted, while J. P. Morgan and Company were willing to handle the loan so long as the State Department controlled the collection of customs. In December 1909 the bankers and the Hondurans agreed on a $10 million loan contract, and Knox believed that success in Honduras was very near.[11]

The Morgan contract, however, was conditional on the execution of a treaty between the United States and Honduras granting the specified customs control; the loan agreement would go into effect only when the treaty did so. The provision for a United States–appointed collector of customs aroused strong opposition to Washington's draft treaty in the Honduran congress, leaving the faltering Dávila at a loss as to what to do. Many Hondurans saw the whole scheme as a device to erect a United States protectorate over their country. Negotiations stalled, and Huntington-Wilson fumed at the delay. At Washington's urging, the Hondurans finally signed the treaty in January 1911, but the Honduran congress continued to oppose both the treaty and the loan contract, and would act on neither. Meanwhile the Dávila government fell to its opponents. As if all this were not enough, the treaty met with disfavor even in the United States Senate, where a powerful Progressive bloc was deeply suspicious of the ties between American diplomacy and Wall Street bankers. By 1912 Knox's Honduran scheme was dead, never to be revived, and Honduras continued in its old disorderly ways.[12]

If the attempt to apply dollar diplomacy to Honduras was a fiasco, Haiti was the scene of a distinct success for the Taft-Knox policies. As had been the case in Honduras, Haiti's government attempted in 1910 to overhaul its finances. These had been largely controlled by the Banque Nationale d'Haïti, a French corporation which had just lost its charter as a result of management scandals. As the Banque underwent reorganization, an international rivalry developed; German interests demanded a share in the new Banque, while United States bankers protested their own exclusion. Philander Knox followed these developments closely, and soon intervened diplomatically. In September 1910 he inquired of the Haitian government whether the arrangements under consideration would create a banking monopoly which excluded American commercial banks, and whether they envisaged Banque control over customs. The United States, he implied, would oppose either.[13]

By October, the State Department had developed an impressive slate of objections to the proposed bank and loan contracts in Haiti. Since the customs would be pledged as security for loans, the French government might find it necessary at some point to secure the customs, Adee wrote the United States minister at Port-au-Prince. "The Government of the United States must view with disfavor any contract which would lead to the possible intervention of European powers in political affairs of American republics, including intervention by control of the customs." Adee also objected to several other aspects of the new proposals: the virtually sovereign powers proposed for the Banque, which would function as the national treasury; the inadequate provisions for repayment of foreign debts; the banking monopoly which would be created; and the unfavorable terms provided Haiti, whose new interest-bearing bonds would be discounted to 72 percent of face value. Finally, while the Haitians paid the Banque a percentage on the funds it handled as a service charge, the Banque paid the government no interest whatever for using its money! Adee's critique was prophetic, for the Haitians themselves would subsequently level almost all of his criticisms against the Banque once they had experienced its operations.[14]

As the year ended, however, the State Department reconsidered its opposition to the Haitian Banque schemes in the light of a new development: the French had agreed to admit United States banks into their arrangements. They offered shares in the bank and the refunding loan to the prominent New York banking firm of Speyer and Company, to the National City Bank of New York, and to two German-American banks. Each would get a 5 percent interest in both contracts, while a Berlin bank received a similar share. In January 1911, the State Department dropped its objections, citing "the explanations offered and assurances given by the American banks." The new arrangements were still highly unfavorable to Haiti, but no longer to the United States, which thus cheerfully accepted them.[15]

The American bankers had pushed their way into the Banque Nationale

d'Haïti only with strong diplomatic backing from Washington, and because
the State Department threatened to block any plans which excluded them. The
Haitians understood the significance of this clearly enough. When General
Cincinnatus Leconte became president in August of 1911, he sent a high official to United States Minister Henry W. Furniss to deny reports that he was
partial to the Germans. Furniss relayed a key part of the message to Washington: "General Leconte desired the good will of the American Government
and recognized that Haiti was within its sphere of influence. He was desirous
of being in perfect accord with the United States." Leconte demonstrated that
"perfect accord" by dropping two proposed cabinet appointments when Furniss claimed that the men named were tied to German interests.[16]

Some of the American bankers involved in Haiti had their own ideas of
the significance of Knox's actions. In 1915, the State Department received a
long memorandum from Roger Farnham of the National City Bank, which
argued that the State Department had entered into a tacit understanding with
the bankers in 1910. One part of this supposed understanding held that the
Banque Nationale should assist in developing Haitian-American trade. Beyond
that, Farnham declared, while it was nowhere written, "it never-the-less was
generally understood by the American interests involved that, should the occasion arise, the American interests would receive from their Government such
prompt and full support as the Department might deem necessary in the circumstances." In the years to come, another administration would go far to
validate Farnham's claims.[17]

While Knox and Huntington-Wilson attempted to stabilize the Caribbean
and expand United States influence through the establishment of various economic controls, their policies in Nicaragua went far beyond dollar diplomacy
to encompass armed intervention. Suspending its disapproval of revolutions,
the State Department used all of its influence to ensure the overthrow of President José Santos Zelaya, and then went to progressively greater lengths in
order to quell the disorders resulting from the fall of the dictator. In the end it
resorted to military invasion to achieve its goals.

Nicaragua's strong man since 1893, Zelaya was unpopular in Washington
for a number of reasons. When it had seemed likely that the isthmian canal
would be built in Nicaragua, he had been tough and determined in rejecting
any United States encroachment on his country's sovereignty over the canal
zone. When the United States shifted to the Panamá route in 1903, Zelaya felt
betrayed and concluded that he had little to gain from the United States. Suspicious of foreign influence and overtly anti-Yankee, Zelaya's official *Diario
de Nicaragua* called in May 1909 for an alliance with Japan to check United
States power. On their side, Washington policy makers believed that Zelaya's
long-standing adventurism in Central America was a primary cause of the continuing international tensions there. In the summer of 1909 he was threatening

the Salvadorean coast with his gunboats, while attempting to meddle in presidential elections in Costa Rica. The Nicaraguan president was at the same time seeking a large loan in London, in defiance of Washington's desire that Caribbean governments do any future borrowing in the United States. Furthermore, United States businessmen at Bluefields, the economic center of Nicaragua's Caribbean coast, complained of Zelaya's heavy taxation, while his sale of private monopolies to favored rivals in a variety of economic activities threatened their very existence.[18]

The incoming Taft-Knox administration was not long in showing its own attitude toward the troublesome dictator. During its first months in office the State Department recalled its chargé in Managua, and used diplomatic pressure to attempt to block the sale of Nicaraguan bonds in London, though with little success. This was a mere prelude, however, to its actions when a revolt against Zelaya broke out in Bluefields in October 1909. The leader of the revolt, General Juan J. Estrada, was governor of the Department of Zelaya, which the dictator had named after himself and which included all of eastern Nicaragua. Lightly populated and physically isolated, the so-called Mosquito Coast had enjoyed an economic boom since the 1880s in and about Bluefields, built upon Yankee enterprise in rubber, bananas, and gold. Both its United States businessmen and its Indian and black coastal population resented being ruled from Managua; since Zelaya's effective incorporation of the area in 1894 it had been a hotbed of revolt. General Estrada could count upon solid support from the local population, while being somewhat protected by his distance from the centers of power. He had secretly approached the United States consul at Bluefields in July 1909 to seek advance help and approval for his projected uprising. While the consul was favorably inclined, the State Department made no response to Estrada's feeler, but the ambitious general had done well in collecting funds: $90,000 from Zelaya's bitter rival, President Estrada Cabrera of Guatemala, and probably far more from the American firms in Bluefields. However, Zelaya's later charge that the State Department actively helped to foment the revolt was untrue.[19]

The American colony in Bluefields expected concrete benefits from its investment in Estrada's revolt. As the United States consul there explained, their intent was to separate the Mosquito Coast region into an independent republic with Estrada president. Liberated from Managua's control, the foreign business community expected freedom from taxes, monopolies, and onerous regulations. "Entire population jubilant at the overthrow of the Zelaya control on the coast . . . foreign business interests enthusiastic," the consul reported as the revolt began. Preserving its correct posture, the State Department responded with an order to do nothing which hinted at official recognition of Estrada's regime.[20]

The energetic Zelaya moved at once to crush the threat in the east, sending a military force down the San Juan River from Lake Nicaragua to the coast. His troops met only light resistance from the Estrada camp, but took some prisoners in the skirmishing. Among these were two United States citizens serving Estrada as demolition experts, who were executed by Zelaya's personal order on November 19. Given this excuse to act against Zelaya, Knox promptly dropped his neutrality and held a meeting to consider the options. Huntington-Wilson insisted that Zelaya should not wriggle out of the trap in which he had put himself, and warned against demanding any specific terms of the dictator for fear he might find a way to meet them. The assistant secretary favored the forcible seizure of Corinto and Managua, but was overruled by the others present. For the moment, it was decided, any sanctions would be purely diplomatic.[21]

At this point the Mexican government offered joint action in the Nicaraguan case, as they had in the days of Root and Roosevelt. On bad terms with Guatemala's Estrada Cabrera, the Mexicans were therefore friendly to Zelaya, and sought to preserve his Liberal party's control even if the president himself had to go. Knox and Huntington-Wilson had lost interest in working with Mexico, however, as they found that government's purposes diverging from their own, and they now wanted to crush the entire Liberal apparatus in Nicaragua. Rebuffing the Mexican overture, Knox acted unilaterally instead. On December 1 he handed the Nicaraguan chargé d'affaires his passports, along with an extraordinary note which savagely attacked Zelaya's regime as "a blot upon the history of Nicaragua." Accusing Zelaya of keeping Central America in turmoil, Knox also charged him with brutal repression in his own country, and claimed that "the revolution represents the ideals and the will of a majority of the Nicaraguan people." Demanding reparation for the death of the two American mercenaries, he made it clear that he would hold Zelaya to harsher terms of settlement than he would a victorious Estrada regime.[22]

At the same time that he broke relations with Nicaragua, Knox arranged with the navy for the dispatch of a special Nicaraguan expeditionary force, commanded by Rear Admiral William W. Kimball and composed of a few warships and about a thousand marines. Kimball was ordered not to land any marines without instructions, but to lie off Corinto on the Pacific coast in readiness for action. For a time, it seemed unnecessary that the State Department do anything more. The Estrada forces did well in their own territory, and soon controlled almost the entire eastern district. They also seized the few small armed vessels which the government kept on the east coast, which in a roadless region dependent on water transportation made them safe against attack. Blocked from an early victory and fearing United States armed intervention, Zelaya resigned in December 1909. He chose as his successor José Madríz, a former judge of the Central American court, who was duly elected president by the Nicaraguan congress.[23]

Mexico's President Porfirio Díaz had joined Zelaya's Liberal party supporters in urging the president's resignation and recommending Madríz for the presidency. Díaz and the Liberals hoped that the choice of an able and respected civilian who had not been close to Zelaya would satisfy the United States. The navy's Admiral Kimball thought the choice a good one, and irritated the State Department by his declared preference for Madríz as head of state, as well as his practice of regularly puncturing in his reports the inflated claims of the Estrada camp. Washington nevertheless set its face against Madríz on the ground that the choice of any Liberal as president would merely mean the continuance of the Zelaya group in power, and bring no real improvement. The civil war therefore continued, settling into a stalemate as neither side proved capable of penetrating the other's territory.[24]

In May 1910 the Madríz government broke the deadlock by purchasing and arming a steamer which outgunned Estrada's cockleshells. At once the rebels were vulnerable, and in May a seaborne government force arrived off Bluefields and seized the entrance to its lagoon. Bottled up by the enemy, Estrada's lot seemed hopeless; the Madríz government was formally recognized by Germany, Denmark, Mexico, Cuba, Venezuela, and Panamá, while Great Britain deferred recognition only at the request of the United States.[25]

At this point, the United States Navy took a hand, and quite literally saved the revolution. The gunboat *Paducah* was at Bluefields when the Madríz force arrived, and her commander issued a proclamation forbidding armed conflict in the town on the ground that it would endanger foreign life and property. He refused to allow the government gunboat to bombard Bluefields, and limited occupation of the town to one hundred armed men. To keep the town, Estrada had merely to move all but one hundred of his men inland, where the government troops were unable to reach them. The Madríz commander then seized the customhouse, located several miles from Bluefields where its lagoon connected with the sea. This action threatened Estrada's supplies and revenues, but once more *Paducah* intervened. There must be no interference with free shipping, said a new decree, and the Estrada regime alone had the right to collect customs there. The American position was that both sides were mere factions, for Madríz was unrecognized, and that Estrada had effective control of the town.[26]

Frustrated, the Madríz force sailed away, and the revolutionaries found new hope. Secure in their sanctuary, they could hold out indefinitely, while the failure to take Bluefields left the Madríz regime discredited. Meanwhile fresh uprisings surfaced in the population centers of western Nicaragua, too, and by late summer the position of the Madríz government was hopeless. Madríz resigned on August 20, 1910, and a week later Estrada entered the capital in triumph.[27]

Expecting quick recognition from Washington, the provisional president soon learned that he would receive it only at a price. The State Department cabled him the text of a message which he was to return to them over his own name. The message promised national elections in six months, asked the State Department to help arrange an American loan, and offered to secure the loan with a portion of the customs receipts. The collection of the customs, in turn, would be "conducted in such manner as may be agreed upon between Nicaragua and the United States." It was clear that, having gotten rid of Zelaya, the State Department meant to impose Dominican-style customs controls on Nicaragua in the belief that they would bring political stability. Estrada was reluctant to accept such controls, but after days of stalling he signed and returned the State Department's text.[28]

The State Department in turn sent Thomas C. Dawson, who had negotiated the Dominican customs agreement in 1905 and was currently minister to Panamá. Arriving in Managua in mid-October 1910, Dawson learned that the Zelaya Liberals were the majority party in Nicaragua, while Estrada's supporters were already breaking into factions. A presidential election, as at first planned, now seemed unprofitable; Estrada was popularly regarded as a renegade Liberal while his Conservative generals lacked any broad support. Even so, two of the generals, Luis Mena and Emiliano Chamorro, had become rivals for the presidency. To finesse the situation, Dawson proposed a constituent assembly which could rewrite the electoral laws and, at the same time, name Estrada as constitutional president for a two-year term. Also, all of the revolutionary leaders must promise to unite on a Conservative presidential candidate when Estrada's term ended. Given a pledge that Estrada would not succeed himself, the two rivals agreed on Dawson's program, each confident that he would take power in two years. As vice-president, Dawson selected Adolfo Díaz, a little-known Conservative who had long been employed by an American mining company in the Bluefields district and who had channeled large amounts of American money into the Estrada movement. The so-called Dawson agreements also provided for an American loan secured by customs receipts, and guaranteed foreign business interests against government-granted monopolies, excessive taxation, and other abuses of the Zelaya era. By November 1910, the agreements had received the approval of all the revolutionary leaders, while the constituent assembly dutifully carried out its work in December.[29]

The Estrada government was unpopular from the first in Nicaragua, the more so because most Nicaraguans resented the United States influence which Estrada brought with him to Managua. Estrada himself soon fell prey to his Conservative rivals. General Chamorro quickly gained control of the constituent assembly, while as minister of war, Luis Mena controlled the army. Estrada dissolved the assembly to check Chamorro, but even the new United States minister failed to sustain him when he attempted to arrest Mena. Estrada was soon ousted by the army commanders, and Vice-President Adolfo Díaz took over the presidency in May 1911. While Díaz had the support of the State Department, as a Conservative he lacked appeal to the country's Liberal majority, while facing the same Conservative rivals who had brought down Estrada. He was a weak reed, and it was only after long indecision that Washington decided to maintain him in power in the face of a challenge from Mena.[30]

Under Díaz, the Nicaraguan government went ahead with the projected financial negotiations. In June 1911, it signed the Knox-Castrillo Treaty with the United States providing for refunding the national debt through a loan secured by customs revenues. The collector general of customs would be chosen from a list of nominees prepared by the bankers handling the loan and approved by the president of the United States, an arrangement similar to that proposed for Honduras. The newly elected Nicaraguan national assembly approved this treaty, but the United States Senate failed to act upon it even though President Taft sent a special message urging ratification. As in the Honduran case, Progressive senators deeply distrusted Wall Street's role in dollar diplomacy, and Knox, though himself a former senator, was a chilly and ineffective lobbyist with that body.[31]

While New York bankers had contracted for $15 million Nicaraguan loan, the contracts were contingent on the Senate's approval of the Knox-Castrillo Treaty. This was not forthcoming, yet the Nicaraguans still needed money. Díaz and his cronies had drained the treasury by paying themselves and their relatives exaggerated claims for damages by the Zelaya regime. The bankers therefore agreed to a smaller short-term loan of $1.5 million, secured by the same customs arrangements as would have obtained under the treaty. The bankers would also establish a Nicaraguan national bank and carry out currency reforms, for the Díaz regime maintained itself by printing floods of depreciated paper money. Secretary Knox agreed to all this while contending that the State Department promised no special protection to the bankers. This time it was the Nicaraguan assembly which objected. Luis Mena's supporters in that body, at that time a majority, refused to approve the loan contract unless Mena was assured of the presidency. In October 1911 the assembly solemnly elected Mena president, even though his term would not begin for fifteen months, and the loan contract went through.[32]

Even this arrangement did not solve the country's financial problems, however, for government revenues continued to fall below expenditures. After much negotiation, the New York bankers agreed to advance another $750,000, but only with stringent conditions. The government must pay no more claims without the approval of a mixed Nicaraguan-American claims commission, in which the American members made up a majority. The government must give the bankers a lien, with an option to buy, on 51 percent of the stock of the national railroad. And the bankers must at once be given the actual management of the railroad, retaining it until all of their loans were repaid. Since the new national bank was already in the New Yorkers' hands, and their agents were collecting the customs, Nicaraguans understandably feared that their government and its chief assets had been sold out to Wall Street.[33]

By early 1912 Díaz feared for his future so seriously that he suggested a treaty resembling the Platt Amendment, in which the United States would have the right to intervene in Nicaragua's internal affairs to restore peace and order. Knox had no objection, but in view of the Senate's opposition to his earlier treaties he was forced to put the idea aside. Not long afterward, in March 1912, the secretary of state visited Nicaragua in the course of a Caribbean tour. Díaz received him fulsomely, announcing that Nicaragua could find peace and justice only with Washington's help. Díaz's countrymen were less enthusiastic; Knox's visit to the national assembly was notable for the thinly veiled hostility of many members and the assembly president's blunt expression of anti-American suspicions. If the secretary of state had hoped to make the country's quarreling leaders come together, his visit was a clear failure.[34]

Events moved steadily downward after the Knox visit. By May, rumors were flying of a Liberal uprising, while Mena's attitude toward Díaz became openly threatening. Chamorro joined forces with Díaz to block his rival's ambitions, securing the election of a Chamorrista as assembly president. With his claim to the presidency in jeopardy, Mena wooed the Liberal camp and picked up Zelayista support. The minister of war was known to be stockpiling arms and ammunition. Fearing that Mena would seize the chief government fortress in the capital, Díaz attempted to surround and arrest him late in July, but Mena escaped to launch a revolution. At the beginning of August, Mena's own forces were augmented by armed units of the resurgent Liberals, and the Díaz government was hard pressed. The rebels surrounded Managua and bombarded it for four days, trying twice to take the city by storm. The defenders held, commanded by General Chamorro, but an estimated eight hundred to a thousand people lost their lives in the fighting, including well over one hundred civilian victims of the rebel shelling. Meanwhile, a government force of several hundred men was annihilated in Leon, the traditional Liberal stronghold.[35]

At the beginning of the fighting, Díaz requested United States troops on the ground that he was unable to protect foreign life and property. One hundred sailors soon arrived at the capital, and in mid-August, following the rebel assaults on Managua, three hundred and fifty United States Marines came to join them. The United States minister, who had by now denounced Mena and demanded his surrender, asked for another two thousand troops at once, and a rapid buildup ensued. Knox was absent from Washington, but Huntington-Wilson appealed to President Taft for strong action against the rebels: "To sit by and see them triumph," he declared, would "be a blow to our prestige in all the neighboring republics." Taft ultimately responded with a statement of support for Nicaragua's constituted government; the United States had a "moral mandate" to use its power to restore order, he said, under the terms of the Washington Conventions of 1907 and Díaz's request for United States troops.[36]

Meanwhile Admiral William H. Southerland, commander in chief of the Pacific Fleet, had taken charge of United States forces in Nicaragua. Southerland's plan was relatively simple: to occupy the main railroad line that connected the country's principal cities from Corinto on the west coast to Granada on Lake Nicaragua. Deprived of the railroad, he believed, the rebels could not move and supply their armies. The marines began to execute this plan on September 19, but the State Department rebelled when it found Southerland acting as a neutral intervener and refusing the use of the railroad to both sides equally. Huntington-Wilson's new appeal to Taft saw this overruled, and the Mena revolution began to come apart. Mena himself fell seriously ill, while the evident intention of the United States to defend the government by force demoralized his followers. Mena surrendered on September 24, leaving only a small Liberal army in the field.[37]

Up to then, Southerland had aimed to defeat the revolution without putting his forces into actual combat, by seizing key points and controlling the national railroad. In this he had succeeded; the revolt was substantially beaten when Mena gave up. But when the remaining Liberal force of several hundred men seized what was considered an impregnable position above Masaya, the admiral was compelled to act. The rebel position dominated the railroad line, halting traffic, while the several thousand government troops at hand were disinclined to storm the hill. Obeying direct orders from Washington, Southerland sent in the marines, who drove off the rebels in a dawn attack. After this victory, and the marines' capture of Leon, the revolt ended on October 8, 1912.[38]

The war had cost more than two thousand lives, and its political results were not popular in Nicaragua. The British consul general summed it up as follows: "A barbarous and futile combat, it has established no principle, pacified none of the discordant political elements of the country, and has left Nicaragua morally and financially weakened." It also left the United States dominant in Nicaragua. A total of 2,350 United States sailors and marines had gone ashore during the revolt, at that time the largest American armed force ever to land on foreign soil in peacetime. Although they were gone again by the end of autumn, except for a symbolic legation guard of 100 marines, Nicaraguans knew that the Yankees could quickly come again. Washington had acted to remove Zelaya, Madríz, and Mena in turn from the political scene, while Díaz retained power only through United States support. Americans controlled the country's government finances, its railroad system, and the economy of the east coast. Even without ratification of the Knox-Castrillo Treaty, Nicaragua had become a protectorate of the United States.[39]

As these events ran their course in the summer and fall of 1912, a new crisis arose elsewhere in the Caribbean. The Taft administration's policies in Central America had been deeply influenced by the example of the Roosevelt administration's actions in the Dominican Republic. To the distress of the State Department, those policies were endangered by a Dominican political breakdown during the last year of the Taft-Knox regime. Washington's attempts to check the drift toward anarchy brought the United States further into the internal affairs of the Dominican Republic, and prepared the way for even more drastic measures under President Woodrow Wilson.

The Morales government in Santo Domingo had fallen at the end of 1905. The new president, Ramón Cáceres, quickly restored order, and went on to rule through six years of comparative stability. The popular Cáceres faced the usual revolts, but was easily able to master them. His unpopular but able minister of finance, Federico Velásquez, brought the government needed administrative and financial skills. This combination of Cáceres' charisma and Velásquez' competence created a regime of unusual strength, further bolstered by the financial improvement deriving from the 1905 customs arrangement with the United States. By 1911, however, the very strength of these leaders had become their downfall. Since Cáceres could not be overthrown, some of his rivals concluded, then he must be assassinated. Indifferent to personal danger, Cáceres took no precautions against attack, and a band of plotters had no difficulty in fatally shooting him on November 19, 1911.[40]

Colonel Alfredo Victoria commanded the army troops in the capital at the time of Cáceres' death. It was he who took charge and restored order, caught and killed the principal assassin, and emerged in a dominant position over the government. The youthful colonel had not yet reached thirty-five, the minimum age required to be president, so he forced the congress to elect his uncle, Eladio Victoria, to that post as provisional president. Shortly thereafter the elder Victoria became president for a full term through a fraudulent election, while Alfredo Victoria made himself minister of war and of the interior and placed his brother in command of the army. Dominating his ineffectual uncle, the younger Victoria became the real ruler of the Dominican Republic.[41]

Within a few months, rival leaders rose in revolt all over the country, which fell into a state of continuing strife. Victoria commanded little popular support, but for a time benefited from Cáceres' reorganization of the army, which alone kept him in power. However, the widespread fighting interfered with the collection of customs and forced the abandonment of some customhouses on the Haitian frontier. At the same time, the costs of maintaining the government by force soon unbalanced the budget and drained the treasury. In less than a year, all of the debt repayment achieved since 1905 was wiped out by fresh deficits. The country had lost both political and financial stability, while the precious customs arrangements were in jeopardy. By September 1912, the United States minister thought the situation hopeless without American intervention to install a new government.[42]

September 1912 was the very month during which American marines intervened in Nicaragua to crush the Mena revolution. It was awkward to have to consider another Caribbean emergency at the same time, but the State Department, like its minister in Santo Domingo, felt that Dominican affairs were rapidly nearing a crisis. In Knox's absence, it again fell to Huntington-Wilson to alert the president, which he did on September 19. A return to constant revolutions, oppression, corruption, and fiscal collapse in the Dominican Republic, he wrote Taft, would discredit the entire American policy there: ". . . such an eventuality, involving also a disastrous set-back to the somewhat similar policy the administration has pursued in Nicaragua and Honduras, would, indeed, be a very severe blow to American diplomacy." The current situation was a difficult one; the Victoria regime was an unattractive and unpopular despotism, but the revolutionists were little better, and at any rate revolution was to be discouraged. Huntington-Wilson therefore advanced a number of specific recommendations for United States actions.

Chief among the assistant secretary's suggestions was the ouster of Alfredo Victoria, the real power in the government. His uncle might be allowed to finish his term as president, but he must release political prisoners, give amnesty to any rebels who surrendered, cooperate closely with the customs administration and the United States minister, and reform his government's worst abuses. Should the Victorias refuse these terms, the United States must decide whether to "sit by and see its whole Dominican policy fail and carry with its failure the wreck of the broad policy pursued in Central America," or to enforce its demands through sanctions short of war. The most promising of the latter would be to withhold customs receipts from the government, which would ensure its fall. Finally, Huntington-Wilson urged that William T. S. Doyle, chief of the State Department's Latin American Division, should be sent to Santo Domingo to urge these demands and back up the American minister there.[43]

With Taft's approval, not one but two special commissioners went to Santo Domingo: Doyle and Brigadier General Frank McIntyre, chief of the War Department's Bureau of Insular Affairs. The two envoys arrived at the Dominican capital aboard a naval vessel on October 2, accompanied by 750 marines to add weight to their "suggestions." After over two weeks of intense talks, the Victorias accepted Washington's demands. The political situation failed to improve, however, while the commissioners complained that the elder Victoria was not meeting their conditions in good faith. They concluded that the president would have to go, an object accomplished by telling him that his government would get no customs receipts after November 20. He resigned within a week, and Knox's State Department had collected another political scalp.[44]

Victoria's resignation enabled the Americans to secure a general truce among the rival revolutionary leaders, who feared a United States military occupation. The two American commissioners sought a nonpartisan provisional president acceptable to all, who would serve for two years and then preside over elections for a constitutional successor. Their choice fell upon Adolfo Nouel, the archbishop of Santo Domingo, whose kindliness and charm had made him widely popular. The Dominican congress confirmed this choice in December, and Nouel took office amid relative calm.[45]

His term was short-lived, as the new president showed himself unequal to his task. The archbishop had never wanted the presidency, and had accepted it only to prevent an American occupation. He lacked firmness and political judgment, but was at once buffeted by conflicting demands from rival leaders. By trying to satisfy everyone he alienated all, and two weeks after taking office he announced that he would resign. Temporarily dissuaded by the American minister, he continued to seek escape in spite of a personal appeal from President Taft to remain in office. In January 1913, Nouel pleaded with the Americans to support him in calling for early elections to choose a successor. Knox wished a general electoral reform first, however, and pressed the archbishop to serve his full two years. Since Nouel was clearly unwilling to do so, was an ineffective leader, and faced the imminent prospect of civil war, Knox's insistence showed an unintelligent rigidity on his part. It made no difference; Nouel fled the capital and resigned to take ship for Europe in March, as the Taft administration left office.[46]

The Taft-Knox record in the Caribbean had not been a happy one. In January 1912, shortly after the murder of President Cáceres in the Dominican Republic, Philander Knox made a major speech in New York to appeal for support of his Honduran and Nicaraguan treaties. "If these conventions are put into operation," he declared,

what has happened in the Dominican Republic will be repeated in the Republics of Nicaragua and Honduras, which are the key to the peace of the whole of Central America, and within a few years the revolutions which keep these countries in a state of constant unrest will be eliminated; the neutrality of Honduras and Nicaragua in Central American affairs will become an accomplished fact; and the peace of the rest of Central America will be immensely strengthened.[47]

A year later, such optimistic prophecies were impossible. Neither the Honduran nor the Nicaraguan treaty had been approved by the Senate; the United States had mounted an armed invasion of Nicaragua to impose peace; and the Dominican model had fallen into such straits that a military occupation had been only narrowly averted there. The illusion that stability could be imposed on the Caribbean through financial controls alone had been shattered, and the next administration would take the more readily to military intervention as a result.

Chapter 10

---·◦◦◦·---

Ideology, Dollars, and Realpolitik

The replacement of William Howard Taft in the presidency by Woodrow Wilson promised major changes in the Caribbean policy of the United States. Wilson represented the Progressive wing of the Democratic party, and Progressives had been affronted by dollar diplomacy with its close working relationship between the State Department and the Wall Street banking fraternity. Wilson's new secretary of state, William Jennings Bryan, was one of the founders of the Progressive movement in America. Three times the Democratic nominee for president, he had run in 1896 on a sweeping platform of domestic reform, while in the 1900 campaign he had also denounced imperialist expansion. As candidate and president, Wilson himself spoke of the nation's duties to its neighbors to the south in altruistic tones far different from those used by Knox or Huntington-Wilson. Both Wilson and Bryan disapproved of the policies of their predecessors, and meant to take new directions in foreign policy.

It is therefore significant that the new administration's first formal pronouncement on Caribbean policy stressed continuity as well as change. During the presidential campaign, the State Department had come to fear that the defeat of the hard-handed Taft-Knox regime coupled with Wilson's antiimperialist rhetoric might encourage revolutionaries throughout the Caribbean who had previously been held in check by the fear of United States reprisals against disturbers of the peace. Huntington-Wilson was in panic, and used an intermediary to ask that Wilson publicly let it be known that he too would act in favor of stability. Wilson accordingly released a statement to the press a week after his inauguration. Declaring that his government desired friendly cooperation with the other nations of the hemisphere, he warned that such cooperation was possible only with states whose governments were characterized by freedom, justice, and orderly constitutional processes. "We can have no sympathy with those who seek to seize the power of government to advance their own personal interests or ambition," Wilson said. "As friends, therefore, we shall prefer those who act in the interests of peace and honor, who protect private rights and respect the restraints of constitutional provision." The statement reflected the now-entrenched opposition of the United States to revolutions in the Caribbean, while also expressing the sense of ideological mission which Wilson brought to his foreign policies. It therefore looked both backward and forward, blending the past with the present.[1]

Some months later, in October 1913, Wilson made a more significant commentary on Caribbean policy. In a major speech at Mobile, Alabama, he promised to help emancipate Latin America from the yoke of foreign economic exploitation. Forced by their poverty and underdevelopment to grant concessions to foreign capitalists, he said, the region's smaller and poorer states had seen alien interests come to dominate their internal affairs.

They have had harder bargains driven with them in the matter of loans than any other peoples in the world. Interest has been exacted of them that was not exacted of anybody else, because the risk was said to be greater; and then securities were taken that destroyed the risk—an admirable arrangement for those who were forcing the terms!

Even so, the peoples so burdened had shown qualities of dignity, courage, and self-respect which deserved every encouragement. Now their rescue was at hand, supported by the future policies of the United States: "We must prove ourselves their friends and champions, upon terms of equality and honor," for "you cannot be friends upon any other terms than upon the terms of equality." In a slap at Taft's dollar diplomacy, Wilson noted that "it is a very perilous thing to determine the foreign policy of a nation in the terms of material interest. It is not only unfair to those with whom you are dealing, but it is degrading as regards your own actions."[2]

This statement, together with that issued in March, summed up the initial aspirations of Wilson and Bryan in the Caribbean. The purpose of United States policies there, they suggested, should be to promote constitutional democracy while seeking to dismantle the accumulated special privileges of foreign enterprises. The United States should act in a spirit of altruism, treating the Caribbean states as equals and subordinating its own material interests to the region's needs. Such an approach would indeed have meant a major shift from that of the previous administration, but it was to prove an inaccurate and incomplete forecast of the Wilson-Bryan Caribbean policies.

The fact was that Wilson and Bryan had developed their original concepts in something like a vacuum. Wilson had no experience or expertise in international relations and knew nothing about Latin America. He was fully aware of this; in an oft-quoted statement, he told a friend shortly before his inauguration that "it would be the irony of fate if my administration had to deal chiefly with foreign affairs." As secretary of state, Bryan was only slightly less unprepared. He had, it is true, developed an interest in foreign policy as a leading antiimperialist, and had monitored major American diplomatic developments since 1898. He had also traveled a good deal, and even become interested in Latin America, visiting both Cuba and Mexico three times before 1913. In 1910 he had spent three months on a long journey through the Caribbean and South America, and he had made several short vacation trips to Jamaica and Puerto Rico. Yet Bryan, too, lacked diplomatic experience and firsthand knowledge of the direction of foreign affairs. Like Wilson an idealist, he hoped to use his new position to promote peace, further the spread of democracy, and make the international behavior of the United States a model for the rest of the world to emulate.[3]

Like every new administration, however, Wilson's soon found itself buffeted by unexpected events, hobbled by previous commitments, and constrained by perceived national interests in ways unanticipated by its leaders. And more than most new leaders, Wilson and Bryan had failed to foresee that there would necessarily be tensions between some of their own competing goals. Nor did they reject every tenet of their predecessors, despite their "new era" rhetoric. It is notable, for example, that Woodrow Wilson believed as firmly as Knox and Taft in the need to cultivate export markets in order to sustain domestic employment and prosperity. During the 1912 campaign, he declared that "our domestic markets no longer suffice. We need foreign markets." Like Taft and Knox, he expected the Panama Canal to create a boom in Latin American markets, and intended that the United States reap the benefits. As he told a New York audience, "America is . . . producing a great deal more than there is a domestic market for, and . . . if she doesn't get bigger foreign markets she will burst her jacket."[4]

Wilson's interest in foreign markets was not limited to campaign speeches, for his administration soon took steps to expand United States foreign trade, particularly with Latin America. Secretary of Commerce William C. Redfield, a former congressman from New York and past president of the American Manufacturers' Export Association, was behind many of these. In numerous speeches to business groups he promised government support in seeking markets abroad. More concretely, Redfield created a system of overseas commercial attachés to drum up trade, expanded and reorganized the Bureau of Foreign and Domestic Commerce, and worked closely with the newly formed National Foreign Trade Council when the latter was created by private business concerns in 1914.[5]

In 1913, half of all United States foreign investments were in Latin America,

Woodrow Wilson. Courtesy of the State Historical Society of Wisconsin

while in that same year the region bought $135 million worth of American manufactured goods. While many United States products sold well in the Caribbean region, they faced strong British and German competition. Since the United States was only one of several leading suppliers, but by far the leading buyer of Caribbean products, it had a regional net trade deficit which reached $42 million in 1912. United States exporters to Latin America were handicapped by the financial dominance there of Great Britain, and to a lesser extent Germany; branch banks owned in these two countries provided much of the region's credit, and used their considerable influence to direct trade toward their homelands. United States law, on the other hand, had long forbidden foreign branch banking by American firms. In an attempt to promote American banking competition in the hemisphere, the Federal Reserve Act of 1913 included provisions which legalized foreign branch banking and allowed national banks to deal in foreign exchange instruments. In 1914 the National City Bank of New York became the first to apply for a charter to open foreign branches, and by 1917 it had opened five of them in the Caribbean region alone. As a result of such actions the dollar joined the pound and the mark as an exchange medium, threatening Anglo-German banking hegemony.[6]

The onset of the First World War in August 1914 gravely disrupted international trade and credit, especially in economically dependent regions like Latin America. European exports, credit, international investment, and shipping suddenly shrank or dried up entirely. The British Navy barred Germany from an area where she had been a major supplier, while British factories were diverted to war production. Latin America faced economic chaos, and required a rapid reorientation of her trade patterns. Among the first to see the advantages which the new situation offered the United States was William Gibbs McAdoo, secretary of the treasury and son-in-law of the president. McAdoo intended that United States manufacturers, investors, bankers, and shippers move into the vacuum left by the departing British and Germans. In 1915 he won the president's support for a Pan-American Financial Conference, held in Washington from May 24 to 29 and funded by a congressional appropriation of $50,000.[7]

The chief goal of the conference was to offer United States commercial credit and merchant shipping to the eighteen Latin American countries represented there. Redfield strongly supported McAdoo's conference plans, while Wilson and Bryan joined McAdoo and Redfield in addressing the nearly two hundred delegates who attended. These Latin American representatives welcomed the proffered new connections, and agreed to establish an international commission to expedite hemispheric trade. It was owing to the wartime situation that United States trade with Latin America boomed, but the government actively attempted to aid that boom. The results were indisputable. In the Caribbean region, United States trade increased fourfold between 1912 and 1921 and left the Americans far ahead of their competitors in the postwar period.[8]

While the Wilson administration was actively concerned for the economic interests of the United States, both before and during the war, its leaders saw it as taking a course basically different from that of Republican dollar diplomacy. They viewed the latter as exploitative and selfish, while their own measures represented to them an enlightened self-interest which benefited all concerned. It was Bryan who most directly attempted to formulate a nonexploitative fi-

William Jennings Bryan. Courtesy of the State Historical Society of Wisconsin

nancial policy for the Caribbean, starting in the summer of 1913. His bold proposal, intended originally for Nicaragua but later broadened to include the entire region, was that the United States government lend its own treasury funds at low interest to Caribbean governments.

Bryan's plan, urged privately on Wilson, called for the Treasury Department to issue special government bonds at 3 percent and lend the funds thus obtained to Latin American governments at 4.5 percent, using the profits to help retire the loans. Such a scheme would wholly eliminate the need for private bankers and their exactions, ensure the Latin American regimes dependable credit at the lowest rates of interest, and maximize United States influence. It would make possible, Bryan thought, the economic development of the region without the too customary parasitism of usurious demands from foreign lenders and special concessions to foreign investors. The secretary of state raised his scheme several times in private correspondence with the president, naming Nicaragua, Ecuador, Panamá, and finally all of Central America as suggested beneficiaries. At last, in March 1914, Wilson returned a final negative. The plan, he wrote Bryan, would "strike the whole country . . . as a novel and radical proposal," and complicate the president's already crowded legislative agenda. Kendrick Clements has suggested that Wilson may also have been concerned about the problem of defaults on the loans, given the long regional record of governments unable to pay their obligations. In such a case the United States government would be forced to choose between losing its money or intervening to ensure repayment.[9]

While the president rejected Bryan's idea of direct government loans to Caribbean countries, he quickly became concerned with the international risks stemming from Caribbean government borrowing. Bryan found Wilson more receptive when he warned in 1913 that the real independence of the southern republics was

> just as much menaced today by foreign financial interests as it was a century ago by the political aspirations of foreign governments. . . . When a local despot is held in authority by powerful financial interests, and is furnished money for the employment of soldiers, the people are as helpless as if a foreign army had landed on their shores.

While Bryan was referring to the case of Mexico, the Wilson administration soon came to see European financial controls as the most threatening avenue for general violations of the Monroe Doctrine.[10]

The fullest statement of this concern came in a long State Department memorandum to the president in November 1915. A covering letter from Robert Lansing, Bryan's successor as secretary of state, noted that perceived threats to the Monroe Doctrine had long been confined to the occupation of territory by European states through conquest or cession. This perception, however, had become too narrow. "Recently the financing of revolutions and corruption of governments by European capitalists have frequently thrown the control of these governments into the hands of a European power," Lansing asserted. Such financially based control could be as great a menace to United States security as more overt forms. To avoid it, the United States might have to intervene "to establish a stable and honest government and to prevent the revenues of the republic from becoming the prize of revolution and of the foreigners who finance it."[11]

The accompanying memorandum delved more deeply into the issues which

Lansing had raised. Preventive intervention by the United States to enforce the Monroe Doctrine, it said, "amounts to an assertion of the primacy of the United States in the Western Hemisphere." Such primacy necessarily conflicted with the principle of the equality of nations, a principle central to widespread recent talk about Pan-Americanism. It must be recognized, therefore, that the Monroe Doctrine was incompatible with Pan-Americanism and must prevail over it. The doctrine was "founded . . . upon a fact, namely, the superior power of the United States to compel submission to its will whenever conditions arise involving European control over American territory." The United States defended its hemisphere from European penetration primarily to serve its own interests: "The integrity of other American nations is an incident, not an end." This might seem a selfish view of the doctrine, but "to assert it for a nobler purpose is to proclaim a new doctrine." Such gritty language was far more characteristic of Lansing than of Wilson or Bryan, but the paper's no-nonsense conclusions summarized current State Department thinking. If they contradicted Wilson's 1913 statement that "you cannot be friends upon any other terms than upon the terms of equality," the president does not seem to have raised the issue.[12]

The Wilson administration's Caribbean policies developed continuity with the past as a result of its desire to increase American export markets in Latin America, and its fear that European financial influence in the Caribbean would end in actual control of some of the more vulnerable countries there. To these forces for continuity were added two developments which bore heavily on Wilson's policy perceptions: the Mexican Revolution and the outbreak of the First World War in Europe.

The Mexican Revolution transformed a situation, which had come to be taken for granted in the United States, of stability and booming foreign investment south of the Rio Grande. Longtime President Porfirio Díaz had capped the Mexican volcano since 1876, while his generosity to capitalists was proverbial. By 1913, United States investment in Mexico had reached a billion dollars; concentrated largely in the north, it had brought about major developments in cattle ranching, mining, railroad construction, and most recently oil wells. Tens of thousands of United States citizens lived south of the border, while Mexican-American trade totaled over two hundred and fifty million dollars per year. Root and Roosevelt had sought to use Mexico's stability and ties with the United States as a basis for cooperation in their Central American policies and as an example to inspire Caribbean leaders. By 1911 that opportunity had ended, as Mexico fell into disorder.[13]

In May 1911 the eighty-year-old Díaz went into exile, overthrown by a diverse coalition of reformers, would-be successors, and regional bosses. The mild-mannered Francisco I. Madero, who won the presidency in a rare honest election, had been an early spokesman of the revolutionary movement, but it soon passed him by. Radical reformers like Emiliano Zapata called for land for the peasants, counterrevolutionary plotters attempted to restore the Díaz imperium, and Mexicans fell into quarreling factions. In February 1913 Madero's ablest general, Victoriano Huerta, betrayed him to his enemies and seized the presidency for himself. Both Madero and his vice-president were promptly murdered by their guards, while Huerta ruled as a military strong man. But the forcas now unleashed were not so easily bridled; much of the coalition which had brought down Díaz re-formed to oppose Huerta, and Mexico was swept by a complex military struggle which would rage over the entire land and last for years.[14]

The new Wilson administration had therefore to deal with cataclysmic events in a country with which the United States shared a long common border and in which it had invested impressive amounts of its money and enterprise. The inevitable problems of applying the neutrality laws to the Mexican conflict, of threats to foreign life and property, and of disruption of economic activities of all sorts in Mexico required that Washington monitor and respond to the successive phases of the Mexican drama. In addition, Wilson was outraged that what he saw as the birth of Mexican democracy under Madero should be brutally suppressed by a counterrevolutionary army boss. He was shocked at the murder of Madero, for which he held Huerta directly responsible, and angry that United States Ambassador Henry Lane Wilson had consistently opposed Madero while apparently aiding Huerta's plot to overthrow him. And finally, both president and State Department worried that the destruction of order and stability in the region's largest Latin American state might promote instability in nearby countries.[15]

In the summer of 1913, Wilson and Bryan asked the opposing Mexican leaders to agree to a truce, hold early and free elections, and thus choose a democratic successor to Huerta, who was expected voluntarily to give up the presidency. When this starry-eyed scheme met the inevitable rejection, the administration moved steadily into the Mexican morass, determined to oust the hated Huerta. By the spring of 1914 the United States government had espoused the cause of Huerta's enemies and sent troops to capture Veracruz, Mexico's chief seaport, in retaliation for fancied insults from Huerta. The Mexican president fell in July, and the Wilson policies seemed successful until the victorious anti-Huerta coalition began to war with itself. In 1915 the fiercest fighting so far saw the forces of Venustiano Carranza ultimately smash those of Francisco ("Pancho") Villa. The latter, enraged at Wilson's recognition of Carranza as president, murdered United States citizens and even attacked the border town of Columbus, New Mexico, arousing a sensation in the United States. In 1916, therefore, Wilson ordered thousands of army troops across the border under General John J. Pershing, the second armed invasion of Mexico by the United States in two years.[16]

For the entire four years of his first term as president, Woodrow Wilson was forced to spend endless hours wrestling with Mexican problems. At times he took the United States perilously close to the brink of war with its neighbor, while undeclared limited war characterized his more radical measures. The president often seemed to sympathize with the aspirations of Mexico's reformers, but much of the time he was merely frustrated by the intractable challenges of revolutionary violence. Indisputably, however, Wilson and his policy makers took from the Mexican revolution a new urgency in their quest for stability in the Caribbean proper. They were determined that the fires which wasted Mexico must not be lighted in Central America and the islands of the Caribbean.

Visiting British diplomat Sir William Tyrell discussed these matters personally with Wilson late in 1913. As he reported to London, the president was "very anxious" to ensure that the neighboring republics "should have fairly decent rulers and that men like Castro [the former president of Venezuela] and Huerta should be barred. With this object in view, the President made up his mind to teach these countries a lesson by insisting on the removal of Huerta. . . ." Wilson was "under no illusion with regard to the capacity of Mexicans for maladministration," but felt that "Huerta . . . exceeded the limit of what is permissible." Any attempt to implement such a policy, Tyrell mused, must lead to a de facto United States protectorate over the entire region, but he thought that Wilson failed to realize it.[17]

Six months later, British Ambassador Cecil Arthur Spring Rice interpreted Wilson's Veracruz intervention for the Foreign Office. As he noted, the president's Mexican policy now went well beyond the ouster of Huerta; Wilson was determined that "the party of oppression should be eliminated and the party of freedom and emancipation take its place." According to Wilson's own public statements, it was the duty of the United States to bring internal purification to its neighbor. "Since the days of the Holy Alliance it is doubtful that any government has thus declared its mission to reform the moral shortcomings of foreign nations, and this declaration is likely to cause some anxiety among the nations of this continent," Spring Rice wrote. As both Englishmen had noted, the civil war in Mexico had engaged the ideologue in Wilson, and led him to marry the search for stability to a quest for democratic reform.[18]

A second major influence on Wilsonian Caribbean policy was the outbreak of war in Europe in August 1914. For the first few months Americans, like Europeans, expected the war to be short, but by 1915 it was becoming clear that the world faced the bloodiest, most destructive conflict in history, and that the outcome would alter the global balance of power. In commonsense terms, the fact that every great power but the United States was involved in the struggle by mid-1915 meant that there could be no outside threat to the western hemisphere while the war lasted. It should particularly have meant that the perennial "German threat" was at least temporarily shelved. In fact, however, the pervasive presence of great-power conflict sharpened American security fears, and even strengthened apprehensions about German ambitions in the Caribbean.

The issue of Germany's unlimited submarine warfare against merchant ships came to the fore in the United States when the British liner *Lusitania* sank in May 1915, and 1,200 lives were lost. Wilson and his advisers grappled with the submarine problem for the next two years, and it was one of the leading factors drawing the United States into war with Germany in 1917. German U-boat warfare led many Americans to regard Germany once more as a sinister threat to hemispheric security. A recurrent theme was that the Germans might seize Caribbean bases for their submarines, a fear which led the navy in 1916 to revive its own requests for a base at Samaná Bay in the Dominican Republic. Robert Lansing, then counselor of the State Department, had raised such fears as early as 1914, and they remained strong throughout the war. Early in 1917 Wilson recorded his uncertainty as to whether Cuba should follow the United States lead and break relations with Germany; he feared that Germany might use the action as an excuse to attack Cuba or seize a submarine base there. With the German army locked in a death struggle in Europe and her navy sealed off from the Atlantic by a British blockade, one wonders how Berlin could possibly have mounted military operations in the Caribbean, even if the Germans had been unconcerned about driving the United States into the coalition against her. Nevertheless, the American fears were unquestionably genuine, if somewhat irrational.[19]

A further manifestation of Washington's fears of Germany was a final, and successful, attempt to purchase the Danish West Indies, or Virgin Islands. An 1867 purchase treaty had failed to secure the approval of the United States Senate. A similar treaty in 1902 had been rejected by the Danish parliament, an action which many Americans attributed to German influence. In 1915 the State Department resumed negotiations for the purchase of the islands. The United States did not need them for naval bases; the only motive for acquiring them was to keep them out of German hands. Secretary of State Lansing believed that if Germany were successful in the war, it would follow an expansionist policy, and might well absorb its small neighbor to the north. When the Danish minister rather bluntly asked if the United States meant to seize the islands even without a purchase treaty, Lansing replied that this was probable if Germany annexed Denmark, or threatened to acquire her Caribbean colony in any other way. Making the best of the situation, the Danes asked $30 million for the three small islands, and ultimately received $25 million in a 1916 purchase treaty which, this time, the Senate approved.[20]

Not only wartime alarms, therefore, but concern about the world's postwar power structure fueled Washington's desire to keep the Carribean under control. Nor was it only the administration which worried about the postwar future. A *Chicago Tribune* editorial in 1915 predicted that whatever the outcome, the war in Europe would alter the previous balance of power, ushering in a postwar era of colonial rivalry. The United States, the *Tribune* warned, would do well to prepare for such rivalry beforehand: "If we are wise we shall get a better control over events in Central America and the Caribbean than we have now, and get it while we are comparatively free from interference." In a similar vein, Admiral William B. Caperton, commander in chief of the Pacific fleet, wrote the Navy Department: "Now is the time for us to tighten the grasp on these wavering Southern Republics . . . we have no one to interfere at present, and by the time the world is at peace again, we should have firmly established our position, and our connections with these countries." As the former commander of armed interventions in Haiti and the Dominican Republic, the admiral expressed a point of view then common to many naval officers.[21]

The terrible war in Europe, the long and violent Mexican Revolution next door, the deeply rooted policies and commitments of earlier administrations, the pressures of economic interest—all of these had a part in moving Wilson and Bryan, originally a pair of peace-minded idealists, away from professions of altruism and into an escalating series of military interventions throughout the Caribbean. Even so, how could men of their professed beliefs come so quickly to agree upon armed invasions of Mexico and Haiti? How could Wilson go on to send troops into the Dominican Republic and Cuba? How could Bryan embrace Knox's budding protectorate in Nicaragua, and formalize it in a treaty reminiscent of dollar diplomacy? Arthur S. Link, the eminent Wilson scholar, finds merely the normal contrast between profession and practice, aggravated by naïveté, prior commitments, and the special pressures of the times. Dana Munro's authoritative study concludes that Wilson and Bryan were unable to reconcile their idealism with the perceived demands of national security. A penetrating analysis by Sidney Bell stresses the extent to which economic interest shaped the Wilsonian policies, and shrewdly traces the many assumptions which Wilson shared with his predecessors. Kendrick A. Clements holds that Bryan adopted forceful measures in the Caribbean because he believed deeply in the possibility of reform there but became frustrated at the obstructionism of the local leaders and the snaillike pace of progress. All of these approaches contain much truth, and together they go far to explain the conundrum of Wilsonian behavior in the Caribbean.[22]

Central to any explanation of Wilson's Caribbean policies is his acceptance of some traditional imperialist concepts, including the role of American tutelage and the need to eliminate revolutions. The seeming contrast between Wilson's advocacy of democratic self-government in Europe and his heavy-handedness closer to home is best explained by his belief in the inequality of peoples and societies, a belief shared with most Americans of his day. Woodrow Wilson never thought or pretended that every country was ready for self-government. Europe was ready for it; the "backward" peoples were not. At the turn of the century he had stated publicly that the new colonies of Puerto Rico and the Philippines would require "prolonged and tedious" preparation for self-rule. To prematurely give them complete individual liberty or national freedom would be no blessing, "but a curse, to undeveloped peoples, still in the childhood of their political growth." Like England, the United States had a duty to bring to backward peoples the commerce and ideas of the European world of progress, and to teach them, in the long run, order, self-control, and the principles of liberty.[23]

By Wilson's day the United States was routinely interfering not only with colonies like Puerto Rico and former colonies like Cuba, but with nations which had long enjoyed formal independence and sovereignty. His predecessors had discerned, however, that some states were more equal than others. As Theodore Roosevelt explained: "In international matters to make believe that nations are equal when they are not equal is as productive of far-reaching harm as to make the same pretense about individuals in a community." For example, it would be "the silliest kind of silliness" to ask Mexico, Venezuela, Honduras, or Nicaragua to join the United States in guaranteeing the Monroe Doctrine—"like asking the Apaches and the Utes to guarantee it." Yet it had become entirely proper to make such a request of Argentina, Brazil, or Chile, Roosevelt believed. Those states had "achieved positions of such assured . . . progress, of such political stability and power and economic prosperity" that the United States need concern itself no more about protecting them. Unfortunately, he concluded, no such developments characterized the countries which surrounded the Panama Canal and its approaches.[24]

The main lesson was that nations which could achieve political stability should be rewarded and recognized, while those which could not must be taken in hand. This was already orthodox doctrine in Washington when Wilson came to office, for by then opposition to revolution was already central to United States Caribbean policy. If Wilson's distaste for revolution was accentuated by the one in Mexico, the Roosevelt administration had been similarly affronted by the Cuban uprising of 1906 which led to the second intervention. As Roosevelt wrote at the time, "not only do I dread the loss of life and property, but I dread the creation of a revolutionary habit, and the creation of a class of people who take to disturbance and destruction as an exciting and pleasant business, steadily, altho intermittently, to be followed." In the same context, Senator Henry Cabot Lodge had confessed to "disgust with the Cubans . . . the general feeling is that they ought to be taken by the neck and shaken until they behave themselves."[25]

How had the leaders of a nation born of revolution, one in which revolution had been a "good" word until the mid-nineteenth century, come to such a fixed antirevolutionary posture? The roots were many. The Civil War had seen the Southern Confederacy claim the right of revolution, and the rest of the nation spend four bloody years refuting the claim on the battlefield. This alone cast an entirely new light on the subject, and other modifications followed. In the late nineteenth century the United States began to identify with the rich and developed nations, to claim the protection of international law for its citizens and enterprises in the undeveloped world, and finally to seize a colonial empire for itself. The Filipinos' armed struggle for independence from the United States cast the latter in the role of a colonial power forcefully crushing revolution. All of this reflected changed American attitudes, but it was in the Caribbean during the early twentieth century that the nation's leadership developed a fully articulated antirevolutionary stance.

To Wilson's generation, the degree of a nation's freedom from recurrent revolution was interpreted as a direct index of its level of civilization and capacity for progress. Elihu Root concluded in 1907 that the capacity to unite on great matters marked the civilized society, while "strife about formal or comparatively unimportant differences" distinguished the backward. "Every great nation seems to pass at some period through a storm belt of incapacity to unite. The races that are capable of development beyond that point rule the world; the races that are not capable of it go down. . . ." It had seemed doubtful that the Latin Americans "could ever acquire any more than the most rudimentary capacity for consistent organization," but portions of that region had eventually showed signs of achieving the capacity to unite. Central America, however, represented an area which lagged behind.[26]

Woodrow Wilson shared these currents of thought and brought them to bear on the revolutions in Mexico and the Caribbean. In a 1913 circular note to the European powers explaining his policies, Wilson expressed himself with unmistakable clarity:

> The purpose of the United States is solely and simply to secure peace and order in Central America by seeing to it that the processes of self-government there are not interrupted or set aside. Usurpations like that of General Huerta [in Mexico] menace the peace and development of America as nothing else could. They not only render the development of ordered self-government impossible; they also tend to set law entirely aside, to put the lives and fortunes of citizens and foreigners alike in constant jeopardy, to invalidate contracts and concessions in any way the usurper may desire for his own profit, and to impair both the national credit and all the foundations of business, domestic or foreign. *It is the purpose of the United States, therefore, to discredit and defeat such usurpations whenever they occur.*[27]

One premise of the antirevolutionary position was that Caribbean revolutions had no real content. As Wilson had put it, revolutions were made by usurpers, "those who seek to seize the power of government to advance their own personal interests or ambition." This assumption was the keystone of the various plans to stop revolutions through customs receiverships, which would protect government revenues from selfish or opportunistic seizure. It reflected a belief that the countries concerned could do little to help themselves except to keep order and cooperate with foreign enterprise; salvation must ultimately come from the outside. To American and European observers, the endemic civil wars and political struggles of the Caribbean involved no significant programs or ideologies, and the difference between one faction and another was that between Tweedledee and Tweedledum. Very often this was true. It was clearly untrue in the case of the Mexican Revolution, as Wilson was able to see, but other exceptions were rarely admitted. Yet the tensions between nationalism and foreign development, cultural conservatism and modernism, planter and businessman, frequently played a role in the broils of Caribbean politics.[28]

Related to the belief that the Caribbean countries could find progress only with the leadership of the United States was the assumption that an identity of interests existed between the two. In announcing his corollary to Congress in 1904, Theodore Roosevelt had declared: "Our interests and those of our southern neighbors are in reality identical. They have great natural riches, and if within their borders the reign of law and justice obtains, prosperity is sure to come to them." It would come, of course, through Yankee enterprise, and everyone would share in its benefits. Wilson believed this no less than Roosevelt and Root, Taft and Knox. It was proper that American dollars and know-how should make profits abroad; aside from being fair and just, it strengthened the great engine of change which would bring the good life to backward peoples everywhere.[29]

By 1915 Wilson could instruct Bryan to tell Haiti's leaders "as firmly and definitely as is consistent with courtesy and kindness that the United States cannot consent to stand by and permit revolutionary conditions constantly to exist there." The Haitians "ought . . . to insist upon an agreement for a popular election under our supervision and to be told that the result of the election would be upheld by the United States to the utmost." [30]

Seen in perspective, Wilson represented the final capstone of the antirevolutionary edifice which had been building steadily for a generation or more. As he and his contemporaries saw it, orderly and stable governments were necessary to the achievement of liberty and freedom, to any real economic development, and to the attainment of social goals such as public health and education. Revolution alone, in and of itself, was the principal barrier to progress in the Caribbean region; nothing of consequence could be done there until revolutions were stopped. Wilson concurred fully in these views, and they ultimately defined his Caribbean diplomacy. In the end, the rhetoric of idealism and altruism which differentiated him from so many of his policy-making contemporaries proved ineffectual in the face of his acceptance of so much of the mainstream consensus.

Even at the time, however, a few expressed doubts about the new orthodoxy. The young Dana Munro, not yet a State Department official and maker of Caribbean policy, was a skeptic in 1918. "The mere discouragement of revolutions," he wrote then, "offers no solution for the most serious of Central America's political problems, for it provides no guarantee of good government and no peaceful method of removing authorities whose rule may have become intolerable." As Munro already knew, to offer imported Yankee-supervised elections as a substitute was to misunderstand the nature of Caribbean politics.[31]

Chapter 11

———·⌘·———

Wilsonism in Action

In its first two years in office, the Wilson administration attempted at least two specific steps designed to usher in a new age of hemispheric harmony. The first of these, regarded as symbolically important by both Wilson and Bryan, was a projected treaty with Colombia that would wipe away the stain of Theodore Roosevelt's "Panamá steal." The second was the so-called Pan-American Treaty, which Wilson visualized as a program for permanent peace and harmony in the western hemisphere. Both failed, and with them went some of the rosier hopes for a changed relationship between the United States and Latin America.

Negotiations about reparations to Colombia for the loss of Panamá had begun in the latter days of the Taft administration, but were bedeviled by Colombia's demand for a United States apology. This came more easily from a Democratic administration than a Republican one, and Wilson's was prepared to concede it; the new negotiations accordingly went well. In April 1914 the two governments agreed upon a treaty which provided for payment of a $25 million indemnity from the United States to Colombia, and expressed the "sincere regret" of the former for past troubles. News of the treaty was welcomed throughout Latin America as evidence that the United States may have abandoned "big sticking" in the Caribbean. In the United States, however, it set off a violent debate. Theodore Roosevelt, furious at the implicit condemnation of his actions, called the treaty "a crime against the United States," and rallied his supporters to oppose it. Senate Republicans responded to the call, while the Senate's foreign relations committee bottled up the treaty until 1916. Even then, after considerable watering down, the treaty lay neglected while the full Senate refused to consider it. In March 1917 the Senate returned the treaty to committee, signaling its final demise.[1]

The second new Wilsonian plan was far grander than the abortive Colombian treaty initiative, for it would have meant no less than the conversion of the Monroe Doctrine from a unilateral United States policy to a set of multilateral hemispheric commitments. Such a transformation had been proposed by the Colombian government in 1912, to the displeasure of the Taft administration. Soon afterward, Yale University's Professor Hiram Bingham, Latin Americanist and discoverer of the lost Inca city of Macchu Picchu in Peru, sparked a national debate on the issue. In 1913 Bingham publicly attacked the Monroe Doctrine as an "obsolete shibboleth." Declaring that European threats to the hemisphere were a thing of the past, he advocated cooperation between the United States and the leading South American powers if it should ever be necessary to repel outside threats or to intervene within the hemisphere to quell serious disorders. While Bingham's position came under heavy fire from a wide range of opponents, it reflected a growing recognition in the United States that not all of Latin America was disorderly or backward.[2]

This new viewpoint was evident in Wilson's vision of a "Pan-American Treaty," to which he devoted serious efforts in 1915. Presidential adviser and intimate Colonel Edward M. House first suggested the scheme to Wilson late in 1914, and the two wrote out a draft treaty on December 16 of that year. The treaty's provisions were breathtaking. The American republics were to join in a mutual guarantee of each others' territory, while all would also be guaranteed complete political independence under republican forms of government. The treaty provided for the settlement of all outstanding boundary disputes by arbitration, with a one-year time limit on the arbitral proceedings. Each government would undertake to control the sale and shipment of munitions from its own territory to that of the other American states. All disputes not settled by normal diplomatic methods must be submitted to an international commission for a year's investigation, and then sent to arbitration, before any of the parties involved could declare war. (This last provision, it was true, contained the familiar escape clause excepting issues affecting the "honor, independence, or vital interests" of the nations concerned.) The plan not only could bring peace and stability to the western hemisphere, its authors thought, but also could serve as a model for European nations after the current war ended.[3]

Wilson and his aides hoped first to gain the support of South America's dominant "ABC powers," Argentina, Brazil, and Chile. Once these leaders had accepted the treaty, a general diplomatic campaign could be launched to bring in the others, but without the three leaders the prospects for general adoption seemed grim. First House, then Bryan and Lansing in turn, went to work at winning over the three, and with some success. The governments of Argentina and Brazil soon responded favorably, but Chile's leaders feared that the treaty's obligations would prejudice their long-standing dispute with Peru over the Tacna–Arica district. Chile, the stronger of the two, held actual possession and was not eager to risk the result of outside arbitration. In spite of some waverings, the Chileans never really came around, and as time passed, Wilson's actions in the Caribbean further soured the atmosphere. Eventually the project faded away; the Monroe Doctrine survived untransformed, while inter-American disputes continued to flourish. As Arthur Link has noted, the Pan-American treaty showed Wilson's willingness to treat stable and orderly American states as equals, but it was hardly consistent with his determination to discipline the disorderly ones at need. Thus the treaty failed to be persuasive as a blueprint for a new Caribbean policy.[4]

Ironically, before either the Colombian reparations treaty or the Pan-American plan had been fully launched, Secretary of State William Jennings Bryan found himself under attack for advocating a policy of imperialism and dollar diplomacy in Nicaragua. By mid-1913 Bryan was on the defensive, while a wave of panic swept Central America at the possibility of a general United States take-over of all the countries there. This Nicaraguan episode, which would bring the administration three years of trouble and embarrassment, best illustrates the dichotomy between the altruistic aims and the mundane practices of the Wilson regime.

It was the imminent bankruptcy of the Nicaraguan government which forced Bryan and the State Department so quickly to become reinvolved in the current problems of that troubled state. The crisis, as well as its proposed solution, was inherited from the Taft administration, as Bryan would repeatedly point out. The Knox-Castrillo Treaty of 1911 had provided for a large American loan to Nicaragua, secured by a Dominican-style customs receivership. When the United States Senate rejected this treaty, Brown Brothers and J. and W. Seligman, the New York bankers involved, had refused to go forward with the loan. Desperate for funds, the Managua regime pleaded for a stop-gap arrangement in the form of a small advance on the proposed larger sum. After cobbling together their own substitute form of customs control, which the State Department approved but refused to enforce or guarantee, the bankers granted Managua the first of a series of small, short-term loans. During the ensuing years the Nicaraguan government failed to improve its financial condition, drained as it was by the service of a large foreign debt, the costs of subduing the Mena revolution of 1912, and the formidable raids made on the treasury by its own ruling clique. The resulting condition was equally unsatisfactory to the Nicaraguan government and the American bankers, as the latter gained increasing influence in Nicaragua but felt financially insecure there.[5]

Meanwhile the poverty of the Managua regime left it weakened and humiliated. With most of its revenues pledged in advance to servicing existing obligations, the Nicaraguan government was forced to abandon public works half finished and let the salaries of government employees go unpaid for months at a time. Since teachers' pay got the lowest priority of all, the school system collapsed entirely. Fearing threats from both within and outside of the country, the regime could not maintain a credible armed force for its own protection, which made it even more dependent on the United States. It was therefore no wonder that the Nicaraguan leaders thirsted for new financial resources by 1913.[6]

In the closing weeks of the Taft administration, Secretary of State Philander Knox had attempted to ease the financial pressure in Managua by negotiating a treaty under which the United States would purchase an exclusive option on the Nicaraguan canal route for $3 million. This sum would also buy the right to build a naval base in the Gulf of Fonseca on the Pacific coast, and a ninety-nine-year lease on the two small Corn Islands in the Caribbean. The primary reason for this purchase treaty was to create a vehicle to provide money for Nicaragua; presumably, the United States Congress could be induced to part with the $3 million as a means to enhance United States security on the isthmus.[7]

This second Knox arrangement with Nicaragua, the Chamorro-Weitzel Treaty, had not yet come before the Senate when Wilson took office, and Bryan had therefore to consider whether to support its ratification or withdraw it. His new subordinates in the State Department, particularly those temporarily held over from the previous administration, insisted that the Knox treaty, or something like it, was essential to prevent the collapse of the Díaz regime in Managua. Bryan himself regarded Central American stability as essential to United States security, and was therefore unwilling to see another overturn in Nicaragua. If the United States government rejected the treaty and withheld the money which it provided for, Nicaragua's leaders would have to mortgage their country even more deeply to Wall Street for substitute funds, a prospect which also disturbed Bryan. It all seemed to come down to a choice between endorsing the Taft-Knox diplomacy which Bryan had so disliked, or turning again to the bankers whom he equally disliked. The only other visible alternative, to allow the Díaz regime to stand or fall on its own and accept the result, meant a return to instability, which was defined as unacceptable. Seeking some way out of the dilemma, Bryan at this time developed his scheme for direct treasury loans to Latin American governments, which Wilson finally rejected. Ultimately, Bryan chose the Knox treaty as the lesser evil.[8]

Initially, Bryan hoped that the treaty's provision for paying the Nicaraguans $3 million would encourage the bankers to make a future loan on terms less onerous than those of the failed Knox-Castrillo loan treaty. Those terms, he thought, had impinged on Nicaragua's sovereignty. Yet during new negotiations to redraft the second Knox treaty, Bryan accepted provisions similar to those in the Platt Amendment which had made Cuba a protectorate of the United States. These new provisions were the work of the Nicaraguans themselves. Fearing overthrow from within, the Díaz government suggested that the treaty give the United States the same right of intervention which Washington used to prevent revolution in Cuba. If a similar policy should be applied to their own country, the Managua incumbents could feel more secure from their enemies.[9]

As Bryan later explained to Wilson, he agreed to the suggested "Platt Amendment" provisions in part because he hoped that they would strengthen Nicaragua's public credit. Lenders had customarily charged a high rate of interest in such countries because of the risks created by chronic instability, Bryan charged, and then attempted to persuade their own governments to act to remove those risks. "If we can eliminate the risk before the loan is made, the people will receive a pecuniary benefit from the lower rate of interest that stability will secure." Beyond that, while the protectorate provisions came at the request of the Nicaraguans and for their own purposes, Bryan declared, "still I think that it is of advantage to us, in that it will give us the right to do that which we might be called upon to do anyhow. We cannot escape the responsibilities of our position, and this is an opportune time for us to secure the necessary treaty provision. . . ." Strange doctrine for an antiimperialist![10]

Though Wilson approved Bryan's new treaty, it promptly ran into trouble in the Senate. The Progressive wing of that body had been hostile to the Taft-Knox policies in Nicaragua, and its members were dismayed to find one of their own blithely continuing in the same direction. The Platt Amendment provisions aroused special animosity; Bryan reported to the president that "there is quite a determined opposition . . . against any extension of our authority over these countries." Worst of all, in explaining the treaty to the Senate's foreign relations committee, Bryan and committee chairman Augustus O. Bacon of Georgia managed to give the impression that similar treaties were projected for the rest of Central America. What they had meant to say was that any objection to the treaty on the part of Nicaragua's neighbors could be addressed in separate treaties with those countries, but the vagueness of their phraseology led to the misconception. While many Republican senators were pleased, the antiimperialists, led by Idaho's Senator William E. Borah, created an uproar which startled and embarrassed the administration.[11]

An even louder uproar issued from Central America, where political and press spokesmen had already been deeply apprehensive about United States intentions toward the area. These peoples' worst fears were confirmed by an article in the New York Times on July 21, 1913, which announced that the Wilson administration planned a general protectorate for all of Central America. Adding fuel to the flames, the Times editors wired every Central American president to request comment on this supposed development, which the Times staff had deduced from Bryan's and Bacon's statements to the foreign relations committee. The resulting general tumult saw days of demonstrations in every Central American capital, while Washington vainly denied that it had ever meant to impose protectorates on the region. The United States minister to El Salvador predicted that Senate ratification of Bryan's Nicaraguan treaty would set off Salvadoran disturbances which might "assume ungovernable proportions," and called for a gunboat. The chargé at San José found that "a large majority of the Costa Ricans" believed that the United States intended to control their country; the Masonic Lodge of San José had even called a meeting to discuss the crisis.[12]

In August the foreign relations committee disapproved the treaty by a vote of eight to four, while indicating that it might be acceptable without its protectorate features. Meanwhile the Managua government, seeing its rescue indefinitely deferred, satisfied the bankers in the only way left to it, by selling them a 51 percent interest in the national railway and the newly established national bank. Thus the bankers' influence deepened, just as Bryan had feared, while Nicaragua's financial situation remained grave. In the opinion of the British consul in Managua, the main object of American policy in Nicaragua had been "to gather up all of the financial reins at Washington with the able assistance of . . . the bankers and with the purse strings in their possession to control the Government and the country"; now, he reported, "this object has been achieved." While this was not at all Bryan's intention, the Briton's error was understandable.[13]

Still determined to get his treaty ratified, Bryan found President Díaz unwilling to drop its protectorate provisions. The secretary of state then sought to mollify the Senate by demonstrating that those provisions had in fact been inserted by Managua, and therefore represented no attempt on his own part to usurp power. At Bryan's behest, Díaz made a written request that the treaty "be made to embody the substance of the Platt Amendment." The Nicaraguan president argued that such an action would improve the nation's credit, develop her resources, and ensure peace. "I believe revolutions will cease if your government can see its way clear to grant the addition of the amendment as respectfully suggested," he asserted.[14]

This second attempt to get Senate approval of the treaty was more disastrous than the first, as Senate opponents were simply enraged by Bryan's persistence. Senator William Alden Smith of Michigan charged that Nicaragua's revenue-producing institutions had fallen into the grasp of American financiers, and that the Díaz regime was an unpopular one kept in power only by the bayonets of United States marines. Smith made public some details of the Díaz clique's raids on the Nicaraguan treasury which had contributed to the current emergency, and charged that the American bankers who now controlled the national railroad were about to make a large profit by selling it to the United Fruit Company. Senator Borah declared that the treaty was "founded upon deception, misrepresentation, fraud, tyranny, and corruption," and called Díaz "a puppet set up and maintained by American arms." Elihu Root, now a senator from New York, consistently opposed the protectorate features in the treaty, arguing that there was no such need for the Platt Amendment provisions as had been the case in Cuba. Even the strongly pro-administration *New York World* echoed the critics, accusing Bryan of being the dupe of Wall Street bankers and Nicaraguan politicians. The Senate's foreign relations committee began an investigation of all of these charges, and the administration found itself facing the strongest attack yet made against United States policies in the Caribbean.[15]

Under such pressure, Bryan jettisoned the protectorate clauses and renegotiated the treaty with the Nicaraguan minister to the United States, Emiliano Chamorro. However, even this new Bryan-Chamorro Treaty was suspect to the Senate, which failed to act upon it for another year and a half. Senate approval finally came in February 1916, as fear of Germany mounted and the navy's General Board argued the need for the new naval bases which the treaty would make possible. Ratification of the treaty came much too late to save the financial integrity of the Nicaraguan government, while the controversy which it aroused did major damage to the moral authority of Wilsonian Caribbean policy. In attempting to secure a formal protectorate over Nicaragua, Bryan and Wilson not only made a political blunder, but betrayed their avowed anti-imperialist principles.[16]

The damage stemming from ratification of the Bryan-Chamorro Treaty reached its peak in Central America. Bryan had truthfully assured the representatives of the other four Central American states that the Nicaraguan leaders themselves had put the protectorate provisions into the treaty, and that the United States had no intention of foisting similar arrangements on the neighboring countries. Woodrow Wilson grew concerned at the persistence of such fears, and inquired of Bryan: "Is it true that Nicaragua's neighbors have been showing themselves to be very much upset by these proposals and that they have made anything like a joint protest against them?" After reassuring the president, his secretary of state had labored manfully to repair the damage. He amended the treaty to state that none of its provisions should be construed so as to diminish the rights of any neighboring state. He further offered once more to negotiate separate treaties with Costa Rica, Honduras, and Salvador providing restitution for any rights of theirs which might be infringed by the Nicaraguan treaty. Bryan's efforts were in vain, for these states were adamantly opposed to the agreement with Nicaragua, and had hoped that the United States Senate would continue to reject it.[17]

Costa Rica had the strongest grievance. The so-called Nicaraguan canal route was actually shared in part by Costa Rica, which by treaty had perpetual navigation rights in the lower San Juan River. Because that river formed both an essential part of the proposed canal route and a section of the boundary between Costa Rica and Nicaragua, the latter country was formally obligated to consult Costa Rica about the terms of any canal treaty. It had not done so, and the Costa Ricans held with some justice that a joint property had been sold off by only one of the owners. El Salvador and Honduras made the same argument on other grounds. Objecting to a United States naval base in the Gulf of Fonseca, which contained their own ports of La Union and Amapala, the Salvadorans and Hondurans claimed that the gulf was the joint property of the three bordering states, and that no one state had a right to alienate territory on its shores without the assent of the other two.[18]

While the Salvador-Honduras position rested less solidly on international law than Costa Rica's, all of the other Central American states resented Nicaragua's action in abetting the further penetration of their area by the United States. Costa Rica, El Salvador, and Honduras all went to the Central American Court of Justice to challenge the Bryan-Chamorro Treaty's infringement of regional rights. The court found in favor of Costa Rica's claim on September 30, 1916, and of Salvador's on March 2, 1917. It arraigned Nicaragua for violating its neighbors' rights, while carefully noting that it had no jurisdiction over the United States. Amidst great excitement, the Nicaraguan government defied the court, refusing to appear before it and withdrawing its own member from the tribunal. The United States government supported the Nicaraguan stand, sounding the death knell for the court, which never heard another case. It was not the court which was discredited, however, but American policy, which was universally blamed for the debacle. Elihu Root's careful construction had been deliberately razed by the very power which had erected it.[19]

While Wilsonian policies alienated the Central Americans, they became equally upsetting to the peoples of the Caribbean's island countries. By 1916 the United States had taken forcible control of Haiti and the Dominican Republic, while in the following year United States troops would return to Cuba as well. Elihu Root had tried hard to find effective alternatives to the use of force in regulating events in the Caribbean; Philander Knox had initially hoped that economic leverage might do the job by itself. William Jennings Bryan moved sharply toward acceptance of forcible measures, though he had qualms about them, while also finding it necessary to preserve much of his predecessor's dollar diplomacy. Under Robert Lansing the unabashed use of force would become central to the nation's Caribbean policy, and Woodrow Wilson had no visible quarrel with the results.

In Haiti a mounting cycle of revolutionary disorders caught the attention of the State Department. A series of successful revolutions had destabilized Haitian politics at the same time that the outbreak of war in Europe virtually severed the main axis of Haiti's foreign trade, leading to great strains on the export sector of the economy. This combination of pressures pushed the government close to bankruptcy, a risk accentuated by the behavior of the National Bank of Haiti. This French, German, and American institution controlled the government's finances, receiving most of the public revenues and deducting the cost of servicing the foreign debt before passing on the remainder to the government. A depressed economy left little for ever weaker governments to live on, and in 1914 a showdown neared between the political leaders and the bank. In the summer of 1914, the bank's managers announced that they would no longer honor the government's monthly drafts, but would settle mutual accounts at the end of each fiscal year. Caught without funds, the government lacked the means to carry on, and the United States minister judged that the bank must mean either to force the government into complete submission or to precipitate an American intervention to establish a customs receivership.[20]

After the outbreak of the European war, the American faction of the bank syndicate took control under the leadership of the National City Bank of New York. The National City's chief link with Washington was Roger Farnham, a bank official and a personal friend of Boaz Long, the chief of the State Department's Latin American Division. Farnham and Long enlisted Bryan's sympathies none too soon to extricate the bank from potential danger. Late in 1914 the Haitian government threatened to seize its own gold reserves from the bank's vaults in order to finance itself. The bankers, however, held that the gold was legally reserved for the redemption of previous paper issues and not available to the government. Fearing that the Haitians would take their gold by force, the bank officials arranged for the United States gunboat *Machias* to land a party of marines, who removed half a million dollars in bullion to the gunboat whence it was shipped to New York for safekeeping.[21]

Well before this, Bryan was leaning toward resolving the Haitian financial tangle with a Dominican-style customs receivership. On the eve of Sarajevo, the French and German governments had both indicated that they would expect to participate in any customs control which might be established. In the eyes of Wilson and Bryan, this threat of European intervention lent additional urgency to the Haitian problem, and in July 1914 they attempted to act. The current regime of Haitian President Oreste Zamor faced the inevitable revolution—he was the fourth president to hold office since August 1911—and feared imminent overthrow. The State Department offered Zamor a bargain: if the Haitian accepted a customs receivership and an American "financial adviser" who would supervise government disbursements, he would gain the protection of the United States against his domestic enemies.[22]

Reluctant to accept such sweeping controls, Zamor delayed too long. Only in October 1914, when his position had become hopeless, did the president and his advisers decide to grasp at the proffered aid. Washington immediately dispatched a transport carrying eight hundred marines to Port-au-Prince to prop up the tottering regime, but the ship came too late. A revolutionary army already occupied the capital and its chief was organizing a new government, while Zamor had gone into exile. There was nothing to do but bring the marines home.[23]

This near-miss only solidified Bryan's intentions for Haiti. A note express-ing "a willingness to do in Haiti what we are doing in Santo Domingo" went down to the new government of President Davilmar Theodore, initiat-ing another round of secret negotiations over customs control. When word of these talks leaked out, however, members of the Haitian senate physically attacked the foreign minister as he appeared before them. The unfortunate minister barely escaped with his life, while the wave of nationalism which swept the capital seemed to make a customs receivership politically impossi-ble. Theodore was still in need of money, nevertheless; his counterproposal offered mining and commercial concessions to United States citizens in return for State Department aid in securing an American loan. To Bryan this smacked of bribery, and was beside the point in any case, for it would not bring Haiti the stability which he sought.[24]

At the beginning of 1915 Bryan was in a quandary. He wrote Wilson that: "There will be no peace and progress in Haiti until we have some such arrange-ment as we have in Santo Domingo," but he had previously "not felt like compelling acceptance of the plan" in the face of Haitian refusal. He now sug-gested the possibility of sending down a commission to do what had recently been done in the neighboring Dominican Republic: that is, get the leaders to agree on a provisional president who could hold an American-supervised presi-dential election. As in the Dominican case, the winner would get United States recognition and support, while potential revolutionaries would be sternly dis-couraged. "The success of this Government's efforts in Santo Domingo," Bryan thought, "would suggest the application of the same methods to Hayti [*sic*] whenever the time is ripe." Within a week Bryan had the president's ap-proval. "The more I think about that situation the more I am convinced that it is our duty to take immediate action there such as we took in San [*sic*] Do-mingo," Wilson replied. He would send off the necessary commission as soon as possible.[25]

Upon investigation, however, Bryan found that Haitian presidents were not chosen by popular election, but by the national assembly, which made it hard to apply the Dominican scheme as planned. President and secretary agreed to send the commission anyway, but by the time of its arrival Theodore's government had fallen to a new revolution led by Vilbrun Guillaume Sam. The commissioners refused diplomatic recognition to Guillaume until he had agreed to American financial controls, while the new president refused to negotiate about anything until his regime had been recognized. Deadlocked, the commissioners soon went home.[26]

Hard on the heels of this fiasco, Roger Farnham of the National City Bank persuaded Bryan and Wilson that European powers still hoped to control the Haitian government through financial manipulation. In March 1915 Farnham wrote Bryan that a French firm had loaned the Haitians a million dollars. Upon hearing the news, Wilson instantly suspected French government involvement.

Meanwhile Farnham came to Washington to alarm Bryan with the allegation that the French and German governments were acting in collusion in Haiti to subvert the interests of the United States, and might even intend to secure the strategic Môle Saint Nicolas. Unlikely as it might seem that the two warring powers, engaged in a life-and-death struggle in Europe, could be working as partners in Haiti, both Wilson and Bryan believed it. "This whole matter has a most sinister appearance," the president wrote Bryan, ordering the latter "to think out a plan of controlling action which we can take . . . before the tangle gets any greater." [27]

In May 1915 another Washington emissary carried further proposals to the Guillaume regime in Port-au-Prince. He was authorized to promise the government the protection of the United States against internal or external foes, in return for Haitian acceptance of financial supervision by the American legation and of arbitration of all foreign claims against the Haitian government. The Haitians would also be required to deny concessions at Môle Saint Nicolas to any third parties. Once more Guillaume rejected the offer, but by this time his days were numbered. Energetic and ruthless in suppressing opposition, Guillaume Sam had scored important successes against a revolutionary force on Haiti's north coast. He seemed more securely in power than any president for some years, but his excesses of repression sparked an almost spontaneous uprising on July 27 in the capital itself. Surprised by this sudden onslaught, the president ordered the massacre of almost one hundred seventy political prisoners whom he had been holding as a precaution, most of them potential opponents from the nation's elite families. Among the dead were two former presidents, one of them Oreste Zamor, who had left the presidential palace only six months earlier. The general rage at this barbarity sealed Guillaume's doom.[28]

On hearing of these disorders, the navy ordered a warship to Port-au-Prince to protect foreign life and property. The large armored cruiser *Washington* was already on Haiti's north coast observing the fighting there, and aboard her was the commander of the navy's Cruiser Squadron, Rear Admiral William B. Caperton. Ironically, Caperton's arrival at Port-au-Prince precipitated further bloodletting. The wounded Guillaume had fled for sanctuary to the French legation, and for a time the general respect for such sanctuary protected him; as the French minister pointed out to a Haitian mob, most of the country's political leaders owed their lives to such diplomatic shelter during previous crises. At the sight of *Washington* on the horizon, however, the cry arose that the Americans would protect the murderous refugee, and a crowd of those who had lost close relatives in the prison massacre dragged Guillaume from the French legation to take their vengeance while they could. The luckless president was literally torn to pieces by the mob, which paraded the fragments of his body through the streets. By the time *Washington* anchored, the city was in chaos and the diplomatic corps terrified of further violence.[29]

Admiral Caperton ordered a landing party ashore to restore order in the city, a decision soon approved by orders from Washington. On July 28, 1915, 330 sailors and marines from *Washington* took control of the capital. Caperton promptly called for reinforcements, and within days additional ships and men began to converge on Port-au-Prince. The policy makers in Washington had been on the verge of forcible intervention since the previous summer, and took it for granted that the bloody fall of Guillaume Sam at last marked the time for action. An entire marine regiment arrived a week after the initial landing, to be joined by a second regiment in mid-August. By the end of that month Caperton had over two thousand marines in Haiti, and was able to detach units from the capital to occupy the country's other chief coastal towns. At each town the marine commander took control of the customhouse, so that a de facto customs control was established by early September.[30]

Meanwhile the country was without a president. Working without much direction from Washington, Caperton identified a suitably pliable and pro-American candidate and induced the national assembly to elect him. The assembly had customarily ratified the results of the latest successful revolution; capture of the capital normally ensured its conqueror the presidency. As the current conqueror, the admiral was skillful in supplementing his monopoly of force with persuasion, politicking, and implied threats. On August 12, 1915, the assembly formally chose as president Philippe Sudre Dartiguenave, who had pledged his obedience to Caperton in advance. Dartiguenave and the Americans quickly fleshed out a client regime that was to rule Haiti for years, and Washington once more had a government in Port-au-Prince with which to negotiate.[31]

With a client state in place, the State Department lost little time in sending Caperton the draft of a treaty for the Haitians to sign. The new terms made those of 1914 look mild. The United States would name a general receiver to administer the customs and a financial adviser to supervise the treasury. A new national constabulary, organized and commanded by Americans, would replace both the army and the existing civil police. The Haitians could neither increase their public debt nor change their customs duties without Washington's permission. The treaty would remain in force for ten years, to be renewed for another decade if *either* party desired it. Even Dartiguenave's cabinet objected to some of the provisions, but on September 3 Caperton countered by declaring martial law at the secret request of the beleaguered president. The latter finally sacked the leaders of the cabinet resistance, and signed the treaty on September 16.[32]

The treaty still required ratification by the Haitian senate, where the opposition was formidable. Wanting badly to preserve the forms of legality rather than simply imposing the treaty by fiat, Caperton once more utilized threats, promises, and even the bribes customary in Port-au-Prince, to get the Senate's approval. He achieved this in November, but by then resistance to the

Americans had taken other forms than the Byzantine maneuvers of the capital. The warlike mountain peasantry of the north, the *cacos,* mounted an armed struggle against American authority. In October and November United States Marines fought a small but fierce campaign in northern Haiti, and broke the *caco* resistance after killing over two hundred of their number.[33]

The protectorate thus forced upon Haiti would endure for nineteen years, to be liquidated only in 1934. During all of that time the marines remained in Haiti, and their commander acted as virtual ruler of the country. As even Woodrow Wilson recognized, the United States take-over of Haiti was of doubtful propriety. "I fear we have not the legal authority to do what we apparently ought to do; and that if we did do what is necessary it would constitute a case very like that of Mr. Roosevelt's actions in Santo Domingo," the president noted candidly a few days after Caperton's initial landing. He nevertheless went ahead, explaining to his future wife that the alternative was "the most sordid chaos" in Haiti and the risk that the United States might be "perhaps fatally embarrassed." At any rate, he thought, the Haitian intervention would not seriously affront the other Latin Americans, for the Haitians "being negroes . . . are not regarded as of the fraternity!"[34]

A comparable sequence of events in the neighboring Dominican Republic paralleled the American advance to control of Haitian affairs. At first the policy makers in Washington had borrowed from their Dominican experience to find expedients for Haiti, starting with the familiar customs receivership plan. At a later stage, the fact of forceful intervention in Haiti made such a step seem more natural and appropriate in the Dominican Republic. During the years 1914 and 1915 in particular, any major action in either country tended to be reflected afterward in policy proposals for the other. In the end, logically enough, both fell under marine occupations which lasted for years, and which extinguished Dominican self-government even more thoroughly than was the case in Haiti.

The Wilsonians inherited from their predecessors a deeply rooted involvement in Dominican affairs. The American customs receivership was the work of Theodore Roosevelt's administration, while that of Taft and Knox had dealt with a renewed political breakdown by ousting one president and installing another, though only provisional, one. The latter, Archbishop Adolfo Nouel, unequal to his task and dismayed by the pressures of office, resigned his presidency at about the time that Wilson entered upon his own. The new regime in Washington, therefore, had from the first to deal with political crisis in the Dominican Republic.

Archbishop Nouel's successor, José Bordas Valdes, was elected by the Dominican congress as provisional president, to serve for a maximum of one year. His principal duty was to administer national elections, first to choose a constituent assembly to reform the electoral process, then to elect a fully constitutional president and thus end the state of crisis in the country. Once in office, however, Bordas showed himself ambitious to stay in power. Striking a bargain with General Desiderio Arias, an equally ambitious politician with a power base in the north, Bordas betrayed the faction which had pushed through his election and demonstrated little interest in holding elections to select a successor. As followers of Arias took over the government's finest patronage posts, opposition leaders united in a revolt against the usurper. Thus Bordas and Arias faced a formidable alliance headed by the nation's two preeminent party leaders, Horacia Vásquez and Juan Isidro Jiménez.[35]

To the ill-informed newcomers in the State Department, this revolt against Bordas was the perfect occasion to start off on the right foot. Bordas had been properly chosen by his legislature, they reasoned, while the curse of revolution had for too long blighted the Dominican scene. Secretary of State Bryan decided on a hard line, and sent a stern warning down with his new minister to the Dominican Republic: the United States would not recognize any government created by the revolutionary leaders, and if they succeeded in erecting one it would get no part of the customs collections which made up most of the public revenues. To this warning the American minister added a promise of his own: if the rebels laid down their arms, the United States government would guarantee an honest and orderly presidential election within a reasonable time. Moved as much by the carrot as the stick, the revolutionaries prepared to disarm and await the promised electoral contest, but Bordas soon showed that he had no intention of allowing himself to be voted out of office.[36]

The State Department was now in a dilemma. The promise to supervise Dominican elections ran far beyond any powers conveyed under the 1907 customs treaty, while Bordas defiantly refused to accept an official United States election commission. He did accept an unofficial team of observers whose presence helped the opposition to win a majority of seats in the new constituent assembly. Even more influential was a threat from the American legation that fraud in this first election could mean direct United States supervision of the subsequent presidential contest. The pledge given to the opposition leaders was nevertheless unredeemed, for Bordas was clearly intent on clinging to office regardless of the democratic niceties. As if this were not enough, the Dominican government had exhausted its treasury in these constant civil wars, while in the spring of 1914 Arias broke with the president to seek power for himself. Something must be done quickly, it appeared, or the entire United States policy in the Dominican Republic would come to nothing. Bryan accordingly pressed a new demand on the Bordas regime: it must accept a financial adviser appointed by the United States government, who would have final authority over all Dominican disbursements. Bordas agreed in March 1914, moving his country further toward becoming a full-fledged American protectorate.[37]

At the end of March, Bordas' legal year in office had run out, while new fighting began between his followers and those of Arias. In June Bordas attempted to hold the long-promised presidential election with himself as candidate, though the politically fragmented constituent assembly had as yet done nothing about election reforms. In seven of the country's twelve provinces there was not even a pretense at elections, and where they were held they were shamelessly rigged for Bordas. By then, however, public disorder was so total that no one took the farce seriously. The fighting between Bordas and Arias inspired the former opposition leaders to renew their own revolution, which began to make way against both of its rivals. Affairs could hardly become worse, and elaborate American efforts at mediation, tutelage, and reform were without effect.[38]

At this juncture, late in July 1914, President Wilson took a direct hand in the Dominican imbroglio. All hostilities must cease, he announced to the warring leaders; Bordas must resign; the various presidential candidates must agree upon someone to serve as provisional president—if they could not, then the United States would name one; as soon as possible, the provisional government must hold elections, in which the temporary president could not be a candidate; Washington would send observers to judge the honesty of these elections, and if the first attempt was found wanting, it would be voided and more elections held; and once a regularly elected government was chosen, the United States government would allow no further revolutions, for all subsequent changes in government must come through constitutional processes. The president sent commissioners to Santo Domingo to implement this so-called Wilson plan. "No opportunity for argument should be given to any person or faction," Bryan informed them on their departure. "It is desired that you present [the] plan and see it is complied with." [39]

Under the naked threat of intervention, the Dominicans did as they were told; Bordas resigned, a provisional president was chosen, and the election held. It was a close contest between the two old rivals and ex-presidents, Horacio Vásquez and Juan Isidro Jiménez, and Jiménez won. Although the losers charged election fraud, Wilson's commissioners testified to the election's fairness, and Jiménez assumed office in December 1914. The fortunes of American policy now rested on this one man, whom Washington had sworn to uphold against all enemies. He was not a promising figure for such a role; burdened with advancing age and ill health, his strength was visibly failing. Worse yet, he had won the election only with the help of that perennial power seeker, Desiderio Arias, who became minister of war and the power behind the throne. Arias soon attempted to gain control of the government, only to be chastized by Bryan's threat to send the marines against him. He nevertheless remained in the cabinet, industriously building support among members of the Dominican congress and the lesser factional chiefs. And in addition to the threat from Arias, Jiménez found an empty treasury. The government upon which Wilson and Bryan had staked all was clearly not a strong one.[40]

Aware of the vulnerability of the Santo Domingo government, Bryan moved to place it firmly under United States control. Jiménez had already agreed to retain the American financial adviser whom Bordas had accepted; the secretary of state now demanded that this official receive formal status as comptroller of Dominican finances. In addition, Bryan wished the receiver general of customs to collect internal revenues as well as external ones, and the American director of public works to receive complete control over his Dominican subordinates, including the right to hire and fire them. Finally, he suggested that the United States "aid" in organizing a constabulary to replace the army.[41]

The enfeebled Jiménez resisted none of these demands, but an outraged Dominican congress rose in fury against the president's proposed delegation of authority to the financial adviser. Bryan's attempt to force a full protectorate on an already weakened president put Jiménez in an impossible situation. If he refused the American demands, he jeopardized his only reliable support and risked losing his revenues as well. If he agreed to them, as he had, he was discredited throughout the country as the traitor who had sold his country to the Yankees. Washington's clumsy coercions had unified all factions against Jiménez, and pitted congress against president in a contest that would ultimately wreck the government.[42]

In April 1915 the Dominican congress began action to impeach the president, on the grounds that he allowed the financial adviser to exercise powers in violation of the constitution. Bryan again threatened to send marines to Jiménez' aid, but the president began to break down both physically and mentally under the continued pressure. When a Dominican commission came to Washington seeking a compromise on the powers of the American officials, it received only cosmetic concessions. As tensions mounted, local rebellions spread across the country, and in the summer of 1915 a general revolt seemed inevitable.[43]

At this point the vigorous Robert Lansing, newly appointed secretary of state, resolved upon a solution "in line with the treaty with Haiti." He moved at once to quell Dominican disturbances by imposing an imperium similar to that currently being erected in the neighboring republic. A regiment of marines, kept discreetly aboard its transport but silently effective nevertheless, visited trouble spots along the Dominican coast from August to October. When a new appointee, William W. Russell, went to Santo Domingo as United States minister in November 1915, he brought an ultimatum to the Dominican government. According to its terms, a United States–appointed financial adviser must control the treasury, as Bryan had long insisted. Furthermore, the army must be replaced, as in Haiti, by a national constabulary organized and

commanded by United States Marines. Lansing boldly claimed these concessions under the treaty of 1907, though the treaty in fact said nothing of such
matters.[44]

Already facing overthrow at home, Jiménez necessarily refused the American demands, and an uneasy stalemate lasted into the spring of 1916. Determined to have its way, the State Department put additional pressure on Jiménez
by blocking approval of a loan to the Dominican government. As an official of
the department's Division of Latin American Affairs saw it, the entire principle
was at stake

> that control of customs in turbulent countries precludes the possibility of revo-
> lution . . . and should it [the principle] fall it will have, I fear, a far reaching
> effect upon the countries of Central America and particularly upon our present
> relations with Haiti.[45]

By April General Arias, the ambitious minister of war, had become so
openly threatening that Jiménez attempted a surprise seizure of the capital's
fortress. Though a failure, the attempt sent Arias into open rebellion, while
a pro-Arias congress adopted a resolution of impeachment. Rejected on all
sides, Jiménez fled to the countryside and rallied a small group of followers.
At the beginning of May, two United States gunboats arrived carrying marines,
and on May 5, 1916, some three hundred marines and sailors went ashore to
support the deposed president. The long-threatened United States intervention
had finally begun, but almost at once its course deviated sharply from Washington's plans. When the American commander proposed operations to drive
Arias from Santo Domingo, Jiménez declared that he could not be responsible for an attack upon his own people. Pressed hard by the Americans, the
president simply resigned, and the government which the United States was
pledged to sustain had ceased to exist.[46]

It continued in theory, however. Russell, the resourceful American minister,
elevated the four cabinet members who had remained loyal to Jiménez to the
status of an interim "Council of Ministers," which he officially recognized as
the rightful government. This body was legally anomalous, and General Arias
held, not surprisingly, that Jiménez had been constitutionally removed by the
congress and that his rump cabinet had no official status. Arias claimed to represent the legitimate power of congress, and thus the only legal power in the
country. The resulting deadlock was broken on May 12 by the arrival of Admiral Caperton, the recent pacifier of Haiti, aboard another warship. Urged on
by Russell, Caperton landed an additional three hundred troops, then handed
Arias an ultimatum: if he failed to disband his army by 6:00 A.M. on May
15, Caperton's men would enter the city and forcibly disarm them. Although
Arias held Santo Domingo's ancient walls with an irregular force far larger
than Caperton's, he had no stomach for a pitched battle with the marines. On

the night before the deadline, he left the capital with a few hundred followers, and the next day Caperton's troops occupied the city without opposition.[47]

For the second time within a year, Admiral Caperton began efforts to secure a national president through whom the Americans could exercise control. Working closely with Russell, he moved to block congressional action to elect Arias while seeking a more pliable substitute. The problem was that in contrast to Haitians, the Dominicans appeared to harbor no useful collaborationists. Not one leader of stature would give the advance assurances which the Americans required for their approval of a president. "I have never seen such hatred displayed by one people for another as I notice and feel here," Caperton reported. "We positively have not a friend in the land. . . ."[48]

Finding a universal hostility to his occupation, the admiral feared a national uprising and called for reinforcements. As these arrived, Caperton moved to occupy the country's main coastal towns as he had in Haiti. This led to small-scale fighting on the north coast between United States forces and a local resistance. In June, the Fourth Marine Regiment arrived, the largest reinforcement to date, and Caperton decided to send it against Arias in the northern interior. The Dominican lay at Santiago with a thousand men, a potential rallying point for the general resistance which Caperton feared. In July a thousand marines approached the town, having fought two brief but decisive engagements on the way. Abandoned by his men, Arias surrendered, and with two thousand troops in the field Caperton had reasonably firm military control of the country.[49]

This military success did not solve the problem of a successor regime, however. After many weeks of conflict and maneuver, the Dominican congress chose as provisional president Dr. Francisco Henríquez y Carvajal, the brother of a favorite candidate whose election Caperton and Russell had blocked earlier. Henríquez resided in Cuba, and had done so for many years. He was thus untainted with recent factional ties and, more significantly, was out of reach of the Americans prior to his return to his native land. He therefore came to office free of the promises demanded by Washington. The Dominican politicos hoped that the Americans would accept this fait accompli, but they proved to be overly optimistic. When Henríquez arrived in the capital at the end of July, Russell refused to recognize his election until he promised advance acceptance of United States demands; until he did so his government would get no money, and all government funds would be impounded. A three-month endurance contest followed, until November, when the State Department withdrew Russell and proclaimed the establishment of a military government in the Dominican Republic. In Haiti the American military would rule through a local client government. In the Dominican Republic, the lack of willing collaborators eliminated even this thin disguise; United States admirals and generals would rule directly there for the next eight years.[50]

A final instance of using United States troops in the Caribbean found the

Wilson administration much less eager to adopt military means. The occasion was another disputed election in Cuba. President Mario G. Menocal had pledged not to seek reelection, but announced in 1915 that he had changed his mind and would run again the following year. This was unwelcome news to most Cubans, who widely assumed that an incumbent president could, and would, control the electoral machinery to his own advantage. Even Menocal's Conservative party was unenthusiastic; lesser party chieftains thought it their turn to seek the presidency. The rival Liberals, who had the larger following, were furious at the prospect of being cheated of a probably victory. As in 1906, both sides looked to Washington for support.[51]

In fact, State Department officials in Washington were beginning to recognize the dangers of being manipulated by Cuban politicos in such circumstances. In addition, they liked Menocal, a pro–United States businessman who had presided over a sugar boom on the island. They therefore avoided being drawn too deeply into the dispute, even after it became clear that Menocal had stolen the 1916 election through fraud. The Liberals took their case successfully to court, winning an order for new elections in some disputed districts, but they were frustrated by the president's obvious intention to resort once more to strong-arm methods. Predictably, Liberal leaders planned a revolt, meaning either to oust Menocal or force a United States intervention which would do the job for them. However, the government's premature discovery of the rebels' plans early in 1917 enabled it to quash the uprising everywhere but in the eastern end of Cuba. There it hung on, while United States naval officers mediated the surrender of rebel bands, American marines landed to guard key points, and American policy worked in general to aid Menocal without major involvement. Washington was by then doubly anxious to avoid a large-scale occupation because the nation was at the brink of war with Germany; the aim where possible was to get troops out of the Caribbean, not put more in.[52]

The entry of the United States into the European war in April 1917 swept Caribbean events into the background. When the State Department could once more focus on Cuba, Menocal's government had also declared war against Germany and become an ally. The Liberal revolt was virtually dead, leaving in its wake an area of widespread violence and unrest in Oriente Province at the extreme eastern end of the island. As sugar production was considered important to the war effort, it became a United States goal to see this area pacified. Victorious in his struggle to stay in power, Menocal had no wish for another American occupation, and now resisted the dispatch of United States troops to Cuba. In the summer of 1917, however, the State Department hit upon a formula for sending troops which would reassure Menocal while threatening his enemies. To ready its men for war, ran the new line, the United States needed semitropical areas where troops could train the year round, and

Cuba was ideal for the purpose. Gladly accepting this approach, Menocal issued the necessary invitation, and two marine regiments soon arrived to patrol the Oriente countryside. Some marine forces would remain in the area until 1922, and Menocal served out his second term in relative security.[53]

Whether it used American power to supplant indigenous governments, as in Haiti and the Dominican Republic, or to maintain them in office, as in Nicaragua and Cuba, the Wilson administration felt few self-imposed limits on its freedom of action in the Caribbean. Its policy makers consistently showed confidence that they were acting for everyone's best interests. As a new United States minister to the Dominican Republic stated late in 1913, "President Wilson's declaration of principles concerning Latin America reserved the right to enter any Latin American country to see that the people's rights were not lost to them by force or fraud. . . ." In practice the Wilsonians intervened only in Caribbean countries, not "any Latin American country," but within the Caribbean region they were determined to exercise control.[54]

Colonel Edward M. House, Wilson's intimate friend and adviser, recorded a conversation with Secretary of State Robert Lansing which illustrated this point. In November 1915, when the United States was deeply involved in Haiti and the Dominican Republic, Lansing discussed with House the status of the other Caribbean states. According to House's account, "He puts them in the same category with Santo Domingo and Haiti and believes we should take the same measures to bring about order, both financial and civil, as we are taking in those countries. I approved this policy and promised to express this opinion to the President." In fact Washington never went so far, but the evident willingness to do so showed the peculiar position to which Wilsonian idealism had been deflected.[55]

Wilson's Caribbean policies nevertheless reflected an inexorable logic. Well before Woodrow Wilson became president, United States policy had become fixed on stability in the region. Like his predecessors, Wilson faced the reality of instability instead. In Haiti and the Dominican Republic, his administration had to deal with failed political systems which seemed incapable by themselves of ending a state of virtual anarchy. Unless and until the national policy in the Caribbean should be redefined, no United States government could ignore such political collapse, or refrain from attempting to take charge where it existed. Wilson's hopes for a new relationship with the area therefore were dashed by his acceptance of previously existing policy and doctrine. Rather than question the need to impose American control, Wilson was the more inclined to accept it in order to serve his own ideological purposes.

Part III

Aspects of Hegemony

Chapter 12

———··⟨✖⟩··———

The United States Impact on Cuba

The United States presence in the Caribbean took many forms, including private investment, special trade ties, financial supervision of local governments, formal protectorate arrangements, armed interventions, and a variety of political, social, and cultural effects. All of these were present in the Cuban case, which represented the most fully rounded example of Yankee penetration in all its diversity. It is therefore useful to look at the Cuban example, not merely from the point of view of Washington policy makers, but in terms of the United States' impact on Cuba itself. As the twentieth century advanced, Cubans would increasingly claim that to a significant degree, their society was shaped by alien forces from the United States. It is worth considering how and to what extent this was true.

There can be no question as to United States domination of the Cuban economy. By the end of the First World War, this domination was evident in almost every economic sector. Cuba's foreign trade went overwhelmingly to the United States; in 1918, that nation provided 76 percent of Cuba's imports and took 72 percent of its exports, in an exchange totaling almost six hundred million dollars for the year. Sugar was still Cuba's principal export crop, and while the war years saw the growth of a European market for Cuban sugar, the bulk of it still went to the United States under the terms of the 1903 reciprocity treaty. Cuban agriculture not only produced for the American market, but was itself heavily penetrated by American capital. By 1920 the United States investment in Cuban sugar lands and mills reached about four hundred million dollars, while roughly one-half of all Cuban sugar production came from American-owned properties.[1]

In addition, United States interests had acquired substantial control over

Cuba's tobacco exports in 1902, and accounted for almost half of its tobacco production. North American capital also came to loom large in Cuban
railroads, public utilities, mining, banking, and other enterprises. Until 1914
British investments in Cuba had exceeded those of the United States, but were
largely in "passive" holdings in the form of bonded indebtedness. After 1914
the British stake shrank, while American interests mushroomed, and within
a decade had far outstripped those of all other nationalities combined. The
American dollar even became the domestic circulating medium, driving Cuban
pesos out of the market.[2]

While United States investment in Cuba had more than doubled between
1895 and the end of the military occupation in 1902, it grew faster after 1902,
and faster yet after 1910. The security offered investors by the Platt Amendment, the Reciprocity Treaty of 1903, and the assurance of a friendly government in Havana did much to attract American dollars. So did the availability
of good Cuban land on the market. The new opportunities for sugar profits
required capital, but many Cuban landowners were too deeply in debt to meet
their obligations, much less renovate their war-damaged estates. These had little choice but to sell their holdings to pay their debts. Small farmers too lacked
money, seeds, livestock, and credit. The resulting wave of postwar land sales
resulted in a major increase in foreign land ownership, particularly by citizens
of the United States, and in a rapid rise in land prices, which increased seven-
fold in Oriente Province between 1902 and 1905 alone. Land transfers were
accelerated by the action of the American military government in regularizing
Cuban land titles; the expensive surveys and legal actions required to validate
titles gave the advantage to large foreign concerns and swept away thousands
of Cuban squatters and smallholders. Thus the United States occupation and
its policies increased foreign landownership and accentuated the trend toward
large holdings at the expense of small farmers.[3]

The influx of foreign investment in Cuba slackened between 1906 and 1910,
undermined by uneasy financial conditions in the United States, but in 1911 the
dollars began once more to flood in. The steadily rising price of sugar ensured
that this movement would continue, while the outbreak of war in Europe in
1914 sent sugar prices soaring. In 1913, sugar sold on the world market for
2.15 United States cents per pound; in 1914 it leaped to 3.66 cents, and by
1916 hit 4.77 cents, a level never before reached. The Cuban sugar crop of
1913 was the first to surpass two million tons, but only three years later it
totaled over three million, all of it sold at over four cents per pound. This sugar
bonanza brought unprecedented wealth to planters and millers, and fueled an
expansion of sugar production that transformed large areas of the island.[4]

Traditionally, Cuban sugar growing had been based mostly in central Cuba.
The eastern third of the island was more lightly populated than the rest, and
less of its land was cultivated; in 1900, only 22 percent of Oriente Province

was in farmland of any kind. While sugar was the leading crop, Oriente's sugar plantations averaged only 13.2 acres in 1899, and large areas of the province were in forest and fallow land. This land use pattern began to change with the growth of foreign investment after 1898. In the older sugar regions, American investors bought existing estates; in the east, they built up new ones. The unutilized land of Oriente in particular attracted large buyers. In 1901 the United Fruit Company bought some two hundred thousand acres near Nipe Bay on the north coast, and in the following years expanded this impressive base to nearly double its original size. The company intended at first to grow bananas on the new land, but quickly found that sugar was more profitable. At about the same time Congressman R. B. Hawley of Texas, and a group of investors which included Theodore Havemeyer of the "sugar trust", formed a syndicate which became the Cuban-American Sugar Company. In 1902 they too bought heavily near Nipe Bay, and built, in *central* Chaparra, what was then the largest sugar mill in Cuba. By 1910 Cuban-American had expanded the Chaparra property into the world's largest sugar plantation. Located in a remote area and surrounded by forest, the Nipe Bay district attracted other large sugar companies as well, and became the beachhead for a new sugar invasion of Oriente.[5]

The wartime sugar boom had its most spectacular effects in Oriente, where a wild scramble for prospective sugar land began. Soaring land prices induced many more smallholders to sell to the sugar companies. The great forests which occupied much of the area were ruthlessly cut down to clear the land, the precious hardwoods burned in neverending fires that left a permanent smoke pall across the sky. In 1919 the single largest sugar plantation in Oriente contained more acreage than had all of the cultivated land in the province in 1899; in the same year, Oriente's sugar acreage was greater than that in all of Cuba in 1899. What had been a region of lumbering, mining, fishing, grazing, and diversified farming became a one-crop economy, as other crops were pushed onto marginal land or disappeared entirely.[6]

In the older Cuban sugar districts, Cuban suppliers called *colonos* raised much of the cane ground by the great *centrales,* and shared to some extent in the rising sugar prosperity. In the new sugar lands of the east, much more of the cane was grown directly by the millowners, who strove to control all phases of sugar production. They characteristically built their own railroads, docks, workers' housing, and other facilities, seeking maximum autonomy. As a Cuban writer put it:

The *central* is now more than a mere plantation . . . it is a complicated system of land, machinery, transportation, technicians, workers, capital, and people to produce sugar. It is a complete social organism, as live and complex as a city . . . or a baronial keep. . . . And all this huge feudal territory is practically outside the jurisdiction of public law; the norms of private property hold sway there. The owner's power is as complete over this immense estate as though it were just a small plantation or farm. Everything there is private—ownership, industry, mill, houses, stores, police, railroad, port.[7]

Whether in the east or the west, sugar became the basis of the Cuban economy. It brought with it economic domination by the owners of the *centrales*, or great mills, the consolidation of most of the good land into large corporate holdings, the virtual elimination of the rural middle class, and the reduction of much of the peasantry to seasonal wage workers. Employed only a few months a year during the *zafra*, or harvest season, the new rural proletariat existed only precariously for the rest of the year. Their typical diet of rice, beans, and tubers was inadequate for good health, and left them prone to tuberculosis, malaria, and other diseases. The change of land use to export agriculture eliminated Cuba's self-sufficiency in food, forcing the importation of a part of the basic food supply from the United States at increased prices. At the same time, the concentration of capital in sugar production kept Cuban society overwhelmingly rural; in 1919, for example, 80 percent of Oriente's population was engaged in agriculture. While large-scale sugar production had already been the leading economic activity before 1900, it was the massive United States investment after that date which pushed the sugar revolution into the remotest corners of the island and enabled its unbridled development. The unprecedented profits of the war years served to drive out less profitable crops to make way for ever more sugar.[8]

As Oriente Province experienced the most extreme effects of the sugar revolution, it exhibited the most social unrest. The sugar boom brought to Oriente an influx of people which increased the population 60 percent between 1907 and 1919. Many of the older inhabitants lost their land, and most became seasonally employed sugar workers. Living costs rose along with field wages as much of the food supply became dependent on imports, thus undercutting the workers' prosperity during the boom. Displaced, frustrated, and resentful, large numbers of the Oriente peasantry joined the Liberal revolt against Mario Menocal after the latter's fraudulent reelection in 1916. As the revolt failed during February and March 1917, its Liberal leaders fled the country or made their peace with the government, but the aroused *quajiros* of Oriente merely substituted local grievances for the national issues which had motivated the Liberal party. Led by their own local chieftains, they raided estates, destroyed property, and stole cattle in a broad outbreak of social banditry. It was this crude protest which the United States marines were sent to suppress later in 1917, and by 1918 a combination of marine patrols and Cuban government measures had largely restored order.[9]

Elsewhere in Cuba there was less violent reaction to the sugar revolution

Cuban sugar *central*, 1890s. Courtesy of the American Geographical Society Collection, University of Wisconsin–Milwaukee

than in Oriente, but almost every part of the island saw the same forces bringing similar patterns of change. Accompanying the new trends was the appearance in Cuba of large numbers of foreigners, which added to the social stresses. Oddly enough, comparatively few of these were from the United States. Despite the enormous influence of American business penetration, not many Americans resided permanently in Cuba: fewer than seven thousand in 1910. Tourists and business travelers were more numerous, but had a relatively small impact on the island outside of Havana and a few other large towns. Although Americans controlled a disproportionate share of Cuba's large enterprises, they employed local workers to staff them.[10]

By a wide margin, the largest foreign group in Cuba was Spanish. Ironically, the period after Cuba achieved independence had seen the largest Spanish immigration there in history. Almost two hundred thousand Spaniards arrived between 1902 and 1910, a very large number in an island with only two million inhabitants in the latter year. Spaniards had traditionally been Cuba's shopkeepers and middlemen, and these new arrivals reinforced the pattern. Spanish-born merchants dominated wholesale importing and retail selling everywhere, in rural as well as urban areas. They employed other Spaniards as much as possible, and formed a close-knit middle class known for hard work and hard bargaining. In the country they ran the *bodegas*, or rural general stores, advanced money and credit at high interest, and often bought and resold crops. As principal creditors to the peasantry, they were hated by the rural poor. During Oriente's Negro Revolt of 1912, a black insurrection with both political and social overtones, the rebels singled out Spanish shops and property for attack, destroying over a million dollars' worth in a few weeks.[11]

A second major immigration came from the neighboring West Indies to serve as field workers for the sugar harvest. The rapid growth of sugar culture in Camaguey and Oriente provinces created a local labor shortage, met by the domestic migration of workers from other parts of Cuba and by importing foreigners. Until 1910 Cuban law had forbidden nonwhite immigration, but in 1912 the United Fruit Company received special permission to bring in 1,400 Haitian laborers, and in 1914 virtually all restrictions were dropped. A system of contract labor quickly arose which brought in some 180,000 black Haitians and Jamaicans between 1914 and 1921. This pool of cheap labor tended to hold down field wages except during the frantic wartime boom, and created social stresses by introducing alien cultures into the countryside. Even the boom could not prevent rising labor unrest in 1918, and a new union activism which mounted two general strikes in the following year.[12]

By the First World War, Cuba had an economy based upon the production of sugar by large corporations. Foreigners dominated in the ownership of these enterprises, United States capital being far in the lead. Although the Cuban elite still owned considerable holdings, these usually took the form of shares in foreign-based companies, while many former owners sold out entirely and lived on the fortunes thus acquired. In general, what was left of the old Creole society survived on North American terms. At the next level of business activity, the Spanish community dominated in merchandising, importing, and small-scale rural credit. Only the bottom of the economic pyramid, represented mainly by the rural wage workers, was truly Cuban. Most Cubans lived and worked in a society shaped by outsiders; in time they knew and resented this. In the words of the Cuban scholar Fernando Ortiz Fernández, "Cuba will never be really independent until it can free itself from the coils of the serpent of colonial economy that fattens on its soil but strangles its inhabitants and winds itself about the palm tree of our republican coat of arms, converting it into the sign of the Yankee dollar." Only the continuing sugar boom could make the system tolerable; when the boom collapsed in the twenties, many Cubans ceased to believe that the sugar monoculture had ever been to their benefit.[13]

In spite of Cuban resentment at United States political and economic power, a visible Americanization was evident in Havana and the larger provincial towns. Though long faithful to Parisian culture, the Cuban elite looked increasingly to American consumption patterns and styles of living. By the First World War many wealthy Cubans sent their sons to be educated in the United States rather than Europe. Havana's fashionable new suburb of Vedado contained houses with Yankee-style plumbing and electric lights, while the streets of the capital were thick with automobiles, and the Ford agency flourished. The face of the city became less Spanish and more North American with every decade. Well-to-do Cuban young people aspired to some of the personal freedom enjoyed by their youthful brethren to the north. In working-class districts, children could be seen playing baseball, that fascinating game introduced by the United States Army and taken up by Cuban boys wherever they possessed a stick and a ball. In Havana's business district, the staccato of the typewriter and the telephone's strident ring sounded through barred windows and shaded arcades. Billboards and electric signs reflected the latest methods of Yankee advertising, while large department stores reminded observers of those in Chicago, Boston, and Philadelphia. Havana had become a queer mixture of Spanish and North American cultures, while other Cuban cities more faintly reflected the Yankee influence.[14]

Cuba's politics was, if anything, even more fragmented than its culture. Its politics was, first of all, severely truncated. Many of the larger national issues were predetermined by the United States, which regulated Cuba's foreign relations and, with less success, its government finances. As we have seen, a combination of market factors and Yankee dollars had massively reshaped the island's economy without significant reference to its political system. The sugar economy was simply a fact, beyond the power of Cuban governments to change; at any rate, Washington would have disapproved of excessive meddling with the private economy. Cubans could not even take up arms to struggle for power, the most basic of political acts, without having the end result determined by foreigners. Their leaders might learn to manipulate the effects of the Platt Amendment with varying degrees of skill, attempting to use United States intervention for local and partisan purposes, but the ultimate decision always lay in Washington. As Jules Benjamin has noted, it was a politics largely devoid of major content: "In effect, the Cubans were not to have politics, only elections." [15]

If the content of politics was limited, so was entry into political careers. A poor, semiliterate, mostly rural population looked to a remarkably narrow segment of society for its public leadership. The old plantation elite had tended to leave politics to others, a tendency which strengthened under the republic. Cubans who became wealthy in business normally stayed away from active political careers. Gaining wealth, a principal object of such careers, was for the rich somewhat redundant, while men of substance needed to stay on good terms with the government whatever its makeup or party alignment. North Americans repeatedly mourned the refusal of the "better classes" to get involved, but a few exceptions like President Mario Menocal merely proved the rule. Nor was the commercial middle class, with its strong Spanish roots, very

In the American Club, Havana, 1890s. Courtesy of the American Geographical Society Collection, University of Wisconsin–Milwaukee

interested in partisan politics. The real centers of economic power, on the other hand, were foreign. Thus the island's major economic interest groups closely monitored politics, but did not themselves participate.[16]

Those at the bottom of Cuba's economic pyramid, like those at the top, rarely pursued political careers. This applied particularly to black Cubans, who had constituted a large majority of the soldiers in the Liberation Army of 1895–98. Representing roughly one-third of the island's people, the black population was mostly rural and poor. They and their leaders hoped for a share of public patronage and political influence after 1898, but were repeatedly disappointed. Embittered by consistently broken promises, they formed the Independent party of Color in 1907, which was outlawed three years later when it threatened to make trouble for the government. In 1912 the Negro Revolt broke out, centered in Oriente Province, to make good black political demands, but the Havana authorities were able to crush it, after which they massacred thousands of Negroes in a campaign of terror and intimidation. Cuba continued to be ruled, not by the soldiers of the Liberation Army, but by their erstwhile leaders.[17]

For three decades after 1898, Cuban political leadership was the near-monopoly of the officer corps of the Liberation Army. The army veterans succeeded in securing most of the desirable places in the first military occupation, and led in organizing the republic's first political parties. Thereafter, as the limits of Cuba's independence became clear, the War of Liberation stood

Cuban cane cutters, 1890s. Courtesy of the American Geographical Society Collection, University of Wisconsin–Milwaukee

almost alone as the symbol of national pride, and its heroes occupied a ground not open to succeeding generations. The struggle against Spain, at least, had been genuinely Cuban, and all Cubans could thrill to its memory.[18]

Even after that thrill began to fade, the former army officers ran the government. They were soon deeply entrenched in the civil service, and formally organized to defend their dominance. In 1912 the "veteran's movement" demanded that *all* civil appointments go to Liberation Army veterans and their descendants, bringing such pressure on the government that congress suspended the civil service law and the president appointed a special committee to screen out nonveterans. Concerned that the veterans' bullying could threaten the national authority, the United States State Department stepped in and threatened to take a hand, upon which the veterans withdrew their demands. They had overreached themselves in seeking a total monopoly of office, but they long continued to enjoy the bulk of political spoils.[19]

The struggle for office was the more bitter because alternate career opportunities were so limited. Cuban government, whatever its limitations, was the only remaining field of enterprise which was wholly Cuban, and it therefore absorbed the energies of many who would in other circumstances have made their careers in the business world. In politics, management skills gave way to charisma, rational calculation to impassioned appeals, but economic motivation continued to play a leading role.

In Cuba, as in other Caribbean nations, the government was the leading provider of employment and source of wealth for much of the educated class. For the many families who had lost their lands through debt, war losses, and lack of capital, there was little other recourse. To the political activist, success for one's own party could mean status, prosperity, even power, while failure cut off all avenues to government largess. Dominated by the officer corps of 1898, the *politicos* sought material advancement and security for themselves above all else. Irene Wright, a long-term North American observer, concluded in 1910 that Cuba had

> the most expensive government on earth, and those who operate it (the Cuban office-holding class) have every reason to labor to make it even more so, since its extravagancies run to salaries, which they receive, and to even more outrageous contracts and concessions, on which they get liberal "rake-offs."

The burden of this extravagance, Wright continued, rested upon the foreign-owned export economy and upon the ultimate consumers, the poor Cubans who made up most of the population. This was a severe judgment, but it was indisputable that Cuban official corruption became notorious, and a source of shame to many Cubans.[20]

Resentful of United States influence and disillusioned by the venality of Cuban politics, Cubans came to blame even their governmental corruption upon the Yankees. The administration of Tomás Estrada Palma (1902–1906) had been characterized on the whole by financial integrity, and when the second United States intervention took over in 1906 it allegedly found a full treasury. It was this second occupation, headed by Charles E. Magoon, which the Cubans blamed for fixing the pattern of future public corruption. Conciliatory and well-meaning, Magoon attempted to calm the passions of the 1906 August revolution by giving something to everyone. Seeing the *politicos* as the key to stability, he rewarded them with sinecures, patronage, and public works programs. As Irene Wright saw it at the time, Magoon had orders from Washington to keep Cuba quiet, and to do so he simply bought off potential troublemakers. According to his critics, he swelled the ranks of government employees, emptied the treasury to build roads, bridges, and waterworks, and placed large treasury loans with favored New York bankers. Allegedly the cat's-paw of Frank Steinhart and North American business interests, Magoon was accused of letting shady construction contracts which especially benefited Steinhart's interests and connections.[21]

The Cuban treasury surplus stood at twenty-six million dollars early in 1906; Magoon's provisional government left less than three million in 1909, against debts of almost twelve million. To Cubans, it appeared that Magoon had looted the treasury to buy peace, and had set off a riot of pork-barreling that defied all efforts to stop it after he was gone. According to historian Herminio Portell-Vilá,

The idea that the government budget was the first national industry, afterwards carried to inconceivable extremes by the Cuban governments of the second republic . . . was a consequence of the weakness of Magoon and his advisers and of the notion that to keep the occupied people tranquil all compromises were little.

Certainly the administration of President José Miguel Gómez (1909–13), which followed Magoon's regime, raised corruption to new levels. There was thus a clear contrast between the relative honesty of government under Estrada Palma and the general crookedness of Gómez and his successors, neatly divided by Magoon's interventionist rule.[22]

The Cuban charges did not go undisputed, however. Magoon's defenders pointed out that Estrada Palma himself dissipated much of his treasury surplus in attempting to put down the 1906 rebellion. Magoon's controversial bond issues were largely intended to complete paving, water, and sewer projects already under way when he arrived, and the charges concerning shady contracts lacked proof. Magoon's tenure had coincided with an economic recession in the United States and poor crop years in Cuba, which brought bad times and lowered government revenues. Most effective was the countercharge that payoffs and patronage, shady contracts and sinecures, were a part of Cuban reality from colonial times, and that Magoon had simply worked with the system as he found it. In British scholar Hugh Thomas' biting words, "The arguments of Cuban historians, later copied by guilt-ridden North Americans, that Magoon taught the Cubans corruption are among the most hilarious examples ever of self-deception."[23]

Whatever the sources of Cuban corruption, Cuban or North American, no one disputed that Washington dominated Havana in those matters which affected United States interests. The British minister reported in 1910 that Cuba's foreign policy was wholly governed from Washington: "Though independent in name the Island is in the position of a lap-dog whose owner keeps a tight hold on the string." The British themselves had had occasion to feel the truth of the minister's statement. The terms of an Anglo-Cuban trade treaty signed in May 1905 reflected United States interference; on orders from the State Department, United States Minister Herbert Squiers had kept enough pressure on the Cubans to block the treaty's ratification until all reference to customs rates had been removed from it. By the time the emasculated version was ratified, the British cared little whether it lived or died, for their goal had been to protect their Cuban sales from increased tariff barriers.[24]

The Cubans themselves had been irritated, however, by Squiers's persistent prodding. A cabinet minister called at the American legation to tell Squiers that his access to the president should be subject to the same limits as that of any of the other diplomats in Havana. Squiers then "very plainly told Mr. Zaldo . . . that the position of the American Minister was quite different . . .; that I am here on a quite different basis, as is well understood. . . ."[25]

It was nevertheless true that from 1902 to 1906, Washington was disposed to give the Cubans a good deal of leeway in their domestic affairs. This changed with the second occupation of 1906–1909, after which Taft and Knox devised the so-called "preventive policy." Taft defined this as "doing all within [our] power to induce Cuba to avoid every reason that would make intervention possible at any time." In practice this meant close supervision by the American legation of the day-to-day actions of the Cuban government. The State Department saw this as "preventive intervention" to head off disruptive developments, rather than intervening after the fact to undo their results. Elihu Root had given a formal assurance in 1901 that the United States' right of intervention under the Platt Amendment was "not synonymous with the intermeddling or interference with the affairs of the Cuban government," but in fact that was exactly what it became.[26]

In 1913 the proper scope of United States authority in Cuba became the subject of an illuminating exchange between William Jennings Bryan and Woodrow Wilson. While attempting to master the details of his new duties, the secretary of state found that the late Gómez administration had granted a concession to some North Americans to build a bridge across the entrance to Havana harbor. In Washington, however, both the War Department and the Navy Department had voiced opposition to the project, and the State Department therefore protested so strongly as to bring construction to a halt. Bryan could find no authority in the Platt Amendment to justify interference in such a matter, and was troubled by the peremptory tone employed by his predecessor. "I think that the language used by the Department . . . is stronger than we should employ in giving advice," he wrote Wilson. "While it purports to be advice, it might easily be construed as a command." But the president had no such qualms. "If we are to stand guardian of the independence and safety of Cuba, we are surely entitled to a definite opinion as to matters of defense and also to give urgent advice with regard to such matters," he replied. With such an attitude, advice and commands were much the same.[27]

Cuba's Negro Revolt of 1912 illustrated two specific aspects of the United States position in Cuba: the manifold ramifications of the threat of intervention and North American insistence on the protection of foreign property. The outbreak of the revolt shocked and surprised most Cubans, giving rise to sensational rumors about its origins. The prevalent thinking held that the ostensible leaders of the revolt were incapable of organizing such a large-scale movement, an estimate in which the United States minister concurred. Those involved, it was assumed, must therefore be the dupes of some larger conspiracy, and the most widely repeated story put Frank Steinhart, entrepreneur and former American consul general, at its center. Steinhart was thought to have profited greatly under the provisional government of Charles Magoon, who was usually pictured as his tool; it was therefore easy to conclude that

Steinhart desired another United States intervention, and had joined his influence and resources with others who similarly hoped to profit after bringing about the revolt. This accusation actually appeared in a Havana newspaper, though the names of the supposed principals were represented only by initials. Even Manuel Sanguily, Cuban minister of foreign affairs, suspected "certain foreigners of prominence who had greatly prospered during the first intervention and naturally desired a return to old conditions" of plotting the rebellion.[28]

If the revolt were really aimed at instigating another United States intervention, such an aim would best be achieved by the wholesale destruction of foreign property, but the rebels were in fact trying to avoid unnecessary property destruction except for that of the hated Spanish merchants. In retrospect it seems clear that the Negro Revolt was solely the work of the blacks and their leaders in eastern Cuba. Yet the blacks themselves apparently wished the Americans to take a hand in events. Their leader, General Evariste Estenoz, sent a message to a nearby American consul which reportedly stated that "rather than be governed by the Cubans in the way we have been it would be much preferable to be governed by strangers." Furthermore, Estenoz wanted a representative of the United States present during any negotiations between himself and the Cuban authorities. Only if the United States guaranteed fulfillment of its terms could he accept a negotiated peace, he said; the Cuban government had betrayed its promises far too often to be credible. In the event there would be no negotiation, for Estenoz was soon to die in battle along with most of his troops, but his tentative appeal to North American power fit the established pattern of Cuban political struggles.[29]

A second revealing facet of the Negro Revolt episode lay in the State Department's repeated insistence that foreign property must be protected, and that failure to do so would bring United States intervention. In practice Washington sent warships and marines to aid in this function without formal intervention, to the relief of the Gómez government, but the threat of intervention never lapsed. In the midst of the revolt Philander Knox instructed A. M. Beaupre, the United States minister to Cuba, to "vigorously impress upon the President of Cuba that a continued failure on the part of his Government adequately to protect life and property will inevitably compel this Government to intervene in Cuba. . . ."[30]

The American minister's reply to Knox voiced concern about the burden thus placed upon the Cuban authorities. The area of fighting, he noted, contained foreign properties of enormous value, all potentially in jeopardy. Foreign owners clamored for military protection and complained bitterly of its lack. Yet the Cuban government would have had to dismantle its field forces to fully meet all these demands. At the same time, the Cuban-owned property in Oriente got no protection at all, since foreign demands took up every soldier who could be spared. The Cubans, Beaupre pointed out, labored under a disadvantage which the Spanish had never faced in Cuba. During the War of Liberation, foreigners and natives alike simply had to accept what the war brought them, hoping for eventual indemnity after hostilities ended. Now foreigners were not only favored over natives, but they claimed an absolute right to total property protection, something which no government could provide in times of disorder. The very vastness of foreign property holdings in Cuba made this problem a unique one for its government.[31]

In times of armed struggles like the Negro Revolt, the United States could control events in Cuba through intervention or its threat. In more normal times, the financial controls implied in the Platt Amendment constituted significant tools for the State Department. These were especially potent when the Cuban government needed to borrow large sums of money. The State Department routinely monitored Cuban government loans, and made its consent to them conditional on satisfaction with Cuba's current financial policies. The department had made no serious objection to such loans in 1904, 1909 (a loan authorized by Magoon in the first place), and 1913. A 1917 loan, however, was approved only on condition that Cuba satisfy the claims against it of two North American companies, while approval of a 1923 loan was tied to major budget and tax reforms.[32]

American diplomats in Cuba were fully aware of the coercive possibilities of fiscal supervision. In the closing months of the Gómez regime, Cuban leaders clashed with the American legation over Beaupre's efforts to check the riot of graft with which the administration prepared to leave office. When Gómez attempted to obstruct Beaupre's influence and access to policy makers, the minister immediately thought of the uses of the State Department's loan controls. "It seems hardly credible that it should not have occurred to the Cuban Government that we, in our turn, have . . . advantages . . . in the almost certain event of the Government desiring to place a further loan," he wrote Knox.[33]

Pervasive as United States authority could be, however, most Cubans had long since grown accustomed to it. Eventually, it was not so much the means of control exercised by Washington as the tone of that control which rankled most. As the years passed, North Americans came more and more openly to regard Cuba as simply a colony of the United States. Although both parties observed the outward forms of Cuban sovereignty, neither really believed in them very deeply. The Taft-Knox "preventive policy" of close routine supervision continued with little change under the Wilson administration, while Cuba's declaration of war on Germany in 1917 brought down from Washington a fresh swarm of intelligence operatives, shipping agents, naval officers, and the like. The behavior of these newcomers was even more cavalier than that of the regular Yankee establishment in Cuba, and by 1918 it had seriously alarmed the United States minister there.

That post was then held by William E. Gonzales, an American of Cuban descent who had served in Cuba during the Spanish-American War and returned to edit a newspaper in South Carolina. An early supporter of Woodrow Wilson's presidential ambitions, he had received the Havana appointment both as a reward for political services and in the hope that the Cubans would welcome an American minister of Cuban extraction. In fact Gonzales found himself not particularly popular, but he nevertheless retained a distinct sensibility to Cuban feelings. This led him in 1918 to write a lengthy protest to the State Department about the damage done to Cuban-American relations by the throng of official visitors.[34]

Cuba, he reminded his superiors, had declared war upon Germany soon after the United States did so, without prompting or coercion. It had freely donated a number of interned enemy ships to the United States for use in the common war effort. Its armed forces had readily accepted defense plans drawn up in Washington, and its president had agreed to the continued presence of United States troops in Oriente Province. It had censored foreign mail, arrested suspected enemy agents at Washington's behest, and destroyed enemy propaganda materials arriving via neutral Spain. The Cubans had seen United States agencies reduce their imports of necessities like flour and coal to a fraction of their normal volume, bringing actual hardship to some. In short, Cuba had willingly cooperated in the war effort to an impressive extent.[35]

In return, the Cubans had received a horde of virtual invaders from the north, Gonzales reported.

> During this period there have come to Cuba, and operated here with perfect freedom, agents of the Department of Justice, of the United States Army Intelligence, of the United States Naval Intelligence, of the War Trade Board, and of the Censorship Board, each working more or less independently . . . none of them responsible to the Department of State, none of them having knowledge of the country or the people, and none of them having contributed to the cordiality existing. . . .

These newcomers soon developed "a distinct idea of the right and power to *control,*" an attitude which, if not curbed, would "prove fatal to good feeling and cordiality." The naval intelligence agents "accept[ed] every wild rumor as fact" and "attempt[ed] to secure the arbitrary arrest of all sorts of people on the flimsiest charges." One army intelligence report characterized as a drunkard an influential cabinet minister who had been particularly useful to the State Department, and the Cuban learned of it. Other reports charged even President Menocal with German sympathies. "It is not in human nature," Gonzales declared, "and certainly not in Latin nature, to enthuse over such return for the efforts of the Cuban Administration." There must be a change in both people and methods, or Cuba's spirit of cooperation would be soured and destroyed.[36]

Gonzales' indignation was natural, but the wartime sojourners derived their arrogance from the general perception of their countrymen that Cuba was a subject nation. It was in fact a sovereign state without real sovereignty, while its people's nationalism had been reduced to a facade and a psychological defense mechanism. With a foreign-dominated economy, a foreign-penetrated culture, and a government limited to the politics of graft, the Cuban nation was simply insufficiently Cuban. It had been a Spanish colony with economic ties to the United States; it became a United States colony suffused with Spanish middlemen. Culturally, it was overshadowed by both metropolitan powers. There had never been a purely Cuban society or a genuinely Cuban state. It was no wonder that those Cubans who aspired to create them came finally to think of the task largely in terms of expelling foreign influence.

Chapter 13

Democracy, Constabularies, and Elections

Stability was the general goal of the United States in the Caribbean. How to achieve that stability, and what its purposes were, were more complex questions, even to the men directly engaged in implementing Washington's policies. The army's attitudes about pacifying supervised peoples grew from its recent experience with Plains Indians in the United States. Army officers believed that good behavior should be rewarded and bad behavior punished, both as quickly as possible, with little room for negotiation or compromise. They did not lack humane concern of a paternalistic kind, but turned naturally to force or its threat to overcome resistance to their actions. Such officers saw Hispanic Americans as subject to anarchy, corruption, and excessive individualism, and wished to inculcate a sense of community and order in their place. It is clear that armed forces leaders in the Caribbean served their own values while obeying the orders of their government. Career officers in all three services valued order, good government, and progress. They shared the spirit of the Progressive era, believed in social and racial inequality, and saw disorder as innately evil. They were overwhelmingly middle class in origin, and their values, it has been aptly said, were more those of Main Street than of Wall Street.[1]

The writer and journalist Carleton Beals traveled widely in the Caribbean region between the two world wars, and came to know intimately the military officers and civilian officials who represented the United States there. A crusading liberal who bitterly criticized American interventions in the area, Beals nevertheless acquired a grudging respect for the sincerity of his nation's proconsuls. He compared them to the American Communists of the day in their idealism and their contempt for political realities: "Both believe in the implantation of an ideal upon people by force." According to Beals, the imperialists, as he called them—the United States colonial administrators, financial experts, and military or naval officers in the Caribbean—firmly believed in the superiority of their own society and the inferiority of foreigners. They further believed in "good roads, sanitation, the strict enforcement of law, stability, work, . . . efficiency, the punctilious payment of debts, and democracy." [2]

Active and extroverted, these men seemed unaware of the deep contradictions in the assumptions which guided them. The "imperialist," Beals wrote, "never stops to try to reconcile his inner conviction that backward, dark people are incapable of progress . . . or democracy with his belief that the only possible way for a foreign people to be happy is to be standardized into the mold already created in the United States." While devising schemes for honest elections, the "imperialists" looked mainly to arbitrary power to achieve results. Possession of such power freed them from the constraints of local politics, but also led them to ignore the local political culture and social realities. The resulting attempts to impose alien institutions and norms created havoc within the subject societies. Such an approach was "not even a good insecticide to kill old parasitisms," Beals insisted; it was rather "a new skin laid over old sores," while underneath, corruption continued to eat into the tissues of social life. Yet, Beals concluded his analysis, "the Imperialist at work abroad is muddle-headed but he is fantastically honest; the shining aura of the crusader always mantles all his acts." [3]

The proconsuls of empire in the Caribbean shared many assumptions with political leaders, administrators, and State Department officials in Washington. Most of those in both groups wished to impose stability upon the Caribbean without too obviously violating their professed democratic values, and many expected or hoped actually to enhance democracy by their actions. The interplay, and frequent incompatibility, of these twin goals of democracy and stability was illustrated by two general approaches of American policy in the region: the organization of national constabularies in several countries, and the many United States attempts to reform or supervise elections.

One of the features of Caribbean life which regularly outraged Yankee observers was the use of military power for political purposes. As elsewhere in Latin America, Caribbean regimes were often overthrown by force, which might reside in a national army turning on its own government, or in ad hoc political armies, hired mercenaries, or armed mobs. To North Americans, all were equally unacceptable. In the United States, the military services had always been properly subordinated to civil control. They had been as politically neutral in practice as in theory, their nonpolitical nature taken as a given. Furthermore, there had been no rival military forces in the United States capable of challenging those of the state. The sole exception, the Confederate army, had been the creation of a new civil polity, not a case of a military insubordinate to its state. This record represented the only proper state of affairs, in Yankee eyes, and it was natural that the very different situation in the Caribbean should provoke efforts at reform. If the devil of revolution was to be exorcised, the region's armed forces must be reduced to their proper role of instruments of the civil state. The goal was to create professional, nonpolitical armed forces strong enough to protect their governments against armed revolt, and to disband or destroy any rival forces which might challenge these depoliticized armies.

The first systematic attempts to create such a force came in Cuba. Washington's original intent was to leave the new Cuban republic with no regular army at all. Instead, during the first occupation of 1898–1902, the North Americans organized a Rural Guard, modeled after that of Mexico and designed to serve as a reliable police force. After separate beginnings in several provinces, Military Governor Leonard Wood consolidated the guard into a uniform national constabulary in 1900. At the end of the occupation, the guard numbered sixteen hundred officers and men, scattered in small detachments over scores of posts. When it assumed power, the Cuban government rapidly enlarged this force, bringing it to a strength of nearly three thousand by 1906. In addition, the United States military government had created a body of four hundred artillerists trained to man the nation's coastal defenses. After independence, however, the Cubans retrained this corps as infantrymen and used it as a sort of palace guard for the president.[4]

The Rural Guard's primary purpose was to protect property in the countryside. The great majority of the guard's posts were on private land, frequently offered rent free by the owners to secure police protection. By 1905 there were some 224 posts, with an average of 12 men at each. Lacking large-unit organization and command, heavy weapons, or real military training, the men of the guard were policemen, not soldiers. When the Liberal revolt against Tomás Estrada Palma broke out in 1906, the beleaguered president found the Rural Guard of little use against a suddenly mustered Liberal army many times its size. Although it remained loyal to the government, the guard was not a major factor in the events of that summer, a fact noted by United States policy makers at the time. One of the objects of Charles Magoon's provisional government, therefore, was to create a more effective armed force which could protect its government against rebellion, making another United States intervention unnecessary.[5]

The American occupation authorities saw the Rural Guard as the logical basis for a reorganized force. It had, after all, remained loyal to its government, and was the only large armed body legally existing in Cuba. The provisional government accordingly made plans to further enlarge the guard, concentrate it into fewer and larger units, and enhance its military efficiency. In 1907, several army schools began retraining the guard, and recruiting went forward steadily. This expansion and reform was supervised by the United States Army in Cuba, while President Theodore Roosevelt approved an ultimate guard strength of 10,000 men.[6]

These plans and projects soon became highly controversial, leading to a confrontation between the provisional government and the popular Cuban Liberal party. The Liberals, who had revolted because Estrada Palma's government had defrauded them of an electoral victory in 1905, regarded the Rural Guard as politically hostile to themselves. They feared that a really effective guard, used for political ends, could indefinitely frustrate Liberal hopes of power. To prevent this, Liberal leaders from José Miguel Gómez down urged replacing the guard with a new regular army whose loyalties had yet to be shaped. United States Army advisers in Cuba opposed the Liberal plan, fearing that the proposed new army would be dominated by the Liberals and give them permanent control of the country. Magoon's regime was anxious to avoid conflict with the Liberals, however, and ultimately accepted a compromise. The Rural Guard would be preserved but enlarged no further, while a so-called permanent army, consisting of a single infantry brigade, would also be formed. The two units had separate commands, but the army, established in April 1908, could be reinforced by men from the guard in case of emergency. The North Americans hoped that the two forces would neutralize each other politically, while together being strong to intimidate prospective rebels.[7]

With the end of the second occupation in 1909 and the advent of President Gómez's administration, earlier fears that the Liberals would politicize the army proved prophetic. Gómez soon scrapped the short-lived compromise upon two separate forces, merging the Rural Guard and the army under the overall command of a close crony. He removed the former guard officers and packed the single new force with officers chosen for their Liberal party connections, creating a solid prop for his regime.[8]

Even after Gómez left office and the Conservative party's Mario Menocal became president, the army retained its Liberal loyalties. When the Liberals organized their 1917 revolt in response to Menocal's fraudulent reelection, the pro-Liberal army was assigned a central role in ousting the president. The government's premature discovery of the revolutionary plot enabled it to arrest many senior army commanders, but even so about one quarter of the army actually took the field on the rebels' side. Quick action by the government and steady United States support of Menocal gravely weakened the rebels, and government victories in the field sealed their defeat. However, it had not been a loyal, nonpartisan army which saved the regime; on the contrary, Menocal had nearly fallen victim to the army, and was afterward obliged to remold it to his own political pattern as Gómez had done before him. In Cuba, any hopes for a nonpolitical armed force were dead, and Washington fully recognized the failure.[9]

Despite its fiasco in Cuba, Washington continued to attempt the creation of nonpolitical government forces in other Caribbean countries. The United States interventions in Haiti and the Dominican Republic in particular saw full-fledged national constabularies emerge under marine training and control. In Haiti the intervention of 1915 established a United States protectorate in which a new national constabulary replaced both the army and the civil police. The new organization, to be known as the *Gendarmerie d'Haïti*, was trained and commanded by officers of the United States Marines, placing both law enforcement and military functions under Washington's control.[10]

The Haitian army thus disbanded had a paper strength of over 9,000 officers and men, but in fact little of this manpower really existed. There were, however, no less than 308 generals and 50 colonels on the government's payroll, who benefited by receiving the few funds and supplies allotted to their mostly imaginary troops. As a fighting force the army was negligible, as the frequent violent overthrow of Haitian governments seemed to attest, and it had been maintained largely for patronage purposes. Besides the army, the central government had maintained a decentralized rural police force under the minister of war, and police units in the larger towns under the minister of interior. These too were disbanded, and their functions consolidated under the new organization. In the North American scheme, the gendarmerie was to keep order in the countryside, protect the government from attack, and supplement the strength of the thinly stretched marine occupation force.[11]

The gendarmerie was formally established in September 1915, and recruiting began almost at once. Marine Lieutenant Colonel Smedley D. Butler became the gendarmerie's first commander in December, with a Haitian rank of major general. Butler's officer corps of 120 marines was similarly elevated; captains became colonels, second lieutenants captains, and sergeants lieutenants, in the Haitian service. In its earlier years the gendarmerie had only white marine officers, who had quickly to learn enough of the native Creole to begin training their men. Recruiting proved relatively easy, once the desperately poor Haitians found that the wages promised were actually paid, and that the food and clothing provided were of a quality and quantity never before available to most of them. Illiterate but enthusiastic, the recruits filled out rapidly and gained in physical strength under their new regimen. The gendarmerie was 1,500 strong by February, 1916, and in October reached its full strength of 2,500 Haitian enlisted men. Taught marine drill and discipline, outfitted with surplus marine uniforms and weapons, the Haitian gendarmerie became a curious tropical mutation of the United States Marine Corps.[12]

The new gendarmerie took over its national responsibilities early in 1916, when its predecessor agencies ceased to exist. Within a few months the Dominican intervention of 1916 drew off nearly half the occupation marines in Haiti, leaving fewer than a thousand. The gendarmerie thus became the most pervasive instrument of United States control. As a marine general recalled, "We . . . used the gendarmerie officers as our agents throughout the country." These officers became what amounted to rural district bosses, while marine regulars continued to garrison the main towns. The marine commander and the gendarmerie chief, fellow marines working in close tandem, soon wielded far more power than the client government which the occupation forces had erected in Port-au-Prince. The two secured State Department support for extending the gendarmerie's jurisdiction to road building, sanitation, and other public service duties.[13]

The gendarmerie officer in the field took on many local functions: judge, paymaster, school superintendent, tax collector, and police chief. His authority was unchallenged, overriding that of local and village officials. As the occupation went on, Haitians increasingly complained about the arbitrary, and sometimes brutal, way in which the gendarmerie exercised power. Isolated in the interior, foreign, often the only white men on the scene, its officers felt few checks upon their behavior, and a few committed serious excesses.[14]

The gendarmerie not only provided a framework for rural administration, but joined the marine regulars in putting down a serious rural uprising in 1918–19. The gendarmerie's own role in road building brought on the trouble; its commander reinstated a nineteenth-century law requiring country people to perform forced labor on the roads in lieu of paying a road tax. This system was formally abandoned in 1918 only after thousands of peasants had been dragged from their villages to labor in distant places. Despite the new orders to the contrary, however, it was quietly continued by a gendarmerie commander in the rugged mountain district of the north, an area occupied by the warlike *cacos* and already prone to local feuding and rebellion. To suppress the resulting *caco* outbreak required all the armed forces available in Haiti; when the job was done, some three thousand Haitians had been killed.[15]

Only in the later years of the nineteen-year United States occupation of Haiti were the white marine officers in the gendarmerie replaced with black Haitians, and its name changed to *Garde d'Haïti*. The transfer of the gendarmerie to full Haitian control occurred in 1934, after which it moved steadily toward the exercise of political power; it had, after all, been created as an instrument to control the people. By the 1940s the *garde*'s high command was making and unmaking presidents. It was doing so, however, as a unified and disciplined force; violent revolution, at least, had ended, for the gendarmerie, now become an army, had a monopoly of military power in Haiti. Thus far was its original concept fulfilled; the failure lay in its lack of subordination to civil authority.[16]

In the Dominican Republic events paralleled those in Haiti. The persistence of revolutionary violence in the former country led the State Department to insist throughout 1915 that the Dominican Army also be replaced by a national constabulary, as elsewhere to be organized and commanded by United States Marines. The Dominican refusal to accept either this demand or that for a Washington-appointed financial controller was the chief issue leading to the complete United States take-over in November 1916. Early in 1917 the United States military government at Santo Domingo drew up plans for a new *Guardia Nacional* to replace the former 500-man army. The North American planners were divided as to whether the new organization should be essentially a national police force, like the Cuban Rural Guard, or an army which also exercised police functions. The result was a body which fell between the two stools, too small, dispersed, and lightly armed to constitute a real army, but too military in outlook for a traditional police force.[17]

Established in April 1917, the National Guard was to have about twelve hundred Dominican enlisted men serving, as in Haiti, under United States marine officers. All ranks above lieutenant were to be filled by marines detached for the duty; only company-grade officers were to be Dominican. In practice, recruiting went slowly at both officer and enlisted levels. Dominicans of all classes resented the American occupation and were uneager to serve it, but eventually enough young countrymen were attracted by the relative affluence of fifteen dollars per month and free food and shelter. Potential officers were scarcer; the marines did not really want Dominican officers and recruited only feebly for them, while even those literate Dominicans willing to collaborate were discouraged by the absence of any promotion prospects. As late as 1920, a majority of company officers were drawn from the ranks of marine enlisted men.[18]

United States entry into the European war in April 1917 brought strong pressures to withdraw the marines stationed in the Caribbean for use in France or in training new units at home. In the Dominican Republic, marine manpower fell well below two thousand for the duration of the war, leaving few marines available to train the new guard, or indeed its enlisted-marine company officers. Without adequate training or even some essential equipment, the guard had to take up its duties long before it was ready. Poorly disciplined, its members too often abused the rural population, which disliked it in any case for its collaboration with the occupiers.[19]

With all these shortcomings, the guard found itself seriously challenged in keeping order. The Dominican Republic was a country of decentralized districts and local *caudillos,* a kind of feudal hierarchy in which the central government had kept its claim to authority only by co-opting regional and local chieftains. The choices had been to buy off the local boss, abandon the district to his control, or support a local rival who would owe some fealty if successful in replacing the incumbent. Of the country's many presidents, only Ulises Heureaux in the late nineteenth century and Ramón Cáceres early in the present one had exercised anything approaching a general authority. The United States occupation in 1916, and subsequent assumption of complete political control, affronted all Dominican leaders from the smallest local bosses to regional and national chiefs. The easternmost portion of the country fell into something like permanent rebellion, desultorily conducted by small bands of fifty to two hundred men whom the marines always regarded as "bandits." Faced with this resistance, the North Americans decided to break the power of the *caudillos* everywhere, and they needed the guard to help their undermanned marine ranks in the task—one which further alienated the guard from its own population during several years of small-scale campaigning.[20]

When the United States government began in 1921 to prepare to withdraw from the Dominican Republic, Washington placed a high priority on reforming the guard. As the only national armed force, it would be pivotal in the nation's future. It must quickly be placed under Dominican officers, who must be recruited and trained, and it must be professionalized to ensure its nonpolitical nature. A new military school at Haina began turning out Dominican officers as rapidly as possible under marine instruction, while the guard's enlisted units rotated through other training centers to learn the skills and discipline so long lacking. Renamed the Dominican National Police, the force was better trained, equipped, and disciplined than ever before when the last of the marines left the country in July 1924.[21]

Both presidential candidates in the 1924 Dominican election promised to maintain the nonpartisan character of the National Police, but the American departure in that year left no way to ensure that such promises were kept. The successful candidate, political veteran Horacio Vásquez, attempted to secure the organization's loyalty, but found in time that the man whom he had placed in command of it sought power for himself. Rafael Leonidas Trujillo was a member of the first class of officers graduated at the Haina Military Academy, and became police commander in 1928. Ruthless and intelligent, he had impressive skills of organization and command. In 1930 he used the power of his army to make himself president, and would rule the Dominican Republic with an iron grip until his assassination thirty-one years later. Once again, Washington's imposed constabulary had failed to remain nonpartisan in local hands. What it had done was to create a central force so formidable as to crush the old Dominican system of local and regional *caudillos,* reducing the entire nation to obedience to a single tyrant.[22]

Cuba, Haiti, and the Dominican Republic were not the only places where the United States sought unsuccessfully to remove force from politics. We have seen earlier how Panamá's tiny army disbanded at North American insistence after its commander attempted a coup in 1904. It too was replaced by a national police force which in turn became involved in partisan rivalries. By

1917–18, Panamanian politics had grown so disorderly and the police were so deeply involved in its struggles that Washington resolved to reform the police force. Once again Marine Corps officers introduced professional training and modern equipment and methods, and once again the more efficient organization which emerged came eventually to be the arbiter of political power within its own borders. After 1931, Panamanian constabulary leaders usually determined who was to be president, and for how long.[23]

In Nicaragua, the United States did not utilize the device of a national constabulary until somewhat later. The withdrawal of North American controls in 1925 was followed by renewed political strife and a civil war, which a new armed intervention ended in 1926. Following the familiar pattern, Washington demanded that the regular army give way to a new *Guardia Nacional,* established in 1927, which was organized and trained by the marines. After a second United States withdrawal in 1933, this guard became the center of power in Nicaragua. Its commander, Anistasio Somoza Debayle, ultimately ousted the president, assuming that office himself in 1936. From then until 1979, the Somoza family ruled Nicaragua as a personal fief, secured in power by the forces of the National Guard.[24]

Nowhere had the creation of a national constabulary led to enhanced democracy. The policy did, however, contribute to Caribbean stability, as professional, centralized armed bodies emerged which gave central governments a military power far beyond that of traditional party militias or *caudillos'* private armies. When the new constabularies supported existing regimes, those regimes were normally secure against domestic foes. Only the constabulary commanders could change national leadership through force, and when they did so there could be little resistance. The old bloody civil wars drew to a close, but the new era was too often characterized by infamous tyrannies such as those of Trujillo and Somoza. Contrary to some accounts, these tyrannies were not the deliberate result of United States policies; the policy makers had genuinely intended to divorce force from politics. When they failed at this, however, they accepted stability as an adequate substitute, so long as it was imposed by dictators who were prepared to follow the lead of the United States in local and regional affairs.

While United States policy makers disapproved of the use of force in politics, they were equally frustrated by Caribbean politicians' constant abuses of the electoral process. Democracy depended upon free and honest elections, while electoral fraud frequently drove the wronged party to violent rebellion. Surely American influence could help to make elections more fair, thus promoting democracy and stability together. Such was the guiding assumption, but in practice electoral purification proved as elusive as creating nonpartisan military establishments. What began as a straightforward program of reform ended in a Byzantine tangle of competing goals and pressures.

Elihu Root expressed the North American desire for electoral democracy in his 1907 program for stabilizing Central America. Among the package of agreements adopted by the Central American republics at the Washington conference of that year was a pledge to withhold diplomatic recognition from any regime among them which came to power as a result of a coup d'état or revolution. To obtain recognition from its neighbors, such a regime would have to submit itself to the will of the voters. The governments which adopted this agreement favored it because it raised another obstacle against revolutionary regimes coming to power, to the benefit of incumbents and the status quo. In practice the new policy failed to promote stability, since the difficulty of new regimes' gaining legitimacy simply encouraged their rivals to attack them. It failed equally to ensure honest elections because there was no mechanism for electoral oversight or guarantee of fairness, or desire on the part of local politicians to establish any.[25]

The real problem was that elections had a different function in the Caribbean from that which they had in the United States. Their purpose was not normally to determine who would hold power, but to ratify its possession by those who already exercised it. A government firmly in control was generally assumed to be rigging any elections it might hold. Through control of the armed forces, the police, the electoral machinery, and the courts, an incumbent regime held an advantage unassailable except through successful revolution. When no one had such control and victory was genuinely in doubt, that party usually won which was most successful at barring opposing voters from the polls, padding its own voting ranks, and falsifying the tallies in its own favor. Such successes reflected the reality of power; in Latin eyes, an election served its purpose by clarifying who held the strategic points in the nation's political system, or who could apply superior force to their operation. In this sense, elections were preferable to civil wars or revolutions because they were far less bloody and destructive; an election might involve some force and violence, and take its toll of dead and wounded, but on a much reduced scale.

North Americans attempting to change these realities faced formidable problems of implementation. If the State Department pressed for a free election, the incumbent regime typically gave the contest all of the trappings of legality it safely could, meanwhile bewailing the opposition's own attempts to cheat and thus confusing the picture. Since attempts at election fraud were generally mutual, this could be a very effective tactic. When roughly equal forces contested electoral results, a favorite United States measure was to invite the opposing leaders aboard one of its warships and push them into a compromise, but this in effect was to replace voting with bargaining. At times Washington sent observers to monitor an election, but unless they were empowered to rectify abuses this merely gave the appearance of United States sanction to the winning side without much helping the losers. Direct United States supervision of elections was sometimes attempted, but in addition to being difficult, it represented outside intervention rather than local reform. More commonly, the State Department required its Caribbean protectorates to write elaborate safeguards against abuses into ever more complex electoral laws, only to be dismayed by their clients' skill at finding loopholes in each new legal edifice.[26]

In Panamá, even United States supervision of elections proved no panacea. Political tensions ran high prior to the presidential election of 1908, and vote fraud on the part of the government seemed inevitable. Conservative President Manuel Amador Guerrero favored the election of Ricardo Arias, his minister of foreign affairs. The other chief candidate, José Domingo de Obaldía, was also a member of the government, serving as Panamá's minister to the United States. To offset Amador's backing of Arias, Obaldía allied himself with the opposition Liberal party. The Liberals had long been the majority party in Panamá, but were eclipsed when Conservative leaders organized the successful independence revolution of 1903. There were ample signs that Amador would take strenuous measures to prevent Obaldía's election and the possible resurgence of the Liberals which it entailed, and the government had already practiced flagrant voting fraud in the legislative elections of 1906. Obaldía's supporters therefore appealed to Washington to oversee the 1908 elections.[27]

Theodore Roosevelt accordingly warned that he would not tolerate a rigged election, and if necessary would use the United States' right of intervention to reverse its results. To give credibility to his threat the president ordered 1,200 marines held in readiness on the isthmus. Under heavy pressure from Washington, the Panamanian president grudgingly requested United States supervision of the elections. As a United States electoral commission gathered on the isthmus, Arias withdrew from the race, and Obaldía was elected by default. It was clear to everyone in Panamá that only United States intercession had blocked the government's plan to impose its own candidate through fraud.[28]

Obaldía died in office, to be succeeded by the Conservative Pablo Arosemena. In 1912 Arosemena supported a Conservative candidate to succeed him, while Obaldía's former Liberal supporters put forward their own party leader, Belisario Porras. This time both parties requested United States supervision of the presidential election, to which Washington agreed. Arosemena attempted to use the police to prevent Liberal voting, only to be sharply checked by the North American electoral supervisors. Again the Conservative party lost, and then charged bitterly that the North Americans had favored their opponents by biased and unequal enforcement of the election laws. Having gained power, the Liberals in turn rejected United States supervision of the 1916 election. Their opponents saw this as a clear indication of a government steal, and boycotted the polls, a common Latin American response to any electoral contest viewed as hopeless: if one could not win, one could at least deny the enemy the legitimacy of election. The midterm death of the president in 1918 required new elections, and generated great excitement and disorder. To restore peace, United States troops took control of Panamá City and Colón, after which their government again supervised the presidential election.[29]

This recurrent pattern of electoral supervision did little to develop a workable Panamanian political system, but did arouse local complaints against United States interference. The Liberal party especially was prone to plead for Washington's involvement in elections when out of power, but protest United States "meddling" at all other times. In general, the "outs" desired supervised elections to block the power of governments to reelect themselves. Incumbent regimes were happy to have elections supervised only if they were confident of success anyway, as this would give independent witness to the authenticity of their victory. Losers always charged the United States election authorities with favoring the other side, but might well request American supervision of the next election. One historian has charged that Washington naively allowed itself to be manipulated by Liberal politicians in its long-term involvement in the Panamanian electoral process. Determined as they were to keep order near the Canal Zone, however, United States policy makers could not see what else to do.[30]

Rather than supervise elections, Washington often merely insisted that the electoral process be used. Woodrow Wilson was particularly zealous in this cause, refusing diplomatic recognition to regimes which gained power through the use of force rather than constitutional processes. A notable application of this policy came in Costa Rica, where President Alfredo González Flores was overthrown early in 1917 by Minister of War Federico Tinoco. González had lost popularity and Tinoco's revolt had widespread support, but Wilson set his face against the new regime. The State Department suspected that the United Fruit Company had financed Tinoco, and sent that concern stiffly worded orders to stop interfering in Central American politics. This suspicion further angered Wilson, who rebuffed Secretary of State Robert Lansing's suggestion of softer treatment for Tinoco.[31]

Tinoco strengthened his position by overwhelmingly winning a special presidential election in April 1917, and by declaring war on Germany in the wake of the United States declaration. A United States Senate resolution now recommended that the executive offer Tinoco recognition, but Wilson ignored it. Again Lansing urged the president to reconsider. A recent State Department investigation showed Tinoco to have the support of most of his country's political leaders, and to be following pro–United States policies, Lansing told Wilson, while real evidence of a United Fruit involvement was lacking. Without United States recognition, Costa Rica's war-disrupted economy was cut off from North American loans or credit; there could be neither political nor economic stability there so long as nonrecognition was in effect. But Wilson was adamant: his campaign against revolutions must have first priority. In time, Wilson even closed the American legation in San José.[32]

In 1919 the hard-pressed Tinoco offered to resign in favor of a subordinate, but Wilson insisted that the entire Tinoco faction must go. By then Costa Ricans were anxiously counting the cost of Washington's permanent hostility. An uprising against Tinoco saw most political leaders desert the government, and the former president fled to Jamaica in August 1919. But Wilson, now ill and out of contact, refused to recognize the new regime on the same ground as the old: it had come to power by force. Only after it in turn was regularized by an election did the administration offer recognition, and that only after State Department leaders had pressed Wilson to do so for many months. In August 1920, normal relations finally resumed.[33]

Perhaps the most sustained United States attempt to regularize elections came in Cuba, where electoral disputes created recurring crises. As we have seen, the fraudulent means by which Tomás Estrada Palma secured reelection in 1905 provoked the Liberal opposition to revolt in the following year, bringing on the intervention of 1906–1909. It was clear from the outset, therefore, that electoral reform would be one of the main objects of Governor Magoon and his military subordinates. Under the chairmanship of Colonel Enoch H. Crowder of the United States Army, Cuban political leaders from all major factions sat on a commission which created an electoral system of awesome complexity. Bipartisan boards were to apply and interpret the elaborate new rules, which bristled with safeguards against fraud. The new machinery seemed to work well in the American-supervised elections of November 1908, and the intervention ended early in the next year.[34]

There followed four years of government under the jovial but corrupt President José Miguel Gómez, after which the 1912 elections came off relatively well. The outgoing Gómez had attempted to retain control of his party against the claims of his Liberal rival, Alfredo Zayas. When Zayas won the resulting power struggle, the still popular Gómez threw his support to Mario Menocal, the Conservative party candidate. Menocal then easily defeated Zayas, whose party was badly split. The election thus turned on the maneuverings of factional leaders, and was decided by the coalescence of two major factions against a third; the manipulation of the electoral machinery was not an important factor in the contest. The real test came four years later, when Menocal ran for reelection against the reunited Liberals.[35]

Alfredo Zayas was again the Liberal presidential candidate in 1916, and it was generally accepted that the Liberals would win any honest election. The early vote counting indicated a Zayas landslide, until Menocal's officials seized control of the ballots and cut off access to the Central Election Board. When the government claimed victory, the inevitable crisis flared. Amid talk of revolution, the Menocal forces agreed to adjudicate some of the disputed returns. The Central Election Board found for the Liberals, and with the support of the Cuban Supreme Court ordered new elections in two provinces where abuses had been particularly flagrant. But in these new elections the government again used open force and fraud to hold down the Liberal vote. As it was obvious that Menocal intended to stay in office at all costs, the Liberal leaders sent emissaries to Washington seeking yet another election under United States supervision. Although the State Department had favored Menocal throughout the crisis, Lansing finally sent Havana a blunt demand for electoral guarantees, though not going so far as to propose United States supervision of elections.[36]

How far a reluctant State Department would have gone in restraining Menocal is unclear, but it was saved the necessity by the exposure in February 1917 of a Liberal-army plot to overthrow the government. This prematurely set off a revolt; Washington could now resume its habitual posture of disapproving revolution in Cuba, and use its power on behalf of Menocal. United States policy makers still preferred a negotiated peace to a prolonged armed struggle, however, and saw possibilities in a Liberal offer to negotiate terms. The State Department seriously considered imposing its own settlement of the election dispute, and in March 1917 Lansing pressed Menocal to accept a truce in the fighting in return for granting amnesty and new elections. Immediately thereafter, however, the government captured former president Gómez and almost the entire Liberal field command, virtually ensuring its victory. Menocal was less inclined than ever to make concessions to his enemies, while Lansing and his advisers now saw a quick end to the rebellion as the best way to restore order. While some United States Army and Navy officers were still promising new elections to induce Liberal surrenders, their government decided to let the whole matter drop.[37]

The feebleness of United States efforts to secure fair elections in 1916–17, in the face of the grossest government frauds, left Cubans understandably cynical. Most observers expected similar abuses in the 1920 elections, in which Menocal intended to ensure his replacement by a fellow Conservative. Everything was so obviously in place for another steal that Lansing decided upon further revision of the Cuban election laws in advance of the contest. Colonel Crowder, who had overseen the reforms of 1907–1908, sailed to Cuba in 1919 to try again. The State Department secured a promise of fair elections from Menocal and pressed him to cooperate with Crowder in rewriting the relevant laws. For months Crowder labored to strengthen appeals procedures, tighten voter registration, and provide other safeguards for honest elections. On paper, at least, he made the former abuses impossible.[38]

The Liberal opposition was understandably suspicious of mere legal reforms, declaring that only direct United States supervision of the elections could thwart Conservative plans. Another Liberal delegation went to Washington in the autumn of 1919 to plead for really effective measures from the State Department. As José Miguel Gómez proclaimed, if the United States could intervene in every other facet of Cuban life, the least it could do was to intervene in crooked elections too. All of this was distinctly embarrassing to the State Department, which raised the matter with the unrepentant Menocal. Flatly refusing to accept United States–run elections, Menocal gave his personal pledge that the elections would be fair and honest. Reluctant to provoke an open confrontation, Washington settled for a promise in which it could not have had much confidence.[39]

As the election year unfolded, any remaining hopes for improvement withered rapidly. Menocal ultimately decided that his own party was no longer strong enough to retain power even through voting fraud, but he remained intent upon blocking the election of Gómez, the rebel leader of 1917. He therefore reversed the tactics of 1912 and backed Zayas' wing of the Liberals. Gómez was still a formidable vote-getter, however, and was favored to win in a fair contest. To prevent that, Menocal and Zayas supporters in the Cuban congress pushed through enough changes in the newly enacted Crowder laws to gut their key provisions, an open signal that another steal was coming.[40]

By this time Washington's policy makers understood the problem well enough, and were under no illusions as to Menocal's intentions. A sudden collapse in the wartime sugar boom was bringing widespread economic stress and unemployment in Cuba, making the situation even more volatile. The Liberals threatened to boycott the elections, with the usual implied threat of revolt afterward. If Washington failed to act, Cuban stability might be gravely threatened.[41]

Under these pressures, the State Department denounced election fraud in Cuba and announced its intention to send observers to monitor the 1920 elections. As abuses appeared in the preliminary stages of the election process, Washington lodged protests in Havana, but did nothing else. The Cuban authorities judged correctly from this inaction that the Americans had decided not to intervene forcefully, and therefore perpetrated the usual frauds in spite of the foreign observers. In effect, Washington looked the other way. The State Department had hoped, with little justification, that they could control Menocal and Zayas through moral suasion. Its failure to do so was so complete that Cubans came to believe the United States government to be actually implicated in the frauds.[42]

In fact, the men in the State Department had concluded that such efforts were largely futile in the long run. Furthermore, the end of the war in Europe eliminated the "German threat," while discrediting hemispheric security fears in general. With the war ended, more public attention shifted back to Caribbean affairs, and the level of criticism of the government's policies there rose to an unaccustomedly high level. Taking advantage of this, the Republican party attacked the Wilson administration's record in Haiti and the Dominican Republic, making these issues a part of its 1920 presidential campaign. Reflecting these pressures and their own rising doubts, State Department professionals argued forcefully for less United States interference in the internal affairs of Caribbean countries, and their influence helped bring on the attempted retrenchment of the 1920s in Caribbean interventions. Woodrow Wilson was disabled by a stroke in 1919, and wholly focused on his failed European peace settlement at any rate. Robert Lansing broke with Wilson over the peace treaty and left the cabinet, replaced by an inexperienced and less effective successor. Operating in something like a power vacuum, the State Department's professional staff had an unaccustomed leeway for reshaping Latin American policy. There was much to be said for their new policy, but its early application in Cuba hardly enhanced United States honor or prestige.[43]

In a few cases, the United States had gone beyond the mere toleration of election fraud to rig elections itself. The practice was most blatant in Nicaragua, where Washington long supported a minority party in power to prevent the resurgence of the popular but anti-Yankee Liberals. José Santos Zelaya, the long-time Liberal dictator, disappeared permanently from the political scene with his resignation in 1909, but he had been anathema to United States policy makers and they were determined that none of his followers should succeed him. The Liberals had joined with dissident Conservatives to attack the government in the Mena revolution of 1912, reinforcing Washington's distaste for them. The presidential elections of 1912 and 1916, therefore, were parallel exercises in manipulation.

In 1912, most Conservatives supported General Emiliano Chamorro, but Provisional President Adolfo Díaz wished to extend his short tenure in office by a full constitutional term. To head off a party split, United States Minister George T. Weitzel imposed an agreement by which Chamorro went to Washington as Nicaraguan minister to the United States while Díaz became the Conservative presidential candidate. Having arbitrarily reunited the Conservatives, Weitzel informed the Liberal leaders that no candidate they might nominate would be allowed to run. Held soon after the 1912 revolution, while the United States marines who had helped to defeat the rebels were still much in evidence, the election was closely controlled by the Díaz regime. Liberal voters were simply disfranchised, and only a few thousand known supporters of the government were allowed to vote. There was only one candidate in any case, so the result was hardly in question, and Díaz received his full term.[44]

Four years later the State Department faced the same twin problems of bitter internal rivalries in the Conservative camp and a popular preference for the Liberals. General Chamorro again demanded the Conservative presidential nomination, while President Díaz was still determined to block his rival's succession. Debarred from running himself, Díaz threw his weight behind

Minister of Finance Carlos Cuadra Pasos, the least popular of presidential aspirants. The Liberals meanwhile nominated Julian Irias, Zelaya's former right-hand man and a popular leader in his own right. If the United States government did not interfere, it was clear that Díaz meant to use his control of the electoral machinery to make Cuadra Pasos president. This would bring to the presidency a man almost wholly lacking in popular support, whom Washington might well have to sustain through further military intervention. If, on the other hand, the State Department insisted upon an honest election, Irias would unquestionably win and the Liberals would return to power.[45]

As before, the State Department chose neither of these unwelcome alternatives. Irias had gone to Washington in the summer of 1915 to pledge his future adherence to United States policies in return for the promise of a free election, but had failed to overcome a fixed North American hostility. The policy makers looked instead to Emiliano Chamorro, who had been busily cultivating them during his four years in Washington as Nicaraguan minister. Chamorro was the most popular Conservative, and could best unite that party. He was solidly pro-American, and was considered in the State Department to have a moral claim on the presidency after being denied it in 1912. The United States minister in Managua, Benjamin L. Jefferson, accordingly set about the necessary arrangements to elect Chamorro, but he found both the Liberals and the Díaz government defiant. When Jefferson threatened Díaz with the withdrawal of United States support, the president suddenly canceled a ban he had issued against Irias' reentering the country to campaign. As the latter made a triumphal progress from rally to rally, it became clear that Díaz had arranged to ally himself with the Liberals in order to defeat Chamorro, and the American legation found itself losing control of events.[46]

The possibility had been foreseen. The chief of the State Department's Division of Latin American Affairs noted in August 1916 that "we had better henceforth keep the navy as closely in touch with the Nicaraguan situation as we have heretofore in the Haitian and Dominican matters." In mid-September there arrived in Nicaragua Admiral William B. Caperton, recent occupier of Haiti and the Dominican Republic and new commander in chief of the Pacific Fleet. The admiral concentrated three cruisers and a marine regiment at the Pacific port of Corinto, while he himself went on to the capital to join Jefferson. For the next two months he actually lived with the minister at the legation. "Presence of naval forces here very effective in causing tranquillity," Jefferson notified the State Department after Caperton's arrival. Caperton was by now a well-known tamer of Caribbean revolutions, and his mere presence was a major help to Jefferson's negotiations.[47]

Within two days of Caperton's arrival, Díaz had agreed to support the Chamorro candidacy at a price: Cuadra Pasos must go to Washington to replace Chamorro, while the new cabinet must yield several portfolios to the *Cuad-*

ristas. This agreed upon, there remained the problem of Julian Irias, whose popularity surged as he toured the country. It was Jefferson who suggested the course of action next adopted. On September 20, Jefferson and Caperton called both candidates to the legation, where Jefferson laid down the American terms. First of all, the next president must fully accept the entire system of treaties and financial arrangements existing between Nicaragua and the United States, and promise to maintain peace and order. Since Irias had earlier indicated his acceptance of these terms, they had in themselves no invidious effect. The remaining conditions, however, definitively ruled out the Liberal candidate. The successful aspirant, Jefferson said, must be free of any taint of revolutionary activity and, most pointed of all, "must give satisfactory proof of not having taken an active and objectionable part in the administration of President Zelaya." [48]

Irias had apparently expected something of the sort. He announced the end of his candidacy in a manifesto which made public Jefferson's demands and denounced United States domination of his country. Most Liberals boycotted the election, held in October, as Chamorro's victory was a foregone conclusion. Irias took his case directly to the United States, appealing to Woodrow Wilson to reverse his diplomats' machinations. Denied a hearing in Washington, Irias went on to New York and gave his story to the press, which aired it fully in the autumn of 1916. Admiral Caperton responded vigorously to the resulting criticism, insisting that Jefferson's actions, in which he had been closely associated, were completely proper. All legal voters had been free to participate in the election, he argued, and the votes were accurately counted. The election was therefore honest—even if it involved only one candidate, who had been selected by the government of the United States! [49]

In its attempts to implant fair elections on Caribbean political systems, the United States was seriously handicapped by the inconsistency of its commitment to effective reform, as in Cuba, and even more by its own departures from the path of virtue, as in the Nicaraguan elections. Caribbean peoples found it difficult to believe that Washington was ever genuinely neutral, even when that happened to be the case. Yet election reform, like army reform, failed for more deeply seated reasons than mere Yankee ineptitude or bad faith. The projected reforms aimed at changing the very spirit and purpose of the institutions involved, to do which would have required a fundamental transformation of Caribbean politics. Could such an unlikely transformation have been achieved, the reforms would have been superfluous; without it, they were futile.

On the United States side, realistic thinking was hampered by a reluctance to admit that stability and democracy might not always be harmonious goals; that it might at times be necessary to choose one at the expense of the other. Though the choice was in fact regularly made, the official theory that the two goals went hand in hand was slow to change. Ideological allegiance to fostering democracy reached its peak in the Wilson administration, during which United States actions in the Caribbean most regularly violated democratic norms. The military occupations of Haiti and the Dominican Republic, the toleration of election fraud in Cuba, and the actual imposition of Washington's candidates in Nicaragua were difficult to reconcile with the official ideology. The contradictions became too obvious to overlook, as Washington chose in practice to promote stability, not democracy. By the end of the Wilson administration, the first of a new cohort of State Department policy makers tacitly wrote off the promotion of democracy as a vital goal. These new voices proposed less, not more, Yankee interference in the Caribbean. They would intervene if they had to—but only to preserve stability, and that only to further United States interests in the area.

Chapter 14

Agents of Hegemony

United States domination of the Caribbean was accomplished not merely by abstract policies, but by specific men and organizations, both public and private. Over the years a corps of experienced "Caribbean hands" grew up both within and outside of the governmental service, working within complex institutional frameworks. To tell the whole story of North American hegemony in the region, it is necessary to examine some of the agencies and individuals involved.

The implementation of Caribbean policy and the day-to-day supervision of Caribbean affairs on behalf of the United States government was largely entrusted to the Department of State and to the armed forces. In theory the former laid down policy guidelines which the latter sometimes helped to carry out, but in practice the relationship was seldom so simple. On-the-spot policy, made as often by army or navy officers as by diplomats, frequently became Washington's official position. The information and advice upon which Washington acted came from naval officers as well as diplomats. The army had an important institutional role in some United States dependencies, the navy or marines in others. While the State Department and the armed forces often cooperated with notable harmony, they also could work at cross purposes. Furthermore, during the early twentieth century, both institutions were undergoing important long-term changes.

The State Department lay nearest the center of Caribbean policy formation. That department, at home and abroad, comprised three main bodies: the headquarters staff in Washington, with its top policy makers; the diplomatic corps with its missions at forty-odd foreign capitals; and the consular corps, scattered around the globe at hundreds of commercial centers and port cities.

The latter two were separate personnel pools until the creation in 1925 of the present Foreign Service of the United States, and they performed separate and different functions. Consuls had traditionally been responsible for the protection of the American merchant marine and for American citizens abroad, while during the later nineteenth century they came to aid in customs collection by certifying the value of foreign goods exported from their districts to the United States. By the turn of the century, however, the most valued consular functions were promoting United States exports and reporting commercial and market information for their districts. After 1880 the State Department published consular commercial reports on a monthly basis, and after 1898 some of the same material was released daily, often to be reprinted in the press. By 1912, 40 percent of a consul's efficiency rating was based upon his commercial reporting.[1]

In many Caribbean posts, consular duties included a diplomatic dimension. In times of war and revolution, the United States consul in a trouble spot was expected to restrain local violence and protect foreign life and property. If he could not do this by representations to warring leaders, he could call in the navy to impose order, but this was a last resort. Many a consul developed diplomatic and negotiating skills out of necessity, as well as acquiring a detailed knowledge of United States enterprises in his district. As former consul Willard Beaulac later recalled of his first Central American post, "The *raison d'être* of the American consulate, I learned, was bananas and politics— Honduran politics, that is."[2]

Diplomats represented the interests of the United States government, as consuls represented the interests of that government's citizens and their businesses and properties abroad. They served as channels of communication and negotiation with other governments, reported on developments in their host countries, and fulfilled ceremonial functions at courts and capitals. A diplomatic mission consisted minimally of a head of mission with the rank of minister or ambassador, and at least a few local employees to do housekeeping and clerical work. Many missions also had junior diplomats called diplomatic secretaries to share the post's duties; a particularly busy or important capital could rate as many as three of these.

Presiding over these foreign missions and consulates was the secretary of state and his staff in Washington. The actual policy makers at departmental headquarters were not numerous: the secretary of state, three assistant secretaries, the counselor of the department (a post created in 1909), and the heads of the four geographical divisions established during the Taft administration. Almost all of these men were political appointees who changed with each new administration; only the venerable Alvey A. Adee, a long-time assistant secretary, stayed on through every political shift between 1877 and 1924 to provide much-needed continuity.[3]

The level of experience in this policy-making group varied greatly. Of the five secretaries of state who spanned the years from 1898 to 1917, John Hay had served several years as a diplomatic secretary in his youth, and had most recently been ambassador to Great Britain. Elihu Root had gained some pseudodiplomatic experience as secretary of war through his responsibility for the administration of Cuba, Puerto Rico, and the Philippines. Philander Knox had been Roosevelt's attorney general, but had no previous diplomatic experience; neither did William Jennings Bryan, a professional politician and three-time Democratic candidate for president. Robert Lansing, however, had practiced international law and represented his government in several arbitration cases, as well as serving as counselor of the department prior to his appointment as secretary. Every one of these secretaries had studied law and been admitted to the bar in his youth (though Hay and Bryan had soon turned to other pursuits), a circumstance which helps to explain the strong legalistic strain in their diplomacy. But then, a large proportion of public men were lawyers, including those connected with diplomacy.[4]

The State Department was still a relatively small agency, particularly at its Washington headquarters, but it was growing rapidly. In the decade after 1898, the department's Washington personnel grew from 82 to 167, then rose to 210 as a result of a major reorganization in 1909. During the same decade the number of diplomatic secretaries in foreign posts increased from 24 to 60, while the total reached 122 by 1918. Since the number of diplomatic missions changed only from 41 to 47 in the same twenty years, the aim was clearly to strengthen the staffing of existing foreign missions. Meanwhile the First World War had expanded the department's work load; Washington headquarters personnel jumped from 208 in 1914 to 440 in 1918, making a fivefold increase in just two decades. The overseas staff, on the other hand, failed to increase. On the eve of the war, the entire force of American diplomats and consuls abroad numbered fewer than 450 persons, and the total was substantially the same in 1918.[5]

Diplomatic representation in the Caribbean likewise multiplied. At the turn of the century, only two United States ministers served in all of Central America. One normally resided in Guatemala City but was also accredited to Honduras; the other lived in Nicaragua or Costa Rica, accredited to both of those states plus El Salvador. Similarly, a single minister, resident in Port-au-Prince, served for both Haiti and the Dominican Republic. This latter arrangement ceased in 1904, when a separate legation with its own minister opened in Santo Domingo. In 1907–1908 the five Central American states each got their own resident minister. Cuba of course had received a resident minister upon achieving independence in 1902, as did Panamá in 1903, while Colombia and Venezuela had long had separate diplomatic missions. Thus the five ministers posted to the Caribbean region in 1898 grew to eleven a decade later.[6]

It was common knowledge that the United States diplomatic corps was not ideally staffed in the late nineteenth and early twentieth centuries. Inadequately supported by Congress, the men of the foreign service normally received pay and allowances too small to cover the costs of their posts. As a result, only the wealthy could afford to be ambassador in the leading capitals, making up the deficit out of their own pockets; even diplomatic secretaries usually had private incomes. Furthermore, appointments depended upon political patronage, and one's tenure in office was apt to end after the next election. Nothing like a professional foreign service existed in the United States until 1925, when Congress finally established one by law. Under such circumstances the resulting agency could hardly aspire to peak efficiency.[7]

A recent study nevertheless shows that heads of diplomatic missions during this period constituted a cross section of the nation's elite. In a sample of over three hundred heads of mission and consuls general between 1890 and 1910, over two-thirds had been lawyers, journalists, businessmen, or educators. About three-fourths had graduated from a four-year college or university, this at a time when only one American in twenty went to school beyond the age of seventeen. Surprisingly, a narrow majority of the sampling held more than one overseas assignment, while by 1910 one-third of the total had at least ten years' diplomatic experience. Since another third had served from five to ten years, to describe them all as short-term amateurs is clearly inaccurate, while collectively the foreign service appointees had a rather high level of education and social position. All of them were men; women did not yet attain to such posts. The typical foreign service appointees were college-educated professional or business men, middle-aged, white, and hailing mostly from the Northeast or Middle West.[8]

It was still true, however, that diplomatic appointments were made for political reasons, and that few formal qualifications were required. Theodore Roosevelt managed to raise the level of the diplomatic service by promoting for merit from within it, while sixteen years of Republican party rule enabled some career continuity from 1897 to 1913. The advent of the Democratic Wilson administration erased such continuity, however, as William Jennings Bryan rushed to replace incumbents with "deserving Democrats." One of them, James Mark Sullivan, named minister to the Dominican Republic, was ultimately removed as unfit. Afterward, in defending Sullivan's appointment to the president, Bryan admitted that Sullivan was the only one of twenty-seven foreign ministers and consuls in Santo Domingo who could not speak Spanish. But language competence had not figured in any of the other Wilsonian diplomatic appointments, the secretary of state pointed out: "I am sure that very few of our ministers to South America can speak Spanish." Furthermore, Bryan noted, Santo Domingo was an uninviting post for which few had applied, while Sullivan was at least a Catholic, and therefore "religiously in sympathy with the people."[9]

A year earlier, Bryan had urged that the administration appoint Democrats because distinction puts them in a position to do something in the future. We have been quite short of prefixes, while Republicans have been able to introduce Secretary so-and-so; Ambassador so-and-so; and Minister so-and-so. . . . We have usually had to confine ourselves to "Mister" or "Honorable."

For Bryan, at least, the balance between political and technical qualifications for diplomatic appointments clearly favored the former. A leading Wilson scholar, Arthur S. Link, has vividly described Bryan's onslaught on the diplomatic corps: ". . . in the greatest debauchery of the Foreign Service in the twentieth century he dismissed all the Ministers who had earned their posts by merit and training and installed an aggregation of friends and party hacks." The average experience of the twelve departing heads of mission in Central and South America was over fifteen years, and all of them spoke the language of the country in which they served. By contrast, not one of their replacements spoke Spanish or another local language and none had any diplomatic experience.[10]

United States diplomats, however selected, exercised real power in the Caribbean region. They became virtual proconsuls in Cuba, Panamá, Haiti, the Dominican Republic, and Nicaragua, and nowhere did they lack substantial influence and prestige. This position normally brought local social prominence as well, and social duties ranked high among a diplomat's responsibilities. Perhaps because of the relative inexperience of so many, the social performance of American diplomats abroad was at best uneven, a fact attested to by their British colleagues. Each British head of mission had to report annually on the abilities and characteristics of the other heads of mission at his post, and the resulting comments were frequently enlightening. William Gonzales, it appears, at first neglected his social duties as minister to Cuba and consequently made enemies, but later rectified the error and became popular. Minister to Panamá Thomas C. Dawson, who had served as head of the State Department's Latin American Division, fared poorly with his British colleague, who thought him an "unpolished and ordinary American diplomat." He was not personally popular, "and his wife, who is a Brazilian mulatress, is tolerated only because she is the wife of the American Minister."[11]

Even superior social skills often fell prey to diplomatic stress, however. Elliot Northcote, minister to Colombia, and his wife were popular and hospitable, but handicapped socially by the strong anti-American feelings in Bogotá resulting from the loss of Panamá. Similarly, Dawson's successor in Panamá, Percival Dodge, and his wife made themselves very popular with both the local and foreign communities "by their tact, refined manners, and amiability of character." But then the United States supervised Panamá's 1912 presidential election; the losing Conservative party held the loyalty of most of the socially dominant families in Panamá City. Blaming the Americans for their party's defeat, the local elite virtually boycotted the Dodge's social efforts thereafter.[12]

The diplomats' physical surroundings did not necessarily reflect their importance. The United States government rarely owned the buildings used for its embassies and legations, or the residences of ambassadors and ministers; heads of mission had to find and rent quarters on a very modest official allowance. Thus the nature of a legation building depended upon the private resources of the current minister, and his willingness to part with them. When Norval Richardson went to Havana as second secretary of the legation in 1909, he found it located on the second floor of a shabby two-story building, the first floor of which was occupied by a large and noisy family of Cubans. Knowing that the legation was the principal center of power in Cuba, Richardson was struck by its total lack of dignity. A few months after his arrival, however, a new minister came down and promptly rectified the fault, renting one of the handsomest old mansions in Havana.[13]

Richardson also found a heavy work load. Though nominally second secretary, there was no first secretary present during most of his two-year stay in Havana. The minister, a single diplomatic secretary, and a stenographer together handled all the duties, diplomatic and clerical, of the legation. Since Havana was the busiest and most important post in the Caribbean region, this hardly represented lavish staffing. Ironically, Richardson transferred from Havana to Copenhagen and found virtually the same number of personnel with very little work to do. After his departure, however, Havana got its missing first secretary, and later a second stenographer as well.[14]

Richardson's experience in joining the diplomatic service in 1909 is also instructive. The aspiring diplomatic secretary needed to secure a letter of recommendation from a senator, and pass a departmental examination in international law, diplomatic usage, and one modern language. Instituted by Elihu Root in 1905, this examination eliminated one-third of the group of twenty-four candidates to which Richardson belonged, proving that it exercised a definite screening function. After passing the examination, the survivors spent two months in training at the State Department, learning more about diplomatic routines and paper work than about international politics.[15]

Aside from Roots' screening examination and a general raising of salaries, reforms in the diplomatic service were largely blocked by congressional opposition. The consular service did better. The consulates' aid in marketing United States exports gave them a perceived practical importance and a business-based support which the diplomats lacked. The belief that an efficient consular service could directly help the economy spurred efforts at reforms and moved Congress toward approving them. A turning point came in 1906, when Elihu Root seized on a long-standing reform program and attempted to push it through Congress. He had to settle for only a fraction of the program, but in the so-called Lodge Act, Congress provided for much increased consular salaries, the regular inspection of consulates, and the end of the fee system, by which consuls received part of their compensation in the form of set fees for their services to businesses and individuals.[16]

In passing the Lodge Act, Congress deleted provisions for appointment through competitive examination and promotion by merit, a lack which Roosevelt made good in the short run by executive order. To appease the Democratic "solid South," the Roosevelt administration gave that section a fairer share of consular appointments than had previous Republican administrations, a change crystallized and magnified by the Democratic electoral victory of 1912. While the coming of the Wilson administration saw a wholesale turnover in diplomatic personnel, the Wilsonians were forced to respect the business world's interest in the consular service and left it almost untouched. In 1915 Congress agreed at last to appoint consuls to a general grade rather than a specific geographic post, making it much easier to transfer them and thus facilitating promotion for merit.[17]

Such a foreign service, fast growing and in the throes of reform and reorganization, produced officials of widely varying quality. Perhaps the worst diplomatic appointment of the Wilson administration was that of James Mark Sullivan as minister to the Dominican Republic. Sullivan was a New York lawyer and politician who had been a prizefight promoter and possessed unsavory gambling connections. He also had excellent contacts in the Democratic power structure, including Wilson's own private secretary, Joseph Tumulty. As Bryan noted, there were not many aspirants for the Dominican post, while Sullivan mustered very strong backing in his bid for it. Much of this backing, it later emerged, was organized by a lobbyist for the North American owners of the National Bank of Santo Domingo. That bank coveted the deposits of the United States customs receivership, and supported Sullivan in return for his promise to have them transferred to the bank when he occupied the Santo Domingo legation.[18]

Once in office, Sullivan fulfilled his end of the bargain, though Walker W. Vick, the receiver general of the customs, soon grew dissatisfied with the National Bank's performance and returned the funds to their former repository. Vick became deeply suspicious of Sullivan, and in the spring of 1914 returned to Washington to lay serious charges before Bryan and Wilson. The president of the National Bank, he reported, lived next door to the legation and was notoriously intimate with the minister. It was widely rumored that Sullivan and the bank's officials secured Dominican contracts for American businessmen in return for a percentage of their profits. The minister was also a close crony of President José Bordas Valdes, who was said by some to have "bought up" Sullivan for one hundred thousand dollars. A nephew of Sullivan's got a government contract to repair a bridge, received five thousand dollars, but did no work whatever. The list went on, and Vick insisted that a major scandal was brewing.[19]

Wilson and Bryan rejected Vick's accusations even though other Americans in Santo Domingo corroborated them. Frustrated, Vick finally took his story to the *New York World*, which put it on the front pages in a series of exposés. The publicity forced Wilson to investigate; though he named a loyal Democratic supporter to head the investigation, hearings early in 1915 confirmed many of Vick's charges. Sullivan lost his job in the end, and the Wilson administration suffered a serious embarrassment.[20]

Other political appointees did far better in diplomacy. One example was Thomas C. Dawson, who rose to prominence in the shaping of Caribbean policy. An Iowa lawyer and active Republican, Dawson had helped to carry his county for William McKinley in the 1896 election. He was also a friend and former classmate of Charles G. Dawes, a McKinley insider and protégé of the president. When Dawson decided to seek a diplomatic post as a reward for his political labors, his contacts were sufficient to secure him appointment as legation secretary in Rio de Janeiro. He arrived in Brazil early in 1898, to take up a new career at the age of thirty-two.[21]

The Brazilian government was then considering significant changes in its tariff policies, and Dawson's detailed analysis of the possible results for United States–Brazilian trade drew favorable notice in the State Department. He further strengthened his position by returning to the United States on leave in 1900 to work for McKinley's reelection. By this time Dawson aspired to a higher position than diplomatic secretary, but repeated requests to Washington brought nothing better. Meanwhile he married a Brazilian woman—that "mulatress" whom the British minister to Panamá later thought a blot on his social standing—and made a serious effort to learn about the region. In 1903–1904, Dawson published a two-volume work entitled *The South American Republics*, stressing the commercial possibilities of South America as a market for United States exports and justifying Theodore Roosevelt's Panamá coup as a proper use of United States power.[22]

In 1904 Dawson finally got a mission of his own, becoming minister to the Dominican Republic. Santo Domingo had heretofore been covered from Port-au-Prince; one person, since the Civil War normally a black man, had served as minister to both Haiti and its neighbor. The Dominican debt crisis having made Santo Domingo a sensitive post, however, the State Department decided to give it a resident diplomat. Dawson was to be not only United States minister but consul general as well, uniting all representational functions in his person.

The timing was fortunate. The new minister's three-year tenure in Santo Domingo coincided with the climax of the debt crisis and the inauguration of the American customs receivership there. By achieving his government's goals under very difficult circumstances, Dawson ensured the success of his diplomatic career. The price was high, however; by 1907 his health was failing from prolonged tension and overwork, worsened by the effects of a tropical climate. The minister had run his legation virtually single-handed. Lacking a diplomatic secretary, and with only one clerk for legation and consulate combined, Dawson had to do all of his own typing and translating, often late at night when his diplomatic duties were done. He also complained that the post's $5,000 salary and $1,400 in fees per year were inadequate to maintain a proper station in the capital's society. After his departure the State Department belatedly responded to Dawson's appeals, sending down a diplomatic secretary and adding an extra clerk to the payroll, as well as doubling the minister's salary to $10,000, so that his successor led an easier life.[23]

Dawson's next post was that of minister to Colombia, where he spent almost two years negotiating a set of tripartite treaties designed to settle the issues left outstanding between Colombia, Panamá, and the United States in the wake of Panamanian independence. While his efforts ultimately produced the desired agreements, they came to naught when the Colombian congress refused to ratify them in 1909. By then Dawson had been transferred to Chile, but was there only briefly before being recalled to Washington to become the first head of the State Department's newly created Division of Latin American Affairs. As a regional policymaker in the Taft administration, Dawson was deeply involved in the decisions to support the Estrada rebellion against Zelaya in Nicaragua, and to erect a new protectorate there.

After a year at the State Department, Dawson again went abroad in 1910 as minister to Panamá. From this post he served as a sort of roving regional troubleshooter, having become the State Department's most trusted diplomatic agent in the Caribbean. During his tenure at Panamá City he went to Managua to impose the Dawson Agreements on the rival Nicaraguan chieftains and avert —or more accurately, delay—new violence in that troubled country. In 1911 he mediated a similar political struggle in Honduras, meeting factional leaders aboard a United States warship to end a civil war there. After a special mission to Venezuela later that year, he returned to Washington for another stint of headquarters duty, but died of accumulated ailments in the spring of 1912.[24]

Dawson's career ran counter to the tradition that diplomatic appointees lost their jobs with the end of the administration which appointed them. It exemplified the newer trend toward continuity of service and promotion for merit so strongly favored by Theodore Roosevelt, and less enthusiastically accepted by the Taft administration. Though initially politically recruited, Dawson came to represent professionalism in the foreign service and served as a role model for other ambitious young men who joined it.

In their efforts to build a nucleus of Caribbean expertise, Washington's policymakers looked beyond the confines of any one government agency. Charles E. Magoon, for example, a Nebraska lawyer, began his public career as Law Officer of the War Department's newly established Bureau of Insular

Affairs, serving there from 1899 to 1904. Having won the approval of Secretary of War Elihu Root, Magoon received progressively larger responsibilities as a member of the Isthmian Canal Commission, governor of the Panama Canal Zone, and minister to Panamá. His success in these duties led to his selection as provisional governor of Cuba during the second occupation of 1906–1909.[25]

Another protégé of the Bureau of Insular Affairs was Charles A. Conant, a prominent financial journalist and authority on currency and exchange issues. In 1901 the War Department recruited Conant to go out to the Philippines and devise a new system of currency for the islands, a task which occupied him for most of the following year. The new Philippine pesos were promptly dubbed "conants" by the Filipinos, and their author became Washington's favorite expert on foreign money. Between 1903 and 1912 he represented the United States on three separate international commissions dealing with problems of money and exchange, one of them charged with aiding Mexico's conversion to the gold standard in 1903. Conant also advised Washington on currency reforms in Panamá and Nicaragua, and served as a director of the Nicaraguan National Bank. He died in Havana in 1915, while preparing recommendations for changes in the Cuban currency.[26]

William I. Buchanan worked for the State Department, not the War Department, but closely combined careers in business and diplomacy. Beginning life as a salesman and convention manager, Buchanan gained a solid grounding in diplomacy as minister to Argentina from 1894 to 1899. In 1901 he joined the New York Life Insurance Company as an overseas lobbyist and consultant, concentrating on efforts to head off adverse legislation in the many countries where the company did business, and particularly those of Latin America. For a time he took on similar functions for the Westinghouse Company, while continuing his connection with New York Life until his death in 1909.[27]

These business tasks, however, were regularly interrupted by calls for short-term duty with the State Department. In 1902 Buchanan was one of the United States delegates to the second Pan-American conference, held in Mexico City. Late in 1903, John Hay asked Buchanan to serve briefly as the first United States minister to Panamá, in order to establish the desired basis for Panamanian-American relations at the outset. Buchanan spent only two months on that mission, but continued to advise on Panamanian issues after his supposed return to private life.[28]

From 1906 to 1909, Buchanan held eight special assignments for the State Department; he was virtually a full-time diplomat. In 1906 he headed the United States delegation to the Third Pan-American Conference in Rio de Janeiro, then became minister to Colombia. At the Second Hague Conference in 1907 he was the designated adviser to the Latin American states, which were attending such a function for the first time. Later that year he acted as his government's official representative at Root's Central American Peace Conference in Washington, and in 1908 he made a Central American goodwill tour to encourage implementation of the agreements adopted there. Finally, less than a year before his death, Buchanan went to Venezuela as United States minister, to renew diplomatic relations after their rupture in 1908 during Theodore Roosevelt's dispute with then president Cipriano Castro. He had never abandoned his position with New York Life, however, and died in London while on business for that company in 1909. The life insurance company had employed him at least partly because of his State Department connections, which Buchanan did not hesitate to use vigorously in advancing his client's interests.[29]

Such were the civilians who carried out United States policies in the Caribbean. Some had worked for the War Department, constituting the thin edge of a wedge of influence mainly embodied in the personnel of the armed forces. The military were drawn into the Caribbean picture in a variety of ways, one being the vacuum created by the lack of a central colonial office to oversee the new United States colonies and protectorates. In 1898 the War Department found itself directly administering Cuba, Puerto Rico, and the Philippines. In December of that year, it created a Division of Customs and Insular Affairs, which two years later became the Bureau of Insular Affairs. This agency handled paper work and provided counsel for the army in its civil affairs responsibilities overseas, and became a source of expertise for other agencies as well. When asked, the bureau gave the State Department technical advice for use in various Caribbean protectorates, and recruited specialists like Conant for that purpose. In 1907 it took over supervision of the Dominican customs receivership, and in 1920 added the Haitian customs receivership to its charges.[30]

In Panamá the army's role was specialized but influential. The War Department and its military commanders in the Canal Zone often unilaterally took steps that affected United States–Panamanian relations. The generals, for example, opposed the building of road and rail networks in Panamá on the ground that they might enable an enemy invasion force to reach the canal. The resulting lack of internal communications long slowed Panamá's economic development. The War Department also made vigorous use of the provision of the Hay–Bunau-Varilla Treaty which empowered the United States to expropriate lands and waters outside the Canal Zone "which may be necessary or convenient" for building or defending the canal. During the First World War the army irritated the Panamanian government by repeatedly taking over defense sites without prior notification, but the crowning blow came three days after the armistice, when it demanded most of beautiful Taboga Island, Panamá City's prized garden spot and health resort. The zone's commanding general told the Panamanians that he simply had no discretion in the matter, as the War Department had ordered it! This time, however, the government of

Panamá made a major diplomatic assault, and the army ultimately had to settle for only 30 acres out of the island's 1,400.[31]

In Cuba, the army also exercised significant power for many years. The military occupation commanders and Secretary of War Elihu Root were central to formulating Cuban policy during the first occupation of 1899–1902. The second occupation of 1906–1909 was under the civilian direction of Charles E. Magoon, but the army put five thousand men into Cuba to keep the peace. In addition, some army officers again served directly in the Cuban government as "advisers" to the heads of the principal administrative departments, the major police agencies, and the Sanitation Department. At the end of 1908, the army had fifty-eight officers thus serving with the provisional government. After 1909, however, the army's leaders shifted their emphasis from colonial concerns in the Caribbean and the Philippines to a more traditional interest in planning for war with another power, and Cuban affairs receded to secondary rank.[32]

In spite of the army's declining interest, it continued to play a significant role in Cuba, particularly through the activities of General Enoch H. Crowder. Crowder made his career in the Judge Advocate General's Department as a military lawyer and administrator, and was therefore naturally involved in colonial matters. He served in the Philippines as a staff officer from 1898 to 1901, and played a prominent part in the Cuban occupation of 1906–1909. There he "advised" the Cuban departments of State and Justice, while heading the Advisory Law Commission which rewrote the electoral and civil service laws of Cuba. As a presumed expert on Cuban elections, he returned to Havana in 1919 to rewrite the electoral laws a second time and to recommend other reforms aimed at heading off a crisis during the 1920 elections. The subsequent emasculation of these reforms by the Cuban congress and the flagrant election frauds of the 1920 presidential contest enabled Alfredo Zayas to win control of the Havana regime, and eventually brought General Crowder back to Cuba as well.[33]

By this time Crowder was a celebrity in the United States, having written and administered the 1917 draft law which raised the wartime army. His prestige and Cuban experience led to his return to Cuba early in 1921 as personal representative of President Wilson, with orders to head off violence on the part of Zayas' outraged opponents. Arriving without formal notice aboard a United States battleship, Crowder attempted to impose the familiar compromise of holding new corrective elections in disputed districts, but the anti-Zayas Liberals boycotted them, fearing another betrayal from Washington. Zayas therefore retained power, but in circumstances so tense that the incoming administration of Warren G. Harding left Crowder in Havana, still as special representative of the United States president. Soon the Zayas regime embarked on an ambitious program of official graft, the Cuban economy collapsed in a postwar slump, and Crowder stayed on to wage a strenuous power struggle with the Cuban president.[34]

In February 1922 Crowder began a new reform campaign with the first of what would eventually be thirteen "memoranda" to Zayas attacking the latter's financial and governmental abuses. In June the general forced the resignation of Zayas' key cabinet members and secured their replacement by a handpicked group known collectively as the "honest cabinet," in part using the Cuban desire for a large new government loan as a lever. Crowder refused to approve the loan until a sweeping government cleanup was completed. When he finally approved it early in 1923, however, Crowder found his leverage greatly reduced, while Zayas was grimly determined to reestablish control of his government. Within a few months he had fired the "honest cabinet" and seen his congress repeal much of Crowder's reform legislation. The general hinted at intervention, but the State Department disavowed any such intent, and Zayas had won over his Yankee rival. Crowder nevertheless stayed on in Cuba as ambassador until 1927, no longer in the army and without the full support of the State Department. In Crowder, Washington had been rattling an empty scabbard, and the Cubans soon knew it.[35]

While the army carried more weight in Panamá and Cuba, the navy routinely performed pseudodiplomatic and administrative duties all over the Caribbean. In this context the Marine Corps constituted an important arm of the Navy Department. The navy and marines together virtually ran Haiti after 1915, while the marines largely governed the Dominican Republic from 1916 to 1924. The marines mounted interventions in Nicaragua in 1912 and Cuba in 1917. With the army they supervised elections and helped to garrison Panamá; with the navy they carried out scores of lesser peace-keeping operations about the region. A small specialized force, the Marine Corps expanded steadily from fewer than three thousand men early in 1898 to over eleven thousand in 1916. At any given time, marine units were distributed in shipboard assignments on naval vessels, occupation and landing-force duties, overseas garrisons, and shore duty in the United States. Ready forces were usually held at Philadelphia, Brooklyn, or Guantánamo Bay, available for quick movement to trouble spots. After 1901 the corps made increasing use of floating battalions and regiments, already aboard transports, which could anchor in a sensitive locality without actually landing troops.[36]

Utilized for both large- and small-scale operations, the marines more frequently saw combat in the early twentieth century than either the army or the navy, while some marine officers became intimately acquainted with Caribbean affairs. The overlapping careers of Littleton W. T. Waller and Smedley D. Butler illustrate both features. Waller, the older of the two, joined the marines in 1880. He won a decoration fighting in Cuba in 1898, and was promoted for gallantry in China during the Boxer Rebellion of 1900. In 1901 Waller, then a major, commanded a small marine force on the island of Samar during the Philippine insurrection. After hard combat and harrowing experiences, and while seriously ill with fever, Waller ordered eleven Filipino prisoners executed for the alleged murder of marines. In a cause célèbre, he was himself court-martialed for murder, and although he was acquitted, the affair cast a shadow over the rest of his career. He nevertheless commanded marine units in Cuba in 1906 and in the Veracruz intervention in Mexico in 1914. Later in his career he was the principal marine commander in Haiti during 1915 and 1916, retiring as a major general in 1920.[37]

Smedley Butler, an admiring younger colleague of the swashbuckling Waller, was the son of a congressman who for many years chaired the House Naval Affairs Committee. Joining the marines in 1898, he saw no combat in the Spanish-American War but was twice wounded in fighting near Tientsin during the Boxer Rebellion. After subsequent duty in Honduras, Panamá, and the Philippines, he played a conspicuous field role in the 1912 Nicaraguan intervention, where he earned the sobriquet Old Gimlet Eye. Rising rapidly, he received one Medal of Honor for his actions at Veracruz in 1914, and an unprecedented second one for action against native resistance in Haiti in 1915. Organizer and first commander of the Haitian gendarmerie, he was Waller's chief subordinate in the early years of the Haitian occupation. Given a nonfighting base command in France during the First World War, he ultimately won promotion to major general, and retired in 1931.[38]

Both men typified the Marine Corps's fighting tradition and its considerable commitment to Caribbean intervention. Both were physically small, feisty individuals whose rough and ready methods proved effective at cowing "natives" wherever found; fearless and charismatic, they were also abrasive and authoritarian. But neither was responsible for the campaigns in which he fought; they fought with equal readiness whenever and wherever ordered, and turned to civil administration only when their superiors demanded it. They nevertheless were a part of a connection so intimate that Americans came automatically to think of the marines upon hearing of any new troubles in the Caribbean.

However, the Marine Corps was the junior member in its arbitrary partnership with the navy. Marine commanders in the field ordinarily took orders from the admirals of the senior service, and commanders of naval vessels interfered in local affairs much oftener than ground troops were landed. Naval officers had long acted as ad hoc representatives of their government in sudden crises, particularly in the less developed areas of the globe; occasionally ship captains had to make on-the-spot decisions with direct political consequences. Furthermore, naval officers were an important source of diplomatic intelligence. Whenever an American warship stopped in a foreign port, its commander was required to report on political developments there. The Navy Department routinely forwarded these reports to the State Department, where they received much the same attention as that department's own reports. In fact, the political evaluations of experienced naval officers often carried more weight than those of less qualified consular officials, and acted as an independent check on State's own reporting system.[39]

Naval officers constituted a select and close-knit group. They were drawn mostly from the upper-middle and middle classes, were largely of Anglo-Saxon or Teutonic descent, and belonged to protestant religious sects, Episcopalians being dominant. They were similarly conditioned by their naval academy training and their subsequent duty assignments at sea and ashore. The navy was a career service, by 1900 just recovering from a post-Civil War officer glut that had made promotion glacially slow for decades. Even in 1906 the navy's youngest captain was fifty-five years old, while admirals' stripes were rarely attainable much before the age of sixty. In 1899, however, a newly created "plucking board" began its task of weeding out unsatisfactory captains, while by 1916 the adoption of formal screening at each promotion level fully introduced the "up or out" system by which officers repeatedly passed over for promotion had to retire. In the early twentieth century, therefore, the navy was transforming a rigid seniority system into one of selective promotion for merit, and the naval officer corps gained new competence and prestige as a result.[40]

In the Caribbean region the navy played a leading role in Washington's continuing efforts to restrain political violence. One common practice was to forbid warfare in the immediate vicinity of United States citizens or property. In April 1907, for example, the commander of U.S.S. *Marietta* refused to allow a Nicaraguan warship to bombard the Honduran banana port of La Ceiba on the ground that such shelling would endanger American life and property. In his report the officer involved laid down a principle: "To admit the sovereign rights of any so-called government, . . . to officials on this coast today . . . would be to invite anarchy and to surrender all protection for foreign interests." [41]

Admiral William B. Caperton pursued a similar course early in 1915 during a successful revolutionary campaign to overthrow the Haitian government. At the beginning of the war the Admiral warned both sides that their forces must not loot or burn towns, or needlessly endanger foreign life or property. The rival leaders agreed, and were surprised to find, as the fighting moved down the coast toward the capital, that one of Caperton's warships lay waiting in each new coastal town that passed within the combat area. Thus closely supervised the brief civil war was a model of order and propriety, at least as far as foreign interests were concerned. A few months later, when a new struggle erupted, Caperton flatly forbade fighting in Cap-Haïtien, and as a result the decisive battle for the town occurred three miles away from it.[42]

In 1904, prior to any of the above cases, Commander A. C. Dillingham in

U.S.S. *Detroit* had banned revolutionary conflict at Sosua in the Dominican Republic. Because the United Fruit Company had a large banana plantation there, Dillingham told the opposing Dominican commanders that "outside of this line you can fight; inside of this line is American property, this I defend." Later that year at Puerto Plata, Dillingham announced that he would take charge of the local fort, while the hostile forces must go outside the town for battle. Whichever side won would receive possession, he promised, and when the government troops triumphed, he duly gave them the fort and the town.[43]

These actions had marked Dillingham's advent into Dominican politics. Impressed by his forcefulness, the United States minister praised him in dispatches to Washington, while Dillingham's constant patrolling soon brought him into contact with most of the country's top factional leaders. This officer's growing part in the unfolding Dominican crisis demonstrated the navy's intimate relationship to Caribbean crisis. In August 1904 Dillingham acted as mediator between the current Morales government and General Desiderio Arias, the ambitious boss of the country's north coast. The resulting Dillingham Agreement headed off a new civil war and added to the commander's local prestige, at the same time building his reputation in Washington as an authority on Dominican politics.[44]

Dillingham moved into the center of Dominican tensions in January 1905, when Theodore Roosevelt sent him to join Minister Thomas C. Dawson in negotiating an American customs protectorate agreement. Far from resenting this intrusion on his turf, Dawson welcomed the naval man and lauded his "energy, tact, frankness and decision" in his official reports. The two worked smoothly together, agreeing on all essentials, Dillingham doing most of the initial talking. Indeed, in the crucial early stages of the negotiations, the officer was probably more important than the diplomat; most of the Dominican politicos had already experienced Dillingham's direct methods and seen the ships and guns which made them effective. As in the case of Admiral Caperton and the Nicaraguan election of 1916, merely calling in the naval commander evoked a vivid image of the threat that lay behind United States demands.[45]

The navy itself was early to recognize the diplomatic side of its Caribbean responsibilities. In 1902 the Navy Department created the Caribbean Division of the North Atlantic Squadron specifically for such work. Initially composed of half a dozen small cruisers and gunboats, the command was not normally expected to operate as a unit, but rather to provide vessels as needed to visit trouble spots throughout the region and bring their message of American power. Later known as the Cruiser Squadron or the Special Service Squadron, for several decades this small arm of the navy served an essentially diplomatic function, but always with the capability of using force.

The order establishing the new command exhorted its officers to cultivate more friendly relations with the peoples of the Caribbean through "greater intercourse with the natives and their officials, by being familiar with their language and habits, and by the avoidance of any assumption of superiority." While the order laudably stressed this latter point, the squadron's very functions made it difficult to achieve. Admiral Caperton stretched these functions to the limit in 1915–16, when as commander of the squadron he launched two major interventions—in Haiti and the Dominican Republic—in less than a year.[46]

A seminal study by Richard D. Challener found some years ago that the army, and more especially the navy, had significant input in forming and implementing United States foreign policy in the early twentieth century. This occurred without much institutional framework for integrating civilian and military viewpoints, largely through the personal efforts of presidents and policymakers and the inevitable role of the armed forces in enforcing policy decisions. It was particularly visible in the Caribbean region, where civilians were often as caught up in security fears as service heads. Admirals, generals, and politicians shared many assumptions about their country's role in the world, the expressions of which were mutually supporting. If there was a "military mind," Challener insists, not all military men had it; more importantly, civilian leaders were almost equally apt to think in terms of using force. The more significant difference may well have been that the armed forces better understood the limits of military power than their civilian chiefs.[47]

The United States impact on the Caribbean world came not only from official government actions, but from private interests as well. As we saw earlier, Minor Keith's railroad and banana empire in Central America, the sugar economy built in Cuba by men like Edward Atkins, or the work of bankers' agents like the National City Bank's Roger Farnham could equally shape the Caribbean reality. Besides these larger operators, each principal town or city had its Yankee manufacturers' agents selling Ford automobiles, Singer sewing machines, and Victor phonographs, its electric companies and ice plants, its mining offices or streetcar lines. This subculture of American penetration produced some notable characters, a few of whom are difficult to classify under any standard category. Two related examples help to show the outer limits of Americans' activity.

General Lee Christmas was once a legend in Central America, and his name survives dimly as a reminder of a departed day. In its own way, Christmas' career was unique. Born Leon Winfield Christmas in 1863, he went to work for the railroad in his native Louisiana. At twenty-one he was promoted to engineer, a job he lost in 1891 for wrecking his train while drunk. After three years of vagrancy, Christmas was hired as an engineer by the Honduran National Railroad, which ran about sixty miles inland from Puerto Cortés on the north coast. In 1897 a small insurrectionary force seized Puerto Cortés and forced Christmas, at gunpoint, to take it inland on a train. The train in turn was counterattacked by government troops, and to save his life Christmas picked up a rifle and joined in the defense. He fought so formidably that the rebels offered him a captain's commission, starting him on his subsequent course of political soldiering. The rebellion soon collapsed, however, and Christmas fled with other survivors of his cause across the mountains to Guatemala.[48]

In Guatemala the devious President Manuel Estrada Cabrera gave refuge and support to the failed revolutionaries, who were potentially useful to his perpetual designs against the Honduran government. In time the Honduran regime offered a general amnesty, and Christmas even regained his old railroad job. He soon quit the railroad, however, to indulge his considerable appetites for women, liquor, and gambling. He was quietly supported in this by the newly installed President Terencio Sierra, who intended to outstay his legal term in office and wanted a body of proven fighters behind him when the inevitable crisis came. In 1902 the president made Christmas chief of police in Tegucigalpa, the capital city, and began to prepare for a showdown. Manuel Bonilla emerged as Sierra's main rival for power; unluckily for the incumbent, Bonilla had meanwhile become Christmas' best friend. Early in 1903 the erstwhile police chief deserted his patron and defected to Bonilla, taking along almost all of his 185-man force to join Bonilla's army.[49]

In the ensuing war, Christmas was second in command of one of Bonilla's armies. He played a stellar part in the principal battle in his area, turning the tide by annihilating an enemy flanking force. Bonilla won the war and the presidency, while Christmas again became Tegucigalpa's police chief, this time with the accompanying rank of brigadier general. But the wheel of politics continued to turn, and in 1907 the regime met disaster. Bonilla's domestic enemies allied themselves with Nicaragua's formidable President José Santos Zelaya to form an irresistible combination. Bonilla's army suffered a decisive defeat, and the president fled aboard a United States warship. Christmas, trapped with a smaller force, attempted a dash through the enemy line, but was wounded and captured instead. To his surprise he was not shot; his captors, impressed with his legendary daring and *machismo*, allowed him to return to exile in Guatemala, where he soon recovered from his wounds.[50]

When Manuel Bonilla attempted a comeback revolt in 1910, Lee Christmas was titular commander in chief of his forces, but the movement was a short-lived fiasco and no real forces materialized. It was clear that there had been insufficient preparation, but all was not lost; Bonilla had secret financial backing in the United States, and was prepared to try again. It was at this point that Christmas' activities became linked with those of another remarkable adventurer, Samuel Zemurray.[51]

The young Zemurray, son of poor Bessarabian peasants, came to the United States in 1892 to help his aunt and uncle run a country store in Selma, Alabama. Moving to Mobile in 1899, he became a fruit jobber and began to sell

Lee Christmas as a Honduran general. Courtesy of the American Geographical Society Collection, University of Wisconsin–Milwaukee

bananas. On a trip to New Orleans he noticed that the United Fruit Company threw away large numbers of bananas which were too ripe to ship. He contracted with United Fruit to buy them cheaply, then sold them in nearby towns at below the market price. Zemurray prospered, and in 1900 joined with a partner to buy a small steamer, in which they imported bananas purchased from independent growers in Honduras. Financed in part by United Fruit, the partners bought their own banana land in Honduras, and finally incorporated as the Cuyamel Fruit Company, with Zemurray as president. To secure its position, Cuyamel needed government concessions: a guarantee against increased taxes, permission to build a railroad, and the right to import building materials duty-free. By 1910 this quest for concessions had drawn Zemurray into Honduran politics.[52]

The president of Honduras in 1910 was Miguel Dávila, who had little personal backing and faced an empty treasury and mounting debts. To avoid bankruptcy and gain support against his enemies, Dávila signed a treaty with the United States which provided for refinancing the Honduran debt in return for foreign management of the government's finances. The treaty was very unpopular in Honduras, but Dávila believed that once such an arrangement existed, Washington would protect him against forcible overthrow. He therefore tried desperately to secure congressional approval of his treaty before his domestic opponents could oust him.[53]

It was their common opposition to Dávila which drew together Zemurray and the Bonilla camp. Neither the Dávila regime nor the State Department were likely to approve concessions such as Zemurray sought, which would limit government revenues in a time of stringency. If the Paredes-Knox Convention became binding and Dávila were fixed in office by American power, the banana enterprise could hope for little government help. With the energetic Bonilla already plotting to seize power, it was easy for the two to make common cause. Zemurray's Cuyamel Fruit Company therefore sponsored Bonilla's first, abortive revolt, and was prepared to do a more thorough job next time. Late in 1910 Bonilla and Christmas went to New Orleans to meet secretly with Zemurray, who provided them with a large, fast yacht and the money to procure arms and men.[54]

Although closely watched by federal agents, the two revolutionists managed to sail to Guatemala, pick up a cache of arms, and seize the offshore island of Roatan as a base for their campaign. In January 1911 Bonilla landed at Trujillo on the mainland with almost two hundred men commanded by Christmas. The capture of that town secured the garrison's arms, the customhouse gold, and over three hundred new recruits. Playing for time, Dávila managed to send a strong force to La Ceiba, the next major coastal town to westward, and it was there that the crucial fighting occurred. Not all banana wars were opéras bouffes: at La Ceiba that January, Christmas with fewer than six hundred men attacked a well-led government force twice the size of his own. In the ensuing slaughter the Bonilla army lost one hundred dead and one hundred and fifty wounded, but killed or captured the entire enemy command. With no other troops in the area, the Dávila regime abandoned the north coast and faced an almost hopeless future. To prevent further fighting, the United States government sent Thomas Dawson to hold a peace conference which produced a neutral provisional president and a national election. His prestige restored, Bonilla won the election to resume the presidency in 1912.[55]

For a time Christmas rode high as commander in chief of the Honduran army, remaining in that position after Bonilla's death from illness in 1913 but finally being unseated two years later. His career declining steadily and his patron dead, he was ultimately exiled from Honduras. He returned to Guatemala, where his second patron, President Estrada Cabrera, fell from power and died in 1920. A general without an army, Lee Christmas returned to the United States in failing health, dying in 1924.[56]

Zemurray faced a brighter future. His alliance with the victorious Bonilla ensured that the Cuyamel Fruit Company would receive all the government largess it requested. Through adroit maneuvering, Zemurray managed to remain on good terms with later Honduran governments after Bonilla's death, in part by exploiting common interests. In 1915 he began expanding his banana operations into the Motagua Valley, a disputed area on the Honduran-Guatemalan border. The rival United Fruit Company having already secured concessions in the same district from the Guatemalan government, Zemurray got a Honduran concession in support of his own claim. The Guatemalans sent troops to uphold their sovereignty in the area, and Tegucigalpa followed suit. Soon skirmishes on the border threatened to escalate into real war. The United States offered mediation and discouraged further fighting, but the dispute lingered for years, the handiwork of the mutually reinforcing ambitions of the rival governments and fruit companies.[57]

Under Zemurray's driving leadership, the Cuyamel Fruit Company pioneered in selective fruit breeding, advanced irrigation systems, and other progressive practices, eventually producing better bananas than United Fruit. During the 1920s, Cuyamel became United's principal competitor, but in 1929 Zemurray sold out to his great rival for 300,000 shares of the latter's stock, and retired to New Orleans. The impact of the Great Depression soon brought him out of retirement, however, as United Fruit lost heavily and its stock value plummeted. Afraid that his fortune would be wiped out, Zemurray led a stockholders' revolt, ousted the company's management, and became the managing director himself in 1932. Effective as always, he brought the company successfully through the depression. From his new eminence, Zemurray sounded taps for the bad old days: "I feel guilty about some of the things we did . . . all we cared about was dividends. Well, you can't do business that way today." [58]

Soldier of fortune and business buccaneer, Lee Christmas and Samuel Zemurray were fit partners for one another, but hardly representative of Americans in general in the Caribbean. They nonetheless shared some attributes with their less colorful contemporaries, chiefly energy, self-confidence, and a readiness to impose their wills on local society. Like North Americans in more official positions, they did not shrink from the use of force, and put ends above means in planning their actions. What differentiated them from more formal representatives of their nation was their unabashed quest for personal profit, and their lack of any need for idealistic or ideological justifications of their acts.

Chapter 15

———⸲⸲⸲————

Economic Consequences
of Hegemony

By 1918 the United States had achieved economic hegemony in much of the Caribbean region. This stemmed in part from the flow of American investment into the region. To be sure, until 1914 United States investment was roughly balanced by that of Great Britain. Furthermore, British strength in banking facilities and commercial credit contrasted with the United States weakness overseas in these fields. But North American influence was strengthened by the Yankee preference for direct investment—the extension of United States enterprises or their subsidiaries into foreign countries—rather than the more passive portfolio investment—government and private bonds and minority stockholdings—such as the British tended to prefer. By 1914, according to one estimate, United States direct investment had reached $587 million in Mexico and $371 million in Central America and the Caribbean. The years after 1914 saw the repatriation of much of the British and European money to pay for the war, while American dollars not only stayed on but increased.[1]

If American investment won a clear lead in the Caribbean only during the European war, American market dominance in the region was well established before that event. As one authority wrote in 1916, "Every industry of great importance in the Caribbean finds the United States the greatest buyer of the commodity it produces." In 1920 a National City Bank study concluded that the United States market accounted for over 90 percent of the exports of Mexico, Honduras, and Panamá, over 80 percent of those of Puerto Rico and the Dominican Republic, and over 70 percent of those of Cuba, Guatemala, Costa Rica, and Colombia. Overall, the study found that the United States received 79 percent of all Caribbean exports, including those of the remaining European colonies in the area. It also showed that the region overall bought 74 percent of its imports from the United States, but this figure still reflected the wartime disruption of European suppliers. In more normal times the Caribbean countries might find alternate suppliers of their import needs, but reliable markets for their exports were much harder to come by. This regional market dominance by itself gave the United States a unique position in Caribbean affairs.[2]

Although overshadowed by the British and others in Caribbean banking facilities, the United States moved steadily to regularize the region's currencies. From the McKinley to the Wilson administrations, Washington pushed as many client countries as possible to adopt the gold standard, strengthen their exchange systems, and make their money readily convertible with the dollar. This last object was usually achieved by tying the local currency to the dollar in a fixed ratio. By the early 1920s, the monetary units of Cuba, the Dominican Republic, Panamá, Nicaragua, and Guatemala were all fixed at one United States dollar, that of Honduras at fifty cents, of El Salvador at forty cents, of Costa Rica at twenty-five cents, and of Haiti at twenty cents. The result was a small but secure dollar bloc in opposition to the wider use of British sterling exchange.[3]

While the great bulk of the Caribbean trade was carried in European ships before 1914, most of it moved to and from United States ports. New York was inevitably the most important; some 60 percent of America's imports and nearly 40 percent of its exports passed through New York's harbor in this period. Second in importance, though well behind New York, was New Orleans, more specifically focused on the Central American and West Indian trade. Both ports had large facilities for handling sugar, coffee, bananas, and other tropical products; both were home to concentrations of middlemen and distributers, centers of rail transport, and headquarters of firms interested in Caribbean enterprises. Together they constituted the twin capitals of the American trading empire in the Caribbean, and as such were well known to Latin America's economic elites.[4]

Tied to these and other United States centers was a network of Caribbean port towns whose economies rested largely upon the export of one or more local products to the American mainland. Some were old, long-established ports which had gradually become dependent on United States trade ties; others were relatively new towns which sprang up to meet an emergent export need. Few had very large communities of resident North Americans, even though they were largely products of Yankee markets and enterprise. Collectively, they were a potential force for modernization and foreign cultural penetration, though many such towns had small populations, or were isolated from the main national centers.

One old city which had become a modern export center was Cienfuegos, Cuba's largest sugar-shipping port and one of its larger urban centers. A south

coast town with about forty thousand people in 1912, Cienfuegos shipped virtually all of its sugar to the United States. It shipped little else and imported
little, being supplied overland from Havana and lesser north coast ports. Aside
from sugar factories there were few local industries. Cienfuegos was therefore
a highly specialized community tied to a single product and market. By 1918 it
contained about two hundred fifty resident North Americans, mostly employed
in either the sugar or the construction industries. United States influence was
reflected in the introduction of American automobiles, followed by a flurry of
street paving and road building, which in turn encouraged the use of more
autos. By 1918 the town boasted over three hundred of them, facilitating contact with the countryside. Steamships sailed almost daily for Key West, New
York, or New Orleans, and there was good railroad service to Havana and
Santiago. Well integrated into its world, Cienfuegos faced both inward and
outward, a bridge between two linked economies.[5]

A much newer and smaller export center was Puerto Limón, Costa Rica's
chief port since the completion in 1890 of the national railroad from the central
plateau to the sea. A town of about eight thousand population, Puerto Limón
handled over 90 percent of its nation's foreign trade. Its exports consisted
mostly of bananas shipped by the United Fruit Company to the United States;
of its imports, over half came from the United States in 1910. The number
of resident North Americans fluctuated from under one hundred to about one
hundred and forty, almost all employed either by the fruit company or the
railroad. When war in Europe forced the Hamburg-American Line to suspend
shipping service, the United Fruit Company put its banana fleet under United
States registry and monopolized the local seaborne trade. Puerto Limón's dual
functions as both an export and import channel made it less specialized than
Cienfuegos, but it was nevertheless ultimately dependent on banana exports.[6]

Many Caribbean ports matched the patterns of neither Cienfuegos nor
Puerto Limón except for their intimate trade ties to the United States. In Cuba,
Havana was by far the largest general importing center, about half of the imports handled there coming from the United States. Havana also led in the
export of Cuban cigars and tobacco, with sugar a strong second, the bulk of
both crops going to the United States. The only Caribbean big city, Havana
had a permanent community of two to three thousand resident North Americans prior to the First World War, and was more culturally Americanized than
any other town in the region. Santiago de Cuba, the country's second city with
over fifty thousand people, was the metropolis of Cuba's mining district, ex-
porting almost equal values of sugar and metal ores. As early as 1907, United
States concerns owned properties worth over twelve million dollars in the Santiago area, and by 1912 some five hundred Yankees lived there. Local business
transactions were conducted almost entirely with United States currency. As
the American consul there reported in 1916, "practically all" of the local mer-

chants and planters were "thoroughly familiar with commercial and banking methods in the U.S.," and made frequent trips to New York and other trade centers. Like Havana, Santiago was an old port which had adapted to new trade patterns.[7]

A Central American base of United States trade was Bluefields, Nicaragua, a small but important coastal entrepôt since the 1880s. An early banana port, Bluefields' economy also rested upon rubber, minerals, timber, and assorted tropical products. Tied tightly to New Orleans by its shipping, marketing, and credit arrangements, the town was economically dominated by United States interests and did its business in the English language. Physically and culturally isolated, Bluefields had little contact with Nicaragua's main population centers to the west. It faced only the Caribbean sea-lanes leading north; as one consular report remarked, "The town might be said to be a suburb of New Orleans." Of perhaps two thousand inhabitants, over two hundred were United States citizens in 1913.[8]

There was no single pattern common among the region's seaports. La Ceiba and Puerto Cortés in Honduras, Santo Domingo and San Pedro de Macorís in the Dominican Republic, Bocas del Toro in Panamá, Puerto Barrios in Guatemala, and San Juan in Puerto Rico differed largely in size and specifics, but all shared a dependence upon the export of local products to the United States. In time, such port towns sprang up ready-made to answer the needs of American enterprise. In 1923, consular official Willard Beaulac was ordered to Puerto Castillo in Honduras, but was unable to find it on a map. The reason for this, he found, was that the entire town was just nearing completion, having been built as a unit by the United Fruit Company. When he eventually reached it by coastal schooner, he found an archetypal banana port:

> Puerto Castillo was nearing the end of the construction stage. It was built on filled-in land, a mile or a mile and a half long and less than half as wide, with the Bay of Honduras on one side and the jungle on the other. The newly finished wharf was substantial and modern. Below it was the labor town, a collection of small wooden houses, geometrically arranged. Like all other wooden structures in town, they were built on stilts and painted yellow. In the middle of the town, opposite the wharf and extending several hundred yards on each side of it were the railroad yards. Beyond them, in the direction of the jungle, were the company shops and a fine big modern commissary. . . . Next to the hotel were the company offices; and beyond the offices . . . began Executive Row. . . . A single road traversed the town from end to end. . . . Since nearly all vehicles in town ran on rails, this road had practically no traffic over it. It was carefully and lovingly maintained, however, and helped to overcome the impression that we were living in a railroad yard that had wandered, through error, onto a wide, tropical beach.

The fruit company's building plan included a hospital, a baseball field, and even the consulate building which Beaulac was to occupy. It did not include a

Loading bananas in Costa Rica, ca. 1912. Courtesy of the American Geographical Society Collection, University of Wisconsin–Milwaukee

restaurant, cinema, or other social center. There were at least twenty men for every woman in town; its population totaled about fifteen hundred, of whom West Indian Negroes made up a majority. The only residents who did not work for United Fruit were the customhouse staff, the local *comandante* and a squad of soldiers, and Beaulac himself.[9]

Puerto Castillo was a microcosm of Central American banana development, and was welcomed as such by the Honduran authorities. Liberal concessions to foreign fruit companies were not merely an idiosyncrasy of this or that president, but a long-term policy of successive Honduran governments. Such concessions had been standard since the 1880s, while in 1900 the Honduran congress had ordered the survey and sale of virtually the entire Caribbean littoral. In addition to making government lands available on easy terms, Tegucigalpa used liberal railroad-construction contracts to spur development. Typically, these contracts granted the prospective builder a strip route plus up to 1,250 acres of land per kilometer of road built. Running for ninety-nine years if fulfilled, they also normally granted tax exemptions for the developers, tariff exemptions on imported products needed for construction, and the power to expropriate private property.[10]

The Honduran elite encouraged the take-over of the north coast by North

American corporations for what appeared to be compelling reasons. An entire region of the country which had been almost empty of people, and even emptier of economic enterprise, became productive. Towns and infrastructure appeared as if by magic; railroads materialized, by 1918 well over two hundred miles of new main line and much more in branches; seaports, piers, electric plants, and ocean shipping came to serve the coastal districts. Property and export taxes on all this activity greatly increased government revenues, while the resulting growth of the government opened many more bureaucratic posts for the elite and their dependents. The introduction of technology, skilled workers, capital, and professional management into a backward society seemed to promise a widening ripple of modernization and enterprise which could in time transform the entire country.[11]

A chorus of later observers rejected these justifications as false. Carleton Beals argued over a half century ago that the banana companies contributed nothing whatever to Honduras, but killed competing local enterprises with their railroad monopolies and company stores, while their exemptions from import duties cost the government 30 percent of its potential revenues. Others pointed out that the fruit company railroads never extended beyond the banana districts, serving only company, not national, purposes. Furthermore, Beals and others charged, the companies used their political power to evade fair taxation of their product: Central American coffee, produced by individual farmers, typically paid an export duty of 10–13 percent of its value, while banana exports paid only 1–3 percent. The great fruit companies meddled in local politics, amassed huge and often untaxed landholdings, and never sparked the development of other major economic sectors. And even the jobs undoubtedly created in the coastal districts went largely to cheap foreign labor from the West Indies, at the expense of the natives.[12]

This debate was but one facet of a larger dispute over the value and effects of foreign enterprise in the Caribbean. Criticism of the sugar industry paralleled that of the banana companies, and was even more basic. Sugar long dominated the economies of Cuba and Puerto Rico, became the leading export of the Dominican Republic, and was significant in several other countries. Unlike bananas, which took over only portions of a country, sugar could dominate the entire society. The banana companies operated in largely neglected coastal areas in which few Central Americans lived, and which were poorly integrated into their mainstream national societies. The companies imported most of their laborers from the British West Indies and isolated them in company towns, minimizing their contact with local societies. Important as it was, therefore, the banana boom had a distinctly limited impact upon the countries where it occurred. The contrast with sugar was fundamental, since the latter industry touched upon almost every facet of indigenous economies and societies. We have seen how this occurred in Cuba, and some of the negative results:

economic dependence on the fluctuating world price of a single product, wide-spread seasonal unemployment, the diversion of land from food production and consequent rise in the cost of living, the elimination of an entire class of small farmers, the neglect of other forms of enterprise, and the introduction of excessive foreign influence.

In the case of either bananas or sugar, the resulting economic development was partial, unbalanced, and accompanied by undesirable side effects. United States investment in the region went primarily into tropical agriculture, of which these were the two leading branches. Given the long-term results, it appeared that certain prevailing economic assumptions of the early twentieth century were significantly in error: massive investment in export agriculture failed to bring the Caribbean region most other forms of economic develop-ment, to create a general material prosperity, or to achieve "takeoff" to self-sustained economic growth. It was often argued at the time that the people of the Caribbean were themselves to blame for this. Given orderly constitutional government and honest administration, many held, with revolution thoroughly suppressed and the safety of property ensured, the Caribbean would come into its own and the region's inhabitants would enjoy all the wealth which a bounti-ful nature could provide. According to this view, it was their refusal to accept North American tutelage and to conform to North American political norms which doomed the Caribbean states to continued backwardness and poverty.

To test this assumption it is only necessary to look at the case of Puerto Rico, which became United States territory in 1898. In the Puerto Rican case there was no major governmental fraud or corruption, while public adminis-tration was in the hands of appointees from Washington. The Puerto Ricans, made United States citizens in 1917, enjoyed the blessings of law and order and the security of property. No great public violence threatened their sta-bility, revolution was unknown, and Yankee administrators made good roads and public education their goals. Thus the presumed shortcomings which held back other Caribbean societies could be expected to play little part in Puerto Rico, where purely economic factors might be assumed to have full play.

When Puerto Rico passed under United States control in 1898, a peasantry of small landowners scratched out a bare living in the mountains of the interior while more prosperous farmers grew coffee there. On the coastal lowlands much of the rural population lived as landless workers on locally owned sugar and tobacco plantations or ranches. Already food production had fallen below the island's needs; some food was imported, undernourishment was general, and hookworm and anemia sapped the strength of the working classes. Over 80 percent of the population was illiterate. Dismayed by what he saw, the first United States military governor reported in 1899 that debt peonage was widespread, while the country people lived in primitive dirt-floored huts, had "little food worthy of the name," and in many cases owned "no worldly possessions whatever." Starting from such a low base, Yankee methods had an ideal chance to show what they could do.[13]

The challenge was not ignored; United States capital flowed copiously into Puerto Rico. By 1930, mainland corporations owned 60 percent of the island's sugar industry, 80 percent of the tobacco industry, and 60 percent of banking and public utilities. The so-called "big four" American sugar companies controlled almost half of all sugar lands. Coffee, which had been the island's principal export in 1898, had almost disappeared from the scene, having lost its Spanish market and failed to win a foothold in the United States. Sugar growing filled the void, appropriating most of the good farm land and utilizing some 44 percent of all Puerto Rican crop acreage. By one estimate, as much as one hundred twenty million dollars of private capital came to the island between 1898 and 1930, a massive infusion for a country whose population in 1920 was barely a million and a quarter.[14]

Yet the Puerto Ricans were still poor. Harry Franck, a mainland journalist who toured the island in 1920, found a hard-working people living in dire want. He witnessed a sugar workers' strike for a minimum wage, and endorsed their grievances as valid. He was disillusioned to learn that scarcely a third of school-age children actually attended schools, and that malnutrition and disease still prevailed. Economic growth there might have been, he concluded, but the human record in Puerto Rico was a sorry one.[15]

Franck's negative conclusions were echoed in succeeding surveys of the state of the island. A Brookings Institution research group working in 1928–29 described the condition of the masses as "deplorable." Its report granted that there had been unquestionable progress in highways, sewerage, and water supplies since 1898, and marginal improvement in rural clothing and housing. However, with food and clothing imported from the United States, consumer prices were relatively high, yet the average daily rural wage of around seventy cents provided inadequate purchasing power. The number of children in school had grown more than fivefold, but rural schooling was still poor, and 74 percent of the adult rural population was still illiterate. The researchers doubted that there had been much overall improvement in the Puerto Rican standard of living during the period of United States control. "While it cannot be denied that the influx of capital has increased the efficiency of production and promoted general economic development," the group's report warned, "it does not follow that the benefits of this have accrued to the working people of the Island." [16]

Another scholarly survey blamed the sugar companies for much of Puerto Rico's poverty. After examining the annual dividends paid by the "big four" since early in the century, the authors believed that the companies had usually been very profitable, even though their production costs averaged a third to a half higher than those of the Cuban producers. They had compensated for poorer soil by exploiting their labor; yet, this study argued, the profits had been ample to allow for better wages to the workers and still provide an adequate return on capital.[17]

All three works noted the familiar sugar land phenomena of high seasonal unemployment, high living costs resulting from the diversion of land from food production, and the proletarianization of the rural peasantry. All raised fundamental questions about the local effects of foreign enterprise. If large capital investment, the provision of economic infrastructure, manifold increases in productivity, exports, and foreign trade, and the introduction of modern skills and technology could not bring prosperity and self-sustaining growth to an economy, what could? What had gone wrong? The Puerto Rican case raised other questions as well, questions which bore directly on official United States policies in the area. If a Caribbean society could not achieve decent living standards under direct United States administration, then the quest for regional political stability had been justified by exaggerated claims. Such stability might benefit foreign investors; it might even lessen the danger of European interventions, though that danger had undoubtedly been overestimated; but it was not of itself the key to local prosperity.

Theodore Roosevelt had thought otherwise when he wrote in 1904 that the Caribbean countries had "great natural riches, and if within their borders the reign of law and justice obtains, prosperity is sure to come to them." He believed that good government would encourage foreign investment which, unchecked by violence or corruption, would inevitably lead to prosperity for the host society. The conclusion was typical. As Robert Gilpin has pointed out in *U.S. Power and the Multinational Corporation*, a basic assumption of liberal thought has been that international intercourse was essentially benign, bringing benefit to all parties. Liberal-capitalist assertions that international enterprise was the main engine of economic development in the third world reflected their belief in a cooperative, interdependent world economy. Others—Marxists and mercantilists among them—saw economic relations as conflictual, a zero-sum game in which gains to one side must be balanced by losses to the other. They found confirmation of this in the persistence of underdevelopment and poverty in societies long penetrated by large-scale foreign investment. The foreign enterprises, they claimed, profited at the expense of the host society, which provided raw materials and cheap labor but saw the benefits drained off as repatriated profits. To such critics, an interdependent international economy must in reality be a system of hegemonic exploitation.[18]

In their attempts to refute their critics, the Liberals ignored a contradiction: while they defined international economics as cooperative in nature, it was impossible to define international politics similarly. Gilpin notes that power is always relative, and one state's gain in power is necessarily another's loss. From the purely political perspective, international intercourse is hierarchical and hegemonial, and always a zero-sum game. Even if two states were both gaining in wealth, what was important politically was how these gains affected their relative power. Power, in turn, directly affected the distribution of benefits, and distribution within an economic system is also a zero-sum game. Thus an international economic system includes both economic and political dimensions, which are inseparably intertwined. Liberal attempts to analyze such systems in exclusively free-market terms, Gilpin concludes, evade some central issues through oversimplification.[19]

Within the last twenty years, these issues have been specifically addressed by a body of thought known as dependency theory. Originally developed largely by Latin American intellectuals to explain the problems of their own region, the concept of dependency has become one of the principal ways of looking at the global political economy, and writers and scholars have adopted it in every part of the world. By now a diverse and complex array of sometimes competing formulations, the dependency school embraces both Marxists and non-Marxists, and engenders almost as many disputes among its adherents as between them and their common opponents. It nevertheless possesses a few central tenets to which, in some form, all members of the school adhere.

The central concept of dependency theory is that development and underdevelopment are not, as Liberals believe, merely different "stages of economic growth," but rather differing *functional* roles within a single international economic system. The world economy, according to dependency theorists, is permanently divided into a "core" or metropolitan portion and a "periphery" or neocolonial part. The former is industrial, developed, and wealthy; the latter, agrarian, underdeveloped, and poor. Possessed of capital, technology, and markets, as well as great power, the core peoples are able to dominate those of the periphery, casting them in the roles of producers of raw materials for the core factories and purchasers of those factories' output. In many versions of the theory, the underdevelopment of the periphery is seen as a conscious plot of the core states, which use their dominance to freeze all other societies into permanent subordination, and to drain their surpluses to swell the wealth at the center. Such subordination, in this scheme, is an essential condition of the core's prosperity, which positively requires the impoverishment of the periphery.[20]

Whatever form it takes, the new concept stresses the dependent relationship of the underdeveloped countries to the developed core. The core supplies capital and credit, shapes and manages the international monetary system, and creates a relatively open world trading system. It furnishes the markets for the undeveloped economies' exports and plays the leading role in setting the terms of exchange. It provides manufactured goods for the nonindustrial world, as well as technological and scientific expertise. Its mastery of large-scale business organization and managerial techniques enables it to undertake major enterprises which are closed to the periphery's tradition-bound elites. Holding the economic initiative, it is the core economies which set the direction for all the others. The underdeveloped world, forced to concentrate on primary-product exports, is incapable of self-generated economic development.[21]

All this is summed up in a widely quoted definition formulated by *dependencista* Theotonio Dos Santos: dependency, he writes, is "a situation in which the economy of certain countries is conditioned by the development and expansion of another economy to which the former is subjected." It exists "when some countries (the dominant ones) can expand and can be self-starting, while other countries (the dependent ones) can do this only as a reflection of that expansion. . . ." In short, dependent economies lack the capacity to shape their own growth, and by extension their social structures as well.[22]

Though widely accepted, dependency theory faced a formidable array of criticisms, sometimes from within the movement's own ranks. The debate, while far-ranging in time and space, tended necessarily to turn on differing interpretations of the so-called third world's developmental record. It touched most of the theory's central assumptions, and even led some researchers to reassert earlier claims for foreign enterprise as a necessary developmental force.

Some scholars denied that foreign enterprises were necessarily exploitative. A study of the United Fruit Company some years ago argued that that concern's long-term profits ran close to the average for comparable large domestic corporations within the United States, even though United Fruit faced risks unknown to the domestic economy. A student of British investments in Latin America between 1840 and 1930 similarly concluded that the return on productive investments ran only 1 or 2 percent higher than that on domestic industrial stocks, again despite the higher risks involved. This author argued that Latin Americans would have found it difficult to get similar services on better terms. As for the supposed "drain" of assets back to the core, the testimony was at best mixed. Even if the outflow of profits and dividends exceeded the initial investment, that did not prove that the host country had lost; what counted was how much local wealth had been created which stayed there, and which would not otherwise have existed. The multiplier effect of the concern's local payments, the acquisition of infrastructure and technology, all weighed in the final balance. It was even possible that more money was lost in failed ventures in Latin America than was ever made by successful ones, since the data were inadequate to prove the contrary.[23]

Implicit in dependency theory was the assumption that there had been a better, or even "normal," alternative to dependent economic development; that the latter was *ab*normal, a deviation from what might have been expected to happen. Dependency theorists failed to make clear, however, what was the nature of such an alternative. Few followed E. Bradford Burns in his rejection of virtually all modern development and preference for a premodern society.

Marxists usually implied that conversion to socialism was at least a belated cure for the ills they described, if not an original option, but non-Marxists challenged this claim as well. Had not the Soviet Union erected its own system of economically dependent states in Eastern Europe after the Second World War? And had Cuba, for example, become less dependent on sugar merely by switching from North American to Soviet patronage? Underdeveloped countries, the non-Marxists explained, must import goods which they could not produce locally. To pay for them they must export their own goods, and these must meet the requirements of the world market. Such countries had to produce whatever local products could find a world market and compete within that market with rival producers' goods. Thus every undeveloped country structured its economy to foreign needs, regardless of its politics or bloc membership, for there was no alternative. There was likewise no alternative, they insisted, to foreign enterprise as a source of the capital, skills, and technology needed for development.[24]

A central question was whether foreign economic penetration actually blocked local development. It *might* do so, said Robert Gilpin, for the forces of the core were powerful, and often did seek to preserve their freedom from effective third-world competition. But opposed to this tendency was a contrary one which might offset it: the spread of capital and infrastructure, the migration of labor skills, the diffusion of science and technology, in time made the factors of production mobile. When supported by economic nationalism and effective government intervention, this countertendency could prevail. The object of economic nationalism was to reduce dependency by accelerating the growth of local industry. Once well started, the industrial latecomers had the "advantages of backwardness"—cheap labor and the use of all-new technology—to help them catch up. Gilpin used the recent examples of Taiwan, Hong Kong, and South Korea to illustrate this process.[25]

The British maverick socialist Bill Warren went further, seeking at length to demonstrate that capitalist enterprise in the underdeveloped world was in fact the principal engine of its development. Coming full circle back to the original claims of the industrial world, Warren denounced dependency theory as an economic myth forged for the purposes of third-world nationalism. He further attacked the theory's overgeneralized vagueness and lack of rigor, its use of tautologies for definitions, and its tendency to explain nothing by explaining everything. In this latter critique he was supported by D. C. M. Platt, who charged that the debate on dependency theory had "reached a level of abstraction difficult to associate with what may be understood to have happened in the past."[26]

More fundamentally, the anti-Castro Cuban exile Carlos Alberto Montaner asserted that the dependency issue was a sham because, for places like Cuba, dependency was simply inevitable. For underdeveloped countries, he wrote, the idea of sovereignty, or a nation's right to determine its own destinies, had lost any real meaning. A handful of "civilizing centers" had long since come to shape everyone's life everywhere, with television, antibiotics, computers, birth control, robots, rock music—an endless tide of techniques, influences, and products which steadily changed the world. The United States was the greatest of these centers for change, while Cuba, its near neighbor, was small, "culturally rickety," and hopelessly malleable. According to Montaner, "The least important facets of Cuban-American relations were the insolence of United States ambassadors or the degree of Yankee penetration of the economy." Cubans could shape their own destinies only to the extent that they mastered the new processes and became involved in bringing on the kinds of change now originating in the United States and elsewhere. To do this they needed to become more closely involved with North America, not isolated from it; to consciously embrace their dependency, and break free of it by Americanizing themselves! Curiously, Montaner's views seemed to parallel the thinking of Latin American Liberals a century earlier.[27]

The range of controversy extended to other significant issues as well, but the discussion above suggests its breadth and thrust. On balance, the dependency concept seems distinctly useful, but more persuasive as description than as explanation. Reversing the conclusions of a previous generation which had attributed Caribbean poverty entirely to the shortcomings of the region's own people, *dependencistas* blamed it wholly on foreign influence. Neither approach involved a realistic appraisal of the area's historical development, local resources, or factors of productivity. Both reflected the myth of potential Caribbean riches which had so strongly influenced foreign travelers and writers in the nineteenth century. Ironically, Caribbean leaders, writers, and opinion shapers had come to reject most of the original developmental propaganda while wholeheartedly adopting that part of it which was least demonstrable. They held, as had their earlier North American critics, that their lands were inherently rich; if their wealth had not been realized, someone must have stolen it.

Thus Cuba's Abecedista political movement in the 1930s and 1940s called for the nationalization of foreign property, believing that once the golden stream of profits was dammed up within Cuba rather than drained off to the mainland, prosperity was ensured. Fidel Castro, who absorbed this credo in his youth and acted upon it when he came to power, was one of an entire generation which believed implicitly that a few simple though sweeping measures could make their region wealthy. Meanwhile they added to the many real sins of the foreign enterprisers the imaginary one of failing to bring them a European standard of living. The enterprisers' claims that they could do this had originally reflected a genuine if mistaken optimism, compounded by a more cynical bid for the favors of the region's governments.

Unfortunately, developmentalists and *dependencistas* alike have tended to slight the importance of indigenous factors in analyzing contemporary societies. Political scientist Tony Smith has concluded that the greatest fallacy of dependency theory was its insistence that the "world system" explained everything, an approach which made local histories meaningless. While Smith emphasized the evolution of local political systems as crucial, other historical factors were also essential to understanding the Caribbean. Carlos Rangel insisted that the region's colonial conditioning had played a large part in creating its current dilemma. The formerly Spanish lands, for example, shared a heritage of authoritarian rule, two-class societies with sharply defined elites, the glorification of landownership, a low status for manual and practical skills, and an elite aversion to entrepreneurship. The long-term influence of slavery made physical work seem unworthy of free men, while technical progress grew suspect as a potential source of unwelcome social change. The neofeudal hacienda system, which reduced so many to peonage, prolonged the rigidities of the slave period even after it had ended. Rejecting the emerging spirit of modernism, hispanic schemes of education had little scientific or practical content, instead emphasizing law, theology, philosophy, and the *belles artes*. In addition, Spanish law and practice had encouraged state monopolies and closed economic systems, a tendency visible in independent Latin America's fondness for licenses, local transit taxes, official monopolies, and the general proliferation of costs and formalities which overburdened private business activity.[28]

In more purely economic terms, how well prepared was nineteenth-century Latin America for industrialization and economic development? D. C. M. Platt argues that it was poorly positioned for such development in either absolute or comparative terms. Most of Latin America lacked the very bases of industrialization: skilled labor, industrial fuels, adequate internal transport systems, even capital, as well as strong domestic markets. Japan, by contrast, had available more working capital, a more effective banking system, large urban markets, adequate coal and iron supplies, and a workable system of internal transport. Furthermore, lacking the option of developing export agriculture, modern Japan had no choice but to industrialize. Perhaps factors such as these helped to explain why certain Asian countries—Japan, South Korea, Taiwan—could escape dependency through industrialization, while the Caribbean countries could not.[29]

Beyond this it is difficult to draw firm conclusions. It would be unhistorical to argue that what happened was inevitable, and that no happier alternatives to Caribbean underdevelopment ever existed, though one fails to discern what they may have been. North American hegemony may have foreclosed more promising options simply by ensuring that they were never tried. Without Yankee domination it is possible that a more vigorous economic nationalism on the part of Caribbean governments may have channeled foreign money and enterprise into more diverse and better-balanced forms of development. Yet the deeply rooted positivism of the region's leadership and the lack of well-defined concepts of central economic planning casts grave doubt on such propositions. Nor did the dominant Yankees depart radically from the economic patterns first established by European activity in the region. From the mid-nineteenth century on, converging patterns of economic thought in Latin America and the North Atlantic industrial world joined with existing realities to dictate the course which outside enterprise followed.

It is also possible, as some insist, that the processes of change are even now working to produce true economic growth in the Caribbean. In this view, Mexico's massive industrialization during the 1960s and 1970s is a portent of the future, proof that a vigorous government-led effort can indeed transcend the limits of dependency. Unfortunately, widespread poverty continues to coexist with the new Mexican productivity, as does a crippling foreign debt and an ongoing dependence upon the United States economy. But progress comes slowly, the optimists maintain, and cannot be hurried; already there is a large Mexican middle class, and another generation may see the deprivation of the poorer classes recede before a tide of material plenty. As Brazil is now becoming an autonomous economic giant, and breaking the chains of dependency, so will Mexico follow in the future, the argument goes. At present this can only be speculation, but some questions arise nevertheless. Even if they do break free from dependency, will Brazil and Mexico lead the rest of Latin America into a similar state of grace, or will they merely join the older core states in dominating their still-dependent neighbors? For their part, do the Caribbean countries share the specific resources and advantages which might support a similar success? One cannot say.

What is certain is that the Caribbean region still harbors widespread want, and that whatever its causes, dependency in fact exists. It is clear that the United States government attempted in many ways to impose its own political and economic goals upon the peoples of the Caribbean, and that its claims that this would inevitably benefit both parties proved invalid. Sometimes the local society gained net benefits, but too often the balance sheet was in doubt. In no case did one of Washington's client states in the area escape from poverty or break through to self-sustained economic growth. This failure was not Washington's alone, it is true, but in time it made the contemporary rhetoric of progress ring hollow in the lands to the south, and ultimately brought the charges of the *dependencistas*. These too must be viewed with caution. While it is at best difficult to properly evaluate the United States–Caribbean relationship, it is impossible to do so without clearing away the self-serving myths perpetuated by both sides.

Chapter 16

─────·⟨∞⟩·─────

Hegemony and Nationalism

It is often assumed that foreign hegemony is invariably unwelcome to all who feel its effects. The modern critique of imperialism is twofold: it is exploitative by nature, and it violates the principle of nationalism or self-determination. These charges were less easy to substantiate, however, in the underdeveloped societies of an earlier time. It is by no means obvious, for example, that turn-of-the-century foreign enterprises in the Caribbean were necessarily more exploitative than the area's traditional peonage systems. Seen at close range by ordinary people, the new economic currents promised cash income in neighborhoods formerly limited to subsistence agriculture, and for a fortunate few provided upward mobility to jobs as foremen or skilled workers. For the educated minority they opened at least low-level management and clerical positions, while members of the elite benefited by the growth of government bureaucracies and the increased market for legal, medical, and other services. For some members of the local society, foreign penetration must have created an exhilarating current of opportunity and opened doors to advancement never before visible.

The charge of violating the spirit of nationalism was harder to refute, and was often persuasive even in the last century. It was, however, a time and place of incomplete nationality. Often, what passed for nationalism might be no more than localism or a primitive xenophobia. Most Caribbean countries lacked effective institutional centralization, and many were still defining their national identities. Panamá, for example, abandoned its role as a province of Colombia to pursue a nationalism that in the past had sometimes appeared to be no more than a quest for increased autonomy. Colombia itself was a land of *patrias chicas,* "little homelands" whose people thought largely in terms of their own local district or isolated valley. The Dominican Republic, Spanish in cultural heritage, had endured colonial captivities at the hands of France and Haiti. Though independent since 1844, Dominicans had found what unity they possessed in shared fears of a Haitian reconquest, while up to the turn of the century their country too was hardly more than a collection of disparate regions. At times, Dominican leaders had subordinated their nationalism to a search for a stronger patron state, as in the reannexation to Spain in 1861 or the attempt to annex the country to the United States in 1870. Yet these episodes, as well as the United States occupation of 1916–24, had set off contrary waves of nationalist feeling. In Nicaragua the entire Caribbean coast was racially and culturally alien to the rest of the country, and nurtured a strong local separatism. In Guatemala a more fundamental separation existed, in which half the population lived entirely outside the dominant cultural and political system, speaking only Indian languages and wholly confined to the concerns of their own small districts and villages.[1]

Many, if not most, of the Caribbean's people were so isolated, ignorant, and politically submerged as to be unaware of, or apathetic to, all but the most direct threats to the national integrity. Even educated elites were torn between the nationalist impulse and their desire for progress and prosperity; might it not be the truer patriotism to modernize with foreign help, acquire wealth, skills, and infrastructure, and only then assert the nationalist imperatives against foreigners? To make the question even harder to decide, the United States seemed at times to support local nationalism against its other foreign enemies, and to aid in the struggle for self-rule.

The United States, of course, did not constitute the only threat to Caribbean nationalism. Mexico had been invaded in the nineteenth century by the armed forces of France, Great Britain, and Spain, as well as those of the United States. In the twentieth century, Germany was also suspect; the political leaders of the Dominican Republic preferred United States financial control to German in 1904–1905, for example. Germany, Great Britain, and Italy resorted to force to collect Venezuela's debts to their citizens in 1902–1903. Haiti had several times suffered gunboat coercion from France and Germany as well as the United States. An awareness of these other potential threats at times mitigated reactions to United States interventions, especially when these could be presented as counters to some putative European scheme. Caribbean leaders were keenly aware of their vulnerability, and the United States at least helped to reduce the frequency of incursions from across the Atlantic.[2]

In addition, the new forces actively appealed to many minds. The Europeans and North Americans visibly possessed power and knowledge of a special and advanced kind, and some Latin Americans were eager to share this knowledge, and perhaps to acquire power as a result. On purely intellectual grounds, a few bright young people burned to understand the science, technology, or popular ideology of the outsiders. A quickening economic activity revitalized some old towns and created new ones, liberated trapped minds and aspirations from stultifying village cultures, offered a first vision of material plenty and social progress. Even if only a few responded to these allures, the response could be significant in societies where so many were inert and the circle of involvement was so small.

At first, cultural and intellectual stimulation came mainly from Europe, London and Paris being the chief centers of dissemination. As time passed, North American cultural penetration also widened and deepened. Patterns of consumption, the automotive revolution, the distribution of news through North American press services, the sale of best sellers in English and in translation promoted the prestige and values of the United States. The age of the cinema brought glamorous visual images of an alternate culture. Thousands of Caribbean youths attended the educational institutions of the northern colossus, bringing back new attitudes to traditional elites. Regular denunciation of these developments by intellectuals and elders was in itself evidence of their ubiquity. Whether best defined as modernization or cultural subversion, at least some aspects of the foreign presence were seductive to many.[3]

While it is the negative side of foreign penetration which has received the chief emphasis in recent years, there was nevertheless a positive side as well. The foreigners brought better transportation, contacts with the great outside world, scientific medicine, better public health. They made available a wide array of conveniences and consumer goods for those who could afford them: gas and electric lighting, canned goods, low-priced books, machine-made clothing and shoes, automobiles for the wealthy, better machetes for the poor. At times they offered something more fundamental: the promise of public order. While political instability and disorder were endemic in the Caribbean, every society nurtures a thirst for order as certainly as it fosters forces to the contrary. Cubans, Haitians, Nicaraguans, viewing failed political systems in times of violence, could not but feel some relief when the United States reimposed order and halted mounting bloodshed. Had such interventions not gone too far and lasted too long, as they so often did, they would not have been wholly unwelcome, as the initial ambivalence of local elites regarding them showed. While virtually no one likes alien rule, there was for one reason or another a good deal of acquiescence to the alien presence.

This ambivalence was clearly visible in the case of Haiti, ruled for nineteen years by a United States military occupation. Dantes Bellegarde, a distinguished Haitian writer, educator, and diplomat, expressed it privately as the occupation drew toward its close. "It is painful to make such an admission," he wrote in the early 1930s, "but we must acknowledge that we have lived in horrible disorder. . . . Our financial incompetence due to our extravagant spending, and our powerlessness at maintaining the peace due to our lack of discipline, are the explanations, if not the justification of the American occupation." In 1939, former president Stenio Vincent recalled the nation's mood when the occupation had begun:

> There was, in general, among the Haitians, a sort of discreet understanding to excuse the intervention, hoping that it would liquidate the chaotic situation that existed in the country, substituting an organized life of peace and work. The most intransigent patriots . . . came to consider it as a necessary evil. . . .[4]

In our own time we have forgotten much of this. A sharpened third-world nationalism and the mass mobilization of peoples for political purposes have become the norm, while radio and television enable governments to bring their propaganda to everyone. Rising educational levels and improved transportation have reduced isolation, as has the movement to cities. Marxist modes of analysis, and their popularization throughout the third world, have created a mass awareness of economic exploitation and first-world imperialism. Had all of these developments been present at the turn of the century, the tide of hegemony would have been altered or stemmed, for an effective foreign hegemony is possible only if its subjects are somewhat ambivalent about it. Before the First World War, there was no uniform principle of opposition to such hegemony except in response to obvious infringements of nationalism. Mass mobilization of the public was much more difficult, and local opinion leaders were deeply factionalized and individually torn on the subject of foreign influence. Let us look at United States hegemony in the Caribbean in the light of these complexities rather than current prevailing assumptions.

It bears repeating that the United States had two separate and opposed images in Latin America, appearing as both problem and solution. Local elites regarded themselves as culturally, and perhaps morally, superior to most of the North American engineers, businessmen, and technicians who resided among them, who often seemed socially crude and indifferent to high culture. United States society was frequently denounced as materialistic and greedy, but with equal frequency it was seen to exemplify modern enlightenment. While Yankee imperialism was widely denounced and feared, the North American model of political democracy continued to exert an enormous attraction. Many Latin American intellectuals and leaders deeply admired British and North American achievements, and attempted to emulate the methods while enlisting the aid of those societies. The elites of the Caribbean region aspired to peace and plenty; they expected these to follow hard on the heels of economic development, initiated through the building of railroads and the advent of foreign capital. The necessary capital, technology, and organizational skills could come only from abroad, principally from Britain and the United States, the nations which led in the march of progress.[5]

In 1910 the United States minister to Colombia reported to the State Department a conversation he had had with that nation's foreign minister. Despite Colombia's resentment at the loss of Panamá, the statesman had explained, his government was anxious to cultivate good relations with Washington because Colombia's economic development required close ties with American enterprise. "Doctor Olaya said that it would be his endeavor to attract foreign capital by demonstrating the security of investments in Colombia, as he felt satisfied that in no other manner could the agricultural and mineral resources of the country be developed."[6]

Most Caribbean policy makers of the late nineteenth and early twentieth centuries saw no alternative to foreign-led economic development, nor is any very apparent today. Meanwhile, local elites enjoyed personal benefits from foreign enterprises even as they hoped for national benefits in the future. Monopolizing government offices, they gained from the rapid growth in the size and revenues of government that accompanied the rise of export agriculture with its possibilities for export taxes and foreign loans. In most Caribbean countries, government was by far the biggest locally owned enterprise, and in many, the elite chiefly made their careers there. It was also true, however, that the new economic currents could create new classes which changed the makeup of the national elite.

Costa Rica and the Dominican Republic provide examples of export-based elite creation. By the later nineteenth century the most influential members of the Costa Rican elite were the *cafetaleros,* or coffee growers, of the central plateau. It was they who called for a railroad to the coast to provide an outlet to the Atlantic for their product. At first the coffee came from many small growers throughout the *mesa central,* but as choice coffee land increased in value the pattern of landholding changed. Wealthier growers bought up the best land, and introduced the use of expensive machinery for processing the beans. As the smaller and poorer growers fell behind, a dominant class emerged which soon controlled the government, led in social prestige, and amassed at least modest wealth. Not until after 1900 did coffee fall to less than half of the country's exports in value, and even thereafter the *cafetaleros* retained local dominance, for the fast-growing banana companies of the coast were foreign owned. It was *cafetalero*-dominated governments which encouraged the foreign enterprises, and they meant to share in any resulting prosperity.[7]

In the Dominican Republic, the most productive and important region had once been the Cibao, a north-central district inland from the coast. Its chief export crop was tobacco, shipped through north coast ports such as Puerto Plata. Toward the end of the 1870s, however, export sugar growing appeared in the country's southern and eastern provinces. The Ten Years' War in Cuba had forced some Cuban planters to flee to a safer environment, and Dominican land was cheap. In the 1880s a few Puerto Rican and North American enterprises moved in to swell the Dominican sugar culture, which thereafter grew rapidly in size and productivity. After the turn of the century a sugar-based elite in the south gradually began to challenge the old Cibao leadership in public affairs. More significantly, a country which had long been too lightly populated and decentralized to develop a crystallized national elite had begun to acquire one as a result of export agriculture, improved transport, and enlarged government. Dominican politics thus directly reflected the effects of foreign enterprise.[8]

This linkage is embodied in dependency theory as the "co-optation of the elites." The usual formulation is that the ruling class in each undeveloped country sold out its people to foreign domination because the elite profited as a group from this betrayal. The elites involved were supposedly conscious of acting against the interests of their peoples, believing that foreign enterprise would harm their country, but encouraging it nevertheless for reasons of greed. The evidence is to the contrary: Caribbean elites, like virtually anyone at the time with an educated opinion, firmly believed that they were following the path of progress to the ultimate benefit of all. Meanwhile they also intended to serve their own interests, and did so.

Nationalism was nevertheless a powerful force in the Caribbean, as elsewhere. Clear-cut violations of national sovereignty, as opposed to economic penetration and foreign influence, never failed to awaken a nationalist response. Yet even some power-building activities of the United States government in the Caribbean could appear in an ambiguous or even pro-nationalist guise, confusing or delaying the local nationalist defense. The case of Cuba is the most obvious: United States intervention there came initially in the form of helping the Cubans to throw off Spanish control. The Teller Resolution, passed when Congress declared war, promised to leave Cuba wholly independent and self-governing when the fighting was over and order restored. The promise was then abridged by the Platt Amendment, which demanded that Cuba accept a United States protectorate as the price of ridding itself of Yankee occupation troops. Many Cubans deplored this development, but they could comfort themselves with the achievement of formal independence and hope for the best in the future. Some of Cuba's planter elite actually preferred the promise of order and stability implicit in the new arrangement. Even Máximo Gómez and Tomás Estrada Palma, two of the most prestigious leaders of the late revolution, wished for a limited period of North American tutelage while the new Cuban republic was finding its feet. As a result, Cubans disagreed for years as to whether United States actions had done more to enlarge their freedom or to curtail it.

Panamá presents another case where Washington acted both to exploit local nationalism and then to restrict it. Without North American support and naval protection, the independence revolution of 1903 would quickly have been reversed by Colombian troops, so that independent Panamá was in great part a product of United States action. Yet Panamá too found itself a protectorate, living within bounds set in Washington and lacking even the smallest functions within that part of its territory which comprised the Canal Zone. As it did in Cuba, the United States used its authority in Panamá to supervise elections, put down disorder, and generally truncate the power of the state which it had helped to create.

A more complex policy marks the United States record in Nicaragua before and after the turn of the century. One of the chief priorities of the new regime of President José Santos Zelaya in 1893 was to end British dominance in his country's Mosquito Coast. This eastern third of the nation, facing on the Caribbean, was thinly populated by native Indians and Negroes from the British West Indies. Few Spanish-speaking Nicaraguans lived there, and the region had long enjoyed the substance of autonomy, both under Spanish rule and after independence. By the mid-eighteenth century the Miskito (or Mosquito) Indians had established a kind of satellite kingdom on the Caribbean coast, sponsored by the British and permanently allied with them. Even after the fall of the Spanish empire, the peoples of the coast continued to look to British power to offset any closer authority. For their own purposes the British obliged, proclaiming a "Mosquito Protectorate" from 1844 to 1860, and thereafter guaranteeing the self-government of the Mosquito Reservation in an 1860 treaty with Nicaragua. Within this reserved area, Nicaragua possessed nominal sovereignty but was forced to give up virtually any power to rule.[9]

The United States government liked this state of affairs little better than the Nicaraguans did, being convinced that British efforts to separate the Mosquito Coast (Mosquitia) from Nicaragua proper sprang from an intention to control the outlet of a prospective isthmian canal route. From the 1840s on, Washington's isthmian diplomacy aimed at minimizing British influence in the area, a purpose which furnished a common cause with Nicaragua. When Zelaya began active attempts to regain control of the coast, he counted heavily on the United States backing his challenge to British power. For a time, the rising United States activism in the Caribbean and its anti-British manifestations seemed to play directly into Zelaya's hands.[10]

In 1894 Zelaya sent Nicaraguan troops into the Mosquito Reservation under the pretext of border defense during a war then in progress with Honduras. When the Miskito chief protested the advent of military control, he was ousted, and Nicaraguan officials came out from Managua to take over governmental functions. Facing revolt by both Indians and immigrant blacks, Zelaya sent more troops, which forcibly restored Nicaraguan authority and abruptly deported those whom the Nicaraguans regarded as troublemakers. These were chiefly British Jamaicans, which further irritated a British Foreign Office already angered by Managua's unilateral action in changing a regional status formally defined by an Anglo-Nicaraguan treaty.[11]

The British attempted at first to replace Miskito autonomy with a joint

Anglo-Nicaraguan provisional government for the region, but ultimately accepted full Nicaraguan control. The ensuing expulsion of British subjects, however, offered London an occasion to save face, which it did by sending a naval squadron to seize Nicaragua's west coast port of Corinto until Managua paid a £75,000 indemnity. Unpleasant as this last action was for the Nicaraguans, Great Britain had in fact allowed a small Central American state to eject it from a long-standing de facto protectorate. Everyone had recognized from the start that the British response was crucial, and that Nicaragua could do little about the status of the coast if London chose to take a hard line.[12]

The most obvious reason for British restraint was the vigorous diplomatic support which the United States gave to Nicaragua throughout the Mosquito crisis. Washington vetoed a joint Anglo-Nicaraguan imperium on the coast and made clear its objection to any renewed British protectorate there: Managua must now rule alone. The British ultimately gave in to avoid a confrontation with the United States over a relatively minor interest. The leading Nicaraguan historical accounts of the incident acknowledge the pivotal role of the United States in the extension of Nicaragua's authority over her eastern territory, while President Zelaya himself hailed the significance of Washington's actions at the time.[13]

Washington's support for Nicaraguan authority in Mosquitia ran counter to the interests of its citizens at Bluefields and the recommendations of the United States consul there. The Anglo-American Bluefields business community feared and opposed effective Nicaraguan rule, with its accompanying tariffs, taxes, and monopolies. Up to 1894 they had been virtually untaxed and unregulated, while feeling secure under British protection. Their appeals to maintain the status quo fell on deaf ears in the State Department, however, where the isthmian canal question far outweighed the petty concerns of a few distant planters and merchants. United States policy would never encourage Mosquito separatism from Nicaragua.[14]

The American colony in Bluefields nevertheless continued to foster Mosquito separatism in the years after 1894. Angry at the new taxes and more especially at the plethora of government-sponsored monopolies imposed on them from Managua, local Yankee businessmen encouraged and helped to finance Bluefields-based rebellions in 1899 and 1909. When Washington decided to rid itself of the troublesome Zelaya it gave its support to the 1909 movement, nursing it through to ultimate success in the following year. It did so, however, on terms which differed from the goals in Bluefields, where resident Americans intended the revolt to secure the independence of the east coast from the rest of Nicaragua. The State Department had adopted the revolution but vetoed the separatism, ensuring Managua's continued authority in Mosquitia. At the same time, it moved to impose Washington's authority on Managua in the form of a budding protectorate. Once again, United States policy began by supporting a nationalism which it would eventually constrict.[15]

Once United States infringement of Nicaraguan sovereignty had become blatant, a strong nationalist response emerged. One Nicaraguan writer of the 1920s, Máximo Soto Hall, called the record of United States intervention in his country "a crime without a name," and compared it to the worst excesses of the Spanish conquistadores. The principal difference, he suggested, lay in the hypocrisy of the North Americans, who pretended to believe in freedom and equality. In Soto Hall's analysis, President Zelaya drew Washington's wrath because he had defended his country's independence against the grasping Yankees; his only real crime was a refusal to sell out to the foreigners as Adolfo Díaz did a few years later. By trying to preserve proper control of a prospective Nicaraguan canal zone, and to reduce foreign businessmen to obedience to the law, Zelaya had sealed his own doom. Prior to the American interventions, another 1920s writer asserted, Nicaragua had been a "prosperous and highly progressive country . . . before the vulture buried its beak in her throat, to suck the lifeblood out of her body." Bitterly defiant, such anti-Yankee rhetoric ran thick in the land for many years.[16]

In the same vein, the elites of other countries mounted their own anti-Yankee attacks, beginning in the teens of this century and peaking in the years between the two world wars. After several years of a hard-handed United States occupation, Haitian nationalism surged at the end of the First World War, and Haiti's elite campaigned to turn North American public opinion against its government's policies in their country. In 1921 a widely circulated manifesto from the *Union Patriotique d'Haïti* detailed their grievances. The United States, it said, had forced a protectorate treaty on the unwilling Haitians, then systematically violated its terms; furthermore, after solemnly promising to help in Haiti's economic development, Washington did nothing whatever to make the promise good. Instead of bringing benefit, the arbitrary nature of the occupation authority opened the way for almost routine brutalities against the Haitian population. "Numberless abominable crimes" had been committed, in a "terrible regime of military autocracy." "The Haitian people," the authors charged, had "passed through such sacrifices, tortures, destructions, humiliations, and misery as have never before been known in the course of its unhappy history."[17]

The United States occupation of the Dominican Republic in 1916 provoked a similar response. Such an occupation, Dominican writers complained, was a grave violation of international law, for it followed neither a mutually approved treaty nor a declaration of war: it was therefore an act of naked imperialism. Like the Haitians, they charged the occupation with "the most horrible tortures to a defenseless people" and declared that "the alcoholic caprices of the soldiers and officers of the Army of Occupation filled our cities with infamy and anguish." According to these Dominicans, Woodrow Wilson was a hypocrite who talked at home of peace and international justice while holding a million and a half of their fellow countrymen in virtual slavery.[18]

A major theme of all of these protests was that the imperialists sought illicit economic benefits. Nicaraguans charged that Washington served the interests of Wall Street bankers, who seized control of their country's treasury and railroad system, and of privileged Yankee businessmen who disliked being subjected to legitimate Nicaraguan laws. These interests joined in profiteering shamelessly at Nicaragua's expense, the accusation ran. Haitian protesters and subsequent historians stressed the influence of the National City Bank of New York on the Wilson administration on behalf of its subsidiary, the National Bank of Haiti. The National City Bank was said to be the only beneficiary of the Haitian occupation, which was alleged to be no coincidence: Wilson had sold out to Wall Street, like Taft before him. Some Dominican writers asserted that the occupation of their country in 1916 really resulted from the financial disarray into which its government was once again falling, as it had in 1904–1905. Others charged that the United States military government had used its power to favor foreign sugar companies, and had meddled with the Dominican land laws specifically to enable them to expand their holding at the expense of the natives. In each of these countries, anti-American writers voiced intense suspicions of the personal honesty of those involved in their occupations, and resentment at foreigners taking over positions of power and profit from local elites.[19]

Yet even the expressions of a burgeoning Caribbean nationalism were by no means as simple and unambiguous as such summaries may suggest. A look at some Cuban historians of the first half of the twentieth century is particularly revealing. Certainly these Cuban writers protested those United States policies which limited Cuba's political or economic independence, and charged Washington's agents and policy makers with serious sins of omission and commission. Ramiro Guerra y Sánchez depicted an acquisitive Yankee people who seized control of Caribbean agriculture, forcing millions whom they never saw to toil in the sun for their collective enrichment. The North Americans thus secured tropical products at the lowest possible price and sold them at a large profit, leaving Cubans and others in the region in poverty and civil discord. Emilio Roig de Leuchsenring condemned Washington's misuse of the Platt Amendment, which had been twisted into new meanings after 1906: the North Americans sought to deny Cubans the right of revolution. It was not revolutions which disgraced a people, he insisted, but the dictatorships at which they were aimed—and which Washington all too often supported. While Cuba's stability may temporarily have been shored up by "Plattism," her *nationality* was being ruined, Roig concluded. Herminio Portell-Vilá accused the United States of perpetuating a colonial sugar economy in Cuba which the revolution of 1895–98 had been in the process of transforming into something far better for Cubans. Portell-Vilá's angry account of arbitrary United States political interference and exploitative economic policies in Cuba was a sustained attack upon the Yankee record. Undoubtedly, the voice of outraged nationalism is sufficiently evident in these works.[20]

Yet these same works, and those of other contemporary Cubans, make some very different points as well. Herminio Portell-Vilá rejected the proposition that Cuba's prosperity was a direct function of her close ties to the United States, but in the same breath accepted the relative prosperity of Cuba as compared with her neighbors, and even with the poorer and more backward regions of the United States. He furthermore gave partial credit for this to the United States connection, though claiming at least an equal share for the Cubans themselves. Raúl de Cárdenas y Echarte went further, asserting that United States imperialism was really political, not economic, in purpose, and aimed primarily at guarding North American security. As it affected Cuba, Cárdenas declared, United States policy had been decidedly beneficial, even praiseworthy, in bringing both order and prosperity to the Cuban nation. Cárdenas wrote this at the height of the sugar boom which peaked after the end of the First World War, and may have reached other conclusions had he written a decade later. Yet Cuba did enjoy at least a relative prosperity and rapid economic growth for much of the early twentieth century, however unequally the benefits were distributed, and while it lasted this state of affairs undoubtedly helped reconcile Cubans to the North American presence.[21]

More significantly, there runs through these works an undertone of respect for the United States' ideal of political democracy. Roig de Leuchsenring, for decades a leading Cuban critic of Washington's policies, believed all of his life that the American people were misled by their presidents and unaware of the misuse of American power in Cuba. They had generously supported Cuba's aspirations for freedom and had gone to war in 1898 to bring liberty to Cuba, but a cynical executive subverted this crusade to more sordid ends. Similarly, Cárdenas y Echarte was concerned that the United States military regimes established in Haiti and the Dominican Republic in 1915–16 violated the most deeply held principles of the people who had imposed them. He accounted for this by suggesting that the American people were so fixed on the great events in Europe that they failed to note what their government was really doing in the Caribbean; once more, a willful president was seen to be acting against the democratic sentiments of his own people. When Manuel Márquez Sterling condemned Theodore Roosevelt's Cuban intervention of 1906, on the other hand, he saw it as an honest error in White House thinking: Roosevelt had acted to prevent a falling away from democracy, not realizing that the Cubans themselves could have rectified the problem with far less harm to their future. Márquez Sterling found Roosevelt guilty only of an inadequate mastery of mass psychology, his intentions being portrayed as basically good. Writing in 1914, Francisco Caraballo y Sotolongo optimistically believed that antiimperialism had triumphed in the United States, and that the new administration of

Woodrow Wilson would mark the rejection of forcible intervention and dollar diplomacy. This reversal would return the Monroe Doctrine to its proper form, a system of protecting the American republics against European threats which served equally the purposes of the United States and its sisters to the south. Many years later, even the acidulous Portell-Vilá expressed his esteem for the North American people and separated them from the sins of their government's policies abroad. Despite all that had occurred between them, he wrote, the best interests of both the Cuban and North American peoples lay in coming to a fuller understanding and a mutual respect.[22]

There is in the collective works of these writers a curious ambivalence. All of them knew the United States at first hand, and found something to admire in its society even as they criticized it. While strongly condemning United States interventionism and imperialism, they regularly acknowledged that some North Americans had done good in Cuba, that some of the work of the occupations was well meant, that to some extent foreign economic activity had benefited both sides. They were perennially hopeful that the democratic ideals which they had seen practiced in the Colossus of the North would come to their rescue, that these people whom they knew to value their own freedom would come to see the iniquity of denying it to others. Even at their most aroused, these writers rarely seemed able to achieve a genuine across-the-board hatred of their giant neighbor. By current standards, theirs was a moderate and qualified nationalism, however passionate some of its manifestations. One is touched by their reiterated desire for *proper* close relations with the United States, and saddened by the persistent inability of the latter nation to apply its own domestic ideals to its foreign behavior.

A true picture of the interaction of United States hegemony and Caribbean nationalism is difficult to construct, for the relationship was shifting and complex. There is ample evidence to support any one of several stereotypes, but any interpretation which harmonizes with all of the evidence must be very different from these. The actions of the United States were seen by Caribbean leaders and intellectuals as both positive and negative, welcome and unwelcome. Whether North American economic and political penetration would do more in the long run to forward or retard national development in the region was frequently unclear at the time. There were always those who were consistently anti–United States, those who looked more favorably on that nation, and those who were ambivalent or vacillating. What was never in evidence was a general and consistent hostility to the United States presence in all of its forms.

Conclusion

By 1917 the United States had created the policies, methods, and instruments necessary to maintain its hegemony in the Caribbean region. It had done so for a number of reasons: to ensure its security against European penetration or attack; to achieve economic expansion beyond its borders; and to promote its ideological goals, indulge its prejudices, and improve its self-image. North Americans justified their dominance in much the same terms used by contemporary imperial powers in Europe. Believing themselves and their institutions to be superior to the people and societies of the Caribbean, they claimed to be bringing progress to the latter. Their business enterprises would bring material progress, which in turn would promote the general improvement of local society. Their official policies would promote stability by limiting disorder, fiscal chaos, and revolution. The twin blessings of stability and economic development would serve the interests of the United States and the Caribbean countries equally, and all would advance together, although at different levels of maturity and civilization. So ran the mainstream thinking of the period.

The United States was sufficiently powerful and free from great-power competition to be able to impose its dominance upon the Caribbean region. It could not, however, escape the dilemmas and contradictions inherent in its policies there. How could Washington adjudicate local struggles and stop revolutions without itself being drawn into the domestic strife of the countries concerned? How could it impose its will without the routine use of force? How could it prevent revolutions without guaranteeing the tenure of often tyrannical or corrupt incumbent regimes? How could it promote local democracy while usurping for itself the power of real political decision?

Such questions emerged only with experience, undermining the policy makers' initial confidence in brisk, straightforward solutions. They learned in time that the possession of ultimate power raised as many problems as it solved, and that other peoples' politics are usually as complicated as one's own. Even the lessons of experience failed to shake the conviction of Yankee superiority, however, or to cast doubt on the assumed necessity of United States hegemony in the Caribbean. While the task became visibly more difficult, the leadership's commitment to accomplish it was unwavering. United States hegemony in the Caribbean was the product of a remarkably consistent effort which ran uninterrupted from the administration of William McKinley through that of Woodrow Wilson.

This consistency in the face of a growing knowledge of the difficulties involved stemmed from several convictions. Americans continued to fear the threat of Europe's great powers, particularly Germany, and were determined to prevent any successful foreign incursions into the Caribbean. They were inordinately proud of their Panama Canal project, which they defined as vital to the national security, and they meant to ensure its safety. They had faith in their dynamic economy and pioneering technology, and believed deeply in the benefits of private enterprise. Aside from important matters of self-interest, they thought it simply wrong that any people should obstruct the economic development offered by the foreign enterprisers of the North Atlantic industrial states.

To these convictions must be added some equally strong prejudices. Ethnocentricity and arrogance characterized the North American world view, as did racism and a belief in the inequality of peoples. Most Americans assumed that tropical societies of mixed race had inferior capacity, and must accept the tutelage of a superior people in order to achieve progress. They also believed in their own uniqueness, and their divine mission to reshape the world in their own image. Too often they were unaware of the Latin American point of view; even when they noticed it, it was usually with superiority or contempt. Rarely did Washington really listen to the voices of those subjected to its will, and the government's agents on the spot were rarely much better in this regard.

A further obstacle to understanding was the inability or refusal of North Americans to recognize the true nature of their actions. Imperialism was by definition something practiced by Europeans; the Great Republic was held to be superior to it. Even when European and United States activities seemed clearly comparable, Americans saw their actions as qualitatively different, validated by the universal benefits which they expected them to bring. Their collective self-image simply did not permit them to question their basic assumptions. They really *did* believe their country had a unique mission, and their faith in their own good intentions overrode any lack of obvious success.

Since the United States annexed only Puerto Rico and the Danish Virgin Islands, it was possible to pretend that its other dealings in the Caribbean were

variants of ordinary relations between sovereign states. Even in the protectorates, where this was clearly untrue, the facade of local sovereignty enabled
Washington to disclaim responsibility for those problems which it found intractable or did not wish to address, such as corruption, poverty, ignorance, and
disease. Military occupation regimes had to finance themselves wholly from
local revenues; no United States government funds went to Caribbean client
states, except to pay its garrisons there. Washington could thus assume broad
controls over such states without holding itself responsible for the welfare of
their citizens.

In this refusal to use its own funds in its dependencies, the United States
merely mirrored Europe's colonial practices. There were broader similarities
as well. There was nothing unique in North American attempts to achieve
hegemony over foreign areas thought valuable or strategic. Great powers had
routinely sought "spheres of influence" or subservient client states, as well as
more formal colonies. The United States imperium in the Caribbean was certainly no harsher than that of the British in South Asia, the Russians in Central
Asia, or the French in North Africa. On the whole, it left more political authority to local societies and used less military force than comparable European
hegemonies. What was noteworthy was the reluctance to grant that United
States actions in the Caribbean *were* similar to the power-building activities of
the Europeans elsewhere.

In many respects, the United States succeeded in what it attempted in the
Caribbean. Yankee enterprise and money poured into the region and eventually
passed up its European rivals. Local economic activity boomed and export
levels soared. United States power was supreme in the area. Washington's
efforts *did* reduce the Caribbean's level of political violence and international
tension. Germany never got a foothold there, and neither it nor any other
power challenged the North American claim to Caribbean supremacy.

These are not insignificant achievements, but they must be balanced against
the shortcomings of the United States record. Washington's policies failed
to increase real democracy in the Caribbean, and in many cases were anti-
thetic to its professed democratic principles. None of the Caribbean client
states achieved general prosperity or self-propelled economic development; all
remained poor and dependent. National constabularies created under Washington's orders by United States Marines in several cases became the building
blocks for military dictatorships in the next generation. The undoubted success
in preventing European intervention in the region came rather easily because
no European power seriously challenged the United States there; in fact it is
by no means certain that there *was* a real European threat during much of the
period in question. Certainly on many occasions American leaders and public
alike greatly exaggerated the likelihood of a European incursion.

Much of this is not very different from our own day. Now, as then, many

Americans are deeply concerned about the prospect of rival-power penetration of the Caribbean region, this time by the Soviet Union. Washington still sees the area as a key security zone, and still exerts vigorous efforts to maintain its dominance there. American dollars and enterprise, though under fire here and there, are still vital to the area, which still finds its largest market in the United States. North Americans remain largely deaf to the views and plaints of Caribbean societies, preferring still to project their own perceptions, goals, and fears upon the lands to the south. Nor is it any easier today to find solutions to the sticky problems of how much force to use in imposing our will; how to achieve our regional interests without being dragged into local struggles; how to manipulate other governments without making a mockery of the ideals of self-government and freedom.

These are not simple questions, whether considered then or now. Indisputably, the United States still has a national interest in the fate of the Caribbean and legitimate concerns about developments there. Encouragingly, many Americans now earnestly desire to understand the current crisis in the Caribbean. Washington's policies in the region today face far more public skepticism and debate than was customary in the early twentieth century. It would be a sorry thing, therefore, if the nation continued to chart its course in Caribbean affairs virtually without reference to almost a century of relevant experience. Surely our policy makers can do better than unknowingly repeat the errors of the past, while making the same inflated claims for the benefits of a pax Americana and private enterprise. They must recognize that Central America and the West Indies contain vital and evolving societies with their own goals, perceptions, and problems; that it is misleading and inadequate to see in them a mere arena for East-West conflict. They must question the old, easy assumptions, and reach beyond familiar rhetoric in their formulations. More wisdom is sorely needed, and one place to begin the search for it is in the record of the past.

Notes

———◄●►———

Bibliography

———◄●►———

Index

Notes

CHAPTER 1. *The Caribbean in the 1890s*

1 For general Caribbean background see the following: John Parry and Philip M. Sherlock, *A Short History of the West Indies* (London, 1956); Eric Williams, *From Columbus to Castro: The History of the Caribbean, 1492–1969* (New York, 1970); Robert C. West and John P. Augelli, *Middle America: Its Lands and Peoples* (Englewood Cliffs, N.J., 1966); W. M. Davis, *The Lesser Antilles* (New York, 1926); Franklin W. Knight, *The Caribbean: The Genesis of a Fragmented Nationalism* (New York, 1978); Ralph Lee Woodward, *Central America: A Nation Divided* (New York, 1976).

2 See Ramiro Guerra y Sánchez, *Sugar and Society in the Caribbean* (New Haven, Conn., 1964), 1–67; Lowell J. Ragatz, *The Fall of the Planter Class in the British Caribbean, 1753–1833* (New York, 1928); Leland Jenks, *Our Cuban Colony: A Study in Sugar* (New York, 1928); David McCullough, *The Path between the Seas: The Creation of the Panama Canal, 1870–1914* (New York, 1977), 135–240; Woodward, *Central America: A Nation Divided*, chapters 6 and 7; Hugh Thomas, *Cuba, or the Pursuit of Freedom* (London, 1971), 289–425.

3 James W. G. Walker, *Ocean to Ocean: An Account Personal and Historical of Nicaragua and Its People* (Chicago, 1902), 11–12, 16.

4 William Eleroy Curtis, *The Capitals of Spanish America* (New York, 1888), 122, 123–25, 131.

5 Ibid., 60–63, 90, 95–100.

6 See Edward Dennis Hernández, "Modernization and Dependency in Costa Rica during the Decade of the 1880's" (Ph.D. dissertation, University of California at Los Angeles, 1975), 130–35, for comparative data.

7 For major Cuban developments in this period, see Ramiro Guerra y Sánchez, José M. Perez Cabrera, Juan J. Remos, and Emeterio S. Santovenia, ed., *Historia de la nación cubana*, vol. 7 (of 10 vols.), book 4 (Havana, 1952).

8 See James G. Leyburn, *The Haitian People* (New Haven, Conn., 1941), 32–99,

265–84; Samuel Guy Inman, *Through Santo Domingo and Haiti, a Cruise with the Marines* (New York, 1919), 58–59.

9   See Harry Hoetink, "The Dominican Republic in the Nineteenth Century: Some Notes on Stratification, Immigration, and Race," in *Race and Class in Latin America* edited by Magnus Morner (New York, 1970), 96–121; H. Paul Muto, "The Illusory Promise: The Dominican Republic and the Process of Economic Development, 1900–1930" (Ph.D. dissertation, University of Washington, 1976), 29–37.

10 See Woodward, *Central America: A Nation Divided*, 149–63, 177–83.

11 Curtis, *Capitals of Spanish America*, 60–199; Thomas, *Cuba*, 286–87, 433; Gordon K. Lewis, *Puerto Rico: Freedom and Power in the Caribbean* (New York, 1963), 55.

12 See E. Bradford Burns, *The Poverty of Progress* (Berkeley, Calif., 1980), 18–34; Leopoldo Zea, *The Latin-American Mind* (Norman, Okla., 1963), 33, 77; Woodward, *Central America: A Nation Divided*, 151–52; Hernández, "Modernization and Dependency in Costa Rica," 46–54.

13 Mira Wilkins, *The Emergence of Multinational Enterprise: American Business Abroad from the Colonial Era to 1914* (Cambridge, Mass., 1970), 110, 149–55; Robert W. Dunn, *American Foreign Investments* (New York, 1926), 2–3; Thomas, *Cuba*, 289.

14 Edwin F. Atkins, *Sixty Years in Cuba* (Cambridge, Mass., 1926), 1–30, 54.

15 Guerra y Sánchez et al., *Historia de la nación cubana*, 7:151–63; Atkins, *Sixty Years in Cuba*, 34–39.

16 Atkins, *Sixty Years in Cuba*, 37–38, 67–75, 83.

17 Ibid., 83–88, 94; Jenks, *Our Cuban Colony*, 31.

18 Atkins, *Sixty Years in Cuba*, 120–21, 129–33, 138–39; Thomas, *Cuba*, 289–90; Jenks, *Our Cuban Colony*, 29–30, 33. In time, Atkins also became chairman of the board of the American Sugar Refining Company; see *Who Was Who in America* (Chicago, 1943), 1:34.

19 Jules R. Benjamin, *The United States and Cuba: Hegemony and Dependent Development, 1880–1934* (Pittsburgh, Pa., 1977), 4–5; Atkins, *Sixty Years in Cuba*, 108–9, 143–44; Guerra y Sánchez et al., *Historia de la nación cubana*, 7:164–78.

20 Stacy May and Galo Plaza, *The United Fruit Company in Latin America* (n.p., 1958), 3–7.

21 Thomas L. Karnes, *Tropical Enterprise, the Standard Fruit and Steamship Company in Latin America* (Baton Rouge, La., 1978), 4; Watt Stewart, *Keith and Costa Rica* (Albuquerque, N.M., 1964), 9–12.

22 Stewart, *Keith and Costa Rica*, 18–31.

23 Ibid., 33–40.

24 Ibid., 36–47, 54–59, 81–89.

25 Ibid., 48–89, 111–12, 123–34.

26 Ibid., 90–91, 108–11, 135–36, 143–53.

27 Ibid., 154–59, 171–72, 174–78; May and Plaza, *United Fruit Company*, 5–7.

28 Sumner Welles, *Naboth's Vineyard: The Dominican Republic, 1844–1924*, 2 vols. (New York, 1928), 1:495; 2:502–8, 526–31.

CHAPTER 2. *The Background of United States Policy*

1   See David McCullough, *The Path between the Seas: The Creation of the Panama Canal, 1870–1914* (New York, 1977), 24–38; Dwight C. Miner, *The Fight for the Panama Route* (New York, 1940), 18.

2   McCullough, *Path between the Seas*, 135–240; James D. Richardson, *A Compilation of the Messages and Papers of the Presidents, 1789–1897* (Washington, D.C., 1899), 7:585–86.

3   See Dexter Perkins, *A History of the Monroe Doctrine* (Boston, 1941), 113–38, 161–65.

4   McCullough, *Path between the Seas*, 171–240. For a rather subjective account of the French canal project, see the relevant portions of the work of Philippe Bunau-Varilla, *Panama: The Creation, Destruction and Resurrection* (London, 1913).

5   Miner, *Fight for the Panama Route*, 25–28.

6   See Mary W. Williams, *Anglo-American Isthmian Diplomacy, 1815–1915* (Washington, D.C., 1916), 38–49, 52–53.

7   Lester D. Langley, *The Struggle for the American Mediterranean* (Athens, Ga., 1976), 96–100.

8   Walter LaFeber, *The Panama Canal: The Crisis in Historical Perspective* (New York, 1979), 24–26.

9   David H. Wicks, "Dress Rehearsal: United States Intervention on the Isthmus of Panama, 1885," *Pacific Historical Review* 49 (Nov. 1980): 583–85.

10 Ibid., 585–99.

11 Harold Sprout and Margaret Sprout, *The Rise of American Naval Power, 1776–1918* (Princeton, N.J., 1939), 188–89, 213–21; Robert Seager, "Ten Years before Mahan: The Unofficial Case for the New Navy, 1880–1890," *Mississippi Valley Historical Review* 40 (Dec. 1953): 491–512.

12 Walter R. Herrick, *The American Naval Revolution* (Baton Rouge, La., 1966), 39–42; Benjamin Franklin Cooling, *Benjamin Franklin Tracy, Father of the Modern American Fighting Navy* (Hamden, Conn., 1873), 18–45.

13 Herrick, *American Naval Revolution*, 43–51, 54–56. See also Benjamin F. Cooling, "The Making of a Navalist: Secretary of the Navy Benjamin Franklin Tracy and Sea Power," *U.S. Naval War College Review* 25 (Sept.–Oct., 1972): 83–90.

14 See Alfred Thayer Mahan, "The United States Looking Outward," *Atlantic Monthly* (Dec. 1890), reprinted in *The Interest of America in Sea Power* (Boston, 1897), 3–30; A. T. Volwiler, *Correspondence between Benjamin Harrison and James G. Blaine, 1882–1893* (Philadelphia, 1940), 202, 174; Herrick, *American Naval Revolution*, 93.

15 Herrick, *American Naval Revolution*, 67–68, 87–88; Cooling, *Benjamin Franklin Tracy*, 83.

16 Langley, *Struggle for the American Mediterranean*, 142–45; Sumner Welles, *Naboth's Vineyard: The Dominican Republic, 1844–1924*, 2 vols. (New York, 1928), 1:315–33, 342–58; Alexander de Conde, *A History of American Foreign Policy*, 2 vols. (New York, 1978), 1:244–47.

17 Welles, *Naboth's Vineyard*, 1:359–408.

18   Volwiler, *Correspondence between Harrison and Blaine*, 173; Herrick, *American Naval Revolution*, 91–93.

19   Herrick, *American Naval Revolution*, 93–101; Cooling, *Benjamin Franklin Tracy*, 111–14.

20   Herrick, *American Naval Revolution*, 101–102; Welles, *Naboth's Vineyard*, 1: 478–93.

21   David Healy, "A Hinterland in Search of a Metropolis: The Mosquito Coast, 1894–1910," *International History Review* 3 (Jan. 1981): 20–29; Pedro J. Cuadra Chamorro, *La Reincorporación de la Mosquitia* (León, Nicaragua, 1964), 7–95, 121–51.

22   U.S. Congress, *Congressional Record*, 53d Cong., 3d sess., 1895, 27:3077, 3082–84, 3089; see also Cushman K. Davis, *A Treatise on International Law Including American Diplomacy* (St. Paul, Minn. 1901), 273–86; Henry Cabot Lodge, "England, Venezuela, and the Monroe Doctrine," *North American Review* 160 (June 1895): 651–58.

23   Nelson M. Blake, "Background of Cleveland's Venezuelan Policy," *American Historical Review* 47 (1942): 259–77; Lodge, "England, Venezuela, and the Monroe Doctrine," 653.

24   U.S. Department of State, *Foreign Relations of the United States*, 1895, pt. 1 (Washington, D.C., 1896), 557–60, Richard Olney to Thomas F. Bayard, July 20, 1895.

25   For the Venezuelan crisis, see Ernest R. May, *Imperial Democracy: The Emergence of America as a World Power* (New York, 1961), 33–65; A. E. Campbell, *Great Britain and the United States, 1895–1903* (London, 1960), 11–47.

26   See David Healy, *U.S. Expansionism: The Imperialist Urge in the 1890s* (Madison, Wis., 1970); Walter LaFeber, *The New Empire: An Interpretation of American Expansion, 1860–1898* (Ithaca, N.Y., 1963); May, *Imperial Democracy*, for differing interpretations of 1890s expansionism.

27   Henry Cabot Lodge, "Our Blundering Foreign Policy," *Forum* 19 (March 1895): 8–17; Kirk H. Porter and Donald B. Johnson, eds., *National Party Platforms, 1840–1964* (Urbana, Ill., 1966), 109; Albert K. Steigerwalt, *The National Association of Manufacturers, 1895–1914* (Ann Arbor, Mich., 1964), 43–51, 56.

28   For varying views of the Cuban Revolution, see Edwin F. Atkins, *Sixty Years in Cuba* (Cambridge, Mass., 1926); Frederick Funston, *Memories of Two Wars* (New York, 1911); Horatio Rubens, *Liberty, the Story of Cuba* (New York, 1932); Walter Millis, *The Martial Spirit* (Cambridge, Mass., 1931); Herminio Portell-Vilá, *Historia de Cuba en sus relaciones con los Estados Unidos y Espana*, 4 vol., vol. 3 (Havana, 1938–41); Miguel Varona Guerrero, *La Guerra de Independencia de Cuba, 1895–1898*, (3 vols. (Havana, 1946); and Manuel Piedra Martel, *Memorias de un mambi* (Havana, 1968).

29   U.S., Department of State, *Foreign Relations of the United States* (cited hereafter as *FRUS*), 1896, xxx–xxxvi.

CHAPTER 3. *War in Cuba and Its Fruits*

1 James D. Richardson, *A Compilation of the Messages and Papers of the Presidents* (Washington, D.C., 1899), 10:126–36.

2 For standard studies of public opinion and the press regarding Cuba, see Joseph E. Wisan, *The Cuban Crisis As Reflected in the New York Press, 1895–1898* (New York, 1934); Marcus M. Wilkerson, *Public Opinion and the Spanish-American War*, 1932, reprint (New York, 1967); George W. Auxier, "Middle Western Newspapers and the Spanish-American War, 1895–1898," *Mississippi Valley Historical Review* 26 (March 1940): 523–34.

3 The author selected 48 resolutions as being sufficiently clear-cut for his purpose. However, this number could vary with the inclusion of more ambiguously phrased resolutions. The ones counted date from December 2, 1895, to July 8, 1898; see U.S., Congress, *Congressional Record*, 54th Cong., 1st and 2d sess., 1895–97, and 55th Cong., 1st and 2d sess., 1897–98.

4 See French Ensor Chadwick, *The Relations of the United States and Spain: Diplomacy* (New York, 1909), 411–29, 468–75; Ernest R. May, *Imperial Democracy: The Emergence of America as a Great Power* (New York, 1961), 83–88, 115–16.

5 Walter Millis, *The Martial Spirit* (Cambridge, Mass., 1931), 102–45; Hyman G. Rickover, *How the Battleship* Maine *Was Destroyed* (Washington, D.C., 1976). For reaction to the *Maine* disaster see May, *Imperial Democracy*, 139–47.

6 See Chadwick, *United States and Spain: Diplomacy*, 544–60; May, *Imperial Democracy*, 148–77; David F. Trask, *The War with Spain in 1898* (New York, 1981), 30–44.

7 Root to Cornelius N. Bliss, April 2, 1898, Elihu Root Papers, Library of Congress, Washington, D.C. Bliss showed McKinley the letter.

8 May, *Imperial Democracy*; Richard Hofstadter, "Manifest Destiny and the Philippines," in *America in Crisis*, edited by Daniel Aaron (New York, 1952); William Applemen Williams, *The Tragedy of American Diplomacy* (New York, 1972); William Appleman Williams, *The Roots of the Modern American Empire* (New York, 1969); Walter LaFeber, *The New Empire: An Interpretation of American Expansion, 1860–1898* (Ithaca, N.Y., 1963); H. Wayne Morgan, *America's Road to Empire: The War with Spain and Overseas Expansion* (New York, 1965). For useful historiographical essays on the subject, see Joseph A. Fry, "William McKinley and the Coming of the Spanish-American War: A Study of the Besmirching and Redemption of an Historical Image," *Diplomatic History* 3 (winter 1979): 77–87; Jerald A. Combs, *American Diplomatic History: Two Centuries of Changing Interpretations* (Berkeley, Calif., 1983), 77–83.

9 Julius Pratt, *Expansionists of 1898: The Acquisition of Hawaii and the Spanish Islands* (Baltimore, Md., 1936), 232–78; LaFeber, *The New Empire*, especially 379–93, 403–6.

10 Richardson, *Messages and Papers of the Presidents*, 10:139–50.

11 See David F. Healy, *The United States in Cuba, 1898–1902* (Madison, Wis., 1963), 14–15, 25–27. See also Paul S. Holbo, "The Convergence of Moods and the Cuban-Bond 'Conspiracy' of 1898," *Journal of American History* 55 (1968): 54–72, on the parallel issue of Spanish bonds issued to cover Cuban debts.

12 *Congressional Record*, 55th Cong., 2d sess. 31:3811, 3989.

13 Ibid., 3988–93, 3293, 3776.

14 Ibid., 4017–41, 4062. See also Healy, *United States in Cuba*, 27–29; Paul S. Holbo, "Presidential Leadership in Foreign Affairs: William McKinley and the Turpie-Foraker Amendment," *American Historical Review* 72 (1967): 1321–35.

15 Graham A. Cosmas, *An Army For Empire: The United States Army in the Spanish-American War* (Columbia, Mo., 1971), 80–82, 93–102; Trask, *War with Spain in 1898*, 72–90, 108–9, 145–77.

16 Trask, *War with Spain in 1898*, 162–77; French Ensor Chadwick, *The Relations of the United States and Spain: The Spanish-American War*, 2 vols. (New York, 1911), 2:3–14.

17 Trask, *War with Spain in 1898*, 178–216; Chadwick, *Spanish-American War*, 2:12–26.

18 Chadwick, *Spanish-American War*, 2:69, 75; John Black Atkins, *The War in Cuba* (London, 1899), 100, 108; *New York World*, July 14 and July 20, 1898; *New York Tribune*, August 7, 1898; *Literary Digest* (July 30, 1898), 17:123. For an account of the Santiago campaign see Trask, *War with Spain in 1898*, 217–56.

19 Chadwick, *Spanish-American War*, 2:44, 69, 95; Atkins, *War in Cuba*, 98, 289; Miguel Varona Guerrero, *La Guerra de Independencia de Cuba, 1895–1898*, 3 vols. (Havana, 1946), 3:1627ff.; Herminio Portell-Vilá, *Historia de Cuba en sus relaciones con los Estados Unidos y España*, 4 vols. (Havana, 1938–41), 3:473ff.

20 Emilio Roig de Leuchsenring, *Cuba no debe su independencia a los Estados Unidos* (Havana, 1950), sketches an analytic scheme more fully fleshed out in a number of other works, including *La Guerra Libertadora Cubana de los Treinta Años, 1868–1898: Razón de su victoria* (Havana, 1952); *1895 y 1898: Dos Guerras cubanas: Ensayas de revaloración* (Havana, 1945); *Cuba y los Estados Unidos, 1805–1898: Historia documentado de la actitud disimil de estada y del pueblo norteamericano en relación con la independencia de Cuba* (Havana, 1949); and *El Presidente McKinley y el Gobernador Wood máximas enemigos de Cuba libre* (Havana, 1960). For persuasive support of Roig's interpretation, see Luis A. Perez, *Cuba between Empires, 1898–1902* (Pittsburgh, Pa., 1983), 144–69.

21 Trask, *War with Spain in 1898*, 95–107, 369–422; Henry Cabot Lodge, *Selections from the Correspondence of Theodore Roosevelt and Henry Cabot Lodge*, 2 vols. (New York, 1925), 1:311.

22 Cosmas, *An Army for Empire*, 81, 129, 179–80, 198, 230–36; Russell A. Alger, *The Spanish-American War* (New York, 1901), 60, 298; E. E. Morison, ed., *The Letters of Theodore Roosevelt*, 8 vols. (Cambridge, Mass., 1951), 2:831; Lodge, *Selections from the Correspondence of Roosevelt and Lodge*, 1:311; John A. Garraty, *Henry Cabot Lodge: A Biography* (New York, 1953), 194–95; Reid to C. Inman Barnard, July 23, 1898, Whitelaw Reid Papers, Library of Congress, Washington, D.C. See also John Offner, "The United States and France: Ending the Spanish-American War," *Diplomatic History* 7 (winter 1983):4–5, 14; Trask, *War with Spain in 1898*, 336–68.

23 *FRUS*, 1898, 924–39; H. Wayne Morgan, ed., *Making Peace with Spain: The Diary of Whitelaw Reid, September–December 1898* (Austin, Tex., 1965), 72, 78–80, 87–88, 94–98, 105, 114–15, 139, 160.

24   *FRUS*, 1898, lxvi–lxvii, 687–88; *London Chronicle, London Standard*, and *London Daily Telegraph*, all for December 7, 1898; Garraty, *Henry Cabot Lodge*, 194; *New York Tribune*, December 19, 1898; Robert P. Porter, "The Future of Cuba," *North American Review* 168 (1899):418–23. For McKinley's lack of faith in Cuba's capacity for self-government, see Offner, "The United States and France: Ending the Spanish-American War," 14.

25   Louis A. Perez, Jr., "Cuba: Between Empires," *Pacific Historical Review*, Nov. 1979, 473–500; Pánfilo D. Camacho, *Estrada Palma, el gobernante honrado* (Havana, 1938), 176–77; Estrada Palma to Andrés Moreno de la Torre, February 1, 1898, quoted by Manuel Sanguily, "Sobre la genesis de la Enmienda Platt," *Cuba Contemporánea* 30 (Havana, 1922): 123; García to Estrada Palma, June 27, 1898, *Boletín del Archivo Nacional* 35 (1936): 108–112; Leonard Wood to Elihu Root, February 27 and March 13, 1901, Elihu Root Papers, Library of Congress, Washington, D.C.; *New York Sun*, February 27, 1901.

26   For the organization and functioning of the military government, see Healy, *United States in Cuba*, chapter 5.

27   Robert Bacon and James Brown Scott, eds. *Addresses on Government and Citizenship by Elihu Root* (Cambridge, Mass., 1916), 503–4.

28   *Congressional Record*, 55th Cong. 2d sess., 32:325–27; ibid., 1385; Claude G. Bowers, *Beveridge and the Progressive Era* (Cambridge, Mass., 1932), 69, 73–76.

29   "Report of Major General James H. Wilson, June 20, 1899," quoted by Hermann Hagedorn, *Leonard Wood*, 2 vols. (New York, 1931), 1:421; Wilson to Theodore Roosevelt, July 5, 1899, Theodore Roosevelt Papers, Library of Congress, Washington, D.C.

30   Wood to McKinley, April 27, 1899, William McKinley Papers, Library of Congress, Washington, D.C.; *New York Times*, June 24, 1899.

31   Roosevelt to Henry Cabot Lodge, July 21, 1899, Theodore Roosevelt Papers.

32   See John M. Gates, *Schoolbooks and Krags: The United States Army in the Philippines, 1898–1902* (Westport, Conn., 1973); Henry F. Graff, ed., *American Imperialism and the Philippine Insurrection* (Boston, 1969).

33   Philip C. Jessup, *Elihu Root*, 2 vols. (New York, 1938), 1:286–87; Healy, *United States in Cuba*, 118–20; U.S. Department of War, *Annual Reports of the Secretary of War, 1899–1903* (Washington, D.C., 1904), 41–44.

34   *FRUS*, 1899, xxviii–xxix.

35   Root to John Hay, January 11, 1901, Elihu Root Papers; Senator Orville Platt to Root, February 5, 1901, Elihu Root Papers; Platt to Leonard Wood, April 21, 1901, Leonard Wood Papers, Library of Congress, Washington, D.C.; *New York Sun*, February 8, 1901; Healy, *United States in Cuba*, 154–56, 159, 164.

36   *Congressional Record*, 56th Congr. 2d sess., 34:2954.

37   Wood to Root, March 2, March 3, March 6, and February 27, 1901, Elihu Root Papers; Root to Wood, April 2, 1901, Elihu Root Papers; *New York Sun*, February 25 and February 27, 1901; *New York Tribune*, March 3, 1901; New York *Evening Post*, March 8, 1901.

38   Wood to Root, April 15 and June 12, 1901, Elihu Root Papers; see these same letters for a copy of the "Report of the Committee Appointed To Confer with the Government of the United States, Giving an Account of Its Labors." For Cuban

counterproposals, see these same letters for a copy of the "Report on the Relations Which Ought To Exist between Cuba and the United States, Presented by the Respective Committee, February 26–27, 1901"; Wood to Root, May 26, 1901, Elihu Root Papers; New York *Evening Post*, May 20, 1901.

39 *Congressional Record*, 56th Cong., 2d sess. vol. 34, especially 3132–51 and 3331–36.

40 See Orville Platt to Edwin F. Atkins, June 11, 1901, quoted by Louis A. Coolidge, *An Old Fashioned Senator, Orville H. Platt* (New York, 1910), 348–49.

41 Healy, *United States in Cuba*, 194–96.

42 Annual message of the president, *FRUS*, 1901, xxxi–xxxii; Ray Stannard Baker, "How the Beet-Sugar Industry Is Growing," *Review of Reviews* 23 (1901): 324–28; U.S., Congress, House, Committee on Ways and Means, *Reciprocity with Cuba: Hearings*, 57th Cong. 1st sess., 1902; Root to Wood, March 7, 1902, Leonard Wood Papers; *Congressional Record*, 57th Cong., 1st sess., 35:3036, 3491, 4324, 4419, 4423, 6720, 6838.

43 *FRUS*, 1903, 375–82; *Congressional Record*, 58th Cong., special session, 37:3, 145, 260–64, 341–42; Leland Jenks, *Our Cuban Colony* (New York, 1928), 135–38; U.S., Tariff Commission, *The Effects of the Cuban Reciprocity Treaty of 1902* (Washington, D.C., 1929), 30.

CHAPTER 4. *Assumptions, Biases, and Preconceptions*

1 E. A. Benians, James Butler, and C. E. Carrington, eds., *The Cambridge History of the British Empire* (Cambridge, 1959), 3:7. See also Philip D. Curtin, *The Image of Africa: British Ideas and Action, 1780–1850* (Madison, Wisc., 1964), chapter 10; William L. Langer, *The Diplomacy of Imperialism* (New York, 1935).

2 Herbert Feis, *Europe, the World's Banker, 1870–1914* (New Haven, Conn., 1930), 103–4; David S. Landes, *Bankers and Pashas: International Finance and Economic Imperialism* (New York, 1958), 321–27. See Landes, *Bankers and Pashas*, 1–68, for a notable essay on the rise of international merchant banking.

3 Edwin M. Borchard, *The Diplomatic Protection of Citizens Abroad; or, The Law of International Claims* (New York, 1915), vi, 178, 350; Donald R. Shea, *The Calvo Clause* (Minneapolis, Minn., 1955), 11.

4 Shea, *Calvo Clause*, 16–39. For the British position on the Calvo Clause, see the Foreign Office memorandum attached to the letter from Jenner to the Foreign Office, November 26, 1899, *Foreign Office Records* (hereafter cited as FO) 15/325, no. 20, Public Record Office, Great Britain; and Foreign Office to Jenner, October 22, 1900, FO 15/332, no. 83.

5 See Shea, *Calvo Clause*, 13–14; Feis, *Europe, the World's Banker*, 193–94; William F. Sands, *Our Jungle Diplomacy* (Chapel Hill, N.C., 1944), 176.

6 Feis, *Europe, the World's Banker*, 262–397; Borchard, *Diplomatic Protection of Citizens Abroad*, 314. The so-called Drago Doctrine, first stated in 1902 by Argentine Foreign Minister Luis Drago, was a Latin American attempt to reshape international law regarding government debts; the key wording declared that "the

public debt of an American state can not occasion armed intervention, nor . . . the
. . . occupation of . . . territory." See Shea, *Calvo Clause*, 14–15.

7   Robert F. Smith, *The United States and Revolutionary Nationalism in Mexico,
    1916–1932* (Chicago, 1972), 24.

8   William Eleroy Curtis, *The Capitals of Spanish America* (New York, 1888), 138;
    James W. G. Walker, *Ocean to Ocean* (Chicago, 1902), 16; William L. Merry
    to Secretary of State, December 30, 1906, Records of the Division of Latin
    American Affairs, 1904–1944, Record Group 59, National Archives, Washing-
    ton, D.C.; William Bayard Hale, "With the Knox Mission to Central America,"
    World's Work 24 (June 1912): 192.

9   Murat Halstead, *Pictorial History of America's New Possessions* (Chicago, 1899),
    51, 55–56.

10 W. F. Powell to Secretary of State, December 11, 1903, Dispatches from U.S.
    Ministers to the Dominican Republic, Record Group 59, National Archives, Wash-
    ington, D.C., microfilm, M93/9; Philip Jessup, *Elihu Root*, 2 vols. (New York,
    1938), 1:541.

11 London *Times*, January 24, 1905; Paget to Foreign Office, August 22, 1902, FO
    15/347: confidential print no. 7768, 245–48.

12 Arthur S. Link, ed. *The Papers of Woodrow Wilson*, 57 vols. (Princeton, N.J.,
    1966–87), 29:19, 37:510.

13 Harry A. Franck, *Roaming through the West Indies* (New York, 1920), 116–18.

14 Curtis, *Capitals of Spanish America*, 138; Walker, *Ocean to Ocean*, 16; Paget to
    Foreign Office, August 22, 1902, FO 15/347, 245–48; Jessup, *Elihu Root*, 1:541.

15 London *Times*, January 24, 1905; Walker, *Ocean to Ocean*, 12; Frederick Palmer,
    Central America and Its Problems (New York, 1910), 274–75.

16 George W. Crichfield, *American Supremacy: The Rise and Progress of the Latin
    American Republics and Their Relations to the United States under the Monroe
    Doctrine*, 2 vols. (New York, 1908), 1:7, 383–84, 389; *Book Review Digest, 1907*
    (Minneapolis, Minn., 1909), 99.

17 Benjamin Kidd, *The Control of the Tropics* (New York and London, 1898), 3–5,
    50–54, 57–60, 83–86; *Literary Digest* 17 (1898): 34, 514–15.

18 Frederick Bancroft, *Speeches, Correspondence, and Political Papers of Carl
    Schurz*, 2 vols. (New York, 1913), 2:78, 84–90; Link, *Papers of Woodrow Wil-
    son*, 12:223; E. E. Morison, ed., *The Letters of Theodore Roosevelt*, 8 vols.
    (Cambridge, Mass., 1951–52), 8:852.

19 The cartoons described are all found in the work of John J. Johnson, *Latin America
    in Caricature* (Austin, Tex., 1980), chapters 4 and 5. John W. Blasingame, "The
    Press and American Intervention in Haiti and the Dominican Republic, 1904–
    1920," *Caribbean Studies* 9 (July 1969): 29–31, found similar attitudes toward
    Caribbean peoples.

20 In addition to the sources cited in notes 7 through 11, representative statements
    can be found in the following works: "Our Next Invasion of Cuba," *New York
    World*, July 20, 1898; Charles A. Crampton, "The Opportunity of the Sugar Cane
    Industry," *North American Review* 168 (March 1899): 276–84; "Dollar Diplomacy
    in Our Relations with the Neighboring Republics," New Orleans *Picayune*, June

15, 1911; Irene Wright, *Cuba* (New York, 1910), 502–4; Chester Lloyd Jones, *The Caribbean Interests of the United States* (New York, 1916), 10, 24, 27, 263–64; Otto Schoenrich, *Santo Domingo, A Country with a Future* (New York, 1918), 232–35; Arthur Bullard, *Panama, the Canal, the Country and the People* (New York, 1914), especially p. 78.

21 Joseph Conrad, *Nostromo, A Tale of the Seaboard* (London, 1904), 81. Near the end of the novel, Conrad voices his own skepticism of this view through the mine's medical doctor, who declares: "There is no peace and no rest in the development of material interests. They have their law, and their justice. But it is founded upon expediency, and is inhuman; it is without rectitude, without the continuity and the force that can be found only in a moral principle. . . . the time approaches when all that the Gould Concession stands for shall weigh as heavily upon the people as the barbarism, cruelty, and misrule of a few years back."

22 This widespread assumption has been challenged by Paul Bairoch, "Le Bilan économique du colonialisme: Mythes et realités," *Itinerario* 1 (1980): 35–36, but Bairoch treats the point too briefly to be persuasive.

23 Surprisingly, the author has seen no prior use of this rather obvious argument that recent domestic successes helped to build Americans' optimism about Caribbean agricultural development.

24 Crichfield, *American Supremacy*, 2:491; Link, *Papers of Woodrow Wilson*, 35:71.

25 Morison, *Letters of Theodore Roosevelt*, 1:768–69, 3:31–32, 109, 465, 5:63 (see also 3:52 and 2:1208).

26 Henry Cabot Lodge, *Selections from the Correspondence of Theodore Roosevelt and Henry Cabot Lodge*, 2 vols. (New York, 1925), 1:487.

27 Philip Jessup, *Elihu Root*, 2 vols. (New York, 1938), 1:543, 2:310; Robert Seager and Doris D. Maguire, eds., *The Letters and Papers of Alfred Thayer Mahan*, 3 vols. (Annapolis, Md., 1975), 2:529, 3:291.

28 Lionel M. Gelber, *The Rise of Anglo-American Friendship* (London and New York, 1938), 24, 27–30; Thomas J. McCormick, *China Market: America's Quest for Informal Empire, 1893–1901* (Chicago, 1967), 110–11; Alfred L. P. Dennis, *Adventures in American Diplomacy, 1896–1906* (New York, 1928), 94–98.

29 Thomas A. Bailey, "Dewey and the Germans at Manila Bay," *American Historical Review* 45 (Oct. 1939): 59–81; Holger H. Herwig, *Politics of Frustration: The United States in German Naval Planning, 1898–1941* (Boston, 1976), 29–36.

30 Herwig, *Politics of Frustration*, 67, 69–71.

31 Ibid., 42–66, 85–92; H. H. Herwig and David Trask, "Naval Operations Plans between Germany and the U.S.A., 1898–1913," *The War Plans of the Great Powers, 1880–1914*, edited by Paul M. Kennedy (London, 1979), 42–60.

32 Herwig and Trask, "Naval Operations Plans between Germany and the U.S.A.," 53–56, 61–63; Melvin Small, "The United States and the German 'Threat' to the Hemisphere, 1905–1914," *Americas* 28 (Jan. 1972):254.

33 See Small, "The United States and the German 'Threat,' " 254–261.

34 Herwig and Trask, "Naval Operations Plans between Germany and the U.S.A.," 42, 45, 63–64. Frederick Marks also feels that the Roosevelt administration had solid reasons to fear German aggression (see Marks, *Velvet on Iron: The Diplomacy of Theodore Roosevelt* (Lincoln, Nebr. 1979), 8, 39–53); while Herwig's

Politics of Frustration makes the fullest and most detailed case for a German threat.

35 Small, "The United States and the German 'Threat,' " 252–54, 270.
36 On this point, see Richard D. Challener, *Admirals, Generals, and American Foreign Policy, 1898–1914* (Princeton, N.J., 1973), 399.

CHAPTER 5. *The Isthmian Canal*

1 Alfred C. Richard, "The Panama Canal in American National Consciousness, 1870–1922" (Ph.D. dissertation, Boston University, 1969), 6; David Healy, *U S Expansionism: The Imperialist Urge in the 1890s* (Madison, Wis., 1970), 159–65.
2 See Richard, "Panama Canal in American National Consciousness," pp. 235–37.
3 August Carl Radke, "John Tyler Morgan, an Expansionist Senator, 1877–1907" (Ph.D. dissertation, University of Washington, 1953), 145–46, 319–30.
4 Burton I. Kaufman, "New Orleans and the Panama Canal, 1900–1914," *Louisiana History* 14 (fall 1973): 333–36, 339, 341; *Chicago Tribune*, July 3 and December 6, 1891.
5 Quoted by Murat Halstead, *Pictorial History of America's New Possessions* (Chicago, 1899), 498.
6 William Roger Adams, "Strategy, Diplomacy, and Isthmian Canal Security, 1880–1917" (Ph.D. dissertation, Florida State University, 1974), 27–39.
7 Alfred Thayer Mahan, "The United States Looking Outward," *Atlantic Monthly* 66 (1890): 816–24; Alfred Thayer Mahan, "The Isthmus and Sea Power," *Atlantic Monthly* 72 (1893): 459–72. The quotation is from the first of the two Mahan references.
8 Adams, "Strategy, Diplomacy, and Isthmian Canal Security," 59–63, 75.
9 Dwight C. Miner, *The Fight for the Panama Route* (New York, 1940), 28–29, 85–90; Richard, "Panama Canal in American National Consciousness," 127, 143.
10 Richard, "Panama Canal in American National Consciousness," 26; Salisbury to Pauncefote, February 2, 1899, FO 420/192.
11 Lester D. Langley, *The United States and the Caribbean, 1900–1970* (Athens, Ga., 1980), 22–24; Roosevelt to Hay, February 18, 1900, John Hay Papers, Library of Congress, Washington, D.C.
12 Langley, *United States and Caribbean*, 23; Adams, "Strategy, Diplomacy, and Isthmian Canal Security," 145–46; Richard, "Panama Canal in American National Consciousness," 96–102.
13 Miner, *Fight for the Panama Route*, 26–29; Richard, "Panama Canal in American National Consciousness," 106–12. See also "Corollaries of Expansion, 1, The Nicaraguan Canal," *Literary Digest* 20 (Feb. 10, 1900): 177–78.
14 Langley, *United States and Caribbean*, 31–32; David McCullough, *The Path between the Seas: The Creation of the Panama Canal, 1870–1914* (New York, 1977), 266–67.
15 McCullough, *Path between the Seas*, 261–62; Langley, *United States and Caribbean*, 32; Miner, *Fight for the Panama Route*, 32–87; Charles D. Ameringer, "The Panama Canal Lobby of Philippe Bunau-Varilla and William Nelson Cromwell,"

American Historical Review 67 (Jan. 1963): 346–63. Philippe Bunau-Varilla, *Panama: Creation, Destruction, and Resurrection* (New York, 1914), minimizes the role of everyone but himself.

16 U.S., Congress, *Senate Document 474: Diplomatic History of the Panama Canal*, 63d Cong. 2d sess., 1914, 277–88; McCullough, *Path between the Seas*, 330–32; Challener, *Admirals, Generals, and American Foreign Policy*, 152–54.

17 U.S., Congress, *Senate Document 474*, 295–313, gives the text of the treaty.

18 McCullough, *Path between the Seas*, 333–39; Miner, *Fight for the Panama Route*, 385–88; Welby to Foreign Office, May 11, 1903, FO 420/210; Dana G. Munro, *Intervention and Dollar Diplomacy in the Caribbean, 1900–1921* (Princeton, N.J., 1964), 43, 49; Eduardo Lemaitre, *Panama y su separación de Colombia* (Bogotá, 1971), 401–54.

19 Miner, *Fight for the Panama Route*, 274–75; McCullough, *Path between the Seas*, 337–38.

20 Roosevelt to Hay, September 15, 1903, in the work of E. E. Morison, ed., *The Letters of Theodore Roosevelt*, 8 vols. (Cambridge, Mass., 1951–52), 3:599; same to same, August 19, 1903, ibid., 566; William L. Merry to Secretary of State, October 4, 1905, Dispatches from U.S. Ministers to Central America, 1824–1906, vol. 74, Record Group 59, National Archives, Washington, D.C.

21 Roosevelt to Hay, September 15, 1903, in the work of Morison, *Letters of Theodore Roosevelt*, 3:599; Roosevelt to Albert Shaw, October 10, 1903, ibid., p. 628; *FRUS*, 1903, 189.

22 Hay to Roosevelt, September 13, 1903, John Hay Papers.

23 McCullough, *Path between the Seas*, 341–60; Lemaitre, *Panama y su separación de Colombia*, 502–27; Munro, *Intervention and Dollar Diplomacy*, 51–52; Walter LaFeber, *The Panama Canal: The Crisis in Historical Perspective* (New York, 1978), 28–35.

24 G. A. Mellander, *The United States in Panamanian Politics: The Intriguing Formative Years* (Danville, Ky. 1971), 10–43; Alfred L. P. Dennis, *Adventures in American Diplomacy, 1896–1906* (New York, 1928), 320–42; McCullough, *Path between the Seas*, 361–79; Lemaitre, *Panama y su separación de Colombia*, 528–46.

25 John Major, "Who Wrote the Hay-Bunau-Varilla Convention?" *Diplomatic History* 8 (spring 1984):115–23.

26 Ibid.

27 Mellander, *United States in Panamanian Politics*, 10–43; Dennis, *Adventures in American Diplomacy*, 320–42.

28 Kendrick A. Clements, *William Jennings Bryan, Missionary Isolationist* (Knoxville, Tenn., 1982), 43–44; Hay is quoted by Miner, *Fight for the Panama Route*, 383.

29 Roosevelt to John Bigelow, January 6, 1904, in the work of Morison, *Letters of Theodore Roosevelt*, 3:689. On "I took the Canal Zone," see James F. Vivian, "The 'Taking' of the Panama Canal Zone, Myth and Reality," *Diplomatic History*, 4(winter 1980): 95–100.

30 "The Suppressed Panama Message," *Literary Digest* 27 (Nov. 28, 1903): 727; Roosevelt to William Roscoe Thayer, July 2, 1915, in the work of Morison, *Letters of Theodore Roosevelt*, 8:945. See also Roosevelt to Albert Shaw, November 6,

1903; to Jacob Gould Schurman, November 12, 1903; and to John Basset Moore, January 6, 1904, all ibid., 3:649, 651, 691.

31 For a contrary view, see Frederick Marks, *Velvet on Iron: The Diplomacy of Theodore Roosevelt* (Lincoln, Nebr., 1979), 97–105.

32 The newspaper comments are from the *Literary Digest* 27 (Nov. 14 and Nov. 21, 1903): 649, 689–92. See also Richard, "Panama Canal in National Consciousness," 169, 173–84, 211.

33 McCullough, *Path between the Seas*, 333.

34 Munro, *Intervention and Dollar Diplomacy*, 54.

35 Mellander, *United States in Panamanian Politics*, 45–46, 52–53.

36 Ibid., 51–53. An earlier study, William D. McCain, *The United States and the Republic of Panama* (Durham, N.C., 1937), 62–63, argues that Buchanan alone imposed the article on the Panamanians while the State Department was indifferent to it.

37 *Readers' Guide to Periodical Literature*, vols. 1–3 (Minneapolis, Minn., 1905, 1910, and New York, 1915); McCullough, *Path between the Seas*, 471–72, 476, 537, 559, 585.

38 Cited by Richard, "Panama Canal in American National Consciousness," 238.

CHAPTER 6. *Toward Caribbean Security*

1 Walter LaFeber, *The Panama Canal: The Crisis in Historical Perspective* (New York, 1978), 54–56.

2 The General Board's report is printed by Robert Seager and Doris Maguire, eds. *The Letters and Papers of Alfred Thayer Mahan*, 3 vols. (Annapolis, Md., 1975), 2:581–90. See also William Roger Adams, "Strategy, Diplomacy, and Isthmian Canal Security, 1880–1917" (Ph.D. dissertation, Florida State University, 1974), 122–14; Richard D. Challener, *Admirals, Generals, and American Foreign Policy, 1898–1914* (Princeton, N.J., 1973), 34–36.

3 Seager and Maguire, *Papers of Alfred Thayer Mahan*, 2:584–89; Challener, *Admirals, Generals, and American Foreign Policy*, 36–37, 89–110; Adams, "Strategy, Diplomacy, and Isthmian Canal Security," 114–16; R. B. Bradford, "Coaling Stations for the Navy," *Forum* 26 (Feb. 1899): 732–47.

4 Challener, *Admirals, Generals, and American Foreign Policy*, 37–41, 94–99; Adams, "Strategy, Diplomacy, and Isthmian Canal Security," 137–39.

5 Challener, *Admirals, Generals, and American Foreign Policy*, 85–86; Fred T. Jane, ed., *Jane's Fighting Ships, 1906/07* (London, 1906), 97–106, 386–88.

6 Challener, *Admirals, Generals, and American Foreign Policy*, 41, 43–45, 324–26; Seager and Maguire, *Papers of Alfred Thayer Mahan*, 2:683; Henry L. Stimson, "The Defense of the Panama Canal," *Scribner's* 54 (July 1913): 1–6.

7 Quoted by Adams, "Strategy, Diplomacy, and Isthmian Canal Security," 169.

8 Warren G. Kneer, *Great Britain and the Caribbean, 1901–1913* (East Lansing, Mich., 1975), 8–11; Roosevelt to Sternberg, July 12, 1901, in the work of E. E. Morison, ed., *Letters of Theodore Roosevelt*, 8 vols. (Cambridge, Mass., 1951–52), 3:116 (hereafter cited as *Letters of Theodore Roosevelt*).

9 Kneer, *Great Britain and the Caribbean*, 11–22.

10   Ibid., 24–35; Dana G. Munro, *Intervention and Dollar Diplomacy in the Carib-
     bean, 1900–1921* (Princeton, N.J., 1964), 70–71.

11   Challener, *Admirals, Generals, and American Foreign Policy*, 112–13; Frederick
     W. Marks, *Velvet on Iron: The Diplomacy of Theodore Roosevelt* (Lincoln, Nebr.,
     1979), 40.

12   Alfred L. P. Dennis, *Adventures in American Diplomacy, 1896–1906* (New York,
     1928), 291–92.

13   Roosevelt to Albert Shaw, December 26, 1902, *Letters of Theodore Roosevelt*,
     3:396–97; Marks, *Velvet on Iron*, 40–41.

14   Marks, *Velvet on Iron*, 41–42; Howard K. Beale, *Theodore Roosevelt and the Rise
     of America to World Power* (Baltimore, Md., 1956), 410–28; Kneer, *Great Britain
     and the Caribbean*, 39–40.

15   Kneer, *Great Britain and the Caribbean*, 37–60.

16   Roosevelt to Thayer, August 21, 1916, *Letters of Theodore Roosevelt*, 8:1101–5;
     same to same, August 23 and August 27, 1916, ibid., 1106–7, 1107–8.

17   For a scholarly discussion of these issues, see Samuel Flagg Bemis, *The Latin-
     American Policy of the United States*, reprint (New York, 1967), 146–48; Se-
     ward W. Livermore, "Theodore Roosevelt, the American Navy, and the Venezue-
     lan Crisis of 1902–1903," *American Historical Review* 51 (Apr. 1946): 452–71;
     Paul S. Holbo, "Perilous Obscurity: Public Diplomacy and the Press in the Vene-
     zuelan Crisis, 1902–1903," *Historian* 32 (May 1970): 428–48; Beale, *Theodore
     Roosevelt and the Rise of America to World Power*, 410–28; Challener, *Admirals,
     Generals, and American Foreign Policy*, 111–16; Kneer, *Great Britain and the
     Caribbean*, 8–60. Munro, *Intervention and Dollar Diplomacy*, 73–74, suggests
     that Roosevelt's ultimatum came, not in December 1902 but in February 1903,
     when the Germans prolonged their blockade because of the dispute over arbitration
     terms.

18   Roosevelt to White, August 14, 1906, *Letters of Theodore Roosevelt*, 5:358–59;
     Roosevelt to Reid, June 27, 1906, ibid., 319; Roosevelt to Frederick Scott Oliver,
     July 22, 1915, ibid., 8:956.

19   Marks, *Velvet on Iron*, 42–47.

20   Kneer, *Great Britain and the Caribbean*, 61–62.

21   Roosevelt to Hay, March 13, 1903, *Letters of Theodore Roosevelt*, 3:446.

22   Roosevelt to Root, May 20, 1904, ibid., 4:801. For an earlier short statement
     of the American duty to police the Caribbean, see Roosevelt to William Bayard
     Hale, February 26, 1904, ibid., 4:740.

23   Roosevelt to Root, June 7, 1904, ibid., 4:821.

24   London *Times*, May 26, 1904.

25   Douglas R. Gow, "How Did the Roosevelt Corollary Become Linked to the Do-
     minican Republic?" *Mid-America* 58 (Oct. 1976): 159–65.

26   Theodore Roosevelt, *The Works of Theodore Roosevelt*, 24 vols. (New York,
     1923–26), 17:299.

27   James D. Richardson, *The Messages and Papers of the Presidents*, (Washington,
     1909), 14:6994ff.

28   Roosevelt to Cecil A. Spring-Rice, July 24, 1905, *Letters of Theodore Roosevelt*,
     4:1286.

CHAPTER 7. *The Deepening Quest for Security*

1 Roosevelt to William Bayard Hale, February 26, 1904, *Letters of Theodore Roosevelt*, 4:740.

2 Rayford Logan, *Haiti and the Dominican Republic* (New York, 1968), 48–53; Warren Kneer, *Great Britain and the Caribbean, 1901–1913* (East Lansing, Mich., 1975), 104–5.

3 Logan, *Haiti and the Dominican Republic*, 51–53; Kneer, *Great Britain and the Caribbean*, 105–6; Sumner Welles, *Naboth's Vineyard: The Dominican Republic, 1844–1924*, 2 vol., 1928, reprint (New York, 1966), 2:559–65; Dana G. Munro, *The United States and the Caribbean Area* (Boston, 1934), 103–4.

4 Welles, *Naboth's Vineyard*, 2:563–65; Munro, *United States and Caribbean*, 104–6.

5 Powell to Secretary of State, October 19 and October 29, 1903, Dispatches from U.S. Ministers to the Dominican Republic, 1883–1906, vol. 9, Record Group 59, National Archives, Washington, D.C., (cited hereafter as Dispatches, Dominican Republic).

6 Powell to Secretary of State, December 3 and December 17, 1903, and January 9 and January 26, 1904, ibid.; Welles, *Naboth's Vineyard*, 2:527–34; Luis F. Mejia, *De Lilis a Trujillo: Historia contemporánea de la República Dominica* (Caracas, 1944), 44.

7 Roosevelt to Joseph Bucklin Bishop, February 23, 1904; Roosevelt to Theodore Roosevelt, Jr., February 10, 1904; Roosevelt to Charles William Elliot, April 4, 1904; all in *Letters of Theodore Roosevelt*, 4:734, 724, and 770.

8 Welles, *Naboth's Vineyard*, 2:556–95; Mejia, *De Lilis a Trujillo*, 1–19.

9 Welles, *Naboth's Vineyard*, 2:556–95; Mejia, *De Lilis a Trujillo*, 20–36.

10 Welles, *Naboth's Vineyard*, 2:596–613.

11 Powell to Secretary of State, December 29, 1903, Dispatches, Dominican Republic, vol. 9; same to same, January 4, January 14, January 28, February 2, February 10, and February 16, 1904, ibid., vol. 10.

12 Powell to Secretary of State, February 26 and February 10, 1904, ibid, vol. 10; Welles, *Naboth's Vineyard*, 2:620. See also Mejia, *De Lilis a Trujillo*, 45.

13 Powell to Secretary of State, February 29 and March 14, 1904, Dispatches, Dominican Republic, vol. 11.

14 Powell to Secretary of State, March 13, 1904, ibid.

15 Ibid.

16 Powell to Secretary of State, April 5 and April 18, 1904, ibid.

17 Powell to Secretary of State, April 18 and June 6, 1904, ibid.

18 Glenn J. Kist, "The Role of Thomas C. Dawson in United States Latin American Diplomatic Relations: 1897–1912" (Ph.D. dissertation, Loyola University, Chicago, 1971), 73–75.

19 Ibid., 9–56, 58.

20 Ibid., 76, 79.

21 Dawson to Secretary of State, September 12, 1904, Dispatches, Dominican Republic, vol. 12.

22 Dawson to Secretary of State, September 24, 1904, ibid.

23 Dawson to Secretary of State, September 27, October 6, and October 21, 1904, ibid.
24 Dawson to Secretary of State, October 3, October 21, and November 21, 1904, ibid.
25 Dawson to Secretary of State, December 3, 1904, ibid., vol. 13; Secretary of State to Dawson, December 28, 1904, Diplomatic Instructions, Santo Domingo, 1801–1906, Record Group 59, National Archives, Washington, D.C., microfilm, M77/98.
26 Powell to Secretary of State, November 3 and December 3, 1903, Dispatches, Dominican Republic, vol. 9.
27 Quoted from Kist, "Role of Thomas C. Dawson," 120.
28 Ibid., 143, 167; Dawson to Secretary of State, January 2, 1905, Dispatches, Dominican Republic, vol. 13; Richard Challener, *Admirals, Generals, and American Foreign Policy, 1898–1914* (Princeton, N.J., 1973), 127–34; Mejia, *De Lilis a Trujillo*, 45–46.
29 Dawson to Secretary of State, January 2, January 23, and March 7, 1905, Dispatches, Dominican Republic, vol. 13.
30 Quoted from Welles, *Naboth's Vineyard*, 2:621–23; see also Kist, "Role of Thomas C. Dawson" 146.
31 Roosevelt to Joseph Bucklin Bishop, March 23, 1905, *Letters of Theodore Roosevelt*, 7:1144–45.
32 Dawson to Secretary of State, February 13 and March 7, 1905, Dispatches, Dominican Republic, vol. 13.
33 Dawson to Secretary of State, March 23, 1905, ibid.; same to same, April 1 and April 6, 1905, ibid., vol. 14.
34 Welles, *Naboth's Vineyard*, 2:647–53; Kneer, *Great Britain and the Caribbean*, 112–14.
35 Ibid.
36 Kist, "Role of Thomas C. Dawson," 136; Roosevelt to Taft, April 8, 1905, and Roosevelt to Hay, April 2, 1905, *Letters of Theodore Roosevelt*, 4:1159, 1156–57.
37 Kist, "Role of Thomas C. Dawson," 289; Challener, *Admirals, Generals, and American Foreign Policy*, 132.
38 Roosevelt to Joseph Bucklin Bishop, February 23, 1904, *Letters of Theodore Roosevelt*, 4:734.
39 Kist, "Role of Thomas C. Dawson," 224–31, 255; Welles, *Naboth's Vineyard*, 2:640–78.
40 Roosevelt to Andrew Carnegie, February 26, 1909, *Letters of Theodore Roosevelt*, 6:1539.

CHAPTER 8. *Interventions and Alternatives*

1 G. A. Mellander, *The United States in Panamanian Politics: The Intriguing Formative Years* (Danville, Ill., 1971), 62–67; William D. McCain, *The United States and the Republic of Panama* (Durham, N.C., 1937), 48–60.
2 McCain, *United States and the Republic of Panama*, 63–72; Roosevelt to Taft,

May 11, 1908, and Roosevelt to Truman H. Newberry, June 17, 1908, *Letters of Theodore Roosevelt*, 6:1028, 1082. Both presidential candidates in 1908 came from the ruling Conservative party, but the Liberals supported José Domingo de Obaldía, the winner.

3   James D. Richardson, ed., *Messages and Papers of the Presidents* (Washington, D.C., 1909), 14:6923.

4   David A. Lockmiller, *Magoon in Cuba: A History of the Second Intervention, 1906–1909* (Chapel Hill, N.C., 1938), 17–18; Allan R. Millett, *The Politics of Intervention: The Military Occupation of Cuba, 1906–1909* (Columbus, Ohio, 1968), 46–48; Hugh Thomas, *Cuba, or, The Pursuit of Freedom* (London, 1971), 471; Ramiro Guerra y Sánchez et al., ed., *Historia de la nación cubana*, 10 vols. (Havana, 1952), 8:3–16; Manuel Márquez Sterling, *Proceso historico de la Enmienda Platt* (Havana, 1941), 303–5.

5   Millett, *Politics of Intervention*, 50–53; Lockmiller, *Magoon in Cuba*, 27–31; Thomas, *Cuba*, 473–74; Guerra y Sánchez, *Historia de la nación cubana*, 8:17–22; Herminio Portell-Vilá, *Historia de Cuba en sus relaciones con los Estados Unidos y España*, 4 vol. (Havana, 1938–41), 4:420ff.

6   Millett, *Politics of Intervention*, 59–63; Lockmiller, *Magoon in Cuba*, 33–36; Guerra y Sánchez, *Historia de la nación cubana*, 8:17–19.

7   Millett, *Politics of Intervention*, 68.

8   Ibid., 71–74; Roosevelt to George Otto Trevelyan, September 9, 1906, *Letters of Theodore Roosevelt*, 5:401.

9   Millett, *Politics of Intervention*, 71–75; Lockmiller, *Magoon in Cuba*, 39–42; Roosevelt to George Otto Trevelyan, September 9, 1906, *Letters of Theodore Roosevelt*, 5:401.

10 Roosevelt to Gonzalo de Quesada, September 14, 1906, *Letters of Theodore Roosevelt*, 5:411–12.

11 Millett, *Politics of Intervention*, 66–67, 71–73.

12 Lockmiller, *Magoon in Cuba*, 51–52; Millett, *Politics of Intervention*, pp. 71–73; Bacon is quoted by Millett on p. 40.

13 Millett, *Politics of Intervention*, 76–77, 90–91.

14 Ibid., 78, 81, 92–102; Lockmiller, *Magoon in Cuba*, 46; the Roosevelt quotation is from Whitney T. Perkins, *Constraint of Empire: The United States and Caribbean Interventions* (Westport, Conn., 1981), 15–16; Guerra y Sánchez, *Historia de la nación cubana*, 8:22–37.

15 Roosevelt to Taft, September 21, 22, and 26, 1906, *Letters of Theodore Roosevelt*, 5:415, 419, 425; Guerra y Sánchez, *Historia de la nación cubana*, 8:20–21; Millett, *Politics of Intervention*, 93, 101–2.

16 Lockmiller, *Magoon in Cuba*, 47–49; Roosevelt to Beveridge, October 5, 1906, *Letters of Theodore Roosevelt*, 5:444.

17 Theodore Roosevelt to Kermit Roosevelt, October 23, 1906; same to William Coolidge Lane, April 15, 1907; same to Taft, September 26, 1906; all in *Letters of Theodore Roosevelt*, 5:465, 648, 425.

18 Lockmiller, *Magoon in Cuba*, 58–63; Lester D. Langley, *The United States and the Caribbean, 1900–1970* (Athens, Ga., 1980), 41; Enrique Collazo, *Cuba intervenido* (Havana, 1910), 87–176; Emilio Roig de Leuchsenring, *La Enmienda Platt:*

Su interpretación primativa y sus applicaciones posteriores hasta 1921 (Havana, 1922), 408; Portell-Vilá, *Historia de Cuba en sus relaciones con los Estados Unidos y España*, 4:526; Márquez Sterling, *Proceso Historico de la Enmienda Platt*, 341–47.

19 For samples of this point of view, see Millett, *Politics of Intervention*, 109–12; Perkins, *Constraint of Empire*, 12–17; Root to Andrew Carnegie, March 20, 1902, in the work of Philip Jessup, *Elihu Root*, 2 vols. (New York, 1938), 1:327.

20 Embert J. Hendrickson, "Roosevelt's Second Venezuelan Crisis," *Hispanic American Historical Review* 50 (Aug. 1970): 484–85; Roosevelt to Hay, September 2, 1904, and Roosevelt to Charles H. Tweed, September 7, 1904, *Letters of Theodore Roosevelt*, 4:917, 918.

21 Hendrickson, "Roosevelt's Second Venezuelan Crisis," 485–87; Roosevelt to Hay, April 2, 1905, *Letters of Theodore Roosevelt*, 4:1156–57; Richard Challener, *Admirals, Generals, and American Foreign Policy, 1898–1914* (Princeton, N.J., 1973), 118–19; Frederick Marks, *Velvet on Iron: The Diplomacy of Theodore Roosevelt* (Lincoln, Nebr., 1979), 142.

22 Hendrickson, "Roosevelt's Second Venezuelan Crisis," 489–95; Jessup, *Elihu Root*, 1:493–99; Roosevelt to Root, March 29, 1908, *Letters of Theodore Roosevelt*, 6:984.

23 Hendrickson, "Roosevelt's Second Venezuelan Crisis," 495–98; Jessup, *Elihu Root*, 1:499.

24 Roosevelt to William Bayard Hale, December 3, 1908, *Letters of Theodore Roosevelt*, 6:1408. A similar statement appears in Roosevelt to Taft, August 21, 1907, ibid., 5:761.

25 Roosevelt to Taft, July 3, 1905, *Letters of Theodore Roosevelt*, 4:1260 (see also same to Alice Lee Roosevelt, September 2, 1905, ibid., 5:1); Henry Cabot Lodge, *Selections from the Correspondence of Theodore Roosevelt and Henry Cabot Lodge*, 2 vols. (New York, 1925), 2:170.

26 Jessup, *Elihu Root*, 1:469–71 (Root is quoted on page 471); Roosevelt to Andrew Carnegie, February 26, 1909, *Letters of Theodore Roosevelt*, 6:1539.

27 Quoted by Jessup, *Elihu Root*, 1:468.

28 Root to Senator Ben Tillman, December 13, 1905, in the work of Jessup, *Elihu Root*, 1:469.

29 Root to Charles W. Elliot, June 18, 1906, and Root to Albert Shaw, January 3, 1908, both in Jessup, *Elihu Root*, 1:530, 513.

30 Jessup, *Elihu Root*, 1:475–77; Root to Tillman, December 13, 1905, and Root to Jessup, November 19, 1924, both ibid., 1:469 and 289.

31 James Brown Scott, "Elihu Root," in *The American Secretaries of State and Their Diplomacy*, edited by Samuel F. Bemis (New York, 1958), 9:219–21; Robert Bacon and James Brown Scott, eds., *Men and Policies: Addresses by Elihu Root* (Cambridge, Mass., 1925), 307–8.

32 James Brown Scott, *The Hague Peace Conferences of 1899 and 1907*, 2 vols. (Baltimore, Md., 1909), 1:129, 441–43, 821.

33 Arthur P. Whitaker, *The Western Hemisphere Idea: Its Rise and Decline* (Ithaca, N.Y., 1954), 88–103.

34 Glenn J. Kist, "The Role of Thomas C. Dawson in United States–Latin American

Diplomatic Relations: 1897–1912," (Ph.D. dissertation, Loyola University, Chicago, 1971), 231, 255; Roosevelt to Charles J. Bonapart, September 24, 1905, *Letters of Theodore Roosevelt*, 5:10; Bacon is quoted by Perkins, *Constraint of Empire*, 17.

35 Thomas L. Karnes, *The Failure of Union: Central America, 1824–1960* (Chapel Hill, N.C., 1961), 183–85; Ralph Lee Woodward, Jr., *Central America: A Nation Divided* (New York, 1976), 191–92.

36 Karnes, *Failure of Union*, 183–86; Woodward, *Central America*, 191–92; Jessup, *Elihu Root*, 1:500–502.

37 William L. Merry to Secretary of State, July 15, July 20, and July 22, 1906, Dispatches from United States Ministers to Central America, 1824–1906, vol. 74, Record Group 59, National Archives, Washington, D.C. See also Karnes, *Failure of Union*, 185–87; Woodward, *Central America*, 191–92; Langley, *United States and the Caribbean*, 45–46; Jessup, *Elihu Root*, 1:501–2.

38 Ibid.

39 Karnes, *Failure of Union*, 187–88; Woodward, *Central America*, 192; Langley, *United States and the Caribbean*, 46–48; Jessup, *Elihu Root*, 1:505.

40 Root to Adee, July 1, 1907, in Jessup, *Elihu Root*, 1:505.

41 Karnes, *Failure of Union*, 189–91; Woodward, *Central America*, 193; Jessup, *Elihu Root*, 1:510–12.

42 Ibid.

43 Quoted by Jessup, *Elihu Root*, 1:513.

44 Karnes, *Failure of Union*, 193–95; Woodward, *Central America*, 193–94.

45 Quoted by Jessup, *Elihu Root*, 1:510–11.

46 Roosevelt to Henry L. Stimson, June 27, 1911, and Roosevelt to Andrew Carnegie, February 26, 1909, *Letters of Theodore Roosevelt*, 7:301, 6:1539.

47 From a New York speech of October 3, 1913, printed in *The Works of Theodore Roosevelt* (New York, 1925), 18:399–400. See also A. T. Mahan to Carter Fitzhugh, March 9, 1912, in the work of Robert Seager and Doris Maguire, eds., *The Letters and Papers of Alfred Thayer Mahan*, 3 vols. (Annapolis, Md., 1975), 3:446.

CHAPTER 9. *Dollar Diplomacy*

1 For a detailed description of the diplomatic leadership of the Taft administration, see Walter V. Scholes and Marie V. Scholes, *The Foreign Policies of the Taft Administration* (Columbia, Mo., 1970), 1–21.

2 Ibid., 27–31; Richard D. Challener, *Admirals, Generals, and American Foreign Policy, 1898–1914* (Princeton, N.J., 1973), 265–67; Melvin Small, "The United States and the German 'Threat' to the Hemisphere, 1905–1914," *Americas* 28 (Jan., 1972): 254; Francis M. Huntington-Wilson, *Memoirs of an Ex-Diplomat* (Boston, 1945), 216.

3 "Mr. Huntington-Wilson's Address at Baltimore, May 4, 1911," Philander Knox Papers, Library of Congress, Washington, D.C.; Huntington-Wilson, *Memoirs of an Ex-Diplomat*, 216.

4   Scholes and Scholes, *Foreign Policies of Taft*, 12, 16–17; Huntington-Wilson, *Memoirs of an Ex-Diplomat*, 170, 212–13.

5   Root is quoted by Philip Jessup, *Elihu Root*, 2 vols. (New York, 1938), 2:250–51; Bryce is quoted by Warren Kneer, *Great Britain and the Caribbean, 1901–1913* (East Lansing, Mich., 1975), 162–63.

6   Scholes and Scholes, *Foreign Policies of Taft*, 31, 29, 35–36.

7   John Hay to Leslie Combs, August 29, 1904, Diplomatic Instructions, Central America, 1801–1906, vol. 22, Record Group 59, National Archives, Washington, D.C.; Root to Hay, January 7, 1905, quoted by Jessup, *Elihu Root*, 1:471; Roosevelt to Hay, January 14, 1905, Theodore Roosevelt Papers, Library of Congress, Washington, D.C.

8   Knox is quoted by Scholes and Scholes, *Foreign Policies of Taft*, 35. See also "Memorandum Prepared for Secretary Knox," March 28, 1912, Philander Knox Papers.

9   See Philander C. Knox, "The Monroe Doctrine and Some Incidental Obligations in the Zone of the Caribbean," address before the New York State Bar Association, January 19, 1912, Philander Knox Papers; James Bryce to Sir Edward Grey, May 21, 1910, FO 420/252, confidential print no. 47.

10 Scholes and Scholes, *Foreign Policies of Taft*, 68–69; Kneer, *Great Britain and the Caribbean*, 136–41.

11 Charles Brand, "The Background of Capitalistic Underdevelopment: Honduras to 1913" (Ph.D. dissertation, University of Pittsburgh, 1972), 168–74; Scholes and Scholes, *Foreign Policies of Taft*, 69–71; Kneer, *Great Britain and the Caribbean*, 160–61.

12 Brand, "Background of Capitalistic Underdevelopment," 172–76; Scholes and Scholes, *Foreign Policies of Taft*, 71–72.

13 Henry W. Furniss to Secretary of State, August 29, 1910, and Secretary of State to Furniss, September 27, 1910, Department of State, Division of Information, Confidential Series A (cited hereafter as Confidential Series A), vol. 2, no. 70, Record Group 59, National Archives, Washington, D.C. See also Rayford Logan, *Haiti and the Dominican Republic* (New York, 1968), 115–16.

14 Alvey Adee to Furniss, October 12, 1910, Confidential Series A, vol. 2, no. 70. See also Kneer, *Great Britain and the Caribbean*, note, p. 226.

15 Furniss to Secretary of State, October 22, 1910, Ledenburg, Thalmann and Co. to Secretary of State, November 22, 1910, and Secretary of State to Furniss, January 11, 1911, Confidential Series A, vol. 2, no. 70. See also the testimony of Roger L. Farnham on October 4, 1921, in U.S. Congress, Senate, *Hearings on S.R. 112*, 67th Cong., 1st and 2d sess., 1922, 105–6.

16 Furniss to Secretary of State, August 11, 1911, Confidential Series A, vol. 2, no. 70.

17 "Confidential Memorandum in Respect to American Interests in the National Bank of Haiti, Dictated March 27, 1915," and William Jennings Bryan to Woodrow Wilson, March 27, 1915, Correspondence of Secretary of State Bryan with President Wilson, Record Group 59, National Archives, Washington, D.C.

18 William L. Merry to Secretary of State, July 31, 1909, Division of Latin Ameri-

can Affairs, 1904–1914, Record Group 59, National Archives, Washington, D.C.; David Healy, "A Hinterland in Search of a Metropolis: The Mosquito Coast, 1894–1910," *International History Review* 3 (Jan. 1981) 35–37; Scholes and Scholes, *Foreign Policies of Taft*, 49–50; Challener, *Admirals, Generals, and American Foreign Policy*, 292–94; Dana G. Munro, *Intervention and Dollar Diplomacy in the Caribbean, 1900–1921* (Princeton, N.J., 1964), 170.

19   Scholes and Scholes, *Foreign Policies of Taft*, 49–51; Harold N. Denny, *Dollars for Bullets: The Story of the American Role in Nicaragua* (New York, 1929), 73–79; Kneer, *Great Britain and the Caribbean*, 142–44; Healy, "A Hinterland in Search of a Metropolis," 25–33; José Santos Zelaya, *La Revolución de Nicaragua y los Estados Unidos* (Madrid, 1910), 6–7. Máximo Soto Hall, *Nicaragua y el imperialismo norteamericano* (Buenos Aires, 1928), 38–39, 56–57, charges that U.S. businessmen on the Atlantic Coast fomented the 1909 revolt for purely economic reasons, and financed it with contributions totaling a million dollars.

20   Thomas R. Moffat to Secretary of State, October 12, 1909, and Adee to Moffat, October 13, 1909, Confidential Series A, vol. 1, no. 56.

21   Scholes and Scholes, *Foreign Policies of Taft*, 52–53.

22   Ibid., 53–54; Secretary of State Knox to the Nicaraguan Chargé, December 1, 1909, Confidential Series A, vol. 1, no. 6. For Zelaya's defense of his rule against Knox's charges, see Zelaya, *La Revolución de Nicaragua y los Estados Unidos*, especially 60–69; for contrasting views of the Zelaya regime, see Enrique Aquino, *La Personalidad política del General José Santos Zelaya* (Managua, 1944); and Macario Alvarez Lejarza, *Impresiones y recuerdos de la revolución de 1909 a 1910* (Granada, Nicaragua, 1941).

23   Challener, *Admirals, Generals, and American Foreign Policy*, 295–98; Lionel Carden to Sir Edward Grey, June 9, 1910, FO 420/252/61; Ofsman Quintana Orozco, *Apuntes de historia de Nicaragua* (Managua, 1968), 179–82; Alejandro Cole Chamorro, *Ciento cuarenta y cinco años de historia política en Nicaragua* (Managua, 1967), 71–76.

24   Challener, *Admirals, Generals, and American Foreign Policy*, 295–98; Dana G. Munro, *The Five Republics of Central America* (New York, 1918), 229.

25   Carden to Grey, June 9 and June 19, 1910, FO 420/252/61 and 66; Scholes and Scholes, *Foreign Policies of Taft*, 58.

26   Moffat to Secretary of State, May 17, 1910, Confidential Series A, vol. 1, no. 56.

27   Munro, *Five Republics of Central America*, p. 230; Scholes and Scholes, *Foreign Policies of Taft*, 59–60; Cole Chamorro, *Ciento cuarenta y cinco años de historia política en Nicaragua*, 79–80.

28   José de Olivares to Secretary of State, August 19, 1910, and Huntington-Wilson to Olivares, September 1, 1910, Confidential Series A, vol. 1, no. 56.

29   Glenn J. Kist, "The Role of Thomas C. Dawson in United States–Latin American Diplomatic Relations, 1897–1912" (Ph.D. dissertation, Loyola University, Chicago, 1971), 417–25; Dawson to Secretary of State, October 28 and November 6, 1910, Confidential Series A, vol. 2, no. 63; Knox to Elliot Northcott, January 20, 1911, ibid.; Quintana Orozco, *Apuntes de historia de Nicaragua*, 184–85.

30   "The Mena Revolution in Nicaragua," Confidential Series A, vol. 2, no. 90, 3–6;

Munro, *Intervention and Dollar Diplomacy in the Caribbean*, 189–91; Whitney T. Perkins, *Constraint of Empire: The United States and Caribbean Interventions* (Westport, Conn., 1981), 28–29.

31 Scholes and Scholes, *Foreign Policies of Taft*, 61–62; Munro, *Intervention and Dollar Diplomacy in the Caribbean*, 192–95.

32 Scholes and Scholes, *Foreign Policies of Taft*, 63–64; Munro, *Intervention and Dollar Diplomacy in the Caribbean*, 195–99; Roscoe R. Hill, *Fiscal Intervention in Nicaragua* (New York, 1933), 10–17.

33 Scholes and Scholes, *Foreign Policies of Taft*, 63–64; Munro, *Intervention and Dollar Diplomacy in the Caribbean*, 18–20. For a sustained attack on these United States financial arrangements in Nicaragua, see Rafael de Nogales, *The Looting of Nicaragua* (New York, 1928), especially pp. 9–16, 21–25.

34 Perkins, *Constraint of Empire*, 30–32; Munro, *Intervention and Dollar Diplomacy in the Caribbean*, 199–204.

35 H. Cavendish Venables, "Report on the Nicaraguan Revolution of 1912," dated October 20, 1912, enclosed in George Haggard to Sir Edward Grey, December 3, 1912, FO 420/256, no. 248; "Mena Revolution in Nicaragua," 6–36; Munro, *Intervention and Dollar Diplomacy in the Caribbean*, 205–6; Cole Chamorro, *Ciento cuarento y cinco años de historia política en Nicaragua*, 83–85.

36 Scholes and Scholes, *Foreign Policies of Taft*, 65–66; Challener, *Admirals, Generals, and American Foreign Policy*, 302–8; "Mena Revolution in Nicaragua," 30–40; Munro, *Intervention and Dollar Diplomacy in the Caribbean*, 205–8.

37 "Mena Revolution in Nicaragua," 65–72; Challener, *Admirals, Generals, and American Foreign Policy*, 305–7; Lester Langley, *The Banana Wars: An Inner History of American Empire, 1900–1934* (Lexington, Ky., 1983), 68–74; Cole Chamorro, *Ciento cuarento y cinco años de historia política en Nicaragua*, 83–85; Quintana Orozco, *Apuntes de historia de Nicaragua*, 185–87.

38 "Mena Revolution in Nicaragua," 80–85; Langley, *Banana Wars*, 74–75.

39 Venables, "Report on the Nicaraguan Revolution of 1912;" U.S., Department of the Navy, *Annual Reports of the Secretary of the Navy, 1912*, 1913, 12–13.

40 Sumner Welles, *Naboth's Vineyard: The Dominican Republic, 1844–1924*, 2 vols. (New York, 1928), 2:660–78.

41 Ibid., 2:679–90; "Memorandum on the Dominican Situation, Respectfully Submitted to the President by the Department of State on September 17, 1912," Records of the Department of State Relating to Internal Affairs of the Dominican Republic, 1910–1929, National Archives, Washington, D.C., microfilm (cited hereafter as Decimal Files, Internal Affairs, Dominican Republic), M626/5.

42 Welles, *Naboth's Vineyard*, 2:690–91; "Memorandum on the Dominican Situation;" W. W. Russell to Secretary of State, September 9, 1912, Decimal Files, Internal Affairs, Dominican Republic, M626/4.

43 Huntington-Wilson to Taft, September 19, 1912, Decimal Files, Internal Affairs, Dominican Republic, M626/5.

44 Huntington-Wilson to McIntyre and Doyle, September 24, 1912; McIntyre and Doyle to Secretary of State, October 9, 1912; W. W. Russell to Secretary of State, October 20, 1912; Russell, McIntyre, and Doyle to Secretary of State,

1912, November 20 and November 23, 1912; all Decimal Files, Internal Affairs, Dominican Republic, M626/5.

45 Russell to Secretary of State, December 4, 1912, ibid.; Welles, *Naboth's Vineyard*, 2:699–708.

46 Russell to Secretary of State, January 16, 1913, Decimal Files, Internal Affairs, Dominican Republic, M626/5; Welles, *Naboth's Vineyard*, 2:700–708.

47 "Address of Hon. Philander C. Knox before the New York State Bar Association, New York, N.Y., January 19, 1912," Philander Knox Papers.

CHAPTER 10. *Ideology, Dollars, and Realpolitik*

1 Josephus Daniels diary entry, March 11, 1913, *The Papers of Woodrow Wilson*, edited by Arthur S. Link (Princeton, N.J., 1978), 27:169; Richard Challener, *Admirals, Generals, and American Foreign Policy, 1898–1914* (Princeton, N.J., 1973), 361–62; Arthur S. Link, *Wilson: The New Freedom* (Princeton, N.J., 1956), 319; *Papers of Woodrow Wilson*, 27:172.

2 Woodrow Wilson, "An Address on Latin American Policy in Mobile, Alabama," October 23, 1913, *Papers of Woodrow Wilson*, 28:450.

3 Link, *Wilson: The New Freedom*, 277; Kendrick A. Clements, *William Jennings Bryan, Missionary Isolationist* (Knoxville, Tenn., 1982), 46, 65.

4 See Wilson's speeches of August 7 and September 4, 1912, *Papers of Woodrow Wilson*, 25:16–17, 101.

5 Burton I. Kaufman, *Efficiency and Expansion: Foreign Trade Organization in the Wilson Administration, 1913–1921* (Westport, Conn., 1974), 76–81; Burton I. Kaufman, "United States Trade and Latin America: The Wilson Years," *Journal of American History* 58 (Sept. 1971): 342, 349–50.

6 Kaufman, "United States Trade and Latin America," 345, 348, 351, 344n; Joseph S. Tulchin, *The Aftermath of War: World War I and United States Policy toward Latin America* (New York, 1971), 6–10; Kaufman, *Efficiency and Expansion*, 117–18, 124.

7 Kaufman, "United States Trade and Latin America," 351–55; Tulchin, *Aftermath of War*, 23–25.

8 Kaufman, "United States Trade and Latin America," 355; Tulchin, *Aftermath of War*, 39–42.

9 See Bryan to Wilson, October 28, 1913, and February 21, 1914, and Wilson to Bryan, March 20, 1914, William Jennings Bryan Papers, Library of Congress, Washington, D.C.; Clements, *William Jennings Bryan*, 78–79.

10 Bryan to Wilson, October 28, 1913, William Jennings Bryan Papers.

11 Lansing to Wilson, November 24, 1915, *Papers of Woodrow Wilson*, 35:246–47.

12 "Present Nature and Extent of the Monroe Doctrine," State Department memorandum, November 24, 1915, *Papers of Woodrow Wilson*, 35:247–52.

13 Robert F. Smith, *The United States and Revolutionary Nationalism in Mexico, 1916–1932* (Chicago, 1972), 145; Robert W. Dunn, *American Foreign Investments*

(New York, 1926), 3, 89–90; Oscar P. Austin, *Trading with Our Neighbors in the Caribbean*, Foreign Commerce Series no. 1, (National City Bank of New York, 1920), 56–57.

14 For standard accounts of these events, see Charles C. Cumberland, *The Mexican Revolution: Genesis under Madero* (Austin, Tex., 1952); Kenneth Grieb, *The United States and Huerta* (Lincoln, Nebr., 1969); Michael C. Meyer, *Huerta: A Political Portrait* (Lincoln, Nebr., 1972).

15 See Clements, *William Jennings Bryan*, 91–93; Link, *Wilson: The New Freedom*, 347–78.

16 See Link, *Wilson: The New Freedom*, 347–78; Arthur S. Link, *Wilson: The Struggle for Neutrality* (Princeton, N.J., 1960), 456–94; Arthur S. Link, *Wilson: Confusions and Crises* (Princeton, N.J., 1964), 280–318.

17 Tyrell to Sir Edward Grey, November 14, 1913, *Papers of Woodrow Wilson*, 28:543–44.

18 Spring Rice to Grey, May 25, 1914, ibid., 30:77–78.

19 Challener, *Admirals, Generals, and American Foreign Policy*, 399; Wilson to Lansing, February 6, 1917, *Papers of Woodrow Wilson*, 41:131–32.

20 See Lansing to Wilson, December 4, 1915, and Wilson to Lansing, January 7, 1916, as well as "Memorandum of Robt. Lansing of Conversation with the Danish Minister, November 15, 1915," *Papers of Woodrow Wilson*, 35:284–85, 447, 202–3.

21 The *Tribune* editorial is reprinted in *Literary Digest* 51 (Aug. 14, 1915): 288; Caperton to Rear Admiral William S. Benson, October 30, 1916, is in William B. Caperton Papers, Library of Congress, Washington, D.C.

22 See Link, *Wilson: The Struggle for Neutrality*, 495–96; Dana G. Munro, *Intervention and Dollar Diplomacy in the Caribbean, 1900–1921* (Princeton, N.J., 1964), 534; Sidney Bell, *Righteous Conquest: Woodrow Wilson and the Evolution of the New Diplomacy* (Port Washington, N.Y., 1972), 29–48, 190–93; Clements, *William Jennings Bryan*, 95.

23 Wilson, "Democracy and Efficiency," *Atlantic Monthly* 87 (March 1901): 289–99. See also Wilson, "The Ideals of America," *Atlantic Monthly* 90 (Dec. 1902): 721–34.

24 Theodore Roosevelt to Archibald Bulloch Roosevelt, December 2, 1914, *Letters of Theodore Roosevelt*, 8:852; Roosevelt speech, "The United States and the South American Republics," New York, October 3, 1913, *The Works of Theodore Roosevelt* (New York, 1925), 18:399–400.

25 Roosevelt to George Otto Trevelyan, September 9, 1906, *Letters of Theodore Roosevelt*, 5:401; Lodge to Roosevelt, September 16, 1906, from Henry Cabot Lodge, *Selections from the Correspondence of Theodore Roosevelt and Henry Cabot Lodge*, 2 vols., (New York, 1925), 2:233.

26 Root to Silas McBee, April 10, 1907, from Philip Jessup, *Elihu Root*, 2 vols., (New York, 1938), 1:513–14.

27 See Wilson's circular note of November 24, 1913, in the work of Link, *Wilson: The New Freedom*, 386 (italics added).

28 Wilson, "Statement on Relations with Latin America," March 12, 1913, *Papers of*

Woodrow Wilson, 27:172. Bell, *Righteous Conquest*, 52, argues that Nicaragua's President José Santos Zelaya had a definite program of Central American union and development, while his Washington-backed opponents were mere opportunists.

29 Theodore Roosevelt, Annual Message to Congress, December 6, 1904, *Works of Theodore Roosevelt*, 17:299.

30 Wilson to Bryan, January 13, 1915, quoted by Link, *Wilson: The Struggle for Neutrality*, 528.

31 Dana G. Munro, *The Five Republics of Central America* (New York, 1918), 309.

CHAPTER 11. *Wilsonism in Action*

1 Arthur S. Link, *Wilson: The New Freedom* (Princeton, N.J., 1956), 321–22; Kendrick A. Clements, *William Jennings Bryan, Missionary Isolationist* (Knoxville, Tenn., 1982), 79–81.

2 Thomas L. Karnes, "Hiram Bingham and His Obsolete Shibbolith," *Diplomatic History* 31 (winter 1979): 39–57.

3 Link, *Wilson: The New Freedom*, 324–25; for the original treaty draft see *The Papers of Woodrow Wilson*, edited by Arthur S. Link, 57 vols. (Princeton, N.J., 1966–87), 31:471–72.

4 Link, *Wilson: The New Freedom*, 326–29; *Papers of Woodrow Wilson* 35:54–55.

5 Harold N. Denny, *Dollars for Bullets: The Story of American Rule in Nicaragua* (New York, 1929), 144–46; Roscoe R. Hill, *Fiscal Intervention in Nicaragua* (New York, 1933), 10–13, 18–19.

6 Denny, *Dollars for Bullets*, 154–55; Hill, *Fiscal Intervention in Nicaragua*, 27–29.

7 Link, *Wilson: The New Freedom*, 332.

8 For Bryan's dilemma, see Selig Adler, "Bryan and Wilsonian Caribbean Penetration," *Hispanic American Historical Review* 20 (May 1940): 200–209. See also Link, *Wilson: The New Freedom*, 334–35.

9 Bryan to Wilson, May 24, 1913, William Jennings Bryan Papers, Library of Congress, Washington, D.C.; Link, *Wilson: The New Freedom*, 333; Alejandro Cole Chamorro, *Ciento cuarenta y cinco años de historia política en Nicaragua* (Managua, 1967), 85–93.

10 Bryan to Wilson, January 15 and June 12, 1914, William Jennings Bryan Papers.

11 Bryan to Wilson, July 31, 1913, ibid.; Cecil A. Spring-Rice to Sir Edward Grey, August 4, 1913, FO 420/257, no. 131. See also Link, *Wilson: The New Freedom*, 336–37.

12 *New York Times*, July 21, 1913; Marshall Langhorne to Secretary of State, July 26 and August 2, 1913; William Heimke to Secretary of State, July 12 and July 29, 1913; Hugh R. Wilson to Secretary of State, August 4, 1913; Charles D. White to Secretary of State, August 5, 1913; all in U.S., Department of State, Records of the Department of State Relating to Political Relations between the United States and Central America, 1911–1929, Record Group 59, National Archives, Washington, D.C., microfilm, M673/1.

13   Hill, *Fiscal Intervention in Nicaragua*, 25–26; R. C. Michell to Sir Edward Grey, January 24, 1914, FO 420/258, no. 38.

14   Bryan to Wilson, January 23, 1914, William Jennings Bryan Papers; Diaz to Wilson, February 3, 1914, *Papers of Woodrow Wilson*, 29:222.

15   For detailed reports on the Senate's opposition, see Colville Barclay to Sir Edward Grey, June 25, July 5, and July 18, 1914, FO 420/258, nos. 136, 141, 148. See also Philip Jessup, *Elihu Root*, 2 vols. (New York, 1938), 2:251–52; Link, *Wilson: The New Freedom*, 339.

16   Link, *Wilson: The New Freedom*, 339–40.

17   Bryan to Wilson, January 15, 1914, William Jennings Bryan Papers; Wilson to Bryan, January 20, 1914, *Papers of Woodrow Wilson*, 29:152; memorandum of Bryan's statement in "Proceedings of the First Pan American Financial Conference, Washington, May 24 to 29, 1915," Chandler P. Anderson Papers, Library of Congress, Washington, D.C.

18   Dana G. Munro, *The Five Republics of Central America* (New York, 1918), 254–56.

19   Ibid., 245–57; Link, *Wilson: The New Freedom*, 345–46.

20   Hans Schmidt, *The United States Occupation of Haiti, 1915–1934* (New Brunswick, N.J., 1971), 37–41; David Healy, *Gunboat Diplomacy in the Wilson Era: The U.S. Navy in Haiti, 1915–1916* (Madison, Wis., 1976), 27–30; Rayford Logan, *Haiti and the Dominican Republic* (New York, 1968), 115–16; Dana G. Munro, *The United States and the Caribbean Area* (Boston, 1934), 150–53.

21   Schmidt, *United States Occupation of Haiti*, 50–52; Healy, *Gunboat Diplomacy in the Wilson Era*, 30–31.

22   Healy, *Gunboat Diplomacy in the Wilson Era*, 32–33; Link, *Wilson: The New Freedom*, 521–25.

23   Ibid.

24   Bryan to Wilson, December 12, 1914, with enclosure dated December 11, 1914, *Papers of Woodrow Wilson*, 31:456–57; Arthur Bailly-Blanchard to Bryan, December 12 and December 15, 1914, ibid., 483–86; Bryan to Bailly-Blanchard, December 18, 1914, ibid., 486–87. See also Healy, *Gunboat Diplomacy in the Wilson Era*, 33–34.

25   Bryan to Wilson, January 7, 1915, *Papers of Woodrow Wilson*, 32:27–28; Wilson to Bryan, January 13, 1915, William Jennings Bryan Papers.

26   Bryan to Wilson, February 25, 1915; Bryan to John Franklin Fort, February 27, 1915; Bryan to Bailly-Blanchard, February 27, 1915; all *Papers of Woodrow Wilson*, 32:288–89, 295–96, 297.

27   Bryan to Wilson, March 25 and March 27, 1915; Wilson to Bryan, March 25 and March 31, 1915; all ibid.

28   Bryan to Paul Fuller, Jr., May 6, 1915, ibid., 33:116–17; U.S., Department of State, *Foreign Relations of the United States, 1916*, 1925, 311–20 memorandum, R. B. Davis, Jr., to Secretary of State, January 12, 1916; Healy, *Gunboat Diplomacy in the Wilson Era*, 43–56.

29   Davis, memorandum of January 12, 1916; Healy, *Gunboat Diplomacy in the Wilson Era*, 57–59.

30 Healy, *Gunboat Diplomacy in the Wilson Era*, 59–79, 138–41; William B. Caperton, "History of U.S. Naval Operations under Command of Rear Admiral W. B. Caperton, Commencing January 5, 1915, Ending April 30, 1919," Naval Records Collection, Office of Naval Records and Library, Record Group 45, National Archives, Washington, D.C. (cited hereafter as Caperton, "History of Operations"), 47–62, 99; Edward L. Beach, "Admiral Caperton in Haiti," Naval Records Collection, Office of Naval Records and Library, Record Group 45, National Archives, Washington, D.C., 102–33.

31 Healy, *Gunboat Diplomacy in the Wilson Era*, 102–17; Caperton, "History of Operations," 75–88; Beach, "Admiral Caperton in Haiti," 145–63.

32 Healy, *Gunboat Diplomacy in the Wilson Era*, 133–37, 150–58; Caperton, "History of Operations," 102–4, 98, 110, 133, 144–46.

33 Healy, *Gunboat Diplomacy in the Wilson Era*, 159–70, 175–84; Beach, "Admiral Caperton in Haiti," 184–85; Caperton, "History of Operations," 118–19, 129–48, 152–60, 163–70, 177–213, 216–18.

34 Wilson to Bryan, August 4, 1915, William Jennings Bryan Papers; Wilson to Edith Bolling Galt, August 15, 1915, *Papers of Woodrow Wilson*, 34:208–9. For a standard account of the entire occupation, see Schmidt, *United States Occupation of Haiti*.

35 Sumner Welles, *Naboth's Vineyard: The Dominican Republic, 1844–1924*, 2 vols. (New York, 1966), 2:708–13; Arthur S. Link, *Wilson: The Struggle for Neutrality, 1914–1915* (Princeton, N.J., 1960), 500; Dana G. Munro, *Intervention and Dollar Diplomacy in the Caribbean, 1900–1921* (Princeton, N.J., 1964), 274–80.

36 Bryan to Charles B. Curtis, September 11, 1913; James M. Sullivan to Bryan, September 24 and October 6, 1913; all in Decimal Files, Internal Affairs, Dominican Republic, M626/6. See also Welles, *Naboth's Vineyard*, 2:714–26; Link, *Wilson: The Struggle for Neutrality*, 550–000; Munro, *Intervention and Dollar Diplomacy in the Caribbean*, 277–80.

37 Sullivan to Bryan, October 7, October 31, and December 5, 1913; Bryan to Sullivan, December 2 and December 7, 1913; all in Decimal Files, Internal Affairs, Dominican Republic, M626/6 and 7. See also Welles, *Naboth's Vineyard*, 2:723–33; Link, *Wilson: The Struggle for Neutrality*, 503–7; Munro, *Intervention and Dollar Diplomacy in the Caribbean*, 281–84.

38 Welles, *Naboth's Vineyard*, 2:731–36; Link, *Wilson: The Struggle for Neutrality*, 508–12; Munro, *Intervention and Dollar Diplomacy in the Caribbean*, 285–91.

39 Welles, *Naboth's Vineyard*, 2:735–39; Link, *Wilson: The Struggle for Neutrality*, 512–15 (the quotation is on pp. 514–15).

40 Welles, *Naboth's Vineyard*, 2:739–48; Link, *Wilson: The Struggle for Neutrality*, 538–39; Munro, *Intervention and Dollar Diplomacy in the Caribbean*, 293–98.

41 Welles, *Naboth's Vineyard*, 2:748–52; Link, *Wilson: The Struggle for Neutrality*, 540; Munro, *Intervention and Dollar Diplomacy in the Caribbean*, 296–98.

42 Welles, *Naboth's Vineyard*, 2:748–52.

43 Ibid., 750–56; Link, *Wilson: The Struggle for Neutrality*, 540–41; Munro, *Intervention and Dollar Diplomacy in the Caribbean*, 298–302.

44 Lansing to Wilson, November 24, 1915, Decimal Files, Internal Affairs, Domini-

can Republic, M626/13; Welles, *Naboth's Vineyard*, 2:757–66; Link, *Wilson: The Struggle for Neutrality*, 741–43; Munro, *Intervention and Dollar Diplomacy in the Caribbean*, 302–4.

45 J. B. Wright to Lansing, January 24, 1916, Decimal Files, Internal Affairs, Dominican Republic, M626/13.

46 Russell to Lansing, December 27, 1915, April 15, 16, 27, and 29, 1916, and May 1, 6, and 7, 1916, Decimal Files, Internal Affairs, Dominican Republic, M626/13; Frederick May Wise, *A Marine Tells It to You* (New York, 1929), 138–43.

47 Russell to Lansing, May 7 and May 10, 1916; Lansing to Russell, May 7, 1916; Caperton to Secretary of the Navy, May 12, 1916; all in Decimal Files, Internal Affairs, Dominican Republic, M626/13; Antonio Hoepelman and Juan A. Senior, *Documentos historicos que se refieren a la intervención armada de los Estados Unidos de Norte-América y la implantación de un gobierno militar americano en la República Dominica* (Santo Domingo, 1922), 18–19.

48 Hoepelman and Senior, *Documentos historicos*, 7–10; Welles, *Naboth's Vineyard*, 2:773–74; Caperton, "History of Operations," 258–59; the quotation comes from Caperton to Rear Admiral William S. Benson, June 15, 1916, William S. Caperton Papers, Library of Congress, Washington, D.C.

49 Caperton to Secretary of the Navy, May 18, 1916, and Russell to Lansing, May 18, 1916, Decimal Files, Internal Affairs, Dominican Republic, M626/13; Caperton's Reports of Operations, June 14, June 22, and July 8, 1916, ibid.; Caperton, "History of Operations," 258, 261, 266, 271–72.

50 Russell to Lansing, June 2, 6, 14, and 17, and July 13, 1916, Decimal Files, Internal Affairs, Dominican Republic, M626/13; Welles, *Naboth's Vineyard*, 2:774–90; Link, *Wilson: The Struggle for Neutrality*, 545–47; Munro, *Intervention and Dollar Diplomacy in the Caribbean*, 308–14.

51 Louis A. Perez, Jr., *Intervention, Revolution, and Politics in Cuba, 1913–1921* (Pittsburgh, Pa., 1978), 5–15; George W. Baker, "The Wilson Administration and Cuba, 1913–1921," *Mid-America* 46 (1946): 55; Leo J. Meyer, "The United States and the Cuban Revolution of 1917," *Hispanic American Historical Review* 10 (May 1930): 139–43.

52 Perez, *Intervention, Revolution, and Politics in Cuba*, 16–35; Baker, "The Wilson Administration and Cuba," 55–58; Meyer, "The United States and the Cuban Revolution of 1917," 143–50.

53 Perez, *Intervention, Revolution, and Politics in Cuba*, 36–98; Baker, "The Wilson Administration and Cuba," 58–60; Meyer, "The United States and the Cuban Revolution of 1917," 158–66.

54 James M. Sullivan to Bryan, December 5, 1913, Decimal Files, Internal Affairs, Dominican Republic, M626/7.

55 E. M. House, diary entry for November 28, 1915, *Papers of Woodrow Wilson*, 35:259.

CHAPTER 12. *The United States Impact on Cuba*

1   Oscar P. Austin, *Trading with Our Neighbors in the Caribbean*, Foreign Commerce Series, no. 1, (National City Bank of New York, 1920), 56–57; Robert W. Dunn, *American Foreign Investments* (New York, 1926), 119–20, 122; Louis A. Perez, Jr., *Intervention, Revolution, and Politics in Cuba, 1913–1921* (Pittsburgh, Pa., 1978), 131.

2   Jules R. Benjamin, *The United States and Cuba: Hegemony and Dependent Development, 1880–1934* (Pittsburgh, Pa., 1977), 8–10, 17, notes, pp. 196 and 200; Irene Wright, *Cuba* (New York, 1910), 67.

3   Benjamin, *United States and Cuba*, 9–10; Louis A. Perez, Jr., *Cuba between Empires, 1878–1902* (Pittsburgh, Pa., 1983), 346–47, 357–60; Robert B. Hoernel, "Sugar and Social Change in Oriente, Cuba, 1898–1946," *Journal of Latin American Studies* 8 (Nov. 1976): 226.

4   Hugh Thomas, *Cuba, or the Pursuit of Freedom* (London, 1971), 36–38; Perez, *Intervention, Revolution, and Politics in Cuba*, 4; Ramiro Guerra y Sánchez et al, eds., *Historia de la nación cubana*, 10 vols. (Havana, 1952), 9: 311–24.

5   Hoernel, "Sugar and Social Change in Oriente," 221–22, 229–30; Wright, *Cuba*, 464–69.

6   Hoernel, "Sugar and Social Change in Oriente," 230, 233.

7   Ibid., 240; Fernando Ortiz Fernández, *Cuban Counterpoint: Tobacco and Sugar* (New York, 1947), 52–53. For a detailed description of one large Nipe Bay sugar operation, see Wright, *Cuba*, 470–75.

8   Ramiro Guerra y Sánchez, *Sugar and Society in the Caribbean* (New Haven, Conn., 1964), 73–89; Hoernel, "Sugar and Social Change in Oriente," 235–38.

9   Perez, *Intervention, Revolution, and Politics in Cuba*, 72–98.

10   Wright, *Cuba*, 150; Thomas, *Cuba*, p. 500.

11   Guerra y Sánchez, *Historia de la nación cubana*, 9:303; Thomas, *Cuba*, 497; Allan R. Millett, *The Politics of Intervention* (Columbus, Ohio, 1968), 23; Wright, *Cuba*, 134–35; Hoernel, "Sugar and Social Change in Oriente," 232–34.

12   Hoernel, "Sugar and Social Change in Oriente," 234–35; Guerra y Sánchez, *Historia de la nación cubana*, 9:301; Ortiz Fernandez, *Cuban Counterpoint*, 53–54; Perez, *Intervention, Revolution, and Politics in Cuba*, 72, 98–99.

13   Thomas, *Cuba*, 601; Ortiz Fernandez, *Cuban Counterpoint*, 65.

14   Harry Franck, *Roaming through the West Indies* (New York, 1920), 28–40; Frank G. Carpenter, *Lands of the Caribbean* (New York, 1926), 172–77; Wright, *Cuba*, 150–62; Thomas, *Cuba*, 497–500.

15   Benjamin, *United States and Cuba*, 20.

16   Ibid., 20–21; Millett, *Politics of Intervention*, 27.

17   Thomas, *Cuba*, 514–24; "The Negro Uprising in Cuba," July 9, 1912, Confidential Series A.

18   Thomas, *Cuba*, 599; Benjamin, *United States and Cuba*, 21; Millett, *Politics of Intervention*, 22, 27; Perez, *Intervention, Revolution, and Politics in Cuba*, 6–7.

19   For an analysis of the "veterans' movement," see Stephen Leech to Foreign Office, January 2, January 17, and February 3, 1912, FO 277/179, nos. 2, 10, 21.

20   Perez, *Intervention, Revolution, and Politics in Cuba*, 6–7; Wright, *Cuba*, 166.
21   Millett, *Politics of Intervention*, 205–6, 262; David A. Lockmiller, *Magoon in Cuba: A history of the Second Intervention, 1906–1909* (Chapel Hill, N.C., 1938), 200–213; Wright, *Cuba*, 184–85; Guerra y Sánchez, *Historia de la nación cubana*, 8:36–37; Emilio Roig de Leuchsenring, *La Enmienda Platt: Su Interpretación primativa y sus aplicaciones posteriores hasta 1921* (Havana, 1922), 412–14; Enrique Barbarrosa, *El Proceso de la República: Analisis de la situación política y económica de Cuba bajo el gobierno presidencial de Tomás Estrada Palma y José Miguel Gómez* (Havana, 1911), 77–82, 129. See also Stephen Leech to Foreign Office, October 22, 1909, FO 277/158, no. 123.
22   For representative statements of the case against Magoon, see Herminio Portell-Vilá, *Historia de Cuba en sus relaciones con los Estados Unidos y España*, 4 vols. (Havana, 1938–41), 4:526, 536, 545–46 (the quotation is on p. 536); Guerra y Sánchez, *Historia de la nación cubana*, 8:36–37; Barbarrosa, *Proceso de la República*, 129; and Roig de Leuchsenring, *La Enmienda Platt*, 412–14. See also Thomas, *Cuba*, 504–7.
23   See especially Lockmiller, *Magoon in Cuba*, 200–213; Thomas, *Cuba*, 485.
24   Stephen Leech, "General Report on Cuba for 1909," January 26, 1910, FO 277/169, no. 17; Warren Kneer, *Great Britain and the Caribbean, 1901–1913* (East Lansing, Mich., 1975), 82–90; Portell-Vilá, *Historia de Cuba*, 4:381–92.
25   Squiers to Hay, May 26, 1904, quoted by Portell-Vilá, *Historia de Cuba*, 4:399–400.
26   Taft is quoted by Thomas, *Cuba*, 509–11; the Root statement is from Root to Wood, April 2, 1901, Elihu Root Papers, Library of Congress, Washington, D.C. See also Emilio Roig de Leuchsenring, *Analisis y consecuencias de la intervención norteamericano en los asuntos interiores de Cuba* (Havana, 1923), 13–14.
27   Bryan to Wilson, June 2, 1913, and Wilson to Bryan, June 4, 1913, William Jennings Bryan Papers, Library of Congress, Washington, D.C.
28   A. M. Beaupre to Secretary of State, May 24, 1912, "Negro Uprising in Cuba," Confidential Series A.
29   Consul Holaday (in Santiago de Cuba) to Secretary of State, June 6, 1912, ibid.
30   Knox to Beaupre, June 5, 1912, ibid.
31   Beaupre to Secretary of State, June 6, 1912, ibid.
32   Benjamin, *United States and Cuba*, 23–24.
33   Beaupre to Secretary of State, July 5, 1912, Records of the Department of State Relating to Political Relations between the United States and Cuba, 1910–1929, Record Group 59, National Archives, Washington, D.C., microfilm (cited hereafter as Decimal Files, Relations between the U.S. and Cuba), M509/1. See also Stephen Leech, "Annual Report on Cuba for 1912," April 17, 1913, FO 277/181, no. 79.
34   For an appraisal of Gonzales, see Stephen Leech to Foreign Office, June 30, 1913, FO 277/181, no. 146.
35   Gonzales to Secretary of State, July 30, 1918, Decimal Files, Relations between the U.S. and Cuba, M509/1.
36   Ibid.

CHAPTER 13. *Democracy, Constabularies, and Elections*

1   See Allan R. Millett, *The Politics of Intervention* (Columbus, Ohio, 1968), 7–14, 133–39; Richard D. Challener, *Admirals, Generals, and American Foreign Policy, 1898–1914* (Princeton, N.J., 1973), 12–23; Peter D. Karsten, *The Naval Aristocracy: The Golden Age of Modern Navalism* (New York, 1972), 6–7.

2   Carleton Beals, *Banana Gold* (Philadelphia, 1932), 294.

3   Ibid., 295–96.

4   U.S., Department of War, *Civil Report of General Leonard Wood, Military Governor of Cuba, for 1900* (Havana, 1901), 62–65; same for 1901 (Havana, 1901), p. 48; same for 1902 (Washington, D.C., 1902), 189. See also Louis A. Perez, Jr., "Supervision of a Protectorate: The United States and the Cuban Army, 1898–1908," *Hispanic American Historical Review* 52 (May 1972): 264; Millett, *Politics of Intervention*, 222; Allan R. Millett, "The Rise and Fall of the Cuban Rural Guard, 1898–1912," *Americas* 29 (Oct. 1972): 191–97.

5   Perez, "Supervision of a Protectorate," 260–65; Millett, *Politics of Intervention*, 222–23.

6   Perez, "Supervision of a Protectorate," 264–66; Millett, *Politics of Intervention*, 223–27.

7   Perez, "Supervision of a Protectorate," 267–71; Millett, *Politics of Intervention*, 228–39; Edwin Lieuwen, *Arms and Politics in Latin America* (New York, 1961), 178; Millett, "Rise and Fall of the Cuban Rural Guard," 198–204.

8   Millett, "Rise and Fall of the Cuban Rural Guard," 205–13.

9   Louis A. Perez, Jr., *Intervention, Revolution, and Politics in Cuba, 1913–1921* (Pittsburgh, Pa., 1978), 23–24, 27–29, 47, 57, 118.

10   David Healy, *Gunboat Diplomacy in the Wilson Era: The U.S. Navy in Haiti, 1915–1916* (Madison, Wis., 1976), 134.

11   James H. McCrocklin, *Garde d'Haïti, 1915–1934* (Annapolis, Md., 1956), 55–56.

12   McCrocklin, *Garde d'Haïti*, 61–68; Lowell Thomas, *Old Gimlet Eye: The Adventures of Smedley D. Butler as Told to Lowell Thomas* (New York, 1933), 209–210; Robert D. Heinl, Jr., *Soldiers of the Sea* (Annapolis, Md., 1962), 178–80; Hans Schmidt, *The United States Occupation of Haiti, 1915–1934* (New Brunswick, N.J., 1971), 86–91.

13   Testimony of Brigadier General Eli K. Cole, U.S. Marine Corps, U.S., Congress, Senate, Select Committee on Haiti and Santo Domingo, *Inquiry into the Occupation and Administration of Haiti and Santo Domingo: Hearings on S. R. 112*, 67th Cong., 1st and 2d sess., 1922, (cited hereafter as *Hearings on Haiti and Santo Domingo*), 687; Healy, *Gunboat Diplomacy in the Wilson Era*, 207–8, 210–12.

14   Schmidt, *United States Occupation of Haiti*, 90, 104–6; see *Hearings on Haiti and Santo Domingo*, 27–33, for alleged atrocities.

15   Schmidt, *United States Occupation of Haiti*, 100–104; Heinl, *Soldiers of the Sea*, 235–45. The estimate of Haitian dead is Schmidt's; he convincingly refutes the more widely used figure of 2,000.

16   Lieuwen, *Arms and Politics in Latin America*, 180–81.

17   Sumner Welles, *Naboth's Vineyard: The Dominican Republic, 1844–1924*, 2 vols.,

1928, reprint (New York, 1966); 2:748–66; Arthur S. Link, *Wilson: The Struggle for Neutrality, 1914–1915* (Princeton, N.J., 1960), 741–43; Bruce J. Calder, *The Impact of Intervention: The Dominican Republic during the United States Occupation of 1916–1924* (Austin, Tex., 1984), 54–55.

18 Calder, *Impact of Intervention*, 55–56; Marvin Goldwert, *The Constabulary in the Dominican Republic and Nicaragua* (Gainesville, Fla., 1962), 8–12.

19 Calder, *Impact of Intervention*, 57–58; Stephen M. Fuller and Graham A. Cosmas, *Marines in the Dominican Republic, 1916–1924* (Washington, D.C., 1974), 46–47.

20 Bruce J. Calder, "Caudillos and Gavilleros versus the United States: Guerrilla Insurgency during the Dominican Intervention, 1916–1924," *Hispanic American Historical Review* 58 (Nov. 1978): 649–60. For a detailed account of the campaigning, see Calder, *Impact of Intervention*, 115–82.

21 Calder, *Impact of Intervention*, 58–60; Goldwert, *Constabulary in the Dominican Republic and Nicaragua*, 12–14; Fuller and Cosmas, *Marines in the Dominican Republic*, 47–51.

22 Goldwert, *Constabulary in the Dominican Republic and Nicaragua*, 14–21; Calder, *Impact of Intervention*, 61–62.

23 Steve C. Ropp, *Panamanian Politics, from Guarded Nation to National Guard* (New York, 1982), 25–26. See also Lieuwen, *Arms and Politics in Latin America*, 183–84.

24 Lieuwen, *Arms and Politics in Latin America*, 185–86; Goldwert, *Constabulary in the Dominican Republic and Nicaragua*, 22–47; Neill Macauley, *The Sandino Affair* (Chicago, 1967), 135–37, 173–78.

25 See Theodore P. Wright, Jr., "Free Elections in the Latin American Policy of the United States," *Political Science Quarterly* 74 (Mar. 1959): 92–93.

26 Ibid., 97–103.

27 G. A. Mellander, *The United States in Panamanian Politics: the Intriguing Formative Years* (Danville, Ill., 1971), 129–31, 161; Ropp, *Panamanian Politics*, 17–18.

28 Roosevelt to Taft, May 11, 1908, and Roosevelt to Secretary of the Navy Truman H. Newberry, June 17, 1908, *Letters of Theodore Roosevelt*, 6:1028 and 1082; Mellander, *United States in Panamanian Politics*, 162–86.

29 H. Percival Dodge to Secretary of State, May 20, June 25, July 1, and July 20, 1912, Confidential Series A, no. 85, 5–7, 15–17, 24–27, and 33–38; William D. McCain, *The United States and the Republic of Panama* (Durham, N.C., 1937), 72–74.

30 McCain, *United States and the Republic of Panama*, 74; Mellander, *United States in Panamanian Politics*, 193–94. The charge of manipulation by the Liberals is Mellander's.

31 George W. Baker, "Woodrow Wilson's Use of the Non-Recognition Policy in Costa Rica," *Americas* 22 (July 1965): 3–21; Robert Lansing, *War Memoirs* (Indianapolis, Ind., 1935), 308–9.

32 Baker, "Woodrow Wilson's Use of the Non-Recognition Policy in Costa Rica," 11–15.

33 Ibid., 16–21.

34 Millett, *Politics of Intervention*, 199–201, 254–56; Whitney T. Perkins, *Constraint of Empire* (Westport, Conn., 1981), 18.

35 Ibid.

36 George W. Baker, "The Wilson Administration and Cuba, 1913–1921," *Mid-America* 46 (1964): 55–56; Perez, *Intervention, Revolution, and Politics in Cuba*, 11–26; Dana G. Munro, *Intervention and Dollar Diplomacy in the Caribbean, 1900–1921* (Princeton, N.J., 1964), 489–92.

37 Perez, *Intervention, Revolution, and Politics in Cuba*, 31, 46–47, 55–61; Baker, "Wilson Administration and Cuba," 27; Munro, *Intervention and Dollar Diplomacy in the Caribbean*, 492–97.

38 Baker, "Wilson Administration and Cuba," 60; Perez, *Intervention, Revolution, and Politics in Cuba*, 104–8; Munro, *Intervention and Dollar Diplomacy in the Caribbean*, 503–6.

39 Perez, *Intervention, Revolution, and Politics in Cuba*, 108–11.

40 Ibid., 113–15; Baker, "Wilson Administration and Cuba," 60; Munro, *Intervention and Dollar Diplomacy in the Caribbean*, 508–9.

41 Perez, *Intervention, Revolution, and Politics in Cuba*, 121–23; Munro, *Intervention and Dollar Diplomacy in the Caribbean*, 509–10.

42 Perez, *Intervention, Revolution, and Politics in Cuba*, 123–27; Baker, "Wilson Administration and Cuba," 61; Munro, *Intervention and Dollar Diplomacy in the Caribbean*, 511–18.

43 See Dana G. Munro, *The United States and the Caribbean Republics, 1921–1933* (Princeton, N.J., 1974), 12–15. Munro dates the major change in Caribbean policy as appearing in 1923; the author sees it as beginning earlier, late in the Wilson administration.

44 Joseph O. Baylen, "American Intervention in Nicaragua, 1909–1933: An Appraisal of Objectives and Results," *Southwestern Social Science Quarterly* 35 (Sept. 1954): 133; Dana G. Munro, *The Five Republics of Central America* (New York, 1918), 245.

45 Munro, *Five Republics of Central America*, 249–52; Munro, *Intervention and Dollar Diplomacy in the Caribbean*, 406–8.

46 Munro, *Intervention and Dollar Diplomacy in the Caribbean*, 406–13; Jefferson to Secretary of State, July 18 and September 6, 1916, in Records of the Department of State Relating to the Internal Affairs of Nicaragua, 1910–1929, Record Group 59, National Archives, Washington, D.C., (cited hereafter as Decimal Files, Internal, Nicaragua).

47 J. B. Wright to Jordan Stabler, August 12, 1916, and Jefferson to Secretary of State, September 15, 1916, Decimal Files, Internal, Nicaragua.

48 Jefferson to Secretary of State, September 17 and September 21, 1916, ibid.; Munro, *Intervention and Dollar Diplomacy in the Caribbean*, 411.

49 Jefferson to Secretary of State, September 26, 1916, Decimal Files, Internal, Nicaragua; Enoc Aguardo, Secretary of the Executive Committee of the Liberal party of Nicaragua, to Woodrow Wilson, October 21, 1916, ibid.; New York *Herald*, November 2, 1916; William B. Caperton, "History of U.S. Naval Operations under Command of Rear Admiral W. B. Caperton, Commencing January 5, 1915,

Ending April 30, 1919," Naval Records Collection, Office of Naval Records and Library, Record Group 45, National Archives, Washington, D.C., 284–86. For Caperton's full account of the 1916 Nicaraguan election, see ibid., 277–87.

CHAPTER 14. *Agents of Hegemony*

1 William Barnes and John Heath Morgan, *The Foreign Service of the United States* (Washington, D.C., 1961), 157–58; Richard Hume Werking, *The Master Architects: Building the United States Foreign Service, 1890–1913* (Lexington, Ky., 1977), 163.

2 Willard L. Beaulac, *Career Ambassador* (New York, 1951), 45.

3 Barnes and Morgan, *Foreign Service of the United States*, 159; Werking, *Master Architects*, 15–17.

4 See relevant biographies in *The Dictionary of American Biography* and *The National Cyclopaedia of American Biography*.

5 Barnes and Morgan, *Foreign Service of the United States*, 155–56, 160, 193–94; Rachel West, *The Department of State on the Eve of the First World War* (Athens, Ga., 1978), 4.

6 Compiled from Richardson Dougall and Mary Patricia Chapman, *United States Chiefs of Mission, 1778–1973* (Washington, D.C., 1973).

7 Barnes and Morgan, *Foreign Service of the United States*, 132–46, 162–73; Werking, *Master Architects*, 13–15; Robert D. Schulzinger, *The Making of the Diplomatic Mind: The Training, Outlook, and Style of United States Foreign Service Officers, 1908–1931* (Middletown, Conn., 1975), 5, 15–16.

8 H. E. Mattox, "Research Note on America's Senior Representatives Abroad at the Turn of the Century," *Newsletter of the Society for the Historians of American Foreign Relations* 14 (Dec. 1983): 1–8.

9 Bryan to Wilson, May 19, 1915, *Papers of Woodrow Wilson*, 33:219.

10 Bryan to Wilson, June 22, 1914, William Jennings Bryan Papers, Library of Congress, Washington, D.C.; Arthur S. Link, *Wilson: The New Freedom* (Princeton, N.J., 1956), p. 106.

11 See FO 420/258, no. 116, May 9, 1914; FO 420/257, no. 78, March 27, 1913; and FO 420/254, no. 21, January 28, 1911.

12 See FO 420/252, no. 29, April 6, 1910; and FO 420/257, no. 46, January 14, 1913.

13 Norval Richardson, *My Diplomatic Education* (New York, 1929), 35–36, 51.

14 Ibid., 53, 60–62.

15 Ibid., 6–7, 24–25.

16 Werking, *Master Architects*, 30–35, 93–98.

17 Ibid., 99–106, 246–48.

18 Link, *Wilson: The New Freedom*, 107–8.

19 See Walker W. Vick to Bryan, April 14, 1914, William Jennings Bryan Papers.

20 Link, *Wilson: The New Freedom*, 109–10.

21 Glenn J. Kist, "The Role of Thomas C. Dawson in United States–Latin American

Diplomatic Relations: 1897–1912" (Ph.D. dissertation, Loyola University, Chicago, 1971), 1–17.

22   Ibid., 30–55.

23   Ibid., 56–58, 295–97.

24   Ibid., 304–38, 343–45, 384, 411–32, 441–42.

25   Allan R. Millett, *The Politics of Intervention* (Columbus, Ohio, 1968), 148–50.

26   David Healy, *U S Expansionism: The Imperialist Urge in the 1890s* (Madison, Wis., 1970), 194–95, 206–9; *New York Times*, July 7, 1915.

27   Harold F. Peterson, *Diplomat of the Americas: A Biography of William I. Buchanan* (Albany, N.Y., 1977), 1–237, 262–75.

28   Ibid., 188–257.

29   Ibid., 278–345, 231.

30   See Earl S. Pomeroy, "The American Colonial Office," *Mississippi Valley Historical Review* 30 (1944): 521–32.

31   See "The Safety of the Panama Canal," *The Military Engineer* (July–August 1939), 252; William D. McCain, *The United States and the Republic of Panama* (Durham, N.C., 1937), 144–52, 162.

32   Millett, *Politics of Intervention*, 121–51, 264.

33   David A. Lockmiller, *Enoch H. Crowder: Soldier, Lawyer and Statesman* (Columbia, Mo., 1955), especially 109–20, 218–23, 228–29. See also Millett, *Politics of Intervention*, 151, 197–201; Louis A. Perez, Jr., *Intervention, Revolution, and Politics in Cuba, 1913–1921* (Pittsburgh, Pa., 1978), 107–21.

34   Lockmiller, *Enoch H. Crowder*, 229–41.

35   Ibid., 233–42; Whitney T. Perkins, *Constraint of Empire* (Westport, Conn., 1981), 85–90.

36   See U.S., Department of the Navy, "Report of the Commandant of the United States Marine Corps," *Annual Reports of the Navy Department, 1907–1920*; Robert D. Heinl, Jr., *Soldiers of the Sea: The United States Marine Corps, 1775–1962* (Annapolis, Md., 1962), 146, 159–60; John A. Lejeune, *The Reminiscences of a Marine* (Philadelphia, 1930), 146–48.

37   *Who Was Who*, 1:1293; Joseph L. Schott, *The Ordeal of Samar* (Indianapolis, Ind., 1964), 68–69, 71–76, 139–45. For Waller's service in Haiti, see David Healy, *Gunboat Diplomacy in the Wilson Era: The U.S. Navy in Haiti, 1915–1916* (Madison, Wis., 1976).

38   See *Dictionary of American Biography*, 22:80–82. For a colorful but unreliable memoir, see Lowell Thomas, *"Old Gimlet Eye": The Adventures of Smedley D. Butler as told to Lowell Thomas* (New York, 1933). For Butler in Haiti, see Healy, *Gunboat Diplomacy in the Wilson Era*.

39   Richard D. Challener, *Admirals, Generals, and American Foreign Policy, 1898–1914* (Princeton, N.J., 1973), 63–65; Richard W. Turk, "Strategy and Foreign Policy: The U.S. Navy in the Caribbean, 1865–1913" (Ph.D. dissertation, Fletcher School of Law and Diplomacy, 1968), 199–202.

40   See Peter D. Karsten, *The Naval Aristocracy: The Golden Years of Modern American Navalism* (New York, 1972).

41   Challener, *Admirals, Generals, and American Foreign Policy*, 170–71.

42   Healy, *Gunboat Diplomacy in the Wilson Era*, 23, 37, 47–48, 51.

43   W. F. Powell to Secretary of State, April 29, 1904, U.S. Department of State, Dispatches from United States Ministers to the Dominican Republic, Record Group 59, National Archives, Washington, D.C., microfilm, M93/11.

44   Thomas C. Dawson to Secretary of State, August 9, 1904, ibid.

45   Dawson to Secretary of State, January 23, 1905, ibid.; Sumner Welles, *Naboth's Vineyard: The Dominican Republic, 1844–1924*, 2 vols., 1928, reprint (New York, 1966), 2:623–26.

46   Challener, *Admirals, Generals, and American Foreign Policy*, 152–53; Turk, "Strategy and Foreign Policy," 100–101. The quotation is from Challener, p. 153.

47   Challener, *Admirals, Generals, and American Foreign Policy*, especially 12–25, 401–12.

48   Hermann B. Deutsch, *The Incredible Yanqui: The Career of Lee Christmas* (London, 1931), 6–23. This work is the only full and reliable study of Christmas' career.

49   Ibid., 24–43.

50   Ibid., 47–80; Thomas L. Karnes, *Tropical Enterprise, the Standard Fruit and Steamship Company in Latin America* (Baton Rouge, La., 1978), 38–39.

51   Deutsch, *Incredible Yanqui*, 80–101.

52   Charles D. Kepner and Jay H. Soothill, *The Banana Empire: A Case Study of Economic Imperialism* (New York, 1935), 100–105; Stacy May and Galo Plaza, *The United Fruit Company in Latin America* (n.p., 1958), 15–16; Karnes, *Tropical Enterprise*, 42.

53   Walter V. Scholes and Marie V. Scholes, *The Foreign Policies of the Taft Administration* (Columbia, Mo., 1970), 68–72; Deutsch, *Incredible Yanqui*, 103–7; Karnes, *Tropical Enterprise*, 43–44.

54   Deutsch, *Incredible Yanqui*, 110–25; Karnes, *Tropical Enterprise*, 44; Charles Brand, "The Background of Capitalistic Underdevelopment: Honduras to 1913," (Ph.D. dissertation, University of Pittsburgh, 1972), 177–78.

55   Deutsch, *Incredible Yanqui*, 135–86; Karnes, *Tropical Enterprise*, 44–45; Brand, "Background of Capitalistic Underdevelopment," 178–81. Brand asserts that the United Fruit Company also backed Bonilla's 1911 revolution.

56   Deutsch, *Incredible Yanqui*, 184–205.

57   May and Plaza, *United Fruit Company in Latin America*, pp. 16–17; Karnes, *Tropical Enterprise*, 60.

58   May and Plaza, *United Fruit Company in Latin America*, 2, 17 (the quotation is from p. 2); Kepner and Soothill, *Banana Empire*, 130–31, 152.

CHAPTER 15. *Economic Consequences of Hegemony*

1   Robert W. Dunn, *American Foreign Investments* (New York, 1926), 3, 89–139; Mira Wilkins, *The Emergence of Multinational Enterprise: American Business Abroad from the Colonial Era to 1914* (Cambridge, Mass., 1970), 110, 113, 149–71; Robert Gilpin, *U.S. Power and the Multinational Corporation* (New York,

1975), 10; Burton I. Kaufman, *Efficiency and Expansion: Foreign Trade Organization in the Wilson Administration, 1913–1921* (Westport, Conn., 1974), 6–7.

2   Chester Lloyd Jones, *The Caribbean Interests of the United States* (New York, 1916), 274; Oscar P. Austin, *Trading with Our Neighbors in the Caribbean* (National City Bank of New York, Foreign Commerce Series, no. 1, 1920), especially pp. 56–57.

3   Luis Eduardo Laso, *Evolución de los sistemes monetarios y bancos centrales de América Latina* (Guayaquil, Ecuador, 1972), 37, 52, 56, 58, 68, 70; J. Lawrence Laughlin, *Money and Prices* (New York, 1919), 223–24; Henry C. Wallich, *Monetary Problems of an Export Economy: The Cuban Experience, 1914–1947* (Cambridge, Mass., 1960), 32–33; Harold P. Davis, *Black Democracy: The Story of Haiti*, 2d rev. ed. (New York, 1936), 305; Carl P. Parrini and Martin J. Sklar, "New Thinking about the Market, 1896–1904: Some American Economists on Investment and the Theory of Surplus Capital," *Journal of Economic History* 43 (Sept. 1983): 571–72.

4   See Kaufman, *Efficiency and Expansion*, 8–15.

5   Inspection report of R. M. Bartleman, Cienfuegos, Cuba, April 30, 1907; inspection report of Charles C. Eberhardt, Cienfuegos, February 17–22, 1912; report of same, Cienfuegos, June 25–29, 1918; all in U.S., Department of State, Consular Inspection Reports, 1906–39, Record Group 59, National Archives, Washington, D.C., (cited hereafter as Consular Inspection Reports).

6   Inspection report of Albert A. Morawetz, Port Limon, Costa Rica, January 18, 1908; inspection report of Charles C. Eberhardt, Port Limon, August 18–20, 1910; report of same, Port Limon, September 19–23, 1915; all ibid.

7   Inspection report of R. M. Bartleman, Havana, Cuba, April 12, 1907; inspection report of Charles C. Eberhardt, Havana, February 28–March 8, 1912; report of same, Havana, December 18–23, 1914; inspection report of R. M. Bartleman, Santiago de Cuba, April 24, 1907; inspection report of Charles C. Eberhardt, Santiago, January 19–23, 1912; reports of same, Santiago, February 8–12, 1915; June 12–17, 1916; and June 3–7, 1918; all ibid.

8   Inspection report of Albert R. Morawetz, Bluefields, Nicaragua, January 4, 1908; inspection report of Charles C. Eberhardt, Bluefields, August 7–10, 1910; reports of same, Bluefields, April 28–May 2, 1913; and October 29–November 3, 1915; all ibid. It should be noted that most of the native population of Bluefields was English speaking, while few spoke Spanish.

9   Willard Beaulac, *Career Ambassador* (New York, 1951), 40–52 (the quotation is from 51–52).

10 Charles A. Brand, "The Background of Capitalistic Underdevelopment: Honduras to 1913" (Ph.D. dissertation, University of Pittsburgh, 1972), 129–30, 151–54.

11 Ibid., 52, 123, 135, 184–87.

12 See Carleton Beals, *Banana Gold* (Philadelphia, 1932), 120–21; Charles D. Kepner and Jay H. Soothill, *The Banana Empire: A Case Study in Economic Imperialism* (New York, 1935), 40–41; 156–58; 213, 223–33, 341; and Brand, "Background of Capitalistic Underdevelopment," 127, 134, 156, 165, 184.

13 Victor S. Clark et al., *Porto Rico and Its Problems* (Washington, D.C., 1930),

xvii–xix (quotations are from p. xix); Edward J. Berbusse, *The United States in Puerto Rico, 1898–1900* (Chapel Hill, N.C., 1966), 41, 103–5, 127–28; Gordon K. Lewis, *Puerto Rico: Freedom and Power in the Caribbean* (New York, 1963), 55–59.

14 Lewis, *Puerto Rico*, 88–89; Clark, *Porto Rico and Its Problems*, xxii; Bailey W. Diffie and Justine W. Diffie, *Porto Rico, A Broken Pledge* (New York, 1931), 52; Harry A. Franck, *Roaming through the West Indies* (New York, 1920), 278.

15 Franck, *Roaming through the West Indies*, 267, 269, 274–82, 297.

16 Clark, *Porto Rico and Its Problems*, xix–xxi, 73–77, 420.

17 Diffie and Diffie, *Porto Rico, A Broken Pledge*, especially pp. 62–65 and 86–88.

18 Theodore Roosevelt, annual message to Congress, December 6, 1904, in the work of James D. Richardson, *A Compilation of the Messages and Papers of the Presidents*, 14 vols. (Washington, D.C., 1905), 14:6923ff; Gilpin, *U.S. Power and the Multinational Corporation*, 26–27, 32–33.

19 Gilpin, *U.S. Power and the Multinational Corporation*, 34–35. For a discussion from a somewhat different perspective, see Kenneth E. Boulding on "threat" and "exchange" systems in *Ecodynamics, A New Theory of Societal Evolution* (Beverly Hills, Calif., 1978), chapters 7 and 8, 141–88.

20 See F. Cardoso and E. Faletto, *Dependencia y desarrollo en América Latina* (Mexico City, 1970); Immanuel Wallerstein, *The Modern World System: Capitalist Agriculture and the Origins of a European World Economy in the 16th Century* (New York, 1974); Theotonio Dos Santos, "The Crisis of Development Theory and the Problem of Dependence in Latin America," in *Underdevelopment and Development* edited by H. Bernstein (Harmandsworth, England, 1973); Andre Gunder Frank, *Capitalism and Underdevelopment in Latin America* (New York, 1967).

21 See Gilpin, *U.S. Power and the Multinational Corporation*, 48; Philip J. O'Brien, "A Critique of Latin American theories of dependency," in *Beyond the Sociology of Development: Economy and Society in Latin America and Africa*, edited by Ivar Oxaal, Tony Barnett, and David Booth (London, 1975), 15–16.

22 Theotonio Dos Santos, "The Structure of Dependence," *American Economic Review* 60 (May 1970): 231.

23 Stacy May and Galo Plaza, *The United Fruit Company in Latin America* (n.p., 1958), 112–13; D. C. M. Platt, ed., *Business Imperialism, 1840–1930: An Enquiry Based on British Experience in Latin America* (Oxford, England, 1977), 12 (see also D. K. Fieldhouse, *Unilever Overseas: The Anatomy of a Multinational, 1895–1965* (London, 1978), 577–97); Bill Warren, *Imperialism: Pioneer of Capitalism* (London, 1980), 175; David Ray, "The Dependency Model of Latin American Underdevelopment: Three Basic Fallacies," *Journal of Inter American Studies and World Affairs* 15 (Feb. 1973): 11–12. For the role of exports see also Douglass C. North, "Location Theory and Regional Economic Growth," *Journal of Political Economy* 43 (June 1955): 243–58.

24 Warren, *Imperialism*, 119–20; E. Bradford Burns, *The Poverty of Progress* (Berkeley, Calif., 1980); Ray, "Dependency Model of Latin American Underdevelopment," 14–17.

25 Gilpin, *U.S. Power and the Multinational Corporation*, 51–57.

26   Warren, *Imperialism*, especially 7–10; Platt, *Business Imperialism*, 2.
27   Carlos Alberto Montaner, "The Roots of Anti-Americanism in Cuba," *Caribbean Review* 13 (spring 1984): 13–16, 42–46. See also Montaner, *200 Years of Gringos* (Lanham, Md., 1983), especially p. 50.
28   See Tony Smith, *The Patterns of Imperialism: The United States, Great Britain, and the Late-Industrializing World* (Cambridge, England, 1981), 50–74; Carlos Rangel, *The Latin Americans: Their Love-Hate Relationship with the United States* (New York and London, 1977), 182–205.
29   D. C. M. Platt, "Dependency in Nineteenth-Century Latin America: An Historian Objects," *Latin American Research Review* 15 (1980): 122–23.

CHAPTER 16. *Hegemony and Nationalism*

1   This is not to imply the lack of a vital and active nationalism in the Caribbean nation-states. For a pioneering analysis of that nationalism, see Gordon K. Lewis, *Main Currents in Caribbean Thought* (Baltimore, Md., 1983), especially pp. 239–307.
2   For an interesting discussion on this point see Raúl de Cárdenas y Echarte, *La Política de los Estados Unidos en el Continento Americano* (Havana, 1921), 176, and the extract from F. García Calderón in the work of Alejandro Alvarez, ed., *The Monroe Doctrine* (New York, 1924), 258–59. García Calderón, on balance, finds the United States more dangerous than Germany, while Cárdenas y Echarte reaches the opposite conclusion. (García Calderón was a Peruvian diplomat.)
3   See Ramiro Guerra y Sánchez, *La Expansión territorial de los Estados Unidos* (Havana, 1935), 12–19.
4   Both quotations are from Patrick Bellegarde-Smith, *In the Shadow of Power* (Atlantic Highlands, N.J., 1985), 23, 125.
5   Leopoldo Zea, *The Latin-American Mind* (Norman, Okla., 1963), 77–84; Edward Dennis Hernández, "Modernization and Dependency in Costa Rica during the decade of the 1880's" (Ph.D. dissertation, University of California at Los Angeles, 1975), 45–60; H. Paul Muto, Jr., "The Illusory Promise: The Dominican Republic and the Process of Economic Development, 1900–1930" (Ph.D. dissertation, University of Washington, 1976), 115–32.
6   Elliot Northcott to Secretary of State, Bogotá, August 25, 1910, Confidential Series A, no. 62, "Relations between the U.S. and Colombia," October 7, 1910, Record Group 59, National Archives, Washington, D.C.
7   Hernández, "Modernization and Dependency in Costa Rica," 34–36, 174–75, 189, 194, 202.
8   See Harry Hoetinck, "The Dominican Republic in the Nineteenth Century: Some Notes on Stratification, Immigration, and Race," in *Race and Class in Latin America* edited by Magnus Morner (New York and London, 1970), 106–8, 110–12; Wilfredo Lozano, *La Dominación imperialista en la República Dominica, 1900–1930* (Santo Domingo, 1976), 100–112.
9   See Troy S. Floyd, *The Anglo-Spanish Struggle for Mosquitia* (Albuquerque, N.M., 1967), 1–22, 62–69, 163–89; Ralph Lee Woodward, *Central America,*

a Nation Divided (New York, 1967), 51–59; Lester D. Langley, *Struggle for the American Mediterranean: United States–European Rivalry, 1776–1904* (Athens, Ga., 1976), 83–92; Mary W. Williams, *Anglo-American Isthmian Diplomacy, 1815–1915* (Washington, D.C., 1916), 38–49, 52–110, 264–69.

10 Williams, *Anglo-American Isthmian Diplomacy*, 264–69, 288–89; Langley, *Struggle for the American Mediterranean*, 90–101.

11 Pedro J. Cuadra Chamorro, *La Reincorporación de la Mosquitia* (León, Nicaragua, 1964), 7–159.

12 Cuadra Chamorro, *La Reincorporación de la Mosquitia*, 36–47, 59, 67–69, 99, 157–59.

13 Ibid., 49, 83–85, 92; Emilio Alvarez Lejarza, Andrés Vega Bolaños, and Gustavo Alemán Bolaños, *Como reincorporó Nicaragua su costa oriental* (Managua, 1944), p. 17.

14 Cuadra Chamorro, *La Reincorporación de la Mosquitia*, 64–66, 74–77; Rising Lake Morrow, "A Conflict between the Commercial Interests of the United States and Its Foreign Policy," *Hispanic American Historical Review* 10 (1930): 2–13.

15 David Healy, "A Hinterland in Search of a Metropolis: The Mosquito Coast, 1894–1910," *International History Review* 3 (Jan. 1981): 30–31, 34–43.

16 Máximo Soto Hall, *Nicaragua y el imperialismo norteamericano* (Buenos Aires, 1928), 7–10, 28, 55; Rafael de Nogales, *The Looting of Nicaragua* (New York, 1928), 41.

17 H. Pauléus Sannon, Sténio Vincent, and Perceval Thoby, "Memoir on the Political, Economic, and Financial Conditions Existing in the Republic of Haiti under the American Occupation by the Delegates to the United States of the Union Patriotique d'Haïti," printed in U.S. Congress, Senate, Select Committee on Haiti and Santo Domingo, 67th Cong., 1st and 2d sess., *Hearings on S.R. 112*, 2 vols., 1922, 1:5–33.

18 La Academia Colombina, *Memorial de protesta contra la arbitraria ocupación militar de la República Dominica por tropas de los Estados Unidos de Norte América*, pamphlet (Santo Domingo, 1916); J. Rafael Bordas, *Frente al imperialismo*, pamphlet (Santo Domingo, 1923); Fabio Fiallo, *The Crime of Wilson in Santo Domingo* (Havana, 1940), especially 36–41.

19 Soto Hall, *Nicaragua y el imperialismo norteamericano*, 38–39, 55–57, 97–100; Nogales, *Looting of Nicaragua*, 7, 13–15, 21–32; Policarpo Bonilla, "The Monroe Doctrine," in the work of Alvarez, *Monroe Doctrine*, p. 243; Sannon et al., "Memoir . . . of the Union Patriotique d'Haïti," pp. 1:5–7, 19–20, 21–23; Dantes Bellegarde, *La Résistance Haïtienne* (Montreal, Canada, 1937), 73–84; Hogar Nicolas, *L'Occupation américaine d'Haïti: La Revanche de l'histoire* (Madrid, 1956), 137–89.

20 Guerra y Sánchez, *La Expansión territorial de los Estados Unidos*, 12–19; Emilio Roig de Leuchsenring, *Analisis y consecuencias de la intervención norteamericano en los asuntos interiores de Cuba*, pamphlet (Havana, 1923), 10–15; Herminio Portell-Vilá, *Historia de Cuba en sus relaciones con los Estados Unidos y España*, 4 vols. (Havana, 1938–41), especially 1:13–14, 2:8–10, 4:393. See also Manuel Márquez Sterling, *Proceso historico de la Enmienda Platt* (Havana, 1941); Francisco Carabello y Sotolongo, *El Imperialismo norte-americano* (Havana, 1914).

21 Portell-Vilá, *Historia de Cuba en sus relaciones con los Estados Unidos y España*, 1:11–12; Cárdenas y Echarte, *La Política de los Estados Unidos en el Continento Americano*, 197, 274, 281–83.

22 Emilio Roig de Leuchsenring, *La Enmienda Platt: Su interpretación primativa y sus aplicaciones posteriores hasta 1921* (Havana, 1922), 324–32; Emilio Roig de Leuchsenring, *Cuba no debe su independencia a los Estados Unidos* (Havana, 1950), 6; Emilio Roig de Leuchsenring, *Cuba y Los Estados Unidos, 1805–1898: Historia documentada de la actitud disimil de estada y del pueblo norteamericano en relación con la independencia de Cuba* (Havana, 1949), especially pp. 227, 257, 260; Cárdenas y Echarte, *La Política de los Estados Unidos en el Continento Americano*, 280; Márquez Sterling, *Proceso historico de la Enmienda Platt*, 341–47; Carabello y Sotolongo, *El Imperialismo norte-americano*, 117–20; Portell-Vilá, *Historia de Cuba en sus relaciones con los Estados Unidos y España*, 1:16. Gordon K. Lewis, *Main Currents in Caribbean Thought*, 297–99, comments on José Martí's deep ambivalence about the United States.

Bibliography

———••◦✦◦••———

GOVERNMENT DOCUMENTS

Great Britain. *Foreign Office Records*. Public Record Office, Kew: FO 15, General
   Correspondence, Central America; FO 108, General Correspondence, Cuba; FO
   277, Embassy and Consular Correspondence, Cuba; FO 420, America, South and
   Central.
Richard, James D. *A Compilation of the Messages and Papers of the Presidents*. 14
   vols. Washington, D.C., 1896–1909.
U.S. Congress. *Congressional Record*, 1895–1905.
U.S. Congress, House, Committee on Ways and Means. *Reciprocity with Cuba: Hear-*
   ings. 57th Cong., 1st sess., 1902.
U.S. Congress, Senate. *Diplomatic History of the Panama Canal: Senate Doc. 474*. 63d
   Cong., 2d sess., 1916.
U.S. Congress, Select Committee on Haiti and Santo Domingo. *Inquiry into the Occu-*
   pation and Administration of Haiti and Santo Domingo: Hearings on S.R. 112.
   67th Cong., 1st and 2d sess. 2 vols. 1922.
U.S. Department of the Navy. *Annual Reports of the Navy Department, 1907–1920*.
   1908–1921.
U.S. Department of State. *Foreign Relations of the United States*.
———. General Records of the Department of State. Record Group 59, National
   Archives, Washington, D.C.
Correspondence of Secretary of State Bryan with President Wilson. 1913–1915.
Diplomatic Instructions, Central America. 1801–1906.
Diplomatic Instructions, Santo Domingo. 1801–1906.
Dispatches from United States Ministers to Central America. 1824–1906.
Dispatches from United States Ministers to the Dominican Republic. 1883–1906.
Division of Information. Confidential Series A: Latin America.
Division of Information. Confidential Series M: Miscellaneous.
Division of Latin American Affairs. Files for 1904–1944.
Inspection Reports on Foreign Service Posts. 1906–1939.
Records Relating to Internal Affairs of the Dominican Republic. 1910–29.

Records Relating to Internal Affairs of Nicaragua. 1910–29.
Records Relating to Political Relations between the United States and Central America. 1911–29.
Records Relating to Political Relations between the United States and Cuba. 1910–29.
U.S. Department of War. *Annual Reports of the Secretary of War, 1899–1903.* 1904.
———. *Civil Report of General Leonard Wood, Military Governor of Cuba.* 3 vols. 1900–1902.
U.S. Tariff Commission. The Effects of the Cuban Reciprocity Treaty of 1902. 1929.

PERSONAL PAPERS (ALL IN MANUSCRIPT DIVISION, LIBRARY OF CONGRESS, WASHINGTON, D.C.)

Chandler P. Anderson Papers.
William Jennings Bryan Papers.
William B. Caperton Papers.
John Hay Papers.
Philander C. Knox Papers.
Robert Lansing Papers.
William Gibbs McAdoo Papers.
William McKinley Papers.
Whitelaw Reid Papers.
Theodore Roosevelt Papers.
Elihu Root Papers.
Leonard Wood Papers.

GENERAL BACKGROUND

Beisner, Robert L. *From the Old Diplomacy to the New, 1865–1900.* Arlington Heights, Ill., 1975.
Benians, E. A., James Butler, and C. E. Carrington, eds. *The Cambridge History of the British Empire.* Vol. 3 (of 8 vols). Cambridge, 1959.
Borchard, Edwin M. *The Diplomatic Protection of Citizens Abroad; or, The Law of International Claims.* New York, 1916.
Campbell, A. E. *Great Britain and the United States, 1895–1903.* London, 1960.
Combs, Jerald A. *American Diplomatic History: Two Centuries of Changing Interpretations.* Berkeley, Calif., 1983.
Conrad, Joseph. *Nostromo, A Tale of the Seaboard.* London, 1904.
Cumberland, Charles C. *The Mexican Revolution: Genesis under Madero.* Austin, Tex., 1952.
Curtin, Philip D. *The Image of Africa: British Ideas and Action, 1780–1850.* Madison, Wis., 1964.
Davis, Cushman K. *A Treatise on International Law Including American Diplomacy.* St. Paul, Minn., 1901.
De Conde, Alexander. *A History of American Foreign Policy.* 2 vols. New York, 1978.

Dennis, Alfred L. P. *Adventures in American Diplomacy, 1896–1906*. New York, 1928.
Gelber, Lionel M. *The Rise of Anglo-American Friendship*. London and New York, 1938.
Graham, Richard. *Britain and the Onset of Modernization in Brazil, 1850–1914*. Cambridge, 1968.
Halstead, Murat, ed. *Pictorial History of America's New Possessions*. Chicago, 1899.
Healy, David. *U S Expansionism: The Imperialist Urge in the 1890s*. Madison, Wis., 1970.
Hofstadter, Richard. "Manifest Destiny and the Philippines." In *America in Crisis*, edited by Daniel Aaron. New York, 1952.
Johnson, John J. *Latin America in Caricature*. Austin, Tex., 1980.
Kidd, Benjamin. *The Control of the Tropics*. New York and London, 1898.
LaFeber, Walter. *The New Empire: An Interpretation of American Expansion, 1860–1898*. Ithaca, N.Y., 1963.
Langer, William L. *The Diplomacy of Imperialism*. New York, 1935.
Lieuwen, Edwin. *Arms and Politics in Latin America*. New York, 1961.
May, Ernest R. *Imperial Democracy: The Emergence of America as a Great Power*. New York, 1961.
McCormick, Thomas J. *China Market: America's Quest for Informal Empire, 1893–1901*. Chicago, 1967.
Meyer, Michael C. *Huerta: A Political Portrait*. Lincoln, Nebr., 1972.
Porter, Kirk H., and Donald B. Johnson, eds. *National Party Platforms, 1840–1964*. Urbana, Ill., 1966.
Pratt, Julius W. *America's Colonial Experiment*. New York, 1950.
Quirk, Robert E. *The Mexican Revolution, 1914–1915: The Convention of Aguascalientes*. Bloomington, Ind., 1960.
Rangel, Carlos. *The Latin Americans: Their Love-Hate Relationship with the United States*. New York and London, 1977.
Reuter, Frank T. *Catholic Influence on America's Colonial Policies, 1898–1904*. Austin, Tex., 1967.
Scott, James Brown. *The Hague Peace Conferences of 1899 and 1907*. 2 vols. Baltimore, Md., 1909.
Smith, Robert F. *The United States and Revolutionary Nationalism in Mexico, 1916–1932*. Chicago, 1972.
Williams, William Appleman. *The Roots of Modern American Empire*. New York, 1969.
———. *The Tragedy of American Diplomacy*. New York, 1972.

THE MONROE DOCTRINE AND UNITED STATES LATIN AMERICAN POLICY

Alvarez, Alejandro, ed. *The Monroe Doctrine*. New York, 1924.
Bemis, Samuel Flagg. *The Latin-American Policy of the United States*. 1943. Reprint. New York, 1967.
Blake, Nelson. "Background of Cleveland's Venezuelan Policy." *American Historical Review* 47 (1942): 259–77.

Blassingame, John W. "The Press and American Intervention in Haiti and the Dominican Republic, 1904–1920." *Caribbean Studies* 9 (July 1969): 27–43.

Caraballo y Sotolongo, Francisco. *El Imperialismo norte-americano.* Havana, 1914.

Cárdenas y Echarte, Raúl de. *La Política de los Estados Unidos en el Continento Americano.* Havana, 1921.

Cox, Isaac Joslin. " 'Yankee Imperialism' and Spanish American Solidarity: A Colombian Interpretation." *Hispanic American Historical Review* 4 (May 1921): 256–65.

Crichfield, George W. *American Supremacy: The Rise and Progress of the Latin American Republics and Their Relations to the United States under the Monroe Doctrine.* 2 vols. New York, 1908.

Davis, Norman H. "Wanted: A Consistent Latin American Policy." *Foreign Affairs* 9 (July 1931): 547–69.

Gibbs, William E. "James Weldon Johnson: A Black Perspective on 'Big Stick' Diplomacy." *Diplomatic History* 8 (fall 1984): 329–47.

Greib, Kenneth. *The United States and Huerta.* Lincoln, Nebr., 1969.

Guerra y Sánchez, Ramiro. *La Expansión territorial de los Estados Unidos.* Havana, 1935.

Holbo, Paul S. "The Convergence of Moods and the Cuban-Bond 'Conspiracy' of 1898." *Journal of American History* 55 (1968): 54–72.

Howland, Charles P. *American Relations in the Caribbean.* New Haven, Conn., 1929.

Jones, Chester Lloyd. *Caribbean Interests of the United States.* New York, 1916.

Karnes, Thomas L. "Hiram Bingham and His Obsolete Shibboleth." *Diplomatic History* 3 (winter 1979): 39–57.

Kneer, Warren G. *Great Britain and the Caribbean, 1901–1913: A Study in Anglo-American Relations.* East Lansing, Mich., 1975.

Lodge, Henry Cabot. "England, Venezuela, and the Monroe Doctrine." *North American Review* 160 (June 1895): 651–58.

———. "Our Blundering Foreign Policy." *Forum* 19 (March 1895): 8–17.

Perkins, Dexter. *A History of the Monroe Doctrine.* Boston, 1941.

Ribas, Mario. "A Central American Indictment of the United States." *Current History* 26 (Sept. 1927): 919–24.

Root, Elihu. "The Real Monroe Doctrine." *North American Review* (June 1914): 841–56.

Tulchin, Joseph S. *The Aftermath of War: World War I and United States Policy toward Latin America.* New York, 1971.

Whitaker, Arthur P. *The Western Hemisphere Idea: Its Rise and Decline.* Ithaca, N.Y., 1954.

Woolsey, Theodore S. "An American Concert of Powers." *Scribner's* 45 (March 1909): 364–68.

Wright, Theodore P., Jr. "Free Elections in the Latin American Policy of the United States." *Political Science Quarterly* 74 (March 1959): 89–112.

THE SPANISH-AMERICAN WAR

Alger, Russell A. *The Spanish-American War.* New York, 1901.

Atkins, John Black. *The War in Cuba.* London, 1899.

Auxier, George W. "Middle Western Newspapers and the Spanish-American War, 1895–1898." *Mississippi Valley Historical Review* 26 (March 1940): 523–34.

Chadwick, French Ensor. *The Relations of the United States and Spain: Diplomacy.* New York, 1909.

——. *The Relations of the United States and Spain: The Spanish-American War.* 2 vols. New York, 1911.

Cosmas, Graham A. *An Army for Empire: The United States Army in the Spanish-American War.* Columbia, Mo., 1971.

Freidel, Frank. *Splendid Little War.* Boston, 1958.

Funston, Frederick. *Memories of Two Wars.* New York, 1911.

Millis, Walter. *The Martial Spirit.* Cambridge, Mass., 1931.

Morgan, H. Wayne. *America's Road to Empire: The War with Spain and Overseas Expansion.* New York, 1965a.

——, ed. *Making Peace with Spain: The Diary of Whitelaw Reid, September–December 1898.* Austin, Tex., 1965b.

Offner, John. "The United States and France: Ending the Spanish-American War." *Diplomatic History* 7 (winter 1983): 1–21.

Piedra Martel, Manuel. *Memorias de un mambí.* Havana, 1968.

Portell-Vilá, Herminio. *Historia de la guerra de Cuba y los Estados Unidos contra España.* Havana, 1949.

Pratt, Julius W. *Expansionists of 1898: The Acquisition of Hawaii and the Spanish Islands.* Baltimore, Md., 1936.

Rickover, Hyman G. *How the Battleship* Maine *Was Destroyed.* Washington, D.C., 1976.

Roig de Leuchsenring, Emilio. *1895 y 1898: Dos guerras cubanas: Ensayos de revaloración.* Havana, 1945.

Trask, David F. *The War with Spain in 1898.* New York, 1981.

Varona Guerrero, Miguel. *La Guerra de Independencia de Cuba, 1895–1898.* 3 vols. Havana, 1946.

Wilkerson, Marcus M. *Public Opinion and the Spanish-American War.* 1932. Reprint. New York, 1967.

THE ISTHMIAN CANAL

Adams, William Roger. "Strategy, Diplomacy, and Isthmian Canal Security, 1880–1917." Ph.D. dissertation, Florida State University, 1974.

Ameringer, Charles. "The Panama Canal Lobby of Philippe Bunau-Varilla and William Nelson Cromwell." *American Historical Review* 68 (Jan. 1963): 346–63.

"Corollaries of Expansion, 1, The Nicaraguan Canal." *Literary Digest* 20 (Feb. 10, 1900): 177–78.

Crowell, Jackson. "The United States and a Central American Canal, 1869–1877." *Hispanic American Historical Review* 49 (Feb. 1969): 27–52.

Hill, Roscoe R. "The Nicaraguan Canal Idea to 1913." *Hispanic American Historical Review* 28 (May 1948): 197–211.

Kaufman, Burton I. "New Orleans and the Panama Canal, 1900–1914." *Louisiana History* 14 (fall 1973): 333–46.

La Feber, Walter. *The Panama Canal: The Crisis in Historical Perspective.* New York, 1978.

Mahan, Alfred Thayer. "The Isthmus and Sea Power." *Atlantic Monthly* 72 (1893): 459–72.

McCullough, David. *The Path between the Seas: The Creation of the Panama Canal, 1870–1914.* New York, 1977.

Miner, Dwight C. *The Fight for the Panama Route.* New York, 1940.

Pierson, William Whately, Jr. "The Political Influences of an Interoceanic Canal, 1826–1926." *Hispanic American Historical Review* 6 (Nov. 1926): 205–31.

Richard, Alfred C., Jr. "The Panama Canal in American National Consciousness, 1870–1922." Ph.D. dissertation, Boston University, 1969.

Stimson, Henry L. "The Defence of the Panama Canal." *Scribner's* 54 (July 1913): 1–6.

Vivian, James F. "The 'Taking' of the Panamá Canal Zone: Myth and Reality." *Diplomatic History* 4 (winter 1980): 95–100.

Williams, Mary W. *Anglo-American Isthmian Diplomacy, 1815–1915.* Washington, D.C., 1916.

THE CARIBBEAN REGION

Baker, George W. "Ideals and Realities in the Wilson Administration's Relations with Honduras." *Americas* 21 (1964): 3–19.

———. "The Woodrow Wilson Administration and El Salvadorean Relations, 1913–1921." *Social Studies* 56 (1965a): 97–103.

———. "The Woodrow Wilson Administration and Guatemalan Relations." *Historian* 27 (1965b): 155–69.

———. "Woodrow Wilson's Use of the Non-Recognition Policy in Costa Rica." *Americas* 22 (1965c): 3–21.

Berbusse, Edward J. *The United States in Puerto Rico, 1898–1900.* Chapel Hill, N.C., 1966.

Blaney, Henry R. *The Golden Caribbean.* Boston, 1900.

Bonsal, Stephen. *The American Mediterranean.* New York, 1912.

Brand, Charles A. "The Background of Capitalistic Underdevelopment: Honduras to 1913." Ph.D. dissertation, University of Pittsburgh, 1972.

Carpenter, Frank G. *Lands of the Caribbean.* New York, 1926.

Carr, Raymond. *Puerto Rico: A colonial experiment.* New York, 1984.

Clark, Truman R. "President Taft and the Puerto Rico Appropriation Crisis of 1909." *Americas* 26 (Oct. 1964): 152–70.

Clark, Victor S., et al. *Porto Rico and Its Problems.* Washington, D.C., 1932.

Curtis, William Eleroy. *The Capitals of Spanish America.* New York, 1888.

Davis, W. M. *The Lesser Antilles.* New York, 1926.

Diffie, Bailey W., and Justine W. Diffie. *Porto Rico: A Broken Pledge.* New York, 1931.

Dinwoodie, David H. "Dollar Diplomacy in the Light of the Guatemalan Loan Project, 1909–1913." *Americas* 26 (Jan. 1970): 237–53.

————. "Expedient Diplomacy: The United States and Guatemala, 1898–1920." Ph.D. dissertation, University of Colorado, 1966.

Franck, Harry A. *Roaming through the West Indies*. New York, 1920.

Goldwert, Marvin. *The Constabulary in the Dominican Republic and Nicaragua: Progeny and Legacy of United States Intervention*. Gainesville, Fla., 1962.

Green, William A. "Caribbean Historiography, 1600–1900: The Recent Tide." *Journal of Interdisciplinary History* 7 (winter 1977): 509–30.

Hale, William Bayard. "With the Knox Mission to Central America." *World's Work* 24 (1912): 179–93, 323–36.

Hernández, Edward Dennis. "Modernization and Dependency in Costa Rica during the Decade of the 1880's." Ph.D. dissertation, University of California at Los Angeles, 1975.

Huck, Eugene R., and Edward H. Moseley, eds. *Militarists, Merchants, and Missionaries: United States Expansion in Middle America*. Tuscaloosa, Ala., 1970.

Inman, Samuel Guy. *Through Santo Domingo and Haiti: A Cruise with the Marines*. New York, 1919.

Jones, Chester Lloyd. *Guatemala, Past and Present*. Minneapolis, Minn., 1940.

Karnes, Thomas L. *The Failure of Union: Central America, 1824–1960*. Chapel Hill, N.C., 1961.

Knight, Franklin. *The Caribbean: The Genesis of a Fragmented Nationalism*. New York, 1978.

Koebel, W. H. *Central America*. London, 1917.

Langley, Lester D. *Struggle for the American Mediterranean: United States–European Rivalry, 1776–1904*. Athens, Ga., 1976.

————. *The United States and the Caribbean, 1900–1970*. Athens, Ga., 1980.

Lewis, Gordon K. *Main Currents in Caribbean Thought*. Baltimore, Md., 1983.

————. *Puerto Rico: Freedom and Power in the Caribbean*. New York, 1963.

Logan, Rayford. *Haiti and the Dominican Republic*. New York, 1968.

Moore, J. Hampton. *With Speaker Cannon through the Tropics*. Philadelphia, 1907.

Munro, Dana G. *The Five Republics of Central America*. New York, 1918.

————. *Intervention and Dollar Diplomacy in the Caribbean, 1900–1921*. Princeton, N.J., 1964.

————. *The United States and the Caribbean Area*. Boston, 1934.

————. *The United States and the Caribbean Republics, 1921–1933*. Princeton, N.J., 1974.

Palmer, Frederick. *Central America and Its Problems*. New York, 1910.

Parry, John, and Philip M. Sherlock. *A Short History of the West Indies*. London, 1956.

Perkins, Whitney. *Constraint of Empire: The United States and Caribbean Interventions*. Westport, Conn., 1981.

Ragatz, Lowell J. *The Fall of the Planter Class in the British Caribbean, 1753–1833*. New York, 1928.

Tansill, Charles C. *The Purchase of the Danish West Indies*. Baltimore, Md., 1932.

West, Robert C., and John P. Augelli. *Middle America: Its Lands and People*. Englewood Cliffs, N.J., 1966.

Williams, Eric. *From Columbus to Castro: The History of the Caribbean, 1492–1969*. New York, 1970.

Woodward, Ralph Lee. *Central America: A Nation Divided.* New York, 1976.
Zea, Leopoldo. *The Latin-American Mind.* Norman, Okla., 1963.

INDIVIDUAL COUNTRIES

Cuba

Baker, George W. "The Wilson Administration and Cuba, 1913–1921." *Mid-America* 46 (1964): 48–63.
Barbarrosa, Enrique. *El Proceso de la república, analisis de la situación política y económica de Cuba bajo el gobierno presidential de Tomás Estrada Palma y José Miguel Gómez.* Havana, 1911.
Beals, Carleton. *The Crime of Cuba.* Philadelphia, 1933.
Benjamin, Jules R. *The United States and Cuba: Hegemony and Dependent Development, 1880–1934.* Pittsburgh, Pa., 1977.
Boletín del Archivo Nacional, Año 35. Havana, 1936.
Camacho, Pánfilo D. *Estrada Palma, el gobernante honrado.* Havana, 1938.
Cárdenas y Echarte, Raúl de. *Cuba no puede invocarse en testimonio del imperialismo norteamericano.* Havana, 1917.
Collazo, Enrique. *Cuba intervenida.* Havana, 1910.
Corbitt, Duvon C. "Cuban Revisionist Interpretations of Cuba's Struggle for Independence." *Hispanic American Historical Review* 43 (Aug. 1963): 395–404.
Guerra y Sánchez, Ramiro. *Sugar and Society in the Caribbean.* New Haven, Conn., 1964.
Guerra y Sánchez, Ramiro, José M. Perez Cabrera, Juan J. Remos, and Emeterio S. Santovenia, eds. *Historia de la Nación Cubana.* 10 vols. Havana, 1952.
Healy, David. *The United States in Cuba, 1898–1902.* Madison, Wis., 1963.
Hoernel, Robert B. "Sugar and Social Change in Oriente, Cuba, 1898–1946." *Journal of Latin American Studies* 8 (Nov. 1976): 215–49.
Jenks, Leland. *Our Cuban Colony: A Study in Sugar.* New York, 1928.
Lockmiller, David A. *Magoon in Cuba: A history of the Second Intervention, 1906–1909.* Chapel Hill, N.C., 1938.
Márquez Sterling, Manuel. *Proceso historico de la Enmienda Platt.* Havana, 1941.
Martinez Ortiz, Rafael. *General Leonard Wood's Government in Cuba.* Paris, 1920.
Meyer, Leo J. "The United States and the Cuban Revolution of 1917." *Hispanic American Historical Review* 10 (May 1930): 138–66.
Millett, Allan Reed. *The Politics of Intervention: The Military Occupation of Cuba, 1906–1909.* Columbus, Ohio, 1968.
————. "The Rise and Fall of the Cuban Rural Guard, 1898–1912." *Americas* 29 (Oct. 1972): 191–214.
Montaner, Carlos Alberto. "The Roots of Anti-Americanism in Cuba." *Caribbean Review* 13 (spring 1984): 13–16, 42–46.
————. *200 Years of Gringos.* Lanham, Md., 1983.
Ortiz Fernández, Fernando. *Cuban Counterpoint: Tobacco and Sugar.* New York, 1947.
Parker, William Belmont. *Cubans of To-Day.* New York, 1919.

Perez, Louis A., Jr. "Cuba: Between Empires." *Pacific Historical Review* 40 (Nov. 1979): 473–500.

———. *Cuba between Empires, 1878–1902.* Pittsburgh, Pa., 1983.

———. *Intervention, Revolution, and Politics in Cuba, 1913–1921.* Pittsburgh, Pa., 1979.

———. "Supervision of a Protectorate: The United States and the Cuban Army, 1898–1908." *Hispanic American Historical Review* 52 (May 1972): 250–71.

———. "Vagrants, Beggars, and Bandits: Social Origins of Cuban Separatism, 1878–1895." *American Historical Review* 90 (Dec. 1985): 1092–1121.

Portell-Vilá, Herminio. *Historia de Cuba en sus relaciones con los Estados Unidos y España.* 4 vols. Havana, 1938–1941.

Porter, Robert P. "The Future of Cuba." *North American Review* 168 (1899): 418–23.

Roig de Leuchsenring, Emilio. *Analisis y consecuencias de la intervención norteamericano en los asuntos interiores de Cuba.* Havana, 1923.

———. *Cuba no debe su independencia a los Estados Unidos.* Havana, 1950.

———. *Cuba y los Estados Unidos, 1805–1898: Historia documentado de la actitud disimil de estado y del pueblo norteamericano en relación con la independencia de Cuba.* Havana, 1949.

———. *La Enmienda Platt: Su interpretación primativa y sus aplicaciones posteriores hasta 1921.* Havana, 1922.

———. *La Guerra Libertadora Cubana de los trienta anos, 1868–1898: Razón de su victoria.* Havana, 1952.

———. *El Presidente McKinley y el gobernador Wood: Máximas enemigos de Cuba libre.* Havana, 1960.

Rubens, Horatio. *Liberty: The Story of Cuba.* New York, 1932.

Sanguily, Manuel. "Sobre el genesis de la Enmienda Platt." *Cuba Contemporánea* 30 (Oct. 1922): 119–27.

Scott, James Brown. "The Attitude of the United States toward Political Disturbances in Cuba." *American Journal of International Law* 11 (April 1917): 419–23.

Smith, Robert F. *The United States and Cuba: Business and Diplomacy, 1917–1960.* New Haven, Conn., 1960.

Thomas, Hugh. *Cuba, or the Pursuit of Freedom.* London, 1971.

Wallich, Henry C. *Monetary Problems of an Export Economy: The Cuban Experience, 1914–1947.* Cambridge, Mass., 1960.

Wisan, Joseph E. *The Cuban Crisis As Reflected in the New York Press, 1895–1898.* New York, 1934.

Wright, Irene. *Cuba.* New York, 1910.

Dominican Republic

Academia Colombina, La. *Memorial de protesta contra la arbitraria ocupación militar de la República Dominica por tropas de los Estados Unidos de Norte América.* Santo Domingo, 1916.

Bordas, J. Rafael. *Frente al imperialismo.* Santo Domingo, 1923.

Calder, Bruce J. "Caudillos and Gavrilleros versus the United States: Guerrilla Insurgency during the Dominican Intervention, 1916–1924." *Hispanic American Historical Review* 58 (Nov. 1978): 649–75.

———. *The Impact of Intervention: The Dominican Republic during the U.S. Occupation of 1916–1924.* Austin, Tex., 1984.

————. "Some Aspects of the United States Occupation of the Dominican Republic, 1916–1924." Ph.D. dissertation, University of Texas, 1974.

Ducoudray, Félix Servio. *Los "Gavilleros" del Este: Una Epopeya calumniada.* Santo Domingo, 1976.

Ellis Gambiaso, Federico. *Los Cuatro monstruos de la anexión.* Santo Domingo, 1922.

Fiallo, Fabio. *The Crime of Wilson in Santo Domingo.* Havana, 1940.

Fuller, Stephen M., and Graham Cosmas. *Marines in the Dominican Republic, 1916–1924.* Washington, D.C., 1974.

Henríquez Ureña, Max. *Los Yanquis en Santo Domingo.* Santo Domingo, 1977.

Hoepelman, Antonio, and Juan A. Senior. *Documentos historicos que se refieren a la intervención armada de los Estados Unidos de Norte-América y la implantación de un gobierno militar americano en la República Dominica.* Santo Domingo, 1922.

Hoetinck, Harry. "The Dominican Republic in the Nineteenth Century: Some Notes on Stratification, Immigration, and Race." In *Race and Class in Latin America,* edited by Magnus Morner. New York, 1970.

Juarez, Joseph R. "United States Withdrawal from Santo Domingo." *Hispanic American Historical Review* 42 (May 1962): 152–90.

Lozano, Wilfredo. *La Dominación imperialista en la República Dominica, 1900–1930.* Santo Domingo, 1976.

Mejia, Luis F. *De Lilis a Trujillo: Historia contemporánea de la República Dominica.* Caracas, 1944.

Muto, H. Paul. "The Illusory Promise: The Dominican Republic and the Process of Economic Development, 1900–1930." Ph.D. dissertation, University of Washington, 1976.

Roig de Leuchsenring, Emilio. *La Ocupación de la República Dominica por los Estados Unidos y el dereche de las pequeñas nacionalidades de América.* Havana, 1919.

Schoenrich, Otto. *Santo Domingo, a Country with a Future.* New York, 1918.

Welles, Sumner. *Naboth's Vineyard: The Dominican Republic, 1844–1924.* 2 vols. 1928. Reprint. New York, 1966.

Haiti

Beach, Edward L. *Admiral Caperton in Haiti.* Naval Records Collection, Office of Naval Records and Library. Record Group 45, National Archives, Washington, D.C.

Bellegarde, Dantes. *Haïti et les Etats-Unis devant la justice internationale.* Paris, 1924.

————. *Histoire du peuple haïtien (1492–1952).* Port-au-Prince, 1953.

————. *La Resistance haïtienne.* Montreal, 1937.

Bellegarde-Smith, Patrick. *In the Shadow of Powers: Dantes Bellegarde in Haitian Social Thought.* Atlantic Highlands, N.J., 1985.

Danache, B. *Le Président Dartiguenave et les américains.* Port-au-Prince, 1950.

Davis, Harold P. *Black Democracy: The Story of Haiti.* New York, 1936.

Healy, David. *Gunboat Diplomacy in the Wilson Era: The U.S. Navy in Haiti, 1915–1916.* Madison, Wis., 1976.

Leger, Jacques Nicolas. *Haiti: Her History and Her Detractors.* 1907. Reprint. Westport, Conn., 1970.

Leyburn, James G. *The Haitian People.* New Haven, Conn., 1941.

McCrocklin, James H. *Garde d'Haïti, 1915–1934.* Annapolis, Md., 1956.

Nicolas, Hogar. *L'Occupation américaine d'Haïti: La Revanche de l'histoire*. Madrid, 1956.

Schmidt, Hans. *The United States Occupation of Haiti, 1915–1934*. New Brunswick, N.J., 1971.

Nicaragua

Alvarez Lejarza, Emilio. *Impresiones y recuerdos de la revolución de 1909 a 1910*. Granada, Nicaragua, 1941.

Alvarez Lejarza, Emilio, Andrés Vega Bolaños, and Gustavo Alemán Bolaños. *Como reincorporó Nicaragua su costa oriental*. Managua, 1944.

Aquino, Enrique. *La Intervención en Nicaragua. Colección de artículos publicados en la prensa sobre el problema americanista nicaraguense*. Managua, 1928.

———. *La Personalidad política del General José Santos Zelaya*. Managua, 1944.

Bailey, Thomas A. "Interest in a Nicaraguan Canal, 1903–1931." *Hispanic American Historical Review* 16 (Feb. 1936): 2–28.

Baker, George W. "The Wilson Administration and Nicaragua, 1913–1921." *Americas* 22 (1966): 339–76.

Baylen, Joseph O. "American Intervention in Nicaragua, 1909–1933: An Appraisal of Objectives and Results." *Southwestern Social Science Quarterly* 35 (Sept. 1954): 128–54.

Cole Chamorro, Alejandro. *Ciento cuarenta y cinco años de historia política en Nicaragua*. Managua, 1967.

Cuadra Chamorro, Pedro J. *Le Reincorporación de la Mosquitia*. Granada, Nicaragua, 1944. Reprint. León, Nicaragua 1964.

Denny, Harold N. *Dollars for Bullets: The Story of American Rule in Nicaragua*. New York, 1929.

Dozier, Craig L. *Nicaragua's Mosquito Shore: The Years of British and American Presence*. University, Ala., 1985.

Floyd, Troy S. *The Anglo-Spanish Struggle for Mosquitia*. Albuquerque, N.M., 1967.

Ham, Clifford D. "Americanizing Nicaragua." *Review of Reviews* 53 (1916): 185–91.

Healy, David. "A Hinterland in Search of a Metropolis: The Mosquito Coast, 1894–1910." *International History Review* 3 (Jan. 1981): 20–43.

Hill, Roscoe R. *Fiscal Intervention in Nicaragua*. New York, 1933.

Macauley, Neill. *The Sandino Affair*. Chicago, 1967.

Meyers, Harvey K. *Historical Dictionary of Nicaragua*. Metuchen, N.J., 1972.

Morrow, Rising Lake. "A Conflict between the Commercial Interests of the United States and Its Foreign Policy." *Hispanic American Historical Review* 10 (1930): 2–13.

Munro, Dana G. "Dollar Diplomacy in Nicaragua, 1909–1913." *Hispanic American Historical Review* 38 (May 1958): 209–234.

Nogales, Rafael de. *The Looting of Nicaragua*. New York, 1928.

Powell, Ann I. "Relations between the United States and Nicaragua, 1898–1916." *Hispanic American Historical Review* 8 (1928): 43–64.

Quintana Orozco, Ofsman. *Apuntes de historia de Nicaragua*. Managua, 1968.

Soto Hall, Máximo. *Nicaragua y el imperialismo norteamericano*. Buenos Aires, 1928.

Squier, Ephraim George. *Weikna; Adventures on the Mosquito Shore*. New York, 1855. Reprint. Gainesville, Fla., 1965.

Walker, James G. W. *Ocean to Ocean: An Account Personal and Historical of Nicaragua and Its People*. Chicago, 1902.

Zelaya, José Santos. *Refutation of the Statement of President Taft*. Paris, 1911.

———. *La Revolución de Nicaragua y los Estados Unidos*. Madrid, 1910.

Panamá

Bullard, Arthur. *Panama, the Canal, the Country and the People*. New York, 1914.

Bunau-Varilla, Philippe. *Panama: The Creation, Destruction and Resurrection*. London, 1913.

Collins, John O. *The Panama Guide*. Mount Hope, Canal Zone, 1912.

Lemaitre, Eduardo. *Panamá y su separación de Colombia*. Bogotá, 1971.

Major, John. "Who Wrote the Hay-Bunau-Varilla Convention?" *Diplomatic History* 8 (spring 1984): 115–23.

McCain, William D. *The United States and the Republic of Panama*. Durham, N.C., 1937.

Mellander, G. A. *The United States in Panamanian Politics: The Intriguing Formative Years*. Danville, Ill., 1971.

Ropp, Steve C. *Panamanian Politics, from Guarded Nation to National Guard*. New York, 1982.

"Suppressed Panama Message, The." *Literary Digest* 27 (Nov. 28, 1903): 727.

Wicks, David H. "Dress Rehearsal: United States Intervention on the Isthmus of Panama, 1885." *Pacific Historical Review* 49 (Nov. 1980): 581–605.

ECONOMIC TOPICS

Atkins, Edwin F. *Sixty Years in Cuba*. Cambridge, Mass., 1926.

Austin, Oscar P. *Trading with Our Neighbors in the Caribbean*. Foreign Commerce Series no. 1. National City Bank of New York, 1920.

Baker, Ray Stannard. "How the Beet-Sugar Industry is Growing." *Review of Reviews* 23 (1901): 324–28.

Beals, Carleton. *Banana Gold*. Philadelphia, 1932.

Crampton, Charles A. "The Opportunity of the Sugar Cane Industry." *North American Review* 168 (March 1899): 276–84.

Dunn, Robert W. *American Foreign Investments*. New York, 1926.

Feis, Herbert. *Europe, the World's Banker, 1870–1914*. New Haven, Conn., 1930.

Jones, Chester Lloyd. "Loan Controls in the Caribbean." *Hispanic American Historical Review* 14 (May 1934): 141–62.

Karnes, Thomas. *Tropical Enterprise: Standard Fruit and Steamship Company in Latin America*. Baton Rouge, La., 1979.

Kaufman, Burton I. *Efficiency and Expansion: Foreign Trade Organization in the Wilson Administration, 1913–1921*. Westport, Conn., 1974.

———. "United States Trade and Latin America: The Wilson Years." *Journal of American History* 58 (1971): 342–63.

Kepner, Charles D., and Jay H. Soothill. *The Banana Empire: A Case Study of Economic Imperialism*. New York, 1935.

Landes, David F. *Bankers and Pashas: International Finance and Economic Imperialism*. New York, 1958.

Laso, Luis Eduardo. *Evolución de los sistemas monetarios y bancos centrales de América Latina*. Guayaquil, Ecuador, 1972.

Laughlin, J. Lawrence. *Money and Prices*. New York, 1919.

May, Stacy, and Galo Plaza. *The United Fruit Company in Latin America*. N.p., 1958.

Mayer, Robert. "The Origins of the American Banking Empire in Latin America." *Journal of Interamerican Studies and World Affairs* 15 (Feb. 1973): 60–76.

Mosk, Sanford. "Latin America and the World Economy, 1850–1914." *Inter-American Economic Affairs* 2 (winter 1948): 53–82.

Parrini, Carl P., and Martin J. Sklar. "New Thinking about the Market, 1896–1904: Some American Economists on Investment and the Theory of Surplus Capital." *Journal of Economic History* 43 (Sept. 1983): 559–78.

Rippy, J. Fred. "British Bondholders and the Roosevelt Corollary." *Political Science Quarterly* 49 (1934): 195–206.

Shea, Donald R. *The Calvo Clause*. Minneapolis, Minn., 1955.

Steigerwalt, Albert K. *The National Association of Manufacturers, 1895–1914*. Ann Arbor, Mich., 1964.

Stewart, Watt. *Keith and Costa Rica*. Albuquerque, N.M., 1964.

Wilkins, Mira. *The Emergence of Multinational Enterprise: American Business Abroad from the Colonial Era to 1914*. Cambridge, Mass., 1970.

DEVELOPMENT AND DEPENDENCY THEORY

Bairoch, Paul. "Le Bilan économique du colonialisme: Mythes et réalités." *Itinerario* 1 (1980): 35–36.

Boulding, Kenneth E. *Ecodynamics: A New Theory of Societal Evolution*. Beverly Hills, Calif., 1978.

Burns, E. Bradford. *The Poverty of Progress: Latin America in the 19th Century*. Berkeley and Los Angeles, 1980.

Cardoso, F., and E. Faletto. *Dependencia y desarrollo en América Latina*. Mexico City, 1970.

Chilcote, Ronald H., and Joel C. Edelstein. *Latin America: The Struggle with Dependence and Beyond*. New York, 1974.

Dos Santos, Theotonio. "The Crisis of Development Theory and the Problem of Dependence in Latin America." In *Underdevelopment and Development*, edited by H. Bernstein. Harmondsworth, England, 1973.

———. "The Structure of Dependence." *American Economic Review* 60 (May 1970): 231–36.

Fieldhouse, D. K. *Unilever Overseas: The Anatomy of a Multinational, 1895–1965*. Stanford, Calif., 1978.

Gilpin, Robert. *U.S. Power and the Multinational Corporation*. New York, 1975.

Gunder Frank, Andre. *Capitalism and Underdevelopment in Latin America*. New York, 1967.

North, Douglas C. "Location Theory and Regional Economic Growth." *Journal of Political Economy* 63 (June 1955): 243–58.

Oxaal, Ivar, Tony Bennet, and David Booth, eds. *Beyond the Sociology of Development: Economy and Society in Latin America and Africa*. London, 1975.

Platt, D. C. M. "British Bondholders in Nineteenth Century Latin America: Injury and Remedy." *Inter-American Economic Affairs* 14 (1960): 3–43.

———. *Business Imperialism 1840–1930: An Inquiry Based on British Experience in Latin America*. Cambridge, 1977.

———. "Dependency in Nineteenth-Century Latin America: An Historian Objects." *Latin American Research Review* 15 (1980): 113–30.

Ray, David. "The Dependency Model of Latin American Underdevelopment: Three Basic Fallacies." *Journal of Interamerican Studies and World Affairs* 15 (Feb. 1973): 4–20.

Richardson, Neil R. *Foreign Policy and Economic Dependency*. Austin, Tex., 1978.

Smith, Tony. *The Patterns of Imperialism: The United States, Great Britain, and the Late-Industrializing World*. Cambridge, 1981.

Wallerstein, Immanuel. *The Modern World-System: Capitalist Agriculture and the Origins of the European World-Economy in the Sixteenth Century*. New York, 1974.

Warren, Bill. *Imperialism: Pioneer of Capitalism*. London, 1980.

PRESIDENTS AND ADMINISTRATIONS

Adler, Selig. "Bryan and Wilsonian Caribbean Penetration." *Hispanic American Historical Review* 20 (May 1940): 198–226.

Beale, Howard K. *Theodore Roosevelt and the Rise of America to World Power*. Baltimore, Md., 1956.

Bell, Sydney. *Righteous Conquest: Woodrow Wilson and the Evolution of the New Diplomacy*. Port Washington, N.Y., 1972.

Blum, John M. *Woodrow Wilson and the Politics of Morality*. Boston, 1956.

Cronon, E. David, ed. *The Political Thought of Woodrow Wilson*. Indianapolis, Ind., 1965.

Fry, Joseph A. "William McKinley and the Coming of the Spanish-American War: A Study of the Besmirching and Redemption of a Historical Image." *Diplomatic History* 3 (winter 1979): 77–97.

Gilderhus, Mark. "Wilson, Carranza, and the Monroe Doctrine: A Question in Regional Organization." *Diplomatic History* 7 (spring 1983): 103–16.

Gow, Douglas R. "How did the Roosevelt Corollary Become linked with the Dominican Republic?" *Mid-America* 3 (Oct. 1976): 159–65.

Harbaugh, William H. *Power and Responsibility: The Life and Times of Theodore Roosevelt*. New York, 1961.

Hendrickson, Embert J. "Roosevelt's Second Venezuelan Controversy." *Hispanic American Historical Review* 50 (Aug. 1970): 482–98.

Holbo, Paul S. "Perilous Obscurity: Public Diplomacy and the Press in the Venezuelan Crisis, 1902–1903." *Historian* 32 (May 1970): 428–48.

————. "Presidential Leadership in Foreign Affairs: William McKinley and the Turpie-Foraker Amendment." *American Historical Review* 72 (1967): 1321–35.

Huntington-Wilson, Francis M. *Memoirs of an Ex-Diplomat.* Boston, 1945.

Lansing, Robert. *War Memoirs.* Indianapolis, Ind., 1935.

Leech, Margaret. *In the Days of McKinley.* New York, 1959.

Link, Arthur S., ed. *The Papers of Woodrow Wilson.* 57 vols. Princeton, N.J., 1966–87.

————. *Wilson: Confusions and Crises.* Princeton, N.J., 1964.

————. *Wilson: The New Freedom.* Princeton, N.J., 1956.

————. *Wilson: The Struggle for Neutrality, 1914–1915.* Princeton, N.J., 1960.

Livermore, Seward W. "Theodore Roosevelt, the American Navy, and the Venezuelan Crisis of 1902–1903." *American Historical Review* 51 (Apr. 1946): 452–71.

Lodge, Henry Cabot. *Selections from the Correspondence of Theodore Roosevelt and Henry Cabot Lodge.* 2 vols. New York, 1925.

Marks, Frederick W. *Velvet on Iron: The Diplomacy of Theodore Roosevelt.* Lincoln, Nebr., 1979.

Morgan, H. Wayne. *William McKinley and His America.* Syracuse, N.Y., 1963.

Morison, Elting E., ed. *The Letters of Theodore Roosevelt.* 8 vols. Cambridge, Mass., 1951–52.

Quirk, Robert E. *An Affair of Honor: Woodrow Wilson and the Occupation of Veracruz.* Lexington, Ky., 1962.

Roosevelt, Theodore. *The Works of Theodore Roosevelt.* 24 vols. New York, 1923–26.

Scholes, Walter V., and Marie V. Scholes. *The Foreign Policies of the Taft Administration.* Columbia, Mo., 1970.

Volwiler, A. T. *Correspondence between Benjamin Harrison and James G. Blaine, 1882–1893.* Philadelphia, 1940.

Wilson, Woodrow. "Democracy and Efficiency." *Atlantic Monthly* 87 (Mar. 1901): 289–99.

————. "The Ideals of America." *Atlantic Monthly* 90 (Dec. 1902): 721–34.

————. "The Road Away from Revolution." *Atlantic Monthly* 132 (Aug. 1923): 145–46.

THE STATE DEPARTMENT AND THE FOREIGN SERVICE

Barnes, William, and John Heath Morgan. *The Foreign Service of the United States.* Washington, D.C., 1961.

Beaulac, Willard E. *Career Ambassador.* New York, 1951.

Crane, Katherine. *Mr. Carr of State.* New York, 1960.

Dougal, Richard, and Mary Patricia Chapman. *United States Chiefs of Mission, 1778–1973.* Washington, D.C., 1973.

Griscom, Lloyd C. *Diplomatically Speaking.* Boston, 1940.

Kist, Glenn J. "The Role of Thomas C. Dawson in United States–Latin American Diplomatic Relations: 1897–1912." Ph.D. dissertation, Loyola University of Chicago, 1971.

Mattox, H. E. "Research Note on America's Senior Representatives Abroad at the Turn of the Century." *Newsletter of the Society for Historians of American Foreign Relations* 14 (Dec. 1983): 1–8.

Peterson, Harold. *Diplomat of the Americas: A biography of William I. Buchanan, 1852–1909*. Albany, N.Y., 1976.

Richardson, Norval. *My Diplomatic Education*. New York, 1929.

Sands, William F., with Joseph M. Lalley. *Our Jungle Diplomacy*. Chapel Hill, N.C., 1944.

Schulzinger, Robert D. *The Making of the Diplomatic Mind: The Training, Outlook, and Style of U.S. Foreign Service Officers, 1908–1931*. Middletown, Conn., 1975.

Werking, Richard Hume. *The Master Architects: Building the United States Foreign Service, 1890–1913*. Lexington, Ky., 1977.

West, Rachel. *The Department of State on the Eve of the First World War*. Athens, Ga., 1978.

THE ARMED FORCES

Bailey, Thomas A. "Dewey and the Germans at Manila Bay." *American Historical Review* 45 (Oct. 1939): 59–81.

Bradford, Royal R. "Coaling Stations for the Navy." *Forum* 26 (Feb. 1899): 732–47.

Caperton, William B. *History of U.S. Naval Operations under Command of Rear Admiral W. B. Caperton, Commencing January 5, 1915, Ending April 30, 1919*. Naval Records Collection, Office of Naval Records and Library. Record Group 45, National Archives, Washington, D.C.

Challener, Richard D. *Admirals, Generals, and American Foreign Policy, 1898–1914*. Princeton, N.J., 1973.

Cooling, Benjamin Franklin. *Benjamin Franklin Tracy, Father of the Modern American Fighting Navy*. Hamden, Conn., 1973.

———. "The Making of a Navalist: Secretary of the Navy Benjamin Franklin Tracy and Sea Power." *U.S. Navy War College Review* 25 (Sept.–Oct. 1972): 83–90.

Ellsworth, Harry A. *One Hundred Eighty Landings of United States Marines, 1800–1934*. Washington, D.C., 1974.

Gates, John M. *Schoolbooks and Krags: The United States Army in the Philippines, 1898–1902*. Westport, Conn., 1973.

Graff, Henry F., ed. *American Imperialism and the Philippine Insurrection*. Boston, 1969.

Greene, Fred. "The Military View of American National Policy, 1904–1940." *American Historical Review* 66 (Jan. 1961): 354–77.

Hagedorn, Hermann. *Leonard Wood*. 2 vols. New York, 1931.

Heinl, Robert D. *Soldiers of the Sea: The United States Marine Corps, 1775–1962*. Annapolis, Md., 1962.

Herrick, Walter R., Jr. *The American Naval Revolution*. Baton Rouge, La., 1966.

Herwig, Holger H. *The Politics of Frustration: The United States in German Naval Planning, 1889–1941*. Boston, 1976.

Herwig, Holger H., and David F. Trask. "Naval Operations Plans between Germany and the USA, 1898–1913." In *The War Plans of the Great Powers, 1880–1914*, edited by Paul M. Kennedy. London, 1979.

Jane, Fred T., ed. *Jane's Fighting Ships, 1906/07*. London, 1906.

Karsten, Peter. *The Naval Aristocracy: The Golden Age of Modern American Navalism*. New York, 1972.

Langley, Lester D. *The Banana Wars: An Inner History of American Empire, 1900–1934*. Lexington, Ky., 1983.

Lejeune, John A. *The Reminiscences of a Marine*. Philadelphia, 1930.

Lockmiller, David A. *Enoch H. Crowder: Soldier, Lawyer, and Statesman*. Columbia, Mo., 1955.

Mahan, Alfred Thayer. *The Interest of America in Sea Power*. Boston, 1897.

———. "The United States Looking Outward." *Atlantic Monthly* 66 (1890): 824.

Parker, James. *The Old Army: Memories, 1872–1918*. Philadelphia, Pa., 1929.

Pomeroy, Earl S. "The American Colonial Office." [The U.S. Army's Bureau of Insular Affairs.] *Mississippi Valley Historical Review* 30 (1944): 521–32.

Schott, Joseph L. *The Ordeal of Samar*. Indianapolis, Ind., 1964.

Seager, Robert, II. "Ten Years before Mahan: The Unofficial Case for the New Navy, 1880–1890." *Mississippi Valley Historical Review* 40 (Dec. 1953): 491–512.

Seager, Robert, II, and Doris Maguire, eds. *Letters and Papers of Alfred Thayer Mahan*. 3 vols. Annapolis, Md., 1975.

Small, Melvin. "The United States and the German 'Threat' to the Hemisphere, 1905–1914." *Americas* 28 (Jan. 1972): 252–70.

Sprout, Harold, and Margaret Sprout. *The Rise of American Naval Power, 1776–1918*. Princeton, N.J., 1946.

Thomas, Lowell. *"Old Gimlet Eye": The Adventures of Smedley D. Butler As Told to Lowell Thomas*. New York, 1933.

Turk, Richard W. "Defending the New Empire, 1900–1914." In *In Peace and War: Interpretations of American Naval History, 1775–1984*, edited by Kenneth J. Hagan. 2d ed. Westport, Conn., 1984.

———. "Strategy and Foreign Policy: The United States Navy in the Caribbean, 1865–1913." Ph.D. dissertation, Fletcher School of Law and Diplomacy, 1968.

Wise, Frederick May. *A Marine Tells It to You*. New York, 1929.

SOME OTHER PEOPLE

Bacon, Robert, and James Brown Scott, eds. *Addresses on Government and Citizenship by Elihu Root*. Cambridge, Mass., 1916.

———. *Men and Policies: Addresses by Elihu Root*. Cambridge, Mass., 1925.

Bancroft, Frederick. *Speeches, Correspondence, and Political Papers of Carl Schurz*. 2 vols. New York, 1913.

Bowers, Claude G. *Beveridge and the Progressive Era*. Cambridge, Mass., 1932.

Clements, Kendrick A. *William Jennings Bryan, Missionary Isolationist*. Knoxville, Tenn., 1982.

Coletta, Paolo E. *William Jennings Bryan: Political Evangelist, 1860–1908*. Lincoln, Nebr., 1964.

Coolidge, Louis A. *An Old Fashioned Senator, Orville H. Platt*. New York, 1910.

Deutsch, Hermann B. *The Incredible Yanqui: The Career of Lee Christmas*. London and New York, 1931.

Garraty, John A. *Henry Cabot Lodge: A Biography*. New York, 1953.

Jessup, Philip. *Elihu Root*. 2 vols. New York, 1938.

Radke, August Carl. "John Tyler Morgan, an Expansionist Senator, 1877–1907." Ph.D. dissertation, University of Washington, 1953.

Scott, James Brown. "Elihu Root." In *The American Secretaries of States and Their Diplomacy*, edited by Samuel F. Bemis. Vol. 9 (of 10 vols). New York, 1927–29.

Index

———··⟨⟐⟩··———